China in the Wake of Asia's Financial Crisis

T0295723

This book examines China's response to the Asian financial crisis of 1997, both in its immediate aftermath and in the years since. The crisis caused turmoil throughout Asia's economies, and precipitated wholesale reform of economic and financial policies and institutions across the region. As one of Asia's largest economies, China responded to the crisis more successfully than many others, avoiding devaluation of its currency, whilst undertaking financial reform, restructuring state-owned enterprises, rural development, and social security systems. This book considers all of these issues, showing how the lessons drawn from the crisis have helped shape China's policies of liberalization and market-orientated reform, including its attitude towards globalization and the outside world in general. Based on research conducted by the China Development Research Foundation, one of China's leading think tanks, this book includes contributions from senior policy makers in the Chinese government and from experts participating directly in the government's policy-making process to assess the effects generated by the country's related policies, making it an indispensable account of China's own thinking on its response to the financial crisis.

Wang Mengkui is former President of the Development Research Center of the State Council, and is currently Chairman of the China Development Research Foundation.

Routledge Studies on the Chinese Economy
Series editor: Peter Nolan
University of Cambridge
Founding Series Editors: Peter Nolan, *University of Cambridge* and
Dong Fureng, *Beijing University*

The aim of this series is to publish original, high-quality, research-level work by both new and established scholars in the West and the East, on all aspects of the Chinese economy, including studies of business and economic history.

China in the Wake of Asia's Financial Crisis

Edited by Wang Mengkui

Routledge
Taylor & Francis Group

LONDON AND NEW YORK

First published 2009 by Routledge

2 Park Square, Milton Park, Abingdon, Oxfordshire OX14 4RN
711 Third Avenue, New York, NY 10017

Routledge is an imprint of the Taylor & Francis Group, an informa business

First issued in paperback 2018

Typeset in Times New Roman by Pindar NZ, Auckland, New Zealand

British Library Cataloguing in Publication Data
A catalogue record for this book is available from the British Library

Library of Congress Cataloging-in-Publication Data
China in the wake of Asia's financial crisis / edited by Wang Mengkui.
   p. cm. — (Routledge studies on the Chinese economy series ; 32)
   Includes bibliographical references and index.
   1. Finance—China. 2. Financial crises—Asia. 3. China—Economic
policy. I. Wang, Mengkui.
   HG187.C6C4336 2008
   330.951—dc22   2008025471

ISBN 13: 978-0-415-46469-7 (hbk)
ISBN 13: 978-1-138-60745-3 (pbk)

Contents

Tables and figures

Tables

Figures

Contributors

Chief Editor Wang Mengkui Former Director-General of the Development Research Center of the State Council of China and Board Chairman for the China Development Research Foundation

Authors

Bai Chong-En Director-General, Economics Department of the School of Economics and Management, Tsinghua University

Cai Fang Director-General, Population and Labor Economy Research Institute of the Chinese Academy of Social Sciences

Han Jun Head of the Rural Economy Research Department of the Development Research Center, State Council of China

Huang Ming Research Fellow, Research Center under the China Securities Regulatory Commission

Jia Kang Director-General, Fiscal Science Research Institute under the Ministry of Finance, People's Republic of China

Li Daokui Director-General, Finance Department of the School of Economics and Management, Tsinghua University, and Director-General, Center for China in World Economy of Tsinghua University

Liu Chunhang Deputy Director, Statistics Department, and Deputy Director-General, Research Bureau, China Banking Regulatory Commission

Liu He Deputy Director-General, Administrative Office of the Central Financial and Economic Leading Group, Communist Party of China

Long Guoqiang Deputy Director, Foreign Economy Research Department of the Development Research Center, State Council of China

Qi Bin Director-General, Research Center of the China Securities Regulatory Commission

Wang Meiyan Deputy Research Fellow, Population and Labor Economy Research Institute, Chinese Academy of Social Sciences

Wang Yanzhong Deputy Director-General, Sociology Institute of the Chinese Academy of Social Sciences

Wu Huazhang Professor, China Medical University

Yi Gang Assistant to the Governor of the People's Bank of China

Zhang Delin Director-General, Administrative Office of the State-owned Assets Supervision and Administration Commission of the State Council of China

Zhang Li Director-General, National Education Development Research Center of the Ministry of Education of China

Zhang Zhenzhong Director-General, Health Economy Research Institute under the State Ministry of Health

Project Chief-Coordinator

Lu Mai Secretary-General for China Development Research Foundation

Foreword

A decade ago, when Asia's financial crisis erupted, many people suddenly had doubts about the East Asian economic miracle. Was it the beginning of the end? And could China go unscathed by the crisis, which had a huge negative impact on regions beyond Asia?

Ten years later, the world is witnessing a resumption of Asia's thriving economy, which has not only overcome the consequences of the crisis, but has also managed to put itself back on the path to rapid growth. China weathered the crisis because of proper measures and prudent and stable policies governing the opening of the financial market to the rest of the world. It is reasonable to say that coping with this crisis and learning a lot from the experience enabled China to grasp important opportunities for development and reform, allowing the country to ascend the global economic ladder. As a matter of fact, China's proven accomplishments over the past 10 years in terms of national development and economic reform and in terms of advancing China in the Asian and global economic paradigm have gone far beyond anyone's imagination. China and the rest of Asia are both marching forward along their chosen paths, drawing attention from all parts of the globe.

What has China learned from Asia's financial crisis? How did China fare on the road toward development and reform over the past decade? What will China's socio-economic scene look like in the future? All these questions are of interest to the general public. *China in The Wake of Asia's Financial Crisis* answers most questions about issues such as macroeconomic administration, financial systems, reforms of state-owned enterprises, social construction, and reform of social mechanism management practices in the wake of the crisis. This volume of research presents as detailed a picture as possible of the economic and financial future of China. All the authors are experts in their respective fields, and some are officials who have taken part in the formulation of policies. Readers will not only have access to a convenient interpretation of relevant policies, but will also be presented with an in-depth analysis based on a blend of theories and practice, so as to have a better and more thorough understanding of existing policies and of China's pursuit of development and reform.

History is like a mirror. Without doubt, the circumstances of today are largely different from those of a decade ago. In this era, where a technology-led revolution thrives and where the tide of economic globalization reaches all corners of the earth, China is poised to comprehensively build a prosperous society. It is time to review China's journey to national development and economic reform to get a clearer picture of where China is heading. The lessons learned from Asia's financial crisis are still of major significance. Finance remains the lifeline of economy in modern times. Some critics say that today's world has seen industrial capitalism give way to financial capitalism. The swift evolution of the financial industry, together with the innovation of financial means, has created great impetus to the development of economic power but has also resulted in new risks. Once the financial system suffers problems, sudden or overall breakdowns will likely occur with dire consequences. Although having positively evolved for 10 years, China's financial industry remains a weak link in the country's economic paradigm. In the scenario of fierce competition in world financial circles, China is still a novice. Thus, it is imperative that China continues to pursue reform and development, carry forward financial reforms, consolidate financial supervision and regulation mechanisms, and prevent financial risks. This is also why we have paid specific attention to financial security when conducting our research.

Wang Mengkui
Former President of the Development Research Center of the State Council of China, and current Chairman for the China Development Research Foundation

September 7, 2007

Introduction

China in the Wake of Asia's Financial Crisis comprises 14 chapters divided into four parts.

Part I: China's macroeconomic management after the Asian financial crisis

In "From overcoming deflation to preventing inflation," Liu He explains how Asia's financial crisis decrease of the volume of China's international trade and contributed to a decrease in prices of domestic agricultural products, triggering deflation. Fiscal policies based on expansion reforms featuring restructuring enabled China to enter a new era of economic progress and develop an economy that was open to the rest of the world. China made remarkable economic achievements but then also faced a new challenge: the imbalance between internal and external macroeconomic conditions. China's macroeconomic policy makers had to right the imbalance from top to bottom.

"From proactive to sound fiscal policy: an improvement to china's public finance system," by Jia Kang, provides the background, substance, and effects of expansion-based, proactive fiscal policies, which China adopted after Asia's financial crisis erupted in 1997. The chapter also describes China's shift from proactive fiscal policies to sound fiscal policies after 2003 and details the major measures that were taken along the way. Kang also looks into and analyzes "extrusion effects," the effects of "construction funds raised from national bonds," tax reductions, risks related to national bonds, and other important policy-related issues. Kang sums up China's progress in building the public finance system in the past decade.

Yi Gang, in "Fluctuation of the RMB exchange rates and relevant institutional factors," analyzes the reasons for and institutional factors of changes in Renminbi exchange rates. According to Gang, the increasing competitiveness of China's tradable items is a result of enhanced labor productivity and total factor productivity, progress in building the legal system, and the protection of intellectual property rights, as well as the swift increase in the value of China's assets (which are classified as non-tradable items). Such changes were positive but nevertheless led to imbalances. Rectifying the imbalance requires reliance on adjustments to factual exchange rates. Meanwhile, nominal exchange rates and commodity prices are both helpful for the adjustment of factual exchange rates.

Long Guoqiang, in "China's policy of opening up in the decade after the asian financial crisis," looks back on and analyzes China's opening-up policy in the decade after the Asian financial crisis. Guoqiang also looks at future opening-up policies. China adopted proper countermeasures to minimize the impact of the crisis and played an active role in maintaining financial stability and economic cooperation in the region, thus fortifying the country's influence in the regional economy. In the future, China must meet the needs arising from the country's scientific concept of development, pursue peaceful development, cling to creeds of "mutual-benefit" and "win-win," seize new opportunities, overcome new challenges emerging because of globalization, and adjust opening-up strategies and policies.

Part II: China's financial system and reform of state-owned enterprises after the Asian financial crisis

In "Reform of state-owned commercial banks: from disposing of non-performing assets to institutional reform," Liu Chunhang maintains that state-owned commercial banks play a principal role in China's financial system. Since 1998, state-owned commercial banks in China have set out to adopt a series of significant reforms, which focused on addressing their bad assets. Since 2003, the Bank of China, the China Construction Bank, the Bank of Communications, and the Industrial and Commercial Bank of China have all started an orderly restructuring in line with the joint stock system and have become increasingly aware that their common goal of reform is to build up a clarified ownership system and maintain sound corporate governance practices. In fact, today's banking industry has opened to the outside on a broader scale, and the financial supervision and regulatory mechanism has been constantly developed. The financial environment and infrastructure have improved. Meanwhile, reform and development measures adopted by China's state-owned commercial banks have yielded impressive results, which have been noticed by the rest of the world. However, these banks have also faced harsh challenges arising from the brand new environment. State-owned commercial banks must still lift themselves up by the bootstraps to improve corporate governance and enhance their competitiveness.

In "System reform of China's capital market," Qi Bin and Huang Ming maintain that since the outbreak of Asia's financial crisis, China's capital market has evolved, following a largely rectified, standardized and healthy path. Such evolution is manifested principally in institutional changes. Rectification started in 1997 and lasted about two years. It mainly covered illegal transactions in over-the-counter stocks, securities organizations and stock exchanges, the futures market, and investment funds. In July 1999, the "Securities Law" went into force, finally conferring legal status to China's capital market. Since then, China's capital market has been further standardized and improved as a result of additional reforms. The State Council issued its "Certain Opinions with Regard to Facilitating the

Reform, Opening-up and Steadfast Development of Capital Market" in 2004 and designated them as the national strategy for developing the capital market. The Certain Opinions laid the foundation for further reform and development of the capital market. There were additional reforms, including ones related to equity division, the settlement of outstanding payments and release of securities by listed companies, and governance of securities companies.

Zhang Delin, in "Reform of state-owned enterprises: a three-year disconnect from difficulties leads to system innovation," analyzes the basic route of reform of state-owned enterprises and describes specific measures taken over the course of the decade. Zhang lists the great changes in Chinese state-owned enterprises as a result of reform and development in institutional, operational, macroscopic, microscopic, theoretical, strategic, policy, and legal terms. State-owned enterprises have now played a more important role in and contributed much more strongly to the national economy and social development. Meanwhile, the future reform and development of state-owned enterprises will continue to pursue a path of diversification and consolidation of governance structures from the microscopic perspective and continue to conduct strategic adjustment and optimization of structure and layout from the macroscopic perspective. The chapter examines other actions that helped state-owned enterprises become bigger, stronger and more competitive.

Han Jun, in "China's rural reform and development after the Asian financial crisis," argues that in the decade after the crisis, China made timely adjustments to the goals of policies related to "three-dimensional rural issues," and bolstered the rural economy, with an emphasis on increasing peasants' incomes. Jun describes China's guiding principle of letting industry boost agriculture and letting urban areas help rural areas pursue development. Jun also points out the strategic importance of constructing new rural areas with socialist features as part of China's drive for modernization. China's agricultural sector and rural areas still face a number of harsh restrictions. To help rural areas develop at a faster pace, it is essential to safeguard peasants' rights and interests, accelerate the development of a social security network, narrow gaps between rural and urban areas in terms of their access to basic public services, and build a system for uniformly planning socio-economic development in rural and urban areas.

Part III: Restructuring China's social welfare system

In "Proactive employment policy and labour market development," Cai Fang and Wang Meiyan state that because of a proactive employment policy and reforms in the labor market after the Asian financial crisis, China successfully promoted employment and re-employment, facilitated the flow of laborers, coped with the impact on the labor market, created a new arrangement for market-resource deployment. Recent changes in the relationship between supply and demand require China to urgently fortify regulation of the labor market.

In "Social security policy," Wang Yanzhong points out that in the decade after Asia's financial crisis, China's new social security system evolved with many twists and turns and adapted to the country's efforts in social and economic restructuring. The system has gained a proven structure and properly functional operating mechanism and has become an important force propelling China's socialist market-oriented economic system forward and developing the campaign to build a harmonious socialist society.

In "Reform and Development of the Public Health System," Zhang Zhenzhong and Wu Huazhang say that since 1998, China's proactive financial policies have accelerated the establishment of a public health care system for urban and rural areas. The authors reviews the evolution of reforms in health care in the past few years. They also discuss noteworthy contradictions in the reforms that have already been undertaken and suggest new directions for the future.

In "Educational policies: from expansion and equity to quality," Zhang Li sums up the thoughts of China's education policy makers and describes the impact of policies over the past 10 years. The progress made in the areas of basic, vocational, and higher education is detailed. Drawing on an in-depth analysis of the barriers to the current development of China's education sector, the author explores options for the future.

Part IV: Reflections on the Asian financial crisis and China's opening up to the outside world

In "The 1997 Asian financial crisis: review and reflections," Bai Chong-En looks at lessons learned from Asia's financial crisis. He maintains that if the financial system had been unable to quickly respond to market signals, small problems could have grown into large catastrophes, triggering a much bigger financial crisis. He also argues that too much interference in the economy (and exchange rates) would mask the market's important market signals.

In "China in the Realm of the World Economy," Li Daokui introduces the main measures China took to cope with the Asian financial crisis, including a flexible micro-market mechanism, effective macroeconomic adjustment initiatives, prudent handling of capital flows, and establishment of an effective "firewall." He further points out that financial risks remain, and says developing countries should push for a fairer and more rational new international economic order, strive to prevent micro-financial risks, and reinforce control over macro-financial risks.

Part I

China's macroeconomic management after the Asian financial crisis

1 From overcoming deflation to preventing inflation

Liu He

It has now been a decade since the 1997 Asian financial crisis erupted. During this period the Chinese economy has gone through different cyclical stages, from overcoming deflation to preventing inflation, and worked the miracle of prolonged high growth. With the transition towards a big power, open economy, and the transformation of the social structure, the challenges confronting China are becoming more and more acute. This chapter describes the characteristics of the changes in China's macro economy during the decade, introduces policy orientation and contradictions, and makes policy recommendations for the next stage. The views expressed represent the personal opinions of the author as a scholar and bear no relation to the author's organization or post.

Halting deflation for a rebound of total demand

Between 1992 and 1997, China adhered to market reform and experienced the cyclical fluctuation of economic overheating. During the period, the Chinese government fulfilled, in timely fashion, two major tasks that had a far-reaching effect on the subsequent economic growth. First, by means of effective macroeconomic regulation, the national economy achieved a "soft landing" from the state of high inflation. Second, very forceful and highly fruitful reform was carried out to establish a market economy, including a micro foundation and a macro-regulation framework so that a social consensus acknowledging the market economy could be reached.

At the same time, three problems, directly related to the deflation that was to emerge later, loomed large. First, economic growth gradually became dependent on exports, and the contribution rate of net exports, which used to be negative, became positive, reaching its peak in 1997. Second, production of agricultural products went into surplus. In 1996, China's grain output unexpectedly exceeded 0.5 trillion kilograms, leading to an oversupply and decline in prices of farm products. The production capacity of major industrial products also became excessive, as evidenced by a marked drop in the equipment utilization rate. Third, residents were prepared for the likely effects of reform; in particular, the housing reform that was about to be introduced resulted in higher saving rates among residents.

When the Asian financial crisis broke out suddenly on July 2, 1997, the Thai currency, the Baht, was the first to nose-dive in value. The tide of depreciation quickly spread to Malaysia, South Korea, and Taiwan, seriously impacting world economic growth. The internal and external reasons for the crisis deserve serious examination. Before and after the crisis, Thailand, a small country with an open economy, witnessed economic prosperity brought by the massive foreign debts of its financial system, experienced the stage where the macro economy was maintained by the massive sterilization of the central bank, and survived the trade deficit brought by the shift from the export-oriented myth to excessive consumption. The sudden crisis exposed the latent contradictions in the combination of a lax micro-regulation structure, crony capitalism, and unbalanced macroeconomic variables. International factors also played a significant role. In particular, in the United States, the Clinton administration's efforts to balance the budget, deregulation, and new economic policies, began to work. This was evidenced by a sharp rise in the rate of returns on the American capital market, a strengthened US dollar, more optimistic expectations for the US economy globally, and formation of an Internet bubble larger than that of Asia, which was pivotal in the withdrawal of global capital from Asia. What is implied here is the need to review local crises from a global perspective and the angle of an international financial system dominated by the US dollar.

China was slow to feel the impact of the Asian financial crisis, which was a typical process of market transference and changes in psychological expectations. No obvious impact was felt in 1997, when China had just secured stability in its macro economy. But, from 1998 onward, the negative impact of deflation gradually began to be felt. In the first half of 1998, export growth registered a year-on-year drop of 18.6 percentage points, and the utilization of foreign capital decreased. At that time, China relied on Asian markets for 60 percent of its exports and 70 percent of its foreign capital inflows. These changes undoubtedly produced a considerable disturbance in domestic growth and employment. Investment and consumption dwindled. While consumption grew by only 6.8 percent, a drop of 3.4 percentage points, the contribution of investment to economic growth declined noticeably. And, as the general level of commodity prices fell, commodity retail prices and consumer prices plummeted. A process of accelerated dispersion appeared where the interaction of weakening total demand, the relative total oversupply, and the decrease in the marginal growth of exports, triggered the fall of other demand variables. As we recall it, the leading indicators of China's economy had already begun to change before the Asian financial crisis, which can be understood either as the result of the economic overheating in the previous stage, or as a sign of the deflation to come. How it would develop depended to a great extent on the unpredictable marginal dynamics of the external environment.

The transition from monetary policy to proactive fiscal policy

In reaction to the Asian financial crisis, the first step was the expansion of the monetary policy. In March 1998, the People's Bank of China (the central bank of China) lowered the deposit reserve requirement rate by five percentage points, from 13 percent to 8 percent, which was followed by a number of adjustments to the interest rates of bank savings and loans. The Bank resumed bond repo, increased the loan examination power of commercial banks, and injected capital into state-owned commercial banks, aiming to expand liquidity and promote economic growth. Given the changed social expectations at the time, the monetary policy had done all it could, but had failed to change the general reluctance of commercial banks to provide loans, and played only a limited role in pushing for economic growth. The cliché that the Chinese economy is "easier started up than stopped" seemed outdated and erroneous. The truth is, that once market players have changed their expectations for the future and are fearful of economic recession, the role that monetary policy can play is limited for a very simple reason: it cannot eliminate the external risks that concern market players. Under such circumstances, the Central Government decided to take up the responsibility by launching a proactive fiscal policy in late 1998.

Having carefully analyzed the international environment and current domestic social expectations, the Chinese government accurately judged the overall trend of the world economy and the future development of the regional crisis. It believed that a downward Renminbi (RMB) exchange rate would be no good for anyone, and that the role of monetary policy is an auxiliary one when it is necessary to get out of recession. Therefore, a decision was made to implement a proactive fiscal policy by issuing long-term construction treasury bonds and expanding public investment to kick off domestic aggregate demand. In the following three years, RMB Yuan 360 billion of long-term construction treasury bonds were issued (about RMB Yuan 1 trillion by today's rate), which were used in agriculture, water conservancy, transportation, communications, urban infrastructure, education, and other social undertakings. In implementing its public investment policy, the government focused on the synergy of long-term effects and short-term macro objectives, and worked hard to eliminate structural bottlenecks and create conditions and potentials for sustained growth. It also stressed the need to draw a line between the role of the government and that of the market, giving the market mechanism the widest possible scope and making substantial investment in the fields where government functions needed to be strengthened. Moreover, it emphasized the coordination of economic and social development, and prioritized such social fields as employment, social security, medical care, education, and poverty relief. These excellent approaches to its strategic vision earned the Chinese government favorable comments from the international community. We note here that China's public investment was the largest-ever fiscal expansion made by a central government since the American New Deal in the last century.

While expanding public investment, efforts were made to create rebound in the other variables of aggregate demand and speed up the strategic reform of the economic structure. The relevant measures included a decision to keep the exchange rate stable to prevent the financial crisis from worsening, while the export rebate rate was raised several times to strengthen the export motivation system. Efforts were also made to encourage consumption demand by increasing the salaries of civil servants, instituting a long holiday system, subsidizing laid-off workers, and developing consumption credit business, and measures taken to improve the infrastructure systems, such as social security and medical insurance. In addition, incentive policies were implemented for investment and utilization of foreign capital to accelerate the development of the capital market, encourage enterprises to pursue direct financing, exempt important equipment from import duties, and otherwise actively utilize foreign capital. In the meantime, timely reflections were made on the export oriented industrial strategy, and the development strategy of focusing on expansion of domestic demand was put forward. Also introduced was the development strategy for western regions combined with policies in the agricultural sector to return grain plots to forestry. Overall, a large-scale integration, covering deepened reform, expanded openings, and restructuring, occurred under the proactive fiscal policy, which undoubtedly played a significant role in boosting the future development of the Chinese economy.

Marked results of the proactive fiscal policy

After several years of hard work, great achievements were made in infrastructure construction that attracted worldwide attention. Under the pull of public investment, the economic growth rate returned to the 9.1 percent previously attained in 2002, and there was a stable rise in the consumer price index (CPI) and producer price index (PPI). More importantly, the proactive fiscal policy, with its emphasis on providing public products, filled the entire society with confidence and positive expectations (which were, in themselves, the public products in shortest supply in China during the economic recession). The proactive fiscal policy of the past few years also combines the long-term promotion of market-oriented reform with the short-term target of controlling deflation, unifying the two in an organic way. This effect is still benefiting China today. At a time when international macro economists were debating the pros and cons of Keynesian economics, China could not wait for a conclusion to be drawn in the academic field and had instead pushed its economy one big resolute step forward.

Preventing inflation and striking a balance between international income and expenditure

How China's economy entered an ascending cycle

From 2002, China's economy gradually broke away from the shadow of deflation and entered a new ascending cycle. In the ensuing five years, China's economy has recorded extraordinary performance and achieved unexpected rapid growth. The most eye-catching achievements include the following: in 2006, as its GDP reached RMB Yuan 20.94 trillion, China was ranked fourth in the world in terms of economic aggregate; per capita GDP rose from US$703 in 1996 to US$2,040; its total volume of foreign trade reached US$1,760.7 billion, the third largest in the world; and China's official foreign exchange reserves rose to the highest in the world. Labor productivity and living standards have improved dramatically and China is exerting an unprecedented impact on the world economy. To date, the economy is still in a cyclical ascendancy and its performance continues to receive unprecedented global attention.

From a broader perspective, there are three main reasons why China's economy entered its new ascending cycle. First, it coincided with a new political cycle. The Sixteenth National Congress of the Communist Party of China in 2002 set the grand goal of building a prosperous society, and new leaders at all levels made it their priority to speed up the process of industrialization and urbanization. Second, after its accession to the World Trade Organization (WTO) in 2001, China gradually embarked on the path of a big power open economy. Seizing the opportunities brought by globalization, China pushed ahead with the liberalizing process of trade and capital in a steady and restrained way, to spur reform and development. Third, in the world economy, the Internet bubble had burst, as shown by the return of new technology to the entity economy, a steady rebound of economic growth, quickened transition of international industries dominated by private capital, and improved trade conditions for primary products.

China's accession to the WTO deserves the highest attention. China has gradually developed an "atypical" open economy when compared with the open economies of other big powers. The Chinese economy influences the changes in world commodity prices through the ups and downs of its domestic total demand/supply system, rather than through the typical conduction of currency and interest rates. China's exports eased the pressure of the upward trend in global commodity prices, while its massive imports triggered a rise in the price of primary products. This has changed the long-term trade conditions of the world, caused changes in the relative comparative advantages, and accelerated the global rearrangement of capital. In contrast, the flow of external capital produced a far-reaching structural impact on the domestic economy. This is the main difference between the current economic cycle and the previous cycles.

The Chinese economy has maintained its overall momentum of rapid growth as a result of the fundamental national policy of reform and opening up. The stage of reform completed in the 1990s has created institutional conditions for the present growth and, in particular, reform of the fiscal and taxation system has provided a strong motivation for the development of local governments. The expansive policy implemented to conquer deflation was maintained, which served to accelerate the growth in the cyclical ascending stage. The proactive fiscal policy has created better infrastructure and improved latent growth capability, or increased the curve of production probability. In the imbalance of world economic growth, the phenomenon of excessive global liquidity began to appear and is continuously intensifying so that the world market has expanded and the economy has moved into a boom stage. The growth of domestic per capita income and market reform has resulted in structural and historic market changes. More importantly, all these developments took place in a large eastern country with a population of 1.3 billion that is promoting industrialization, urbanization, marketization, and internalization.

In the ascending stage of the economic cycle, the macro economy of China is always faced with the issue of how to maintain stability. China's domestic economic structure is changing drastically; it is in a stage of rapid growth as the internal/external variables affecting macro economy have abruptly increased, making it more difficult than ever before to reach the goal of stabilization. The Central Government attaches great importance to the stability of the macro economy in the new economic cycle and takes a position that encompasses two significant points. The first is to keep the positive momentum of economic growth by prolonging the duration of the economic ascending cycle, and by protecting and developing the drive of all sectors. The Central Government holds that the Chinese economy is facing a rare strategic opportunity and is in the historic stage of accelerated urbanization and industrialization. It is inevitable that economic growth will pick up; macro regulation is not intended to simply reduce the speed of economic growth, but rather to create conditions to maintain the momentum of the economic acceleration. The second point in the government's position is the adoption of mild-micro regulation and control-point regulation measures in specific macro policies, which is based on the lessons of past experience and the fear of creating an unstable foundation for the acceleration. Under the precondition of maintaining the continuity and stability of policy, appropriate adjustment has been put in place to avoid dampening the expectations of positive economic growth, prevent the excessive force of policy from causing economic fluctuations, and maintain a harmonized coordination of short-term and long-term policies.

When signs of overheated economic growth appeared, the Central Government made two wise decisions that were related to the overall situation. The first was to increase agricultural investment and incentives in time to curb the fall of grain output, crop area, and per unit area yield, for some years. The move played a crucial role in stabilizing the overall situation and the general level of commodity prices. The second decision was to continuously issue long-term treasury bonds, with a focus on the construction of the short-line industries of coal, electricity, oil, and transportation, to dispel the bottleneck restraint of supply structure, give play to the infrastructure built a few years ago, and avoid structural growth in commodity prices. These two decisions constitute the main content of what is to be preserved under the countermeasure calling for both preservation and restriction, and insure the important conditions for prolonging this round of economic ascendancy are maintained.

Compared with the inflation stage prior to the occurrence of the Asian financial crisis, China started from over-investment in both the cycles, which may seem similar at first glance, but were actually poles apart in subsequent years. The over-heating in the early 1990s took the form of a large trade deficit and skyrocketing commodity prices. This time, however, it was expressed through a huge trade surplus. Abundant liquidity did not immediately exhibit itself in the overall level of commodity prices, but more in the rise of asset prices. Although it is not the intention of this paper to make a comparison between the two, it is helpful to touch on this area in order to deepen understanding of the fluctuation of the Chinese macro economy. As shown in Figure 1.1, the four target variables of the macro economy differed greatly in 2006 from what they were in 1995. Although the growth rate and employment did not change much, the overall level of commodity prices

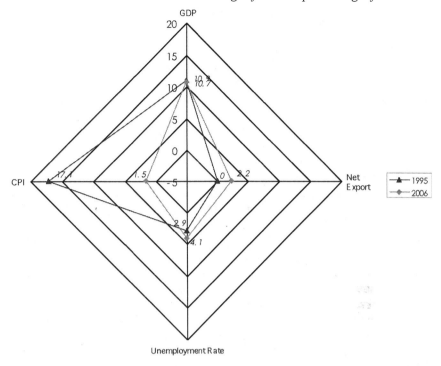

Figure 1.1 Relative changes in four major macroeconomic indicators, 1997–2007.

was extremely different, and the case of international income and expenditure was exactly opposite. The pattern in 1995 featured high inflation and a low trade surplus, leading to a typical overheating of a closed macro economy. The current situation, however, features a coexistence of low commodity prices and a high trade surplus, and a prominent excess of liquidity. The two patterns differ in the background of internationalization and the degree of entry.

Investment began to speed up, reaching 16.9 percent in 2002 and 27.7 percent in 2003. If not for the outbreak of the SARS epidemic in the spring of 2003, over-investment would have been even more prominent. In the third quarter of 2003, over-investment had become serious in some sectors, especially in the heavy industries of steel, cement, and electrolytic aluminum, where the increase in investments had been particularly large. In the related debates two principal views were expressed. One view was that the excess increase in investment should be regarded as an expansion of domestic total demand. The other view regarded the expansion trend of the trade surplus as inevitable, and recommended a sharp rise in the exchange rate of the RMB Yuan since RMB appreciation was not widely expected. These views are valuable. The specifics of the investment expansion include, first, that the increasing demands of the domestic and foreign markets motivated investors at the micro level who had obtained conditions for independent growth – external costs (including environmental protection and social security) that did not become internal costs, rock-bottom land prices, low labor force costs, and a production capacity formation period of an extremely short cycle – that led to very high profits on investment. The relatively undervalued exchange rate encouraged further investment. Second, local governments accelerated industrialization to meet the requirements for improving local economic development conditions. They were given impetus by the fiscal and taxation system, especially revenue from value-added tax, and from selling land obtained at low prices. Third, international capital is always on the look out for good investment opportunities. Abundant liquidity and structural imbalances in the global economy caused a large amount of international investment to switch to China, thereby increasing production capacity in the manufacturing sectors. This round of rapid investment brought with it new challenges: negative environmental impacts brought by extensive economic growth; the sense of crisis and new pressure brought by the drastic price increases on international primary products; the excessive proportion of funds outstanding for foreign exchange; and abundant liquidity brought by a rapidly expanding surplus of international income and expenditure. In fact, these three problems will influence China's future development for at least 20 years.

In the latter half of 2003, the government began to make macro adjustments, persisting in sterilizing the excessive proportion of funds outstanding for foreign exchanges through the central bank and, meanwhile, adopting structural adjustment policies on the supply side, with emphasis on industrial policies and preservation, and restriction countermeasures. The following key adjustments were made: restricting the unfettered expansion of industrial parks and the real estate sector; tightening the controls on land and credit, and addressing the excessive production capacity of some industries by stepped up monitoring of new projects; raising the market access threshold for industries of high energy consumption and high pollution by strictly enforcing environmental protection standards; making moderate adjustments to the prices of resources and products; and taking the necessary administrative measures. Under the conditions of a closed economy implementation of these policies would have been difficult. Under the conditions of an open economy, however, the substitution of external markets and resources watered down the intensity of some policies. That said, the strong program of adjustment and targeting measures gradually began to slow investment in the latter half of 2004, and the strict administration of land achieved the effect of leading domestic investment into a cross-regional and cross-industry transfer.

Along with the adjustment program, the Central Government was aware of the long-term serious consequences of unrestrained investment and extensive growth. Having analyzed future changes and constraints, the government summarized the experience and lessons of developed and developing countries. Taking a scientific outlook of development and with construction of a harmonious society as its goal, China once again achieved timely progress through its governing concept. Taking into account the actual conditions, the government lost no time in combining short- and long-term measures. The Eleventh Five-year Plan set out the development strategy for building a resources-saving and environment-friendly society, called for a faster pace of change in the economic growth paradigm and construction of an innovative country, proposed developmental thinking on the construction of new villages in rural areas and main regions, put forward long-term measures for developing city clusters, worked hard to reduce negative externality, and improved the quality and beneficial results of growth. All these proposals will play an extremely important role in achieving the long-term, healthy development of the nation.

With the extension of this economic pattern, the issues of abundant liquidity and economic aggregate began to draw more attention. Abundant liquidity presented itself as early as 2003. At that time, the central bank took timely sterilizing measures and the operation has now lasted for years. The large quantity of sterilization is unprecedented and the overall effect has received generally positive feedback. However, sterilization is, after all, a passive method and trade surplus is still expanding, rising drastically to US$102 billion in 2005 and US$177.5 billion in 2006. In the first quarter of 2007, the trade surplus had expanded further. The ratio of foreign trade in GDP has exceeded 60 percent, while the speed and quantity of the net inflow in capital accounts are on the rise. Abundant liquidity, or excessive total demand measured with M2, remains prominent.

The reasons for the emergence of abundant liquidity are complicated, and include interwoven long- and short-term factors, and systematic factors. There are at least two long-term factors. First, globalization and lopsided international economic development sped up the cross-border transfer of capital. The trade surplus under current account caused by processing trade capacity formed in China accounts for more than 50 percent of total trade surplus. Second, the relationship between domestic savings and consumption is out of balance. The domestic market is unable to fully consume the huge amount of products coming from new production capacity, which has turned to the international market under the stimulation of an export-oriented policy. The short-term factor relates to the expansion of the international market and the depreciation of the US dollar, which have resulted in improved export trade conditions for Chinese products and more market opportunities so that the distorted economic variables have further increased export profits. In this regard, special attention should be given to the increasing expectations for RMB appreciation, which causes a large amount of inflows of capital to China, through capital accounts or other channels, to form new liquidity pressures after the settlement of exchange rates. Insofar as the factor of system mechanism is concerned, abundant liquidity is related to the less-than-satisfactory formation mechanism of exchange rates and interest rates to the distorted prices of major elements and also to the defects in the fundamental system that caused the domestic phenomena of high savings and low consumption, especially the defects in the fiscal and taxation system, social security systems, and banking system, as well as the structural problems existing in the capital market.

A number of dilemmas arise in finding a solution for abundant liquidity. According to monetarist views, the domestic economy can only come back to a short-term balance when the domestic currency shows a large margin of appreciation. For China, however, the rigidity of the labor market and the high cost of adjustment will result in a heavy social cost. The international community would be unable to bear the shock caused by a sudden rise in commodity prices and break from the supply chain, for there is no other country that can take the place of China, in the short term, to provide the global market with good quality commodities at low prices. Furthermore, even if there are multiple reasonable causes for the sharp appreciation of the RMB, the rise would be difficult given the keen expectations for appreciation. Meanwhile, it should be understood that the exchange rate alone could not solve the global structural conflict of the asymmetrical imbalance between savings and consumption that confronts such a large country. The situation of international imbalance is hard to put right in the short- or medium-term. But, overall, the status quo is going to be sustained, so that any unilateral action will only complicate the situation. The solution to abundant liquidity can only be found by addressing the reality of the structural imbalance in the world economy, and the existing exchange rate policy that the government has undertaken to gradually eradicate the problem through the adjustment of basic prices in the domestic economy and by making improvements to other vital systems.

Some countermeasures have already been taken. In monetary policy, the government continued to ease the pressure of abundant liquidity through the sterilization of the central bank, gradually improved the formation mechanism of the RMB exchange rate through progressive, positive, and controllable fine-tuning of exchange rates, and several hikes in the deposit reserve rate and savings and loan interest rates. In trade policy, the government gradually changed the policy of rewarding exports and limiting imports by adjusting the export rebate rate of some products and the scope of processing trade, while lowering the tariff to encourage an expansion of imports. In investment policy, the government continued to strengthen control over land and credit, raised the market access threshold for some industries of high-energy consumption and high pollution, and speeded up the adjustment of distorted prices of primary products. Along with these moderate short-term measures, the government also attaches weight to the adoption of long-term measures for restructuring. These include, in particular, the creation of conditions for expanding domestic demand through the establishment of a public fiscal system and realization of the equalization of basic public services – for example, accelerated development of social services like education and public health, strengthening the social security and medial insurance systems, removal of agricultural tax, and raising the minimum wage. Overall, these policies are expected to have a far-reaching effect in reducing the surplus of international income and expenditure and addressing abundant liquidity, but that will take time.

Currently, the national economy has maintained a positive momentum of rapid growth and the ascending stage of the economic cycle is continuing. In the first quarter of 2007, the GDP growth rate reached 11.1 percent, an average annual increase of 0.7 percent. The increase of total investment in fixed assets fell from its high position and registered an average annual increase of 23.7 percent, down by four percentage points from 2006. The total volume of retail sales of consumer goods grew at a faster pace, by 14.9 percent. Fiscal revenues increased by 26.7 percent. In January and February, corporate profits increased sharply by 43.8 percent, market commodity prices picked up faster than before, and the CPI recorded a rise of 2.7 percent, up from the same period of 2006 by 1.5 percentage points, or only 0.9 percent growth if the price hike on food and energy is deducted. In addition, living standards continued to improve, as shown by an increase of 16.6 percent and 12.1 percent respectively in the disposable income of urban residents and the cash income of farmers, after deduction of commodity price factors.

But, the problem of abundant liquidity has not yet been solved, the efforts aimed at stabilizing the macro economy still face formidable challenges, and an increased potential for the economy to shift from a somewhat speedy growth to overheating. The major problem for the aggregate relationship is that the excessive surplus of international income and expenditure still exists, which is the root cause of abundant liquidity. In the first quarter of 2007, the trade surplus reached US$46.4 billion, and is likely to exceed US$250 billion for the whole year. Foreign exchange reserves increased by US$135.7 billion, which is much higher than the surplus of current accounts, reflecting the strong expectations for RMB appreciation. The overall price level is gradually rising. The imported prices of supply products and domestic element prices have caused latent inflation pressure to gradually surface. The accelerated rise of asset prices has become an apparent signal of overheating, too. The continuously soaring housing prices and Shanghai Stock Exchange index have attracted worldwide attention. From the perspective of structural relationships, the savings to consumption ratio continues to be distorted. The consumption rate declined to 52 percent in 2005, down by seven percentage points from 1997 when the Asian financial crisis erupted. The domestic savings rate has reached 48 percent and the capital formation rate, 43 percent. While the marginal savings rate of residents rises, and its proportion to total deposits falls, the escalating revenues of enterprises and the government have improved, along with a sharp rise in their savings. The system and mechanism causing investment impulse have not yet been changed. Local governments, and commercial and financial institutions and enterprises, all have a keen desire for investment. In a certain sense, China's economy is like a powerful sports car racing along an expressway, with its deceleration system facing a major challenge.

China's macro economy has moved to a crucial stage, presenting major short-term challenges. Internally, growth is speeding up in both the real economy and the virtual economy. Greater risk may come from the accelerated growth of the virtual economy. If the national economy is likened to a reservoir, the expansion of the water source through the international income and expenditure surplus has increased liquidity so that the water in the reservoir is gradually flowing from the real economy to the virtual economy. If the situation continues in this way, will it affect the soundness of the fundamentals of the economy? Will it create even greater risks? Externally, although the world economy is in a period of rapid growth, there are uncertainties about the US economy, the price of oil is fluctuating at high levels, the private equity fund has increased its cross-border flow and acquisition, the lopsided exchange rate of large countries has caused even stronger trade protectionism, and global inflation pressure has gradually emerged. A sudden change in any of these factors may produce a more intense and infectious effect for domestic markets than that of the Asian financial crisis. In a certain sense, the external impact may be the major force that triggers changes in the current round of the economic cycle.

A more crucial issue is that China's economy has entered a new state of relative imbalance between internal and external factors during a period of rapid growth. Grasping the opportunity to deepen reform becomes an extremely urgent task. It will undoubtedly become much more difficult to promote reform and adjustment, if the contradictions are allowed to pile up, and the pattern of interests consolidate.

Issues worthy of discussion

Looking back at the changes in China's macro-economy in the current round of the economic ascending cycle, and the macro control exercised in the process, we can see that we have accumulated a great deal of beneficial experiences and that several new issues arise, which deserve discussion.

On the relationship between external and internal imbalances

Obviously, China's macro economy is in a state characterized by coexisting external and internal imbalances, the former being the dual surplus of international income and expenditure, and the latter being high domestic savings and low consumption. In terms of their impact on the macro economy, they both affect and cause each other. Against the macro background of the global economic imbalance, high domestic savings and low consumption have made it difficult to consume the huge domestic production capacity that has taken form, created excessive savings, and caused a huge trade surplus. At times when the pattern of savings and consumption remains unchanged, or has worsened, the external imbalance has further exacerbated the internal imbalance. One important basic issue regarding the choices available for the macro economy is whether to start by rectifying the external imbalance to achieve an overall balance, or to start with the domestic imbalance to gradually ease the internal and external imbalance. In the circles of theory and policy, there are many different opinions on this matter. The view of this author is that the external imbalance of China's economy is one aspect of the global imbalance, and, at the same time, the outward expression of the internal imbalance. Therefore, whether from a short- or a long-term perspective, the focus of policy should be on eliminating the internal imbalance for several reasons. The short-term policy of China cannot eliminate the external imbalance, because China's economy is subject not only to structural adjustment of its macro policies, but also to a wide range of international factors. When the internal imbalance is quite obvious, an inordinate pursuit of the external balance will only end up aggravating the internal imbalance, thus expanding the external imbalance. Using the internal imbalance to solve the double imbalances helps promote comprehensive structural reform and will place China's economic growth on a more solid institutional foundation. In spite of the heavy pressure of the external imbalance, the really urgent need is to find a solution for the domestic imbalance. On the other hand, an internal balance also helps promote a global economic balance.

Exchange rate policy and price policy

It is necessary to make a more clear-cut choice between exchange rate policy and price policy to promote the realization of an external balance through the focal adjustment made to the internal imbalance. The Chinese government has persisted in positive, progressive, and controllable reform of the exchange rate formation mechanism thereby deciding the basic route China will follow to solve the imbalance of the macro economy. That is to say, under the precondition of the gradual improvement of the exchange rate formation mechanism and moderate appreciation of the RMB, larger steps will have to be taken to adjust the prices of domestic production output. These steps are as follows: adjustment of prices on important primary products so they reflect the degree of scarcity of resources; making enterprises bear the external cost to unify private and social costs; and the establishment and improvement of the social security system so that the price of labor force can reflect its real cost. The biggest challenge is how to coordinate the conflicts between a stabilized macro-economy and the compensation needed to rectify the social cost. Obviously, the adjustment of any important price will cause losses to some social groups. However, if the price adjustment is inadequate in order to accommodate some vested interests, greater losses will result for the country as a whole. On this issue, there is a need to further intensify the implementation of existing policies.

Aggregate policy and structural policy

As far as the practical process of this round of macroeconomic regulation is concerned, we value the solution of an unbalanced aggregate through restructuring, and have implemented a series of differentiated policies for preservation and restriction, which achieved some effect. Overall, however, it will be hard for macro control based primarily on restructuring to ultimately turn around the pattern of excessive total demand and abundant liquidity, or to prevent the economy from overheating due to excessively fast growth. In retrospect, an important reason behind the multiple contradictions in the economy is an excessive total demand. Therefore, in the next round of macro regulation, we should intensify the regulation of total demand through monetary policy, attach weight to the strategic orientation toward the adjustment of structural policy, reduce unnecessary administrative intervention, and do better at leading market expectations. Given an exchange rate policy that remains unchanged, policy coordination of three aspects is of crucial importance. First, the implementation of an appropriately tightened and timely monetary policy to raise interest rates continuously and, in a stable fashion, to lower the regulation target of the currency supply volume, to intensify sterilization, and to lower the aggregate of liquidity. Second, the implementation of a fiscal policy that aims to expand public expenditure to help reduce savings and expand consumption. Third, the implementation of the trade policy designed to encourage imports, to lower import tariffs, and to reduce the trade surplus.

Relevant considerations

The above is only a brief description of the changes in China's economic continuation from an historical perspective. This is a starting point rather than a conclusion. To give a full picture of a decade of changes in a short paper is an impossible task – although it is hard to stop the pen marking out the future of China from the perspective of an early industrial revolution. A careful analysis points to three main issues in need of further discussion.

The globalized background for the economic growth of China

Since the world entered the stage of the global economy, the policy independence of all countries has been influenced and the degree of mutual reliance between the big powers is higher than ever. The global economy incorporates different development trends. Although the US economy remains the major engine, the relative decline of its share is unavoidable. The UK, Germany, and Japan have completed a new round of structural upgrading and become quality-type economic entities that are insensitive to the fluctuations of the exchange rate. China, India, and some other countries are contributing more and more to world economic growth, but are also faced with many domestic problems. All countries are looking for a new strategic orientation in the global reorganization. The positive growth effect of globalization faces big challenges from the effects of negative distribution. Against this background, we need to reconsider the future position of China's economy and make important strategic choices based on the twenty-first-century challenges of globalization rather than from an over optimistic perspective. We should focus particularly on studying how to foster new competitive edges after China loses its advantages of labor costs and as an aging society with a large population.

Integration of the macro policy and other policies of China

The macro economy policy of China is not simply oriented to monetarism. There is need for complete structural policy integration. Any aspect can function as a logical starting point. If the reduction of the domestic savings rate is the logical starting point, then the establishment of a social security network, adjustment of education policy, reform of income distribution policy, the enhancement of flexibility in the labor market, and the deepening of the financial market are essential policies, with the reform of public finance occupying a core position. From the angle of world changes, China's economic transformation has indeed reached the historical stage of integrating macro with micro policies, economic with social policies, and political with economic policies. There has never been such an inter-reliance between policies as there is today. Without a doubt, it is necessary to put forth thinking and plan measurement under an overall logic, for one can hope to walk smoothly toward the future by finding the way from a vantage point.

The need to maintain and create consensus on reform

Under the pressure of a Cultural Revolution crisis, China formed a consensus on reform. Without market reform, there would not have been the economic prosperity we see in China today. Failure to deepen the reform would make it hard for China's economy to have a bright future. Faced with wide ranging calls for change, today the world feels more profoundly than ever before that the consensus of reform is the most important public product. The common understanding we need to consolidate includes the following aspects. The old track of the traditional planned economy will not work and it is a blessing for China to promote marketization and internationalization in a framework of stable social systems. The key to future plain sailing for China lies in respecting property rights, protecting fair competition, forming social credit, encouraging innovation, and defining the public functions of the government. Motivation rather than equalization should be used to achieve social justice and prevent the occurrence of the two extreme phenomena caused by insufficient sharing of the fruits of development and lack of tolerance for contradictions during the transformation period. Caution should be exercised with respect to the swamp effect on reform resulting from vested interests and loss of interests. It is necessary to insure the decision-making process is more scientific and more democratic. Reform and opening up should be linked more closely to winning international acceptance of goals and routes in the process of globalization.

2 From proactive to sound fiscal policy

An improvement to China's public finance system

Jia Kang

China initiates expansive and proactive fiscal policy after Asian financial crisis

In 1993, China's highest-level decision makers decided to strengthen macro regulation to overcome economic overheating and inflation. Within about three years, the national economy successfully made a "soft landing."

Immediately after the soft landing, controversies arose about the state of the macro economy. Some analysts believed that insufficient aggregate demand had emerged. This view entered the mainstream in early 1998.

However, by the end of the first quarter of 1998, the impact of Southeast Asia's 1997 financial crisis on China had become apparent and, together with a series of domestic problems, contributed to deflationary pressures and led to an urgent need to expand domestic demand. A need arose for urgent measures to prevent a downturn in the economy or even a "flameout" after the soft landing.

The impact of Southeast Asia's financial crisis was worse than expected

On July 2, 1997, Thailand's announcement that it was abandoning its pegged exchange-rate system caused Southeast Asia's economies to burst and sent shockwaves throughout Asia. By 1998, the crisis had spread to Russia and Latin America, and even affected Europe and the United States. The impact on the economies of Asia and other parts of the world was far greater than most people had anticipated.

China's economy was thought to have outperformed other countries in the region during the crisis. But, in the first quarter of 1998, the growth rate of foreign trade with China slowed down noticeably until it became negative in May. In spite of a rebound later, the economy nosedived again at the end of the third quarter. The negative developments alarmed policy makers and others, who came to appreciate the gravity of the situation.

The Asian financial crisis deepened the troughs in China's economic cycle and set the stage for deflation

Chinese economic growth, measured in terms of gross domestic product (GDP), fell from 13.5 percent in 1993 to 8.8 percent in 1997, averaging a one percentage point decrease each year. In early 1998, the rate was nevertheless still regarded relatively desirable. But the downturn did not stop. In the first half of 1998, economic growth rate was merely 7 percent, conspicuously lower than the 8 percent rate targeted for that year. Meanwhile, commodity prices continued to shrink and signs of deflation appeared.

Two decades of market reform enabled China to break away from an "all-around buyers' market"

Before the reform, short supply was typical in China's national economy. After the inception of reform, the mechanism for market-oriented resource allocation took shape, and productivity improved gradually during tremendous liberalization. In the troughs of several economic cycles, China witnessed a partial buyers' market in 1983, a market slump in 1990, and finally a fairly complete buyers' market in 1997–1998, when commodities in short supply decreased in variety but were mostly in line with demand (of course, what should not be forgotten is that housing and mass transit were still in very serious short supply, but the shortages were not reflected in statistics produced by relevant departments). The total quantity of stockpiled products of enterprises continuously rose and reached RMB Yuan 4 trillion in value in 1998, equal to about 50 percent of gross national product (GNP).

At the crucial stage of reform, the strategic reorganization of the state-owned economy resulted in a large number of layoffs and worsened unemployment

After a series of preludes and peripheral moves, the nearly 20 years of reform reached a crucial stage: strategic reorganization of the state-owned economy. In the macro environment of sluggish demand after the soft landing, past preferences and supportive measures designed to rescue loss-suffering enterprises were discarded, creating "survival-of-the-fittest" pressure on enterprises to reorganize, be annexed or file for bankruptcy. This pressure, accompanied by decelerating factors inside and outside the national economy, exacerbated the plight at the micro level and led to about 10 million layoffs a year. How to increase job opportunities and alleviate unemployment has become a major issue for policy makers and all social sectors.

The continuous and intensive use of currency policy yielded unsatisfactory results

To address the problems that occurred during the soft landing, several measures were taken to ease the money supply and stimulate demand. From May 1996 to

1998, the central bank lowered interest rates on deposits and loans seven times, lifted controls over loan limits of state-owned commercial banks in early 1998 (and replaced it with management of asset liability ratio and risks), lowered the reserve rate and promulgated guidance and opinions concerning active loan support, with the aim of expanding the loan demand of enterprises and stimulate investment. Such continuous and intensive use of currency policy could be said to be "all-out," yet it failed to produce sufficiently obvious effects and left relatively limited room for operation.

In summary, decision makers implemented guidelines for increasing government investment to expand domestic demand in 1998 to achieve an 8 percent growth goal for the year and fend off the impact of the Asian financial crisis. Initiation of fiscal policy became an inevitable choice because fiscal policy is the only major reliable tool other than currency policy for a macro regulation system that primarily relies on "indirect regulation" under a market economy.

Key points and the effects of proactive fiscal policy

Implementation of expansive proactive fiscal policy

In April and May 1998, macro statistical data for the first quarter and for the period January through April was released, and all parties concerned gradually reached a common understanding about the situation of the macro economy. Decision makers decided to increase investment and expand domestic demand. Because of the less than satisfactory effect of the currency policy, more considerations were given to more use of fiscal policy for expansion. In mid-June, Minister of Finance Xiang Huaicheng published an important article in the *People's Daily* and *China Financial and Economic News* about his intentions for macroeconomic control and jumpstarting economic growth. The article argued that it was inadvisable to stimulate the economy through tax cuts. Instead, he said, it was necessary to promote the growth of the national economy through timely and appropriate expansion of the financial debt scale and financial expenditures and by increasing investment, stimulating consumption, expanding exports and pushing for reforms to overcome system and policy factors that had curbed effective demand. The relevant departments hastened the study of methods for initiating the fiscal policy and worked out a plan to adjust the original budget, which was submitted to review and adopted at the August session of the Standing Committee of the National People's Congress (NPC).

The budget-adjusting plan included an increased issue of long-term national bonds by RMB Yuan 100 billion. The money raised would be used as special investment within the state budget for the construction of infrastructure. National bonds valued at RMB Yuan 100 billion were issued only to state-owned commercial banks, including the Industrial and Commercial Bank of China (ICBC), the Agricultural Bank of China (ABC), the Bank of China (BOC) and the Construction Bank of China (BOCOM), which respectively subscribed RMB Yuan 50 billion, RMB Yuan 20 billion, RMB Yuan 10 billion, and RMB Yuan 20 billion, with a repayment period of 10 years and an annual interest rate of 5.5 percent. The RMB Yuan 100 billion of debt was split into two parts to be incorporated into the state budget in 1998 and 1999 as financial deficit. Accordingly, expenditure of the 1998 central budget increased by RMB Yuan 50 billion, and the deficit of central finance rose from RMB Yuan 46 billion budgeted at the beginning of the year to RMB Yuan 96 billion. Meanwhile, many of the infrastructure projects to be constructed were those of localities and were not to be undertaken by local governments. But, the Budget Law contained explicit provisions that local governments had no power to raise loans and could not translate debts into the deficits of local financial budgets. Therefore, the State Council decided to loan RMB Yuan 50 billion of the RMB Yuan 100 billion of national bonds to local governments for use.

The budget-adjusting plan also included an adjustment of the RMB Yuan 18 billion originally earmarked in the budget for construction of infrastructure at the beginning of the year to expenditure under current accounts to add investments in science, technology and education, insure the full and timely payment of the basic living expenses of laid-off workers of state-owned enterprises and the pensions of retirees, and increase the expenditure of disaster-relief efforts (at that time, an exceptional flood was forecast in the valleys of the Changjiang River, Nenjiang River and Songhuajiang River.

Such a drastic mid-year adjustment to the financial budget had rarely been seen in the decades since the founding of New China, but was nevertheless in line with Article 54 of the Budget Law and belonged to a flexible "playing to the score" in macro regulation, reflecting the enhanced ability of China to carry out macro regulation.

The decision to issue the RMB Yuan 100 billion of national bonds only to state-owned commercial banks was based on the consideration that at that time, the basic currency supply by the central bank was relatively low, resident savings had increased significantly, commercial banks had a large deposit-loan difference, and commodity prices overall continued to drop, creating a golden opportunity to issue such long-term national bonds to commercial banks.

From January through July that year, the state bank recovered RMB Yuan 66.93 billion more currency than it did in the previous year. The amount of funds taken up by foreign exchange did not increase further, and the basic currency that should be supplied under the national economic plan was in short issuance. Therefore, issuing more national bonds would not cause an over-issuing of currency. By the end of July, the balance of residents' savings had reached RMB Yuan 5.075 trillion, a year-on-year rise of RMB Yuan 743.73 billion, up from the beginning of the year by RMB Yuan 446.98 billion. The intensified restraint mechanism made the commercial banks more cautious in providing loans for any industrial projects that had exceeded demand, thus leading to a considerable difference between savings and loans and increasing the cost of banking operations. Issuing more national bonds to commercial banks would help improve the operating conditions of banks and defuse financial risks. Thanks to the continuous fall of the overall level of commodity prices and repeated downward adjustment of interest rate, the cost of issuing more national bonds also decreased.

The State Council carefully studied the use of the RMB Yuan 100 billion raised from the national bonds that were issued additionally and decided on a number of principles for their use. First, only infrastructure projects could be selected. Generally, no industrial projects would be included. Second, priority would be given to using the funds to speed up projects in progress and those projects for which the feasibility studies and initial preparations had been completed. Third, consideration would be given both to a quick promotion of economic growth and to prevent rushing headlong into action, limiting redundant construction, and pursuing speedy construction. Fourth, new projects would be reported for approval in strict keeping with procedures to be arranged and unified by the Central Government. The new projects arranged from central financing would tend to focus on the central and western regions. Fifth, all projects would be carefully organized and implemented to insure engineering quality.

Project arrangements focused on:

1   increasing investment in cropland water conservancy and ecological environment construction. To prevent and fight floods, efforts were made to consolidate river embankments, repair water-damaged works, protect natural forest resources in the middle and upper reaches of the Changjiang River and Yellow River, and plant more trees for forestation;
2   continuing to accelerate the construction of railways, highways, telecommunications systems and key airports. Railway projects mainly included the double track of the southern section of the Beijing–Kowloon Line. Under the plan for a network composed of five vertical and seven transverse lines, highway construction focused on three vertical lines (Tongjiang–Sanya, Beijing–Zhuhai and Chongqing–Zhanjiang highways), two transverse lines (Lianyungang–Huoerguosi and Shanghai–Chengdu highways); and two important sections (Beijing–Shenyang and Beijing–Shanghai highways). Telecommunication construction focused on the development of digital communications and a mobile communication network;
3   expanding the scale of urban environmental protection and construction of urban infrastructure. The focus was on sewage and rubbish treatment, water supplies, heat and gas, roads and landscaping in large and medium-sized cities;
4   constructing national reserve grain depots with a capacity of 50 billion catties. The investment in the depots directly under state control in the entire year reached 17.5 times the amount that had been planned at the beginning of the year and exceeded the total investment made since the founding of the republic. These depots were mainly constructed by local governments according to unified standard on land provided free of charge by local places. They were exempted from relevant taxes and fees. The State Bureau of Grain Reserve dispatched engineering supervisors to insure the quality of the works. After 1999, the scale of construction increased to a capacity of some 100 billion catties, which could satisfy the storage capacity needed for national reserve grains;

5   carrying out the transformation and construction of a rural power grid and simultaneously hastening the transformation of urban power grid; and

6   expanding the scale of construction of affordable housing. Besides, the funds raised from the additionally issued national bonds were also used for more investment in the construction of public security, procurement and court facilities.

In 1998, when proactive fiscal policy was initiated, RMB Yuan 270 billion of special national bonds (with 30-year terms) were issued to state-owned commercial banks, which actually transformed banks' debts for depositors into the debts of state finance for banks (indirectly for depositors). The funds were then all transferred into the capital accounts of the four state-owned banks, greatly enhancing their capital adequacy ratio and risk-resisting capability.

In 1999, decision makers further adjusted the intensity of implementation and the specific measures of the proactive fiscal policy to address the decrease of investment in fixed assets, a fall in exports and continuously inadequate consumption demand that appeared in the second quarter. There were three aspects to these actions. First, on the basis of the issuing scale originally decided at the beginning of the year, i.e., RMB Yuan 50 billion of long-term national bonds, another RMB Yuan 60 billion of long-term national bonds would be issued subject to review and approval of NPC. Again, the amount was to be shared by the Central Government and localities on a 50 percent basis to expand the central finance deficit by RMB Yuan 30 billion and maintain faster growth in investment demand. The funds from the additional national bonds would mainly find use in ongoing infrastructure projects, technical transformation of some key industries, equipment localization of major projects, industrialization of high technology, environmental protection, ecological improvement and infrastructure for science and education. Discount interest was available for the technical transformation projects of large state-owned enterprises. Second, income distribution policy would be adjusted to increase the income of urban and rural residents, with focus on middle and low-income earners, stimulate consumption demand and appropriately raise the three lines of social security (basic support for laid-off workers of state-owned enterprises, unemployment insurance, and ensuring minimum cost-of-living support for urban residents), increase the income of staff members of government departments and institutions, enhance the welfare of retirees, and strive to resolve overdue pension payments by state-owned enterprise. Throughout the year, financial expenditures in this regard increased by about RMB Yuan 54 billion, directly benefiting more than 84 million people across the nation. Furthermore, practical measures were taken to lighten the burden of farmers and increase income through a variety of channels. Third, the taxation policy would be adjusted to support exports. In response to the impact on trade resulting from changes in the international economic trade environment, China raised export rebates twice in early 1999 and in July for products that were competitive on the world market and that had a high industrial relevance so that the overall rebate rate for export commodities reached more than 15 percent. Besides, to address insufficient investment demand, the policy of collecting fixed-asset investment-regulation tax at a rate reduced by 50 percent in the latter half of the year was implemented.

Starting from August 1, the business tax, deed tax and land value-added tax (VAT) related to real estate were soundly lowered to inspire the driving force of the real estate industry for economic growth and invigorate the large amount of tied-up capital resulting from unoccupied housing. New policies included new provisions for VAT, business tax, import/export taxation, corporate income tax, income tax on foreign investment and foreign enterprise. New policies also include changes to the system for scientific research institutions to promote technological innovation and the development of high technology. Adjustments were made to the taxation policy involving foreign interest to encourage foreign investment, and as of November 1, personal income tax was resumed on interest income from resident savings to promote and stimulate near-term consumption of residents and increase consumption demand.

After the national economy took a turn for the better in the first half of 2000, a decision was made to further intensify the proactive fiscal policy to consolidate the improvements in the economy and to prepare for any uncertainties that might arise in the future. On the basis of the scale of the RMB Yuan 100 billion long-term national bond issue decided at the beginning of the year, the Ministry of Finance (MOF) additionally adjusted the plan and, subject to approval of NPC, issued RMB Yuan 50 billion long-term national bonds in the latter half of the year. These bonds were intended to accelerate the construction of ongoing projects. They covered construction of water conservation and ecological projects, including irrigation infrastructure, construction of new towns for immigrants, reforestation of former grain plots and the planting of grass, protection of natural woods and grasslands, and the start-up of sand treatment works around Beijing and Tianjin; construction of education infrastructure, including dormitories for the increasing number of students enrolled in higher education, and subsidized construction of colleges in the central and western regions; construction of infrastructure projects, including trunk highways, roads in poverty-stricken counties in the central and western regions, railways, grain depots and tourist facilities in the central and western regions; technological transformation of enterprises, industrialization of high-tech industries, localization of environmental protection facilities, technological transformation of military industrial enterprises and major technology projects, such as biological chips and synchronous radiation; and construction of urban environmental protection projects.

The implementation of the proactive fiscal policy continued in 2001, which mainly covered a continued issuance of national bonds for construction of infrastructure; issuance of special national bonds to support the development of the western regions; and appropriately increased incomes of residents (with salary increases for civil servants) to spur consumption.

The additionally issued long-term national bonds for construction amounted to RMB Yuan 150 billion, including RMB Yuan 100 billion as follow-up funds to conclude ongoing projects and RMB Yuan 50 billion as special national bonds to support the construction of key projects in the western regions, such as the kick off of the Qinghai-Tibet Railway. Meanwhile, more investment was made in equipment and high-tech industries, including discount interest for technological transformation.

The policy framework of 2001 continued into 2002, and the funds for national bonds were provided ahead of schedule. In 2003, with support from continued implementation of proactive fiscal policy, China successfully warded off the onslaught of severe acute respiratory syndrome (SARS), and after the third quarter the national economy grew at a rate of 9 percent.

Results of expansive proactive fiscal policy

According to government department estimates, proactive fiscal policy played a marked role in the continuous growth of the Chinese economy, as reflected by its contribution to GDP growth: 1.5 percentage points in 1998, 2 percentage points in 1999, 1.7 percentage points in 2000, 1.8 percentage points in 2001 and 1.5 to 2 percentage points in 2002 through 2004.

In seven years, China had issued RMB Yuan 910 billion of long-term national bonds for construction. By the end of 2004, RMB Yuan 864.3 billion of funds were cumulatively arranged for projects financed through national bonds over this seven-year period: RMB Yuan 259.6 billion for agriculture, forestry, water conservation and ecological construction, accounting for 30 percent of the total; RMB Yuan 171.1 billion for construction of traffic and communications infrastructure, accounting for 19.8 percent; RMB Yuan 131.7 billion for construction of urban infrastructure, accounting for 5 percent; RMB Yuan 35.2 billion for construction of reserve grain depots directly under the Central Government, accounting for 4.1 percent; RMB Yuan 31.2 billion for investment in environmental protection, accounting for 3.6 percent; and RMB Yuan 18 billion for construction of facilities for public security, procurement and courts, accounting for 2.1 percent.

The use of funds for projects financed through national bonds had continuously improved in structure. The period 1999 to 2001 saw a gradual increase or reinforcement of western development, technological transformation of key industries, high-tech industries, return of former grain-producing land to forests or grasslands, education and construction of facilities for public security, procurement and the courts. After 2002, investment shifted to rural areas, and central and western regions and focused on science, technology, education and ecology and the environment, with more attention to the coordinated development of urban and rural areas and their economies.

Investment through national bonds had many results, including:

1   expanded investment demand and promoted economic development. The nearly RMB Yuan 1 trillion in long-term national bonds for construction issued cumulatively after 1998 led localities, departments and enterprises to invest matching project funds and banks to arrange some RMB Yuan 2 trillion of loans, which played a significant role in promoting economic growth;

2   the construction of a number of major infrastructure projects and the completion

of major tasks that had stalled for years, such as large-scale embankment construction along large rivers and lakes, repairs to flood-damaged works, the return of grain plots to farmers who had been dislocated into new towns;

3   improved traffic and transportation at a period in history when China's highways, railways and civil aviation expanded at record speeds, and improved grain storage facilities, which improved the ability of the state to regulate the grains market and insured smooth implementation of the grain reform policy of the Central Government;

4   accelerated technical progress of enterprises and the promotion of industrial upgrading. The funds of national bonds were used to implement a large number of projects of technological transformation, industrialization of high technology and equipment, strongly supporting the reform of state-owned enterprise;

5   adjustment and optimization of regional productivity by enabling the massive development of western regions to take material steps. In arranging the investment of national bonds, focus was placed on the central and western regions. Especially after 2000, the investment channeled to the central and western regions grew noticeably faster than that the eastern regions;

6   improved environmental protection and promotion of sustainable development. A number of water-pollution prevention projects were built in the valleys of rivers and lakes, providing new sewage-treatment capabilities. Ecological actions accelerated, and progress was made in the integrated harnessing of water and prevention of soil erosion; and

7   improved living conditions and the development of social undertakings. The investment of national bonds greatly increased localities' enthusiasm for construction of infrastructure, and conditions improved for power supplies to farms while prices for electricity in rural areas fell, leading to a rise in power consumption.

The shift from proactive to sound fiscal policy

In 2004, after the national economy had evidently gone from a state of relative depression to one of prosperity, fiscal policy promptly changed from an orientation toward expansion and proactive interventions to an orientation that was neutral and sound.

Macro background for fiscal policy transition

With the gradual recovery of the world economy and the propulsion of government investment during the implementation of expansive policy, China's economy shook off the impact of deflation and insufficient demand, starting in 2003. The implementation of proactive fiscal policy and a relaxed, sound currency policy expanded domestic demand and strongly supported accelerated national economic growth. In the meantime, however, the tendency toward excessive investment and low-level redundant construction began to escalate in some industries and regions. In the industries that produced steel, automobiles, electrolytic aluminum and cement, the scale of in-progress and planned projects was too large, and currency credit grew too fast. Resources were increasingly restraining economic growth, causing tension in the supply of coal, power, oil, and other raw materials, as well as transportation. The state therefore took a series of measures to control local economic overheating, including currency-related means (for example, it raised reserve and interest rates). The state also took administrative steps, such as strictly controlling the approval of land use. Judging from conditions in 2004, China's economic development had several characteristics. First, economic growth was close to its potential. GDP grew by 9.3 percent in 2003 and 9.5 percent in 2004. Bottlenecks or limited resources in some industries showed that GDP growth was close to its potential level of output. Second, commodity prices were on the rise. The consumer price index and commodity retail price index rose by 1.2 percent and 0.1 percent, respectively, in 2003 and by 3.9 percent and 2.8 percent, respectively, in 2004. Third, unemployment had reached a plateau. National urban employment increased by 8.59 million people in 2003 and 9.8 million people in 2004, while the registered urban unemployment rate was 4.3 percent in 2003 and 4.2 percent in 2004, down by 0.1 percentage points. Fourth, international income and expenditure remained in the black. Foreign trade surplus was US$25.5 billion in 2003 and US$32 billion in 2004, while foreign exchange reserves reached US$403.3 billion at the end of 2003 and US$609.9 billion at the end of 2004. When the national economy switched phases and showed signs of overheating, China resisted efforts to control excessive growth of investment in fixed assets and prevent inflation to continue the implementation of proactive fiscal policy.

Moreover, prolonged implementation of proactive fiscal policy could have easily resulted in a system regression. The proactive fiscal policy that had been in effect for many years had created an illusion that continuous expansion of financial expenditure had become an essential condition for economic growth. The financial investment of national bonds was used for adjustment of government plans, and investment projects were reported, examined and approved by local governments, level by level.

Meanwhile, banks were required to provide matching loans, and local governments were supposed to arrange matching funds. In this way, the investment system showed a tendency toward being centralized by the Central Government. When the economy already appeared overheated and government was eager to make investments, the continued large-scale arrangement of national bond investment would have complicated not only macroeconomic regulation, but also the efforts to deepen economic reforms. Additionally, China's financial and public risks were gradually mounting. The proactive fiscal policy implemented for years quickly expanded the scale of government debt, as shown by the following figures: the balance of national bonds had reached more than RMB Yuan 2.1 trillion by the end of 2003, accounting for 20 percent of GDP and rising quickly; the amount of construction national bonds issued cumulatively reached RMB Yuan 910 billion; and during the implementation of proactive fiscal policy, banks and local governments provided considerable matching funds, embedding traits of non-performing loans. According to relevant reports, from 1998 to 2002, 10,000 engineering projects were built to help expand domestic demand and restructuring, involving a total investment of RMB Yuan 3.2 trillion. The total scale of the matching funds in the term was over RMB Yuan 2 trillion, embedding factors of increasing the de facto liabilities of local finance and forming a new round of non-performing bank loans. All signs made it clear that a change of the macro fiscal policy was inevitable.

A proposal for sound fiscal policy

On May 27, 2004, Minister of Finance Jin Renqing attended a press conference in Shanghai at the closing ceremony of a Global Poverty Reduction event and answered questions about fiscal policy. For the first time, he pointed to the need for China to shift from an expansive fiscal policy to one that was neutral in preservation and restriction, that is, with the right amount of austerity to insure the healthy development of the economy.

In late July 2004, the Ministry of Finance (MOF) held a symposium of economists to solicit the input of domestic experts about the orientation of China's fiscal policy. The symposium was attended by economists from the People's Bank of China, the State Administration of Taxation, the National Bureau of Statistics, the Development Research Centre of the State Council, the China Academy of Social Sciences, the MOF Research Institute, some universities and non-governmental organizations. The experts believed that China's macro economic situation had changed and that economic growth had entered a new period of expansion. They also believed that the proactive fiscal policy, which had been implemented for more than six years, could not possibly remain unchanged. They believed continued implementation of proactive fiscal policy already deviated from existing needs, thus making timely adjustment imperative. They indicated that to keep pace with the changes in China's economic situation, it would be necessary and even inevitable for fiscal policy to become neutral. But the experts and scholars differed about how to name a fiscal policy of neutral orientation, with suggested alternative terms ranging from "neutral fiscal policy," to "sound fiscal policy," and from "coordinative fiscal policy," to "structural fiscal policy." In early August 2004, the MOF again held a symposium on the orientation of fiscal policy for the next phase to further solicit input of domestic experts and scholars. Present at that symposium were experts and scholars from the Policy Research Office of the Communist Party of China (CPC) Central Committee, China Academy of Social Sciences, Renmin University of China, the MOF research institute and other related units. They generally agreed that proactive fiscal policy had fulfilled its historical mission and that it was high time for it to be retired. Fiscal policy should be adjusted in time to suit the changes in the economic situation. For the next phase, they said, it was necessary to practice a neutral or sound fiscal policy, which would focus on control in matters such as restructuring and promotion of reform.

In July and August 2004, the MOF held symposiums involving the directors of the local departments (bureaus) of finance in Hangzhou of Zhejiang, Huhehaote of Inner Mongolia, and Guiyang of Guizhou to discuss the transition of fiscal policy. Present were the directors of finance of provinces (autonomous regions, municipalities directly under the Central Government and cities specially designated in state planning) and leaders from related MOF departments and bureaus.

On the basis of the input solicited from domestic experts, scholars and working departments, the MOF held an international seminar at the end of November 2004 on the situation of the macro economy and the orientation of China's fiscal policy, with the aim of learning the views of foreign experts and scholars to enable further analysis of the macro economy and accurately take control over the orientation of fiscal policy. Among those present at the seminar were the chief representatives or chief economists from the World Bank Beijing Office, the International Monetary Fund's China Office, the Asian Development Bank's Beijing Office, Deutsche Bank's Asia-Pacific Regional Office, Credit Suisse, and First Boston's Asia-Pacific Regional Office. They agreed with the MOF's view about adjusting the orientation of fiscal policy and expressed the opinion that under the new situation, China should retreat from proactive fiscal policy in 2005 and instead practice neutral fiscal policy. Meanwhile, they suggested that the absolute value of the financial deficit should not be allowed to expand in the following few years as long as no new significant uncontrollable factors appeared. Thus, the proportion of financial deficit to GDP would be lowered with the rapid growth of GDP.

At the economic work conference of the Central Committee held on December 3, 2004, a decision was made to practice sound fiscal policy. Conference participants pointed out that China had achieved remarkable results by following a proactive fiscal policy for seven years in a row and by starting to expand domestic demand. With the marked changes that have taken place in the economic environment in recent years, the focus of proactive fiscal policy has gradually shifted from expanding demand and spurring economic growth to strengthening weak links and adjusting economic structure. It was advisable and necessary to adjust the orientation of fiscal policy to make it sound. At the same time, the conference also stressed that any adjustment to fiscal policy should focus on the appropriate decrease of the financial deficit and the scale of the issuance of long-term construction national bonds, and on an appropriate increase in regular construction investment within the budget of the Central Government. In the area of financial expenditures, they said more support should be given to agriculture, rural areas, farmers, social development, regional coordination and other weak links, with support for deepening reform.

On March 5, 2005, Premier Wen Jiabao delivered a government work report on behalf of the Chinese government at the third session of the tenth NPC. He pointed out that in 2005, China would persist in strengthening and improving macro regulations and would implement a sound fiscal policy. The specific requirements of the policy were also reflected in budget arrangements and in the other relevant deployments of work that had been submitted to the session for review, marking the start of full-scale implementation of sound fiscal policy.

Major measures of sound fiscal policy

The shift toward sound fiscal policy was more than just a change in name. Instead, it was more of a change in the nature and orientation of fiscal policy in macroeconomic regulation. In the change from "proactive" (expansive) to "sound" (neutral), fiscal policy would further play a functional role in the coordinated development of economic society in response to the times. Sound fiscal policy could be summed up in terms of deficit control, structural adjustment, reform promotion, increased income, and expenditure reduction.

Deficit control

Elements of deficit control include a moderate reduction of the Central Government's financial deficit without any drastic compression or excessive tightening or signaling a regulation orientation; the prevention of further inflation or the recurrence of deflation; the alignment of strengthening and improving macro regulation and consolidating the results; and a gradual orientation toward a balance between financial income and expenditure.

In 2005, the state budget arranged a deficit of RMB Yuan 300 billion, down RMB Yuan 19.8 billion from the previous year, and reduced scale of the issuance of long-term construction national bonds to RMB Yuan 80 billion, from RMB Yuan 110 billion in the previous year. In 2006, the Central Government set the financial deficit at RMB Yuan 295 billion, down from the previous year's level of RMB Yuan 4.95 billion, reflecting continued intensity of a policy for aggregate control and appropriate control over the total financial deficit. The Central Government also reduced the scale of the issuance of long-term construction national bonds from RMB Yuan 80 billion in the previous year, to RMB Yuan 60 billion. On the one hand, a certain degree of control intensity was maintained, but on the other hand, a policy signal was conveyed that the government would maintain reasonable control over deficit and investment. In 2007, the Central Government cut the deficit and the scale of long-term construction national bonds arranged in the budget by RMB Yuan 245 billion and RMB Yuan 50 billion, respectively, down by RMB 50 Yuan billion and RMB Yuan 10 billion.

Decisions to avoid drastic cuts to the financial deficit and the scale of long-term construction national bonds were based mainly on comprehensive considerations of factors related to development, including:

1   a need to maintain relative continuity in policy. Construction of projects through national bonds follows a certain cycle and projects that are in progress need follow-up investment. According to statistics, at the end of 2004, the total scale of in-progress projects using funds from national bonds reached RMB Yuan 850 billion. If the funds of national bonds were discontinued abruptly, the projects would be only partially completed, resulting in even heavier losses;
2   the investment in projects through national bonds that contributed to GDP growth in recent years. If the scale of investment in the projects of national

bonds plummeted, it might have a significant negative impact on the economy;

3   a need to appropriately arrange investment to support the grand development of the western regions, the remodeling of old industrial base, in the northeast, for example, and the rise of the central regions;

4   a need for government to pay the relevant reform costs, to perfect the socialist market economy system and push forward with economic and social reforms. Maintaining a certain scale of national bonds benefits the coordination of overall monetary arrangement;

5   the need for a strong physical foundation to put the outlook for scientific development into play and to build a harmonious socialist society. The government must increase expenditure, including that for public works, to strengthen and improve public services and provide an increase in quality public products; and

6   the state of the international and domestic economies, which still face uncertainties, such as changes in geopolitics and fluctuations in oil prices. Therefore, maintaining a certain scale of financial deficit and increased power to regulate would benefit responses to complicated international and domestic situations. The implementation of a sound fiscal policy and a gradual reduction of financial deficit will help sustain and stabilize development of the economy and society.

Restructuring

Without adjusting and compressing the total scale of financial expenditure, efforts will be made to further adjust the structure of such expenditure and the orientation of investment projects through national bonds, which will be preserved, restricted, promoted or controlled. Focus will be on the adjustment and optimization of both increased financial expenditure and existing expenditure. The major measures include:

1   an adjustment to the use of the grain risk fund. Chinese finance used to provide more than RMB Yuan 70 billion of grain subsidies, including RMB Yuan 30.2 billion for a grain risk fund. But the subsidies failed to benefit farmers significantly. Therefore, there exists a need to reform the existing system, starting with a major change in the form of grain subsidies to turn indirect subsidies for links of circulation into the direct subsidies for grain growers, who would directly benefit from them; and

2   an adjustment in the direction and structure of fund use of national bond projects. While there will remain full scope for market mechanisms, China will integrate the funds of national bonds and capital construction funds within the budget, adjust the direction and structure of their use in line with new requirements of the "five centralized arrangements," particularly for scientific development for the deployment of financial resources, a gradual reduction in direct investment in fields of general competition and operations, an increase

in investment in public services and products, and an energetic promotion of the all-around development of the economy and society.

Reform promotion

While China will use fiscal policy to achieve the goal of rationally regulating aggregate and actively optimizing structure, it will use system reform to achieve goals of innovation. On the one hand, this approach will make the reform of finance a success, while on the other hand, using fiscal policy will serve to rationally regulate the aggregate and actively optimizing structure. The approach will also reinforce reform of income distribution, social security, education and public health systems, while creating a solid and fair policy environment for market players, stimulating economic growth, and establishing a long-term mechanism to benefit independent growth and development.

There are six major issues. The first deals with changing VAT from a production type into a consumption type. Ideally, the VAT reform would be piloted in the old industrial base of the northeast and, then, depending on the outcome, would be refined and implemented on a larger scale in more than 20 industrial cities in the central regions selected in the second half of 2007 and then implemented throughout the rest of the country.

The second issue relates to an acceleration of preparations for combining the two laws on corporate income tax: one for domestic enterprises, the other for foreign ones. The reform and opening of China have entered a new phase. Especially since China's accession to the World Trade Organization, the country's market has expanded. However, compared to domestic enterprises, foreign-funded firms bear a heavier burden for taxation, which is contrary to fair competition and deviates from the requirement to enhance utilization of foreign capital in the new period. It is imperative to introduce a new law on corporate income tax to integrate the two systems, make appropriate adjustments to tax rates, practice a unified taxation system and preference policy to create a favorable environment for fair competition between enterprises. The reform will be under way from January 1, 2008.

A third issue is related to the deepening of reforms of rural taxes. In 2005, agricultural tax was abolished in 27 provinces, affecting about 700 million people in rural areas. Starting in 2006, agricultural tax was abolished and replaced with transfer payments. China had sought to abolish agricultural tax in five years but managed to achieve this goal in only three years. Meanwhile, active research was carried out to promote matching reforms, including the reform of township organizations, the management system of rural compulsory education, and the county/township financial management system to set up a long-term mechanism to prevent farmers from having to shoulder any of these burdens.

A fourth issue relates to the perfection of export rebate reforms. Export rebates entailed measures for perfecting mechanisms for clarifying the financial distribution relationship between the central government and localities, and for ensuring that reforms would yield the expected results. This was done to maintain stability in the financial management system for the split tax system in line with the general view that it would result in rapid development in the eastern regions while rationally regulating the distribution of financial resources between different regions to promote a coordinated development. This approach insured a stable source of capital for export rebates and resolved an unequally distributed burden of export rebates and centralized financial resources and facilitated normal development of foreign trade.

A fifth issue related to the continued improvement of systems for income distribution, social security, education, and public health to promote the realization of the five centralized arrangements. With income distribution, it is necessary to consolidate and standardize the order of income distribution, rationally adjust the distribution pattern of national income, and gradually close the excessive gap between some groups by standardizing the income of monopoly industries, pushing distribution system reforms, appropriately raising minimum wages, strengthening the protection of labour rights, reinforcing taxation regulation of excessive income, intensifying transfer payments, increasing the income of low-income groups, and expanding the ratio of middle-income earners. With social security, it is necessary to speed up the construction of a social security system that is compatible with the level of development of China's economy, continue to implement policy incentives for employment and re-employment, beef up pension support and the support for the minimum living standards for laid-off workers of state-owned enterprises and urban residents, and link social security to employment policy. Meanwhile, efforts will be made to expand the coverage of basic old-age insurance and basic medical and unemployment insurance in cities and towns, to gradually experiment with rural old-age insurance and explore the establishment of a minimum living standard system for farmers. With education, it is necessary to increase investment, strengthen compulsory education, especially in rural areas, launch a system for assured investment of funds in compulsory education, and provide more financing and relief for poverty-stricken students in institutions of secondary and higher education. In 2008, free but compulsory education will materialize across the nation. Meanwhile, financial and taxation policies will be leveraged to guide and motivate social resources to invest in schools and stimulate consumption of education services. With medial care and public health, it is necessary to further support and strengthen the construction of urban and rural public health systems, to pilot reforms in the urban health care system, to pilot reforms in rural cooperative medical care, and to accelerate the establishment and improvement of urban and rural medical assistance. At the end of 2004, 150 million people were participating in basic endowment insurance, 199 million in unemployment insurance and 110 million in medical insurance, plus 22.07 million people benefiting from policies that set minimums for living standards in cities.

The sixth issue is related to supporting reforms of state-owned enterprises and the financial system. The establishment of a modern enterprise system to gradually eliminate factors that curb economic growth is the ultimate requirement for sustaining or accelerating development of the economy and gaining command over fiscal policy. Therefore, it is necessary to support the deepening of reforms of state-owned enterprises and of the management of state-owned assets. It is also necessary to continue to push strategic adjustment of the state-owned economy, perfect the system of capital contributors, actively establish an operating budget system for state-owned assets, and bolster the reorganization and transformation of state-owned enterprises. Also required are a splitting of the social functions from enterprises, supporting medium and large-sized state-owned enterprises in separating their primary and secondary business, transforming their secondary business and reassigning and placing redundant personnel, steadily urging the policy-directed closedown and bankruptcy of state-owned enterprises, supporting the deepening of reforms of industrial monopolies, such as railways, electricity supplies, telecommunications, and civil aviation, and supporting accelerated reform of the postal service and urban utilities. Additionally, it is necessary to support market-oriented reforms of the circulation system for commodities, such as cotton, chemical fertilizer and sugar, establish and improve the system for the supervision and management of the state-owned assets of administrative institutions, and perfect the system for the supervision of state-owned assets rather than for business operations, support the reform of the financial system, speed up the solution of the serious delay in reforming the banking system, and establish a modern banking system that meets the needs of a market economy. Meanwhile, it is also necessary to perfect the system for supervising banking, securities and insurance industries to effectively guard against financial risks, to carefully implement financial and taxation policies that support the reform of rural finance and cooperatives, to intensify the financial monitoring of financial institutions, and promote the healthy development of the financial system. In each of the past several years, over RMB Yuan 40 billion of special funds were arranged from the finance of the Central Government to subsidize state-owned enterprises that had been closed down or become insolvent and to enable some state-owned enterprises to split off their social functions. Efforts were actively made to adjust and improve related financial and taxation policies, accelerate the reform of railway and postal systems and hasten the reorganization of electricity, telecommunications and civil aviation. Steps were taken to gradually establish and improve the financial and taxation policy systems that support the development of small and medium-sized enterprises and to step up support to them.

In 1998, RMB Yuan 270 billion of special national bonds were issued to supplement the statutory capital of state-owned commercial banks, raising the capital adequacy ratio of wholly state-owned commercial banks. Financial policies were introduced that expanded the withdrawal of bad-debt reserves and the write-off scope of bad debts, enhancing the ability to fend off risks and the market competitiveness of state-owned commercial banks. After 2003, state foreign exchange reserves were used as government capital contributions to help state-owned commercial banks remodel themselves for joint stock ownership and becoming listed. Meanwhile, support was also provided for reforms of the state-owned insurance enterprises that had already succeeded in being listed overseas. These included BOCOM, BOC, ICBC, the People's Insurance Company of China, the Property and Casualty Insurance Company Limited, China Life Insurance Company Limited, and China Ping An Insurance Group.

Increasing revenue and reducing expenditure

Organizing financial income de jure and ensuring its continuous and stable growth, while strictly controlling expenditure according to budgets and improving benefits of using financial funds are basic activities in financial work. Under current macro-economic conditions, China has an obvious policy orientation and can take two major types of measures. The first measure is to intensify income management to increase revenue. The task of increasing financial income will be a formidable one, considering the policy-related income-reduction factors, such as the future overhaul of VAT, the combination of corporate income tax for domestic and foreign-funded enterprises, the abolishment of the agricultural tax, the continued lowering of tariff rates, and the full guarantee for export rebates. Therefore, it is necessary to take steps to consolidate the mechanism for the stable growth of financial income. To this end, first, effective financial and taxation policies will be leveraged to support economic growth, foster and broaden financial sources and boost the stable and rapid increase of financial income. Second, income management will be strengthened de jure by standardizing taxation policy incentives, resuming taxation after tax honeymoons, and resolutely stopping extreme tax exemption or disguised exemption measures, such as "taxation before refunding." Third, China will further strengthen controls over non-tax income by continuing to clean up administrative fee collection and government funds, correcting, investigating and dealing with arbitrary fee collection, tightening the management of the examination and approval of administrative fee collection and government funds, improving the benefits of state-owned assets (capital), introducing measures for management of non-tax income (for example, through franchises), expanding the issuing scale of lottery, and tapping the potential of non-tax income.

The second type of measure relates to the use of financial funds in a more standardized, safer and more effective way to promote the reduction of financial expenditure. First, one important aspect of fiscal policy implementation is the safeguarding the seriousness and authoritativeness of the budget. Modern manage-ment methods should be fully leveraged to step up supervision, reduce losses and waste, and standardize financial and economic order. Second, it is important to push reforms to socialize the logistics of government agencies, scientifically define the limits of fund supply for institutions, and adjust or optimize the structure of finan-cial expenditure. Third, there is a need to deepen the reform of budget management in a comprehensive way, speed up the establishment of a scientific and standard-ized government income/expenditure classification system, intensify monitoring of budget execution, and gradually establish and improve a system for assessing the results of financial budget. Fourth, there is a need to expand the scope of the reform of the basic expenditure budget, steadily push reform of the real object expense quota of administrative units, practice the rolling management of project budgets, propel the assessment of the results of expenditure projects and actively explore the establishment of the system for assessing the results of financial funds. Fifth, management reform for separated income and expenditure should be continued or expanded, gradually incorporating all eligible administrative fee collections and other non-tax revenues into budget management and increasing the pilot reform department that compiles comprehensive financial budgets. Sixth, reforms should be pushed for a centralized payment system for the Central Government and local treasuries. Seventh, an experiment to direct payment of local special funds by the Central Government should be actively implemented. And seventh, reform of the government procurement system should be deepened to broaden the scope and scale of procurement and strengthen monitoring.

To sum up, as long as China's economy can maintain its rapid performance, the sound fiscal policy of a neutral orientation will continue to be implemented. If the macro economy overheats at any point, the fiscal policy will move in the direction of appropriate expansion. As China's experience suggests, the most likely scenario is for the economy to slow down in the years to come. Sound fiscal policy may require making small, reasonable adjustments over time.

Observations about policy issues

An analysis of whether a "crowding-out" effect is present

After China began to implement an expansive proactive fiscal policy, researchers continually claimed that this macro policy would produce a "crowding-out" effect on non-governmental investment. There were also foreigners who expressed concerns about the possibility of a crowding-out effect resulting from China's efforts to issue national bonds on a large scale and to increase government investment and expenditure.

A crowding-out effect results when the government practices an expansive policy by providing borrowed investment money, which raises interest rates or creates competition with enterprises, commercial banks or individuals for limited credit funds, leading to a decrease in non-governmental investment. Such an effect partially or completely offsets the effect of expansive governmental financial expenditure.

Crowding out is not an inevitable result of governmental regulation through expansive fiscal policy. The proactive fiscal policy implemented by China in the previous years and the analysis of economic performance indicators show that there is no strong evidence of crowding out. This view is supported by three observations. The first relates to the impact of additionally issued national bonds on interest rates. Since May 1996, China has lowered its nominal interest rate several times, but real interest rates have been on the rise, which is not the result of financial expansion. Since China has not subjected its nominal interest rate to the forces of the market, the proactive fiscal policy will not influence the rate's rise or fall. The rise of the real interest rate was caused primarily by falling commodity prices and the failure of the central bank to adjust the nominal interest rate along with changes to commodity prices. Furthermore, the price drop is not the result of financial expansion. Instead, the proactive fiscal policy has somewhat curbed the downward trend in commodity prices.

The second observation is related to the impact of additionally issued national bonds on the amount of credit funds. In recent years, additionally issued national bonds did not vie with non-governmental players for the limited funds. For several years after 1998, the excessive reserve rate of commercial banks topped 70 percent, showing a large gap between savings and loans. The main reasons for excessive funds of commercial banks are sharpened risk awareness, low returns on enterprise investment, pessimistic expectations, and the adjustment made to industrial policies. Besides, such excess occurred after satisfying the borrowing needs of the government.

From the perspective of actual economic operations, non-governmental investment has been influenced mainly by the marginal output (or interest rate) of non-governmental capital and public investment; the rise in the marginal output of non-governmental capital will lead to a scale increase of non-government investment. If public capital is invested in the competitive fields, or those where it can replace production financed by non-governmental capital, the increase in public investment is very likely to crowd out non-governmental investment. However, the primary fields of investment fields in proactive fiscal policy cover ecological and environmental protection, expressways, railways, water supplies, airports, grain depots and rural power grids, which belong to the domain of social public expenditure, resulting in no crowding-out effect on non-governmental investment. On the contrary, construction of infrastructure can improve the external environment for non-governmental investment and the marginal productivity of non-governmental entities to promote non-governmental investment.

The third observation deals with the impact of financial expenditure on resident consumption. There may be some substitutive relationship between government expenditure and resident consumption, meaning that increased government procurement expenditure may crowd out resident consumption. But this can be determined only through an analysis of the structure of financial expenditure. While some financial expenditure on things such as entertainment is indeed substitutive of private consumption, the expenditure on public facilities is a supplement to private consumption. Other public expenditure is both substitutive and supplemental of private consumption in areas such as state expenditure on the inspection of food and drugs, which cuts private quarantine expenditure and increases private expenditure on food and drugs. Through a measurement-model analysis of the relationship between financial procurement expenditure and resident consumption, the relevant departments have found that it is on the whole a mutually supplementary relationship that exists between China's financial procurement expenditure and resident consumption, and expanded government expenditure has an overall expansive effect on demand.

The benefits of using funds of national bonds for construction

The benefits of using funds of long-term national bonds for construction has a direct bearing on the overall effect of proactive fiscal policy and risk control related to expansion of debt scale. The greater the benefits of using funds of national bonds, the closer the effect of expansive policy is toward a high multiplier effect, and the larger the safety space for the expansion of debt scale by the government.

Some scholars compared the funds of national bonds invested with GDP growth in a given year and arrived at the conclusion that the benefits of using the funds of national bonds and government funds were low. This is an unfair comparison because a correct method should instead compare invested funds of national bonds with GDP growth over a period when completed projects of national bonds have generated benefits.

To improve the benefits of using the funds of national bonds, it is necessary to at least prevent erroneous project decisions through adequate feasibility demonstration and rational selections of projects using the funds of national bonds. It is also necessary to manage the coordinating relationship between project construction and all concerned parties through compliance with scientific planning and rational construction standards, to insure that funds for established projects are not diverted and are allocated according to rational progress, and to insure quality.

Since 1998, construction and technological transformation projects supported by funds of national bonds and other matching funds have achieved noteworthy results as a whole. However, an inspection team checked on construction projects and found problems at all levels, from project selection to planning, from dedicated use of funds to engineering quality. For example, a number of construction projects were launched in haste on the basis of existing works with insufficient preparations, thus severely lacking a demonstration of feasibility. Also, some projects did not follow procedures for capital construction and were kicked off before the project proposal was approved. Meanwhile, some projects were inadequately prepared and started arbitrarily in the absence of the necessary conditions, and some urban plans had visible defects and failed to consider water supplies, drainage and sewage treatment. Finally, some projects had serious quality problems and ended up being jerry-built works, regional and departmental protectionism was problematic in project tendering and supervision, and misappropriation of construction funds occurred for some projects in a small number of regions.

To address the above problems, the relevant departments issued the "Circular on Further Strengthening the Engineering Quality Control of Projects Using the Special Funds in the Financial Budget," requiring the establishment of an accountability system in all aspects of construction projects, including prospecting, design, tendering, construction management and final acceptance. It also required suspending funds appropriation for projects where problems had been identified and recovery of misappropriated funds. These measures for checking, supervising, correcting, and punishing, as well as for strengthening management, have played a positive role in increasing the benefits of using funds of national bonds. In fact, in recent years, the incidence of misappropriated funds and poor quality engineering has decreased. The overall benefits of using funds of national bonds cannot be denied.

A basic understanding of tax cuts

The absence of a tax-cut policy after 1998 is the subject of controversy. Conventional wisdom would indicate that an expansive fiscal policy would cover tax cuts and increased expenditure. But in the first few years after 1998, Chinese financial and taxation policies focused only on increased expenditure for a number of reasons. First, at that time, Chinese tax revenues accounted for too small a part of GDP to provide room for tax cuts in terms of the macro tax burden. Tax revenues typically account for 20 percent to 30 percent of GDP in developing countries and even more in developed ones. But in China, the share was only about 11 percent in 1997. Thus, overall, there was little scope for tax cuts. Still, there has been the perception that enterprises and farmers already bear too much tax burden, reinforcing calls for tax cuts. An analysis of this situation, however, revealed that what had been perceived as taxes were actually fees and other charges associated with decentralized arbitrary decision. Meanwhile, most of the gains obtained by various departments as a result of levies related to arbitrary decision had been kept of the books, leading to a multitude of improprieties. Therefore, what China needs to urgently address is the handling of arbitrary fees and improving regulation and monitoring, rather than implementing a tax cut.

Second, the existing taxation system would limit the effects of a tax cut, making such an action pointless. The claim that tax revenues have a stabilizing effect on the economy is only relevant in discussions of the regulatory role of direct taxes (i.e., income tax). Most of China's tax revenues are indirect taxes. Before and after 1997, the three categories of VAT, consumption tax, and business tax together accounted for as much as 65 percent of tax revenues, compared with only around 16 percent for a combination of corporate income tax and personal income tax. Given that nearly one in two enterprises runs at a loss, a reduction in income tax would be meaningless for these faltering firms. Reducing indirect tax would not only decrease financial income by a large margin, but also provide too little stimulation to the economy. Moreover, reducing indirect taxes could also drag down commodity prices and exacerbate deflation.

Third, for a period after 1998, China's economic and taxation environment did not support the use of tax cuts because the market system was not complete, and investment and business actions were not yet on track for standardization, and a number of enterprises were not responsive to signals that there might be a tax cut. In particular, prolonged promotion of local economic growth through an array of tax cuts allowed some inertia. Such practices objectively abetted tax evasion and fraud and neutralized any leveraging of taxation. Regulatory authorities feared that, under such circumstances, any emphasis on tax cuts would not only fail to obtain desired economic effects, but might also disrupt any order in taxation and obstruct the formation and stability of law enforcement in the area of tax revenues.

It is incorrect to believe that increased tax revenues may not exceed GDP growth. Actually, only in periods when the management and tax systems are relatively stable and mature is it possible to avoid major fluctuations in the proportion of tax revenues to GDP. With China's economy, which is still in a state of transition, it would be inadvisable to automatically adopt the framework for a relatively stable proportion of tax revenues to GDP. There has been some reasoning behind the continuous increase of tax revenues after the mid-1990s. First, in a certain sense, the increase has been a normal rebound from the excessive drop in the proportion of tax revenues to GDP in the previous 10 years. Decentralization reforms, tax cuts and profit-transferring arrangements that started in the 1980s caused the proportion of China's tax revenues to GDP to fall nearly 10 percent from what it was in the early 1990s. International experience shows that this ratio reaches more than 20 percent on average in developing countries and is even higher in developed countries. China's tax revenues currently account for only 19 percent of GDP. Therefore, the macro tax burden is not very high.

Of course, as can be seen from specific cases, there does exist a phenomenon of overburdening and excessive levying of taxes. There is therefore an urgent need to enhance enforcement of tax laws and their supervision. In addition, there have been cases of "idle running of loans," or falsification, which appeared to comply with tax revenue targets. One proposal for the future is to create conditions to turn current indicators of tax revenue into predictable guiding indicators like GDP. China may draw on the experience of market economies in the use of short-term government bonds to fill the gap in financial income and expenditure that may result from differences between forecasts for tax revenues and the amount actually levied.

Although there has been little scope for tax cuts in general in China, particularly for several years after 1998, tax exemptions or reductions should not be completely ruled out. For example, policies were introduced successively to increase export rebates, suspend the collection of fixed-asset investment direct tax, to use enterprise investment to offset 40 percent of increased income tax and reduced tax rates for real estate, with the positive effect of encouraging investment and stimulating consumption.

The state also introduced tax incentives to support the development of high technology. What is noteworthy is that this occurred at a time when China was eliminating off-tax collection of fees and canceled three arbitrage-related fees, which mimicked a tax cut. After 2004, regulatory authorities in China gradually abolished agricultural tax, raised the standards for fee deductions from personal income tax, and planned the integration of corporate income tax laws for domestic and foreign enterprises, having the effect of an overall large tax cut.

Risks associated with national bonds

After the initiation of the proactive fiscal policy, the scale of China's national bonds expanded along with the scale of deficits. Questions arose about China's ability to control the expansion and about the prospects for sustaining development of the financial economy.

Judging from nominal indicators, finance faced difficulties in China in those years, but the balance of national bonds nevertheless accounted for a low proportion of GDP. At the end of 1998, the balance of debt accounted for about 10.3 percent of GDP. Taking into account the RMB Yuan 270 billion of special national bonds used to supplement statutory capital of wholly state-owned banks, the proportion was actually no more than 13.6 percent, obviously lower than it was in most other countries. The proportion of the balance outstanding of national bonds to GDP rose slightly, but was still below 20 percent. The major problem haunting China at the time was the reliance of the Central Government's finance on debt (the amount of debt in relation to the amount of expenditure for a year), which was relatively high (once as much as 70 percent). Meanwhile, nominal indicators failed to completely reflect actual conditions. Therefore, it seems necessary to consider that the balance of national bonds/GDP ratio is an indicator that more completely and comprehensively reflects the debt-financing capability of a nation. The heavy reliance of the Central Government's finance on debt that occurred when this indicator was very low is related to existing system factors (such as local governments not being allowed to borrow money) and to the dispersive degree of the government's financial resources (a large amount of off-budget government funds were not reflected in the denominator of the debt-reliance indicator). It is also necessary to consider that the use of additionally issued national bonds for government investment in those years was an anti-cycle financial measure and did not mean that long-term principles of controlling debt scale and compressing deficits had been abandoned. In other words, such an anti-cycle emergency measure cannot be regarded as routine and may not therefore be used without restriction every year. Also necessary to consider was that the expenditure arrangement of expanding investment scale via debt financing also had expenditure rigidity, or a "ratchet effect." The raised expenditure base and construction scale will form the pressure for more financial investment in the subsequent years, including the pressure to repay debt principal and interest. Therefore, it is imperative to carefully coordinate short-term regulation with medium and long-term development to make rational use of funds and avoid the formation of a too steep debt-repayment peak, thereby causing a government debt crisis and an unsustainable scale of expenditure. When national bonds are issued additionally under cool economic conditions, it is advisable to issue more long-term debt (10 to 20 years or longer) to lower the overall fundraising cost of national bonds by leveraging opportunities for low inflation.

It is necessary also to consider that it rationally operating funds raised through debt financing to create the highest level of economic and social benefits is a crucial issue. As has been mentioned above, the management capacity in this regard is not high, and the experience is quite limited, making it important to improve the system, explore forms of special national bonds, and intensify the overall scientific planning in the use of national bond funds, feasibility studies and accountability arrangements throughout the entire process.

Finally, it is necessary to consider that China's nominal indicators of deficit and national bonds inadequately present a complete picture of actual conditions. Therefore, simultaneous considerations must be given to the nominal financial deficit, national bond scale, and latent deficits. In other words, the expansion of nominal scale is in fact likely to limit the scope for absorbing and making up for, in a safe range, the latent deficits and national bonds of public departments (the salaries owed by government at all levels, the accounts receivables of the grain sector, the losses of state-owned enterprises, state-owned banks and non-bank financial institutions, as well as money equal to sovereign debt borrowed by government departments and localities, and the loans of localities at all levels) and contingent government debt (for example, empty pension fund accounts and dead accounts of rural mutual-aid cooperatives). Full attention must be paid to these problems, which should be resolved by comprehensively tackling the root causes and symptoms, and through corresponding reforms to gradually defuse risks. A conclusion (drawn only from observations of nominal indicators of deficits and national bonds) that there is significant room to issue debt in China could easily mislead macro regulation efforts by depleting the amount of space available for debt issuance for the sake of tackling the symptoms rather than reserving the space for addressing root causes, such as the strategic reorganization of the state-owned economy. After 2004, with expansive fiscal policy shifting toward a neutral orientation, the scale of the issuance of national bonds fell, and latent debt was absorbed to an extent, ensuring overall control over risks.

Progress in improving public finance

Public finance, as it is currently known in the western world, is generally considered a financial mode that appeared after the bourgeois revolution as the opposite of and substitute for the "royal finance" of the Middle Ages. It emphasizes rules of political power for wealth management that revolves around "commonality" and "constitutionalism." In China, the establishment of public finance in government management as a clear concept occurred in 1998, the year when proactive fiscal policy was launched.

In the second quarter of 1998, Xiang Huaicheng became minister of finance and made a point to promote public finance. At the national financial work conference later that same year, Li Lanqing, then vice premier in charge of finance and taxation, expressly required the establishment of a public finance framework, making four points:

1   regard public expenditure as a paramount financial task and excel at what should be done while not doing what should not be done;
2   promote fair distribution de jure;
3   make full use of all economic options and tools, such as the budget, tax revenues, and national bonds, for satisfactory indirect macro economic regulation and smooth transfer payments; and
4   regulate deviations in market-allocated resources, materialize state industrial policies, and successfully manage state-owned enterprise and assets.

In short, the points above are guiding principles related to public functions. The first is about solving problems of overactive and inactive performance of government functions and about regarding public expenditure as a priority target. The second is about the need to achieve fair distribution and efficiency for all members of society. The third is about the need to realize indirect macro regulation through economic means and to regulate inter-regional differences with transfer payment. The fourth represents a return to the policy focus emphasized repeatedly in the past: public finance must address the management of industrial policies and make state-owned enterprises and assets successful.

All sides had opened the debate about public finance. The supreme leadership of the Party and the state also emphasized the issue of public finance and incorporated the establishment of a public finance framework into the document of the plenary session of the CPC Central Committee and the state development plan. In recent years, Jin Renqing, the incumbent minister of finance, stressed the need to "shed more sunlight of public finance on the vast rural areas" and called for a review of experience in public finance improvements to guide further development.

Key issues of reform in establishing the framework for public finance

Since the establishment of a public finance framework was proposed in 1998, a series of reform measures have been taken in the financial system to implement system innovation, and the management and technical innovation that is required by public finance.

Reform of departmental budgets (comprehensive budget)

Departmental budgeting requires all departments to include all governmental financial resources under their control (including in-budget and off-budget funds) into the budgets they compile to insure completeness. In 1999, China began this type of reform, and today, the practice is in full force in the central government, provinces, as well as in most places under the provinces' jurisdiction.

Reform for centralized collection and payment by the Treasury for a single account

In most places in China, a system is already in place for the centralized collections and payments by the Treasury. This facilitates process supervision and the efficient operation of financial funds. The Central Government began to implement this reform in August 2001. By November 2005, over 160 departments under the central government and over 3,300 grassroots budget units under its jurisdiction had been included in the scope of the reform for the centralized collection and payment by a single account of the treasury. This was then put into full-scale implementation in 36 provinces and in cities especially designated in state planning, with more than 200 prefecture-level cities and more than 500 counties under them.

Carry out reforms for separation of income and expenditure

In recent years, China carried out a reform to separate income and expenditure. Through this reform, the income of and fees collected by units that exercise public power were de-linked from their own expenditure and welfare and were instead included in special financial accounts and budgets. The expenditure of these units is standardized and separately allocated by the budget. As a result of this reform, progress has been made in the standardization of the management of fee-collecting funds, the cleaning up of government funds projects that have fallen due, rectifying the arbitrary collection of education fees, and reducing the burden on farmers.

The management of separated income and expenditure and the pilot reform for comprehensive budgeting have been carried out in over 40 departments of the Central Government, which redressed the non-standard practices of separately using budgetary/extra-budgetary funds, linking income to expenditure, and continuously enhancing the centralized arrangement and use of in-budget and extra-budgetary funds. At present, preparations are being made for the promulgation of "Interim Regulations on the Management of Governmental Funds," for the revision of the "Regulations on the Management of Financial Bills" and the preliminary studies for "Regulations on the Management of Non-tax Income of Government." Overall, non-tax income of the government will be managed through a separated mode of income and expenditure, including administrative fee collection, governmental funds, income from paid use of state-owned resources (assets), operating income of state-owned assets, the lottery and public welfare fund, and income from fines and confiscations.

Reform of the government procurement system with centralized tendering

In 1999, China began to add centralized government procurement into the departmental budget of the Central Government. The reform of the procurement system is now in full swing in state organs at all levels, institutions and social groups. In the "Catalogue and Standard for Centralized Government Procurement by the Departments of the Central Government" for all years, the applicable range of centralized government procurement has expanded. The current practice of invitations to bid on major government procurement items has restrained and optimized government procurement, improved the efficient use of funds, suppressed corruption, and enhanced regulation, all in line with market mechanisms. The scale of national government procurement increased from RMB Yuan 32.8 billion in 2000 to RMB Yuan 250 billion in 2005 and yielded a savings of about 11 percent.

Reform in the classification of revenue and expenditure

The reform in the classification of revenue and expenditure aims to align the classification of income-to-outlay ratio and the budget-item system with standards generally accepted elsewhere in the world. The reform is also well suited to system reform and provides preconditions for the operation of the "e-Public Finance Project," an information-processing plan. After simulated experiments, the new system for classification of government income and expenditure has been comprehensively put into effect in 2007.

Methods for establishing a financial performance assessment system and performance budgeting

As a requirement for deepening budget reform, performance budgeting can improve the efficiency of government management and impact of financial funds. In recent years, financial authorities have actively researched standardized management measures for performance assessment to delimit the scope, objects and content of assessment, in a bid to initially establish a performance-assessment system and gradually introduce the concept and methodology of performance budgeting into China's management of financial expenditure. The financial department of the Central Government and many localities have selected some projects through which to experiment with performance-budgeting. These experiments will expand, depending on a review of departmental experience. The review will combine the results of the assessment with the compilation of the departmental budgets and change the current phenomena of "valuing distribution" and "neglecting management" in the arrangement of budget funds.

Implementing the e-Public Finance Project

The MOF is organizing the implementation of the e-Public Finance Project, also known as the Government Financial Management Information System (GFMIS), which is designed to create a platform for financial management and supervision, which fully mirrors the government's financial resources and supports scientific decision-making in public finance. The aim is to perfect technical support to and application of a budget compilation and examination system. The planning and implementation of the e-Public Finance Project are pivotal in the reform of financial management. Widespread adoption of the system will allow financial and taxation authorities at all levels to enhance the management of budgetary income and expenditure and to use objective and systematic standardization while eliminating system distortion and lost benefits of public funds resulting from interest-driven or man-made errors.

Measures for intensifying public functions in fiscal policy

Since 1998, during the implementation of proactive fiscal policy and sound fiscal policy on the whole, focus has been on public functions and active solutions to conspicuous problems of absence and unavailability. The following seven key measures should be taken.

Vigorously strengthen construction of public infrastructure, renovation of state land, improvement of agriculture, forestry and water conservation, and environmental protection

Since the initiation of proactive fiscal policy in 1998, China has issued nearly RMB Yuan 1 trillion of long-term national bonds for construction, which have been used mainly for public infrastructure, such as roads, harbors, airports, the rural power grid, an urban clean-energy system, grain depots and affordable housing. Stronger monetary support has targeted the rectification of large rivers and state land. Ecological environmental works have returned cultivated land to forest and grasslands and have protected lakes and natural forests. These national bond projects have effectively eased bottlenecks to the healthy development of the national economy and have intensified conditions for sustainable growth.

The year 2004 saw the shift from proactive fiscal policy to sound fiscal policy. As required by the five centralized arrangements, the financial department adjusted, on its own initiative, the use of national bond funds to reserve some projects and to control other projects to insure subsequent monetary support for major in-progress projects in agriculture, forestry, water conservation, education, science, culture, public health, energy, rural highways, and for constructing the infrastructure and auxiliary conditions related to public health education, scientific and technological progress and social security. Further efforts have been made to highlight and intensify public functions in of the area of financial expenditure.

Promote the formation and gradual perfection of the social security system, provide minimum standards of living for eligible urban residents, launch pilot reforms in the social security system in the northeast, and actively experiment with new rural cooperative medical care

As an important function of public finance in a market economy, social security has received more and more attention in recent years. The financial department has continuously intensified support for the formation and gradual perfection of the social security system. The urban minimum standard of living system was officially started in 1997 and covers about 22 million eligible urban residents. Meanwhile, efforts have been made to establish a minimum standard of living for rural residents[1] with the long-term goal of integrating urban and rural social security systems.

In the second half of 2001, the state began to pilot reforms in Liaoning Province to perfect the urban social security system. Central to this effort is an attempt to ascertain the presence of any personal accounts, lift the standard of allowances from the finances of the Central Government and push endowment insurance for enterprise employees to integrate with unemployment insurance. In 2004, Jilin and Heilongjiang Provinces in the northeast were also identified as pilot provinces for state social security. To this end, the Central Government provided a fixed amount of assistance: RMB Yuan 1.44 billion for Liaoning annually, 2001 through 2003, and RMB Yuan 1.82 billion for Jilin and Heilongjiang annually, in 2004 and 2005.[2]

Meanwhile, to help the large number of farmers avoid "becoming poor and or returning to poverty due to illness," the Central Government began to enthusiastically promote new rural cooperative medical care in 2003.[3] The goal is to create a system that would cover all rural residents by 2008. To speed up the process, it was decided in the second half of 2005 that the Central Government and localities would both add RMB Yuan 10 to the existing RMB Yuan 10 annual subsidy they are both providing for each farmer participating in the cooperative medical care system to increase it to RMB Yuan 20, while the farmers themselves still contribute RMB Yuan 10 each, raising the per capita total from RMB 30 Yuan (10+10+10=30) to RMB 50 Yuan (20+20+10=50). Meanwhile, the territorial scope of financial subsidies by the Central Government has been expanded to incorporate districts under the jurisdiction of cities in the central and western regions, where the majority of the population works in agriculture, and to some poverty-stricken counties (cities) in the eastern regions, which are also taking part in the experiment.

Increase inputs in education, strive to popularize nine years of compulsory education, and clarify the mechanism and schedule for funding compulsory education so that it will be shared by financial departments at all levels

Difficulties in popularizing nine years of compulsory education exist in rural areas. The state therefore requires that any increases in funding for education should be aimed at rural areas to strengthen education and to make nine years of schooling mandatory. In 2005, some students from poor families began to be exempted fees for textbooks and some incidentals and began receiving lodging subsidies during their compulsory education. The state aimed to quickly expand this policy to primary and middle school students of all rural poor families across the nation. To implement the policy, the Central Government and local governments arranged RMB Yuan 7 billion of special funds in 2005, benefiting 34 million rural students in compulsory education in the central and western regions, including 17 million students in 592 state-level, poverty-stricken counties. In 2006, free compulsory education began to be provided in western rural areas, where China covered incidental expenses and provided poverty-stricken students with free textbooks and lodging subsidies. Free compulsory education will be provided for the rural areas in central and eastern regions in 2007. This means that all rural areas of China will soon enjoy free compulsory education.

At present, reforms of the mechanism for ensuring funds for rural compulsory education are ongoing, being guided by the principle of clarifying the responsibility of each level in a joint undertaking by the Central Government and localities, while increasing financial investment, improving the level of coverage and organization. The target is to gradually set up a long-term safeguard for funds for compulsory education in rural areas. After the reform, the Central Government and provincial-level governments will share prorated public funds for compulsory education in the rural areas of western regions, with the former bearing 80 percent of the cost and the latter bearing 20 percent. For central regions, the Central Government will bear 40 percent, while localities will bear 60 percent.

Give strong support to agriculture, rural areas and farmers by providing direct grain allowances, implement policies and take other measures to benefit farmers, gradually reducing agricultural tax until it is completely abolished

Anhui Province took the lead in carrying out pilot reforms in rural taxation in 2000. The reforms consisted of "three cancellations."[4] Then, the coverage of the pilot expanded, and the reforms accelerated. In January 2004, the Central Government announced the gradual reduction in the agricultural tax rate by at least one percentage point each year on average until is cancelled in five years. Meanwhile, tax will also be cancelled for special agricultural products, except tobacco. In 2005, the pace of rural tax reform increased to exempt 592 key counties (targets of state poverty-reduction efforts) from agricultural tax, and to lower agricultural tax rates by another four or two percentage points for those provinces that received a reduction of one or three percentage points, respectively, in 2004, and cancel the animal husbandry tax in the whole country. In 2006, agricultural tax was close to being cancelled throughout the whole country until the end of the year, when the NPC Standing Committee adopted a resolution to abolish the Regulations on Agricultural Tax, ending years of payment of state taxes by farmers. Since cancellation of the agricultural tax, grassroots expenditure has been financed through transfer payments made from the finances of the Central Government, in line with regulations. Previous reforms aimed to standardize taxes and reduce burden, while current reforms are comprehensive and focus on "promoting the reform of township organization, the system of rural compulsory education and the financial system of counties and townships."

Meanwhile, to follow through on the guiding principle of having industry feed agriculture and having rural areas support themselves, great efforts have been made to provide more financial aid. Policy measures have been taken to increase investment that will increase grain output and raise farmers' incomes. The gist of these measures can be described as "two reductions and three subsidies."[5] In 2004, to implement the policy, the Central Government arranged RMB Yuan 31.32 billion of financial subsidies (including RMB Yuan 10 billion of direct subsidies for major grain-producing regions, RMB Yuan 3.7 billion as subsidies for fine breeds and RMB Yuan 300 million as subsidies for purchase of agricultural machines and tools). In the years that followed, the scale of the two reductions and three subsidies expanded and became "comprehensive direct subsidies."

To shed more light on the vast rural areas from a public finance point of view, the state will also shift the focus of infrastructure construction to rural areas, implement a preferential policy for stabilizing prices of agricultural production materials and increase the monetary support for training farm workers.

Increase investment in science and technology, support basic scientific research and independent innovation, and use interest subsidies to promote the technological transformation of large backbone enterprises

To carry through the strategy of vitalizing the nation through science and education, the financial authorities have not only increased investment in science and technology, but have worked hard to optimize the makeup of scientific and technological expenditure. In 2004, allocations for science and technology reached RMB Yuan 109.53 billion, accounting for 3.8 percent of national financial expenditure. The focus has been on increasing investment in basic research, high-tech research, research on social welfare, non-profit scientific research, and continuing support for construction of national scientific research infrastructure. There has also been focus on creating the necessary conditions and financing for a knowledge-innovation project experiment by the China Academy of Sciences. In early 2006, the Central Government promulgated the Outline of a State Plan for Long-term Scientific and Technological Development, which requires, by 2020, that investment in research and development should account for 2.5 percent or more of GDP and the contribution rate of scientific and technological progress should exceed 60 percent during the implementation of an innovative national strategy.

To promote technological transformation of large backbone enterprises, a decision was made to issue more national bonds. RMB Yuan 9 billion was removed from national bonds additionally issued in 1999 and was instead used as interest subsidies for the technological transformation of enterprises. In 2000 and 2001, another RMB Yuan 10.5 billion and RMB Yuan 7.04 billion, respectively, were arranged. The discount interest funds of national bonds have directly supported the technological transformation, reform and development of key backbone enterprises, and boosted restructuring and industrial upgrading. Besides, they have also been accompanied by the investment of social funds and have effectively stimulated domestic demand, obtained a high cost effect and created a multiplier effect with financial funds.[6]

Take initiatives to arrange emergency funding appropriations to fight SARS, bird flu and other sudden disasters

Financial authorities have improved capacity for dealing flexibly with crises. When SARS broke out in 2003, central financial authorities promptly allocated RMB Yuan 2 billion from the budget reserves, and the financial authorities at all levels altogether arranged RMB Yuan 13.6 billion for the prevention and treatment of the disease, effectively stopping an epidemic. Meanwhile, a series of financial and taxation incentives were introduced to help the industries most seriously affected by SARS, such as tourism, catering, civil aviation, hotels and taxis, to overcome difficulties, resume production and persevere through the difficult times.

In 2004, to help prevent and treat bird flu, financial authorities quickly arranged RMB Yuan 848 million, including RMB Yuan 275 million from central finances. The emergency financial policy measures played an important role in safeguarding people's health and safety, protecting social stability, and maintaining enterprises' normal production.

Focus on the grand development of western regions, the revitalization of the old industrial base in the northeast, the rise of the central regions, and the industrial adjustment of cities with depleted resources

To narrow the gap of inter-regional development and implement the strategy for coordinated regional development, the focus of financial fund expenditure has leaned toward the western regions in recent years. From the commencement of the grand development of western regions to 2005, the Central Government cumulatively invested RMB Yuan 55 billion of construction funds, RMB Yuan 75 billion of funds allocated through transfer payments, and RMB Yuan 310 billion of funds of long-term national bonds for construction in western regions, totaling RMB Yuan 1.61 trillion. To support revitalization of the old industrial base in the northeast, the Central Government started the pilot VAT transformation in the northeast and the experimentation with a reform of the urban social security system in 2004. Meanwhile, more monetary support was given to cities with depleted resources to help them make industrial adjustments. In 2005, the Central Government introduced its strategy for the rise of the central regions. Together, these strategic measures will effectively promote coordinated regional development.

Strengthen and improve transfer payments and adopt measures such as the three rewards and one subsidy to ease the financial difficulties of counties and townships and support poverty reduction and development in underdeveloped regions

In the past 10 years or so, the financial difficulties of counties and townships have become noteworthy problems. To alleviate the difficulties and support poverty reduction, public services and growth in underdeveloped regions, financial authorities in recent years have continuously strengthened and improved the transfer payment system, increased the financial (general) transfer payment through a "factor method," explored innovations related to questions of provincial vs. county management and of county vs. township financial management. Financial authorities also intensified matching measures for financial management of counties and townships. In 2005, the Central Government launched a "motivation and restrain mechanism" for transfer payments in line with the principle of "replacing subsidies with rewards" and introduced a policy of "three rewards and one subsidy,"[7] which links rewards from central finance to the actual results of work in localities. To this end, RMB Yuan 15 billion of special funds were arranged out of the central finance to increase a so-called "blood transfusion" and to focus more on so-called "blood making" in a bid to visibly ease financial difficulties of counties and townships within about three years.

Intensify regulation of income distribution through tax revenues

The regulation of income distribution has received a high degree of attention as an important function of public finance in a market economy. In recent years, while China's economy has been developing rapidly and while living standards have been on the rise, the income gap between rich and poor has grown. To address this situation, multiple financial policies and measures have been adopted to intensify policy regulation and improve the distribution mechanism. In 2005, the system of personal income tax was modified to reduce the burden on low-income earners. Preparations are under way to perfect consumption tax and reform the property tax system. Meanwhile, the support of financial funds, through means such as the re-employment program, has been increased to improve care for disadvantaged social groups.

Understanding of basics of China's public finance and outlook

The formation of China's public finance cannot be separated from rational and standardized public income, public expenditure, public policy and public management all with a "public nature." In the absence of a blueprint, it is crucial to find ways to adhere to several basic principles.

As the name suggests, public finance should, first of all, satisfy social or public needs with a focus on financial distribution. In the preliminary state of socialism, it means satisfying public needs through government functions for the common interest and for social progress. It is also closely linked in contemporary times to building a harmonious society and ultimately realizing common wealth with the building of the economy at its core and with developing a prosperous society as a guiding principle. The essence of this basic principle is to appropriately handle the relationship between public and class natures and reinforce the philosophy of Deng Xiaoping: "for 100 years with no waver." The second basic trait of public finance is to satisfy social needs through the supply of public goods and services as the basis for "finance-based administration." The essence of this principle is the management of relations between government and market. Although the market should be a fundamental mechanism for the allocation of resources, it has shortcomings and areas where it does not work at all. The government must fulfill its responsibilities in dealing with market failure, particularly where the market cannot be counted on to effectively provide public goods and services. The "division of work and cooperation" between government and the market will help liberate productive forces, maximize aggregate social welfare and enhance social benefits.

The third basic principle of public finance is the setting up of decision-making and supervision mechanisms for the allocation of public resources while promoting equal civil rights and limiting the manipulation of political power. The essence of this principle relates to matching reforms with the resolution of "political civilization" in modernization. What distinguishes public finance from the finance that used to exist is that government management and the management of public affairs is under legal, democratic and constitutional control.

The fourth basic principle is that public finance uses a budget as the basic management system, which is modern, transparent, complete, agreed upon in advance, strictly enforced, results-oriented and accountable. In its modern sense, a budget is the vehicle for putting into practice all the concepts, principles, objectives and functions of public finance. To sum up, the essence of this principle is to prevent distortion of public power through rational, standardized and tight management.

Given the above, China should take six steps in developing a framework for public finance. First, the state-owned economy should realize strategic reorganization, invigorate large enterprises while relaxing control over small ones, shrink their overall coverage and emphasize quality. Regarding the long term, the Central Government should become involved in competitive fields only in a limited way, that is, for some major projects, like the Baoshan Steelworks, the Beijing–Kowloon Railway and the Three-Gorge Dam, which are long in cycle, cross-regional, of an enormous scale, and strategic significance for optimizing productive forces and upgrading industrial structure. If the Central Government limits its involvement in generally competitive fields (and if local governments cease their involvement), the thorniest issues in the financial system can be addressed, rationalizing the powers of government at all levels and developing a system that is neither excessive nor insufficient.

Second, it is necessary to rationally control the sequence of financial distribution. To achieve this within the framework of public finance, the priority should be to insure the normal running of the state machine subject, with efficiency as a prerequisite. The second priority should be to satisfy public needs for public products and services. The effective supply of these products and services will enhance social investment conditions and standards of living, which in turn will invigorate economic growth. Only then will issues related to policy preferences arise.

Third, it is necessary to form a standardized mechanism for public selection. Decisions about the distribution of financial resources and policy arrangements should be made carefully and properly sequenced. These decisions cannot be made by a small number of government officials. Decision making must increasingly rely on legal procedures and standardized public selection.

Fourth, it is necessary for government departments, including the finance and tax revenue departments, to raise awareness about the standards for the wealth management system to serve the public. In the reform of financial management, views should be exchanged, and innovation in systems should be interactive. It is also necessary to rely on the e-Public Finance Project that has already started to promote the reform budget management with support from modern information technology, which will aid government restraint in and promote supervision of public finance.

Fifth, it is necessary to change the mode of wealth management by striving for new, cost-effective systems. There is the need to draw on international experience, pool social funds and implement industrial policies through participation in shares, discount interest, credit guarantees, build-operate-transfer arrangements and the terms of trade. Projects that benefit from policy preferences should be subject to collective implementation by decision makers and experts and subject to multiple audits (internal and external) to minimize the risk of favoritism through rent-setting and rent-seeking.

Sixth, under the framework of public finance, it is inevitable that a coordinated and complete budget system should take shape gradually in government wealth management. That is, system engineering must be leveraged to form a system that rationally arranges the regulation and application of transfer payments and economic policy tools for public income and expenditure, management of state-owned assets and regional coordination of social security in a compound budget. Such a budget, in a modern sense, should be implemented at the levels of the Central Government, provinces and cities-counties, and reforms for "provinces exercising direct jurisdiction over counties" and "counties managing township finance" should aim to flatten out financial and administrative levels under a principle of "one-level political power having the administrative authority, financial authority, tax bases and budget for that level."

Public finance in its true sense is not new. It emerged in primitive societies. The emergence of classes led to the emergence of a class nature of finance, which came to dominate and eventually negated of public finance. The bourgeois revolution at the end of the Middle Ages took "social compact theory" as an ideological weapon and waved the banner of "freedom, equality and charity" in pursuit of social change, resurrecting the public nature of finance in form and substance under the constraint of power and within the framework of constitutional democracy. The preliminary stage of socialism that came as a result of the socialist revolution will eventually lead to the extinction of states and move toward the public nature of finance and ultimately negate the negation.

Conclusion

In reaction to the Asian financial crisis, China after 1998 began its historic integration of policy regulation and systems development with phased macro regulation and medium and long-term system transition. The achievements of this period are many. For example, in the tide of industrialization, urbanization and the information revolution, market-oriented and globalization-oriented reforms enhanced the government's capacities in areas of management, fiscal policy and fiscal systems, approaching the strategic goal of modernization within a decade. Such enhancements, in the area of finance, were rooted in the development of a mechanism for resource allocation in a market economy. Enhancements in administration and management will undoubtedly lead to more innovative systems that benefit all of society.

Notes

1 By the end of 2004, the system for assured minimum living standards had been established in all urban and rural areas of Beijing, Shanghai, Tianjin, Jiangsu, Zhejiang, Guangdong and Fujian. In rural areas, the system benefits farmers with per capita household incomes below the minimum living standard, with most of the funds shared on a prorated basis by counties, townships and villages. The assured minimum living standard is seen as a systemization of temporary relief efforts. According to data released by the Ministry of Civil Affairs, by July 2005, the number of people enjoying the assured minimum living standard in the rural areas across the country was 5.483 million, compared with 9.063 million through traditional relief programs. RMB Yuan 1.17 billion was spent on the assured minimum living standard in rural areas and RMB Yuan 1.04 billion was spent on regular relief.

2 According to the pilot plan of Liaoning, the scale to be ascertained in the province is equal to 8 percent of personal contribution wages, with the Central Government and localities providing subsidies as per the ratio of 75:25 to fill the gap in pooled funds and insure the timely and full payment of basic pensions to the retirees in the province. From 2001 through 2004, the Central Government provided a fixed amount of assistance (RMB Yuan 1.44 billion), for the province each year. In Jilin and Heilongjiang Provinces, personal accounts are ascertained according to 5 percent of personal contribution wages, and the funds needed were solved with 3.75 percentage points of subsidies from the Central Government and 1.25 percentage points of subsidies from local finance. In 2004 and 2005, the Central Government arranged RMB Yuan 1.82 billion of subsidies for the two provinces annually.

3 By the end of June 2005, 641 counties (cities and districts) across the nation had started the experiment, and 163 million farmers took part in cooperative medical care, with the equivalent of one-time services provided to 119 million people, amounting to RMB Yuan 5.038 billion.

4 Cancellation of the slaughter tax, the township funds subject to centralized arrangements, and education fundraising, which consists of administrative fees and government funds specially collected from farmers. Under the unified regulation, accumulative labor and voluntary labor will be gradually reduced over three years until complete cancellation. Adjust agricultural tax policy and methods for collecting special agricultural product tax and set a new 7 percent ceiling on agricultural tax. Reform methods for collecting and using profits deducted and reserved by villages and collect an agricultural tax surcharge not exceeding 20 percent of agricultural tax to replace the original profit reduction and reservation by villages.

5 Cancellation of the tax on special agricultural products except tobacco, reduce and remit agricultural tax, provide grain-growing farmers with direct subsidies, refine seed subsidies, and refine subsidies for the purchase of large agricultural machines.

6 In 1999, 2000 and 2001, the state arranged an estimated RMB Yuan 26.54 billion of special funds of national bonds, which were used as interest subsidies for technological transformation of enterprises and brought about an investment of RMB Yuan 28.1 billion, showing an effect ratio of 1:10.6.

7 The reward is for efforts made by governments of counties and townships experiencing financial difficulties to increase their tax revenues and financial transfer payments by provincial and municipality-level governments to counties with financial difficulties (including use of financial transfer payments to the provinces from central finance). This aims to generate enthusiasm (among local governments at all levels) for easing the financial difficulties of counties and townships. The reward to the governments of counties and townships for streamlining their organization and personnel aims to encourage them to improve administrative efficiency and lower administrative cost. The reward to major grain-producing counties aims to insure the safety of grains and stimulate enthusiasm of these countries to strive for successful grain production. Subsidies are provided to localities that have excelled in easing financial difficulties of counties and townships to exhibit fairness and to avoid "whipping a quick ox."

3   Renminbi exchange rates and relevant institutional factors

Yi Gang[1]

In recent years China has experienced rapid social and economic development. Against this backdrop there was growing pressure for RMB appreciation, and the trade surplus and foreign exchange reserve increased rapidly. This paper intends to explain the development of RMB exchange rates in the context of productivity growth and institutional factors such as transformation of the foreign exchange rate system, rule of law, and such like.

Development of the RMB exchange rate (1994–present)

On January 1, 1994, China unified the "dual" exchange rate regime into a single one. Previously the official rate had been RMB Yuan 5.8 per US dollar, and this climbed to RMB Yuan 8.7 per US dollar after the exchange rate unification. Some observers argued that China actually depreciated the RMB by 40 percent in 1994. However, this is a misconception.

Before 1994, under the "dual" exchange rate regime, 80 percent of China's foreign exchange trading volume was at the market rate, and only 20 percent at the official rate. The rate of RMB Yuan 8.7 per US dollar was basically the market rate at the end of 1993. During 1993, the supply side of the foreign exchange trading market consisted of two main parts. The first part comprised joint venture firms, which were foreign exchange providers since they could be allowed to retain their foreign exchange. The second comprised domestic export companies, which, as the main foreign exchange quota providers, had excess foreign exchange under the foreign exchange retention system. Under the "dual" exchange rate regime, firms that needed foreign exchange to import could obtain it through any of, or any combination of, the following channels: buying foreign exchange at the market rate; buying a quota from the market and using the quota to buy foreign exchange at the official rate; and applying for a quota from the State Administration of Foreign Exchange to buy foreign exchange at the official rate. The price of the quota was roughly the difference between the official and the market rates. I estimate that the weighted average of the RMB exchange rate depreciated by four percent against the US dollar for the year 1993, compared with RMB Yuan 8.7 per US dollar, which was the starting rate of the new regime at the beginning of 1994 (Table 3.1). The trade surplus in 1994 was only a modest US$5.4 billion, and the trade surplus

Table 3.1 RMB depreciation against the US dollar (1993–1994)

	Official Rate	Market Rate	Weighted Average Rate
	RMB/US$	RMB/US$	RMB/US$
Weight (%)	20	80	
1993.01	5.22	7.00	6.64
1993.02	5.22	8.34	7.72
1993.03	5.22	8.20	7.60
1993.04	5.70	8.20	7.70
1993.05	5.70	8.20	7.70
1993.06	5.70	10.07	9.20
1993.07	5.70	11.20	10.10
1993.08	5.70	10.70	9.70
1993.09	5.70	10.00	9.14
1993.10	5.70	9.00	8.34
1993.11	5.80	8.90	8.28
1993.12	5.80	8.70	8.12
1993 Average	5.60	9.04	8.35
1994 Regime Change	8.70		
Change in exchange rate (%)	-35.67	3.94	**-3.98**

Source: State Administration of Foreign Exchange.

for the period 1995–2004 was fairly stable, reflecting an exchange rate close to equilibrium level. The appreciation pressure that followed was partly driven by productivity gains and institutional factors, and partly by the weakening of the US dollar, especially after 2002.

Since 1994, China has been promoting a market-oriented reform of the RMB exchange rate mechanism. There have been three stages (Figure 3.1):

1994–1996: During the period China managed a single floating exchange rate regime, based on market supply and demand, and the nominal rate of the RMB against the US dollar rose by nearly five percent.

1997–2005: Following the 1997 Asian financial crisis, China maintained stable exchange rates at RMB Yuan 8.28 to one US dollar.

July 2005–present: China reformed the RMB exchange rate regime by moving to a managed floating exchange rate regime based on market supply and demand, with reference to a variety of currencies. The new system features an expanded floating band, an improved spot rate formation mechanism, and the establishment of a forward market, as well as reformed open market operations, and a more market-oriented foreign exchange management mechanism.

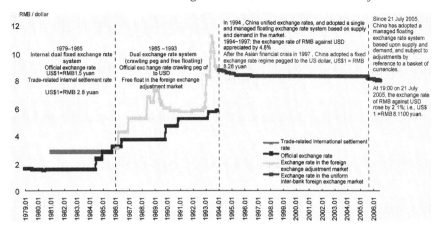

Figure 3.1 Evolution of RMB exchange rate system (1978–present).

Source: People's Bank of China.

From July 21, 2005 to the end of November 2007, the exchange rate of the RMB against the US dollar appreciated by a total of 12 percent. According to the Bank of International Settlements, the nominal effective exchange rate index of the RMB rose by 40.9 percent from January 1994 to February 2002, and decreased by 13.1 percent from February 2002 to July 2005, before rising again by 2.1 percent from July 2005 to November 2007. The real effective exchange rate index of the RMB rose by 58 percent from January 1994 to February 2002, decreased by 16.5 percent from February 2002 to July 2005, and then rose by 6.6 percent from July 2005 to November 2007 (Figure 3.2).

Exchange rate: theory and application in China

The exchange rate is the relative price of two currencies, reflecting the relative prices of factors, assets, and all products in two countries. A country can choose between a fixed or flexible foreign exchange rate regime and the selection, in turn, also impacts on the effectiveness of its monetary and other macroeconomic policies.

Key theories related to the exchange rate regime include the "dualistic conflict" and the "impossible triangle." The former, as explained in the Mundell-Fleming model[2] demonstrates that monetary policy is ineffective in a fixed exchange rate arrangement, but effective under a floating arrangement. That is, the independence of monetary policy conflicts with the fixed exchange rate regime, and it is only possible to have one of them. The theory of the "impossible triangle" (Obstfeld and Taylor 1998) expanded the Mundell-Fleming model, and showed that a government can only select two out of the three goals of an independent monetary policy, a fixed exchange rate, and the free flow of capital.

While the Mundell-Fleming model and Krugman (1994) explain the "corner cases" such as a flexible exchange rate regime or currency board, there is not much

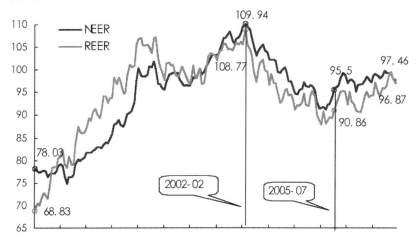

Figure 3.2 Effective exchange rates of the RMB.

Source: Bank of International Settlements.

literature that can interpret the intermediate regimes, as indicated by Frankel (1999). Gang and Xian (2001) developed a more general theory of the "expanded triangle" that can explain both the corner cases and intermediate combinations, arguing that "an economy shall opt for different exchange rate systems in different stages." In cases of insignificant capital flow and less-developed derivative markets, an intermediate solution can help economic entities manage exchange rate risks. But in the case of large-scale capital flow and developed derivative products, a country has to take into consideration speculative attacks and exchange rate risks. When an intermediary arrangement is adopted, the subsequent moral hazards and confidence crises may turn out to be the root causes of a monetary crisis. Therefore, after free capital flow is achieved, the exchange rate regime will acquire added flexibility and float independently or convert to a currency union or currency board arrangement. Eventually, the "corner solution" will prevail.

A large economy like China cannot give up its independent monetary policy. Therefore, China has to choose between a fixed exchange rate and the free flow of capital, in a sense, choosing between stability and efficiency (Gang 2000). In the long term, China is bound to have a free flow of capital and a floating exchange rate regime.

Labor productivity and total factor productivity changes

A number of factors have contributed to the fluctuation of RMB exchange rates. These factors include, among others, labor productivity and total factor productivity. China maintained an average annual GDP growth rate of 9.7 percent from 1978 to 2006, and the rate has exceeded 10 percent since 2003. The key contributing factors are enhanced labor productivity and total factor productivity.

Such enhancements are at the core for China's increased competitiveness, and are the most important contributing factors to the evolution of China's macroeconomic policies, trade surplus, and foreign exchange reserves.

Labor productivity

Labor productivity (total outputs/number of laborers) has skyrocketed from RMB Yuan 1,586 per person in 1990 to RMB Yuan 5,747 per person in 2005, resulting in an annual average growth rate of 8.96 percent (Table 3.2). This is largely due to rapid urbanization, which enhanced the human capital value of rural laborers with better education and increased consciousness. Indeed, urbanization has also upgraded China's industrial structure and technology.

Total factor productivity (TFP)

Total factor productivity in China has also increased (Table 3.3) because of significant improvements in incentive mechanisms and management. The annual growth rate of China's TFP was about 2.14 percent from 1979 to 1999, but this fell to 1.22 percent during 2000 to 2005. The slowing down of the growth rate reflected a trend towards rapid investment and capital formation in China after 2000. As a

Table 3.2 Labor productivity (1990–2005)

Year	GDP (1 billion Yuan, based on fixed price in 1978)	Employment (Millions)	Labor productivity (Yuan/person, based on fixed price in 1978)	Labor productivity (Annual growth rate) %
1990	1026.85	647.49	1585.90	
1991	1121.26	654.91	1712.09	7.96
1995	1830.98	680.65	2690.05	9.94
1998	2373.75	706.37	3360.50	6.59
1999	2554.92	713.94	3578.62	6.49
2000	2769.99	720.85	3842.67	7.38
2001	3000.00	730.25	4108.18	6.91
2002	3272.66	737.40	4438.11	8.03
2003	3600.73	744.32	4837.61	9.00
2004	3963.79	752.00	5271.00	8.96
2005	4357.84	758.25	5747.23	9.03
Average growth rate of labor productivity from 1990 to 2005				8.96

Source: CEIC.

Table 3.3 Total factor productivity (1990–2005)

Year	GDP growth rate (%)	TFP growth rate (%)	TFP index Year 1978 = 100
1990	9.19	-5.82	112.66
1991	14.24	4.79	118.18
1995	10.93	3.42	147.53
1996	10.01	2.61	151.43
1997	9.28	2.10	154.65
1998	7.83	0.30	155.11
1999	7.63	0.54	155.95
2000	8.42	1.59	158.44
2001	8.30	1.13	160.23
2002	9.09	1.26	162.27
2003	10.02	0.99	163.89
2004	10.08	1.30	166.04
2005	10.24	1.03	167.75

Source: Research Bureau of the People's Bank of China.

result, the portion of output explained by capital increased and the unexplained part, the TFP, decreased. Since 1998, the rate of capital return is about 20 percent per year (Bai *et al.* 2007).

Institutional factors

In examining prices and exchange rates in all countries, we observe that the currencies of most developing countries have been undervalued by purchasing power parity (PPP). This shows that there exists a PPP discount for developing countries. However, the PPP does not have a strong explanatory power on exchange rate movements for rather complicated reasons. In this regard, I would emphasize certain aspects of the legal and judicial system – such as property rights protection, social orders, and security issues – as well as social issues like the educational level of the general public, the natural environment, and so on. These factors, when added to commodity quality, currency convertibility, tariff, and transportation costs, explain the PPP discount of a developing country.

China has stepped into the limelight in the global economy in recent years chiefly because of institutional factors, including:

- the implementation of reform and opening-up policies over the past three decades;
- the establishment of a market-oriented economy system;

- the launch of a scientific development principle and a commitment to maintaining a harmonious society;
- the strengthening of the rule of law, and protection of intellectual property rights; and
- the promotion of energy conservation and a healthy environment.

All these endeavors have transformed the world's perception of China, and thus enhanced the value of Chinese products, real estate, and human resources. In short, China's assets and products are becoming more and more valuable as a result of the above institutional changes.

At present, the rest of the world is re-evaluating everything about China. Costs of Chinese labor and raw materials are relatively low, Chinese commodities are available in good quality and low prices, and assets in China are likely to appreciate. Therefore, there is an enormous demand for Chinese products from the rest of the world. This external demand has provided China with a surging trade surplus, overheated investment, the influx of foreign exchange, a relative over-supply of money, and so on. All these factors have already resulted in market disequilibria, which, although it concerns us, has created a state many other developing countries can only dream about.

Effective RMB exchange rate under adjustment

As many have noted, the effective RMB exchange rate is on the low side. In this regard I would like to emphasize that the market is under adjustment, starting with prices, and there is every reason to believe that the RMB exchange rate is moving towards equilibrium.

Since China has already been integrated into the world economy, so long as the disequilibrium exists, the market will adjust. Our experiences in the past 10 years show that certain adjustments – namely price increases and RMB appreciation – were already made to address the imbalance. Either of these two means can solve the problem. They differ in that the general levels of exchange rates and prices are macro variables reflecting relative prices among nations, while the prices of various commodities reflect the parity variations amongst various kinds of commodities within a country. Price adjustments are sticky and price is a sluggish variable. In an economic system where exchange rates are determined by the market, exchange rates can, more often than not, make speedy adjustments to disequilibria, thus acting as a fast-effect variable. In reality, the impact of price increases is felt at home and abroad, while an increase in exchange rates generates its effect abroad only.

Pricing adjustments: rising prices of factors and assets

As demonstrated by Mundell (1961), McKinnon (2005), and the Scandinavian models (Lindbeck 1979), when the wage growth rate is in sync with that of labor productivity or total factor productivity, stable exchange rates will be maintained.

In the past 10 years, except for a relatively low Consumer Price Index, most factors and assets have experienced a comparatively fast increase in prices. First of all, the most important price factor, wages, has been increasing at a fast rate. From 1997 to 2005, the average real wage of Chinesé employees rose by 10.96 percent per annum. During the same period, the wage growth rate in the US and Europe was only two or three percent. Besides wages, raw materials, energy, and real estate in China have all had significant price increases in recent years. From 2003 to 2006, the overall purchasing price indices of raw materials, fuel, and power rose by 32.6 percent, and in 35 medium to large Chinese cities, the average real estate prices have escalated by more than five percent per year. After the prices of labor, raw materials, energy, and assets have all been adjusted upward, China is closer to the point of equilibrium than it was a few years ago.

Ample liquidity and pricing adjustments

In early 2003, the monetary authority found that liquidity was at a relatively high level, and thus began to issue central bank notes and increase the required reserve ratio. From 2003 to 2007, China's foreign exchange reserve increased by roughly US$1 trillion and the monetary authority issued a large number of central bank notes. During the period, the central bank elevated the required reserve ratio 15 times, totalling 8.5 percentage points, and mopped up about RMB Yuan 3.4 trillion liquidity from the market. By the end of 2007, the outstanding central bank notes were worth RMB Yuan 3.9 trillion. That is to say, the liquidity was stabilized by more than RMB Yuan 7 trillion through increasing the required reserve ratio and issuing central bank notes. Besides, the economic growth per annum requires base money of about RMB Yuan 500 billion. From 2003 to 2007, the demand for base money amounted to over RMB Yuan 2 trillion. It thus follows that the Chinese monetary authority has mostly sterilized the redundant liquidity. The current level of excess liquidity is marginal and not as severe as some reports suggest.

It is necessary to keep RMB exchange rates at a rational and balanced level. However, there is no free lunch. Given ample liquidity, the price adjustment process will be accelerated, thus bringing the economy close to equilibrium. This is the implication of the "dualistic conflict" between implementation of an independent monetary policy and maintenance of fixed exchange rates.

Conclusion

The RMB exchange rate is an economic issue. The best way to facilitate its convergence to the equilibrium level is reform. Constructive dialogue helps to speed it up and make the convergence process run more smoothly. However, it should be noted that it takes time to establish an efficient market system. Starting with a very preliminary foreign exchange spot market, which mainly traded through the centralized, automatic matching system, we have developed a fully-fledged, multi-tiered foreign exchange market system since the reform of 2005, including the over-the-counter spot, forward, swap, and other derivative markets. The development of these markets has enabled financial institutions, businesses, and households to adapt to exchange rate fluctuations and hedge exchange rate risks. Exchange rate adjustment is only one factor in correcting the global imbalance. In the experience of Japan and Germany, the trade surplus remained even after a significant appreciation of the yen and the deutsche mark respectively. So besides the exchange rate adjustment, structural adjustments are also important.

To move towards equilibrium, coordinated policy measures are needed for structural adjustment. To resolve imbalances in the balance of payments, measures are required for promoting domestic demand, increasing imports, investing abroad, and accelerating urbanization, in addition to currency appreciation. In fact, many measures can generate impacts similar to currency appreciation, such as imposing environmental protection requirements, enhancing labor standards, strengthening labor protection, and upgrading the judiciary system. All these measures mean higher costs, lower competitiveness, and a reduced trade surplus, which will move the economy towards equilibrium. We must also note that it takes time for these measures to enable structural changes.

Notes

1 Yi Gang is Deputy Governor of the People's Bank of China and professor of Economics at Peking University.
2 The Mundell-Fleming model was set forth by Robert Mundell and Walter Fleming and attempts to describe a small open economy.

References

Bai, C., Xie, C. and Qian, Y. (2007). China's rate of return on capital. *Comparison*, issue 28, pp. 1–22.
Frankel, J. A. (1999). No single currency regime is right for all countries or at all times. National Bureau of Economic Research working paper no. 7338.
Gang, Y. (2000). Selection of the exchange rate system. *Financial Research*, issue 9 (Issue 243), pp. 46–52.
Gang, Y. and Xian, T. (2001). Theoretical foundation of the "corner solution" assumption of the exchange rate system. *Financial Research*, issue 8 (Issue 254), pp. 5–17.
Krugman, P. (1994). The myth of Asia's miracle. *Foreign Affairs*, vol. 73, issue 6 November–December, pp. 62–78.
Lindbeck, A. (1979). 'Inflation and Unemployment in Open Economies'. *Journal of International Economics*, vol. 12, issue 1–2 February, pp. 196–99.
McKinnon, R. (2005). Exchange rate or wage change in international adjustment? Japan and China versus the United States. ZEW [Centre for European Economic Research] discussion paper no. 05–64.
Mundell, R. A. (1961). A theory of optimum currency areas. *American Economic Review*, vol. 51, September, pp. 657–65.
Obstfeld, M. and Taylor, A. M. (1998). The Great Depression as a watershed: international capital mobility over the long run. In: *The Defining Moment: The Great Depression and the American Economy in the Twentieth Century*. Michael D. Bordo, Claudia D. Goldin, and Eugene N. White (eds.). Chicago: University of Chicago Press, pp. 353–402.

4 China's policy of opening up in the decade after the Asian financial crisis

Long Guoqiang

Introduction

China managed to escape unscathed from the Asian financial crisis that started in 1997, partly because of effective policies adopted by the government. The first five years after the crisis were a period of reacting to the crisis, and second five years were a transitory period after having acceded to the World Trade Organization (WTO) in 2001. Late in the transitory period, China's new strategy for opening up had begun to burgeon, yielding "mutual benefits" and resulting in a win-win situation.

It was during the decade after the Asian financial crisis that China pushed forward with its opening up to the outside world. Since China's accession to the WTO, China has greatly liberalized trade and investment and committed itself to become one of the world's most open developing economies.

This decade is also when the opening-up policy of China began to achieve great results. The volume of foreign trade soared from US$325.1 billion in 1997 to US$1.76 trillion in 2006, more than quadrupling the growth rate. Accordingly, in the global system of trade, China jumped from eleventh place to third. As one of the most attractive destinations for cross-border investment, China now ranks third in terms of the amount of foreign investment it draws each year, having increased from US$45.3 billion in 1997 to US$69.5 billion in 2006. China has the world's largest foreign-exchange reserve, which exceeds US$1 trillion.

While having achieved great success, China still faces a number of challenges, including internal and external imbalances in the economy, appreciation pressure on exchange rates, trade frictions, an increasing reliance of strategic resources on international market and the need to achieve economic security. All these require the government to advance with the times, adjust its opening-up strategy, and further leverage the new opportunities arising from globalization to maintain medium and long-term sustainable economic development.

A review of China's opening up after the Asian financial crisis

Policy measures for coping with the crisis

The Asian financial crisis stemmed from a reverse flow of capital from East Asian economies, which affected the region's macro economy. The primary manifestation of this situation was the quick withdrawal of international capital from East Asian countries, which led to currency devaluations, a bursting of bubbles in the capital and real estate markets, and shocks to the real economy which overwhelmed the banking system with massive non-performing assets. Although the Asian financial crisis did not directly strike China, the pressures that accompanied it were keenly felt by the country. Against this backdrop, China was affected to some extent in its efforts to absorb foreign capital. In the years prior to the crisis, foreign direct investment hosted by China under contract reached more than US$70 billion. However, in the three years after the crisis, 1997 to 1999, the figure dropped to US$51 billion, US$52.1 billion and US$41.2 billion, respectively, reflecting foreign investors' tapering interest in China (see Table 4.1).

The Asian financial crisis affected China's exports. Before the crisis, China had been directing about 60 percent of its exports to Asian markets. After the crisis hit, the region's demand for imports from China took a nosedive. At the same time, the crisis caused many East Asian economies to drastically depreciate their exchange rates and intensify competition with Chinese exports in third-world markets. As a result, China's export growth rate plummeted to 0.5 percent in 1998 from 21 percent the previous year (see Table 4.2).

The RMB Yuan exchange rate came under heavy pressure to devaluate. In the financial crisis, neighboring countries generally lowered their exchanges rates by a large margin. For China, the drop-off in foreign investment, the decline in exports and the increased pressure from capital flight all took a toll on the stability of the RMB Yuan exchange rate. In response, the Chinese government took four actions to fend off the impact of the crisis.

Maintenance of a stable RMB Yuan exchange rate and provision of loans for nations stricken by the crisis

Before China reformed and opened its economy, the country had followed an import-substitution strategy and a policy of overestimating the home currency as exchange-rate policy. After the opening up, however, the RMB Yuan exchange depreciated continuously to support the implementation of an export-oriented strategy. In 1993, the official US$–RMB Yuan exchange rate had been 1:5.7 and once reached 1:10 on the foreign-exchange swap market. In 1994, China unified its exchange rate and implemented a manageable floating rate system. The exchange rate of RMB Yuan converted to US$1 to RMB Yuan 8.7. In the three years that followed, the RMB Yuan gradually appreciated slightly and reached US$1 to RMB Yuan 8.27 before the outbreak of the Asian financial crisis.

After the Asian financial crisis occurred, most neighboring economies lowered their exchange rates, putting the RMB Yuan under great pressure for devaluation. If the RMB Yuan had joined the ranks of devaluing currencies, a tide of further competitive devaluation might have been triggered in the region. To maintain regional financial stability and reduce the pressure on neighboring countries affected by the crisis, the Chinese government officially chose not devaluate the RMB Yuan. This policy bolstered investors' confidence in the region and played an important role in stabilizing regional finance. It also enabled China to act as an anchor during the crisis, greatly enhancing China's prestige in the region. Meanwhile, the ensuing regional financial stability also helped reduce pressure to devaluate the RMB Yuan. Therefore, the policy also served the country's own interests.

Furthermore, in spite of its limited financial resources, the Chinese government provided countries affected by the crisis with US$ loans to tide them through their economic difficulties. At that time, international financial institutions, such as the International Monetary Fund, which were dominated by the United States, imposed harsh conditions on affected countries as preconditions for loans. These conditions could not be met immediately, thus delaying loans and exacerbating the losses incurred by these countries. In contrast, the loans of the Chinese government were like "free coal in cold weather" and heightened China's influence in the region.

Tightening control over cross-border capital flows

To maintain the stability of the RMB Yuan exchange rate, China tightened control over capital outflows. Since the RMB Yuan had become freely convertible, the foreign-exchange administration strengthened monitoring of current accounts for accuracy and completeness to curb illegal capital outflows through current items. As a safety measure, China made the RMB Yuan inconvertible under capital accounts. The foreign-exchange administration also introduced diversified measures to control the abnormal outflow of funds under capital items.

Endeavoring to expand exports

Stimulated by the sharp depreciation of RMB Yuan when exchange rates were unified in 1994, Chinese exports had grown rapidly, but the momentum was later dragged down by the Asian financial crisis. In 1998, export growth fell to 0.5 percent from 21 percent the previous year. In response, China formulated a policy of "endeavouring to expand exports." This policy included encouraging the absorption of export-oriented foreign investment, raising the value-added tax (VAT) rebate rate of exports in batches, rewarding export foreign exchange earned through normal trade, expanding coverage of the right of foreign trade for productive enterprises, taking fiscal and financial measures to provide discount interest for export loans and taxation incentives, and providing greater scope in the role played by local governments. Many local policies also offered rewards to exports through normal trade.

Cracking down on smuggling

China took numerous measures to deter smuggling. A margin-account system was implemented for processing trade. Processing trade was placed under various management classifications, depending on the type and management style of enterprises. Export-processing zones were set up and expanded in an attempt to

Table 4.1 Direct foreign investment absorbed by China

Year	Amount of foreign capital under contract, in US$ billion	Amount of foreign capital actually used, in US$ billions
1993	111.44	27.52
1994	82.68	33.77
1995	91.28	37.52
1996	73.28	41.73
1997	51.00	45.26
1998	52.10	45.46
1999	41.22	40.32
2000	62.38	40.72
2001	69.20	46.88
2002	82.77	52.74
2003	115.07	53.51
2004	153.48	60.63
2005	189.07	72.41
2006	200.17	69.47
Total	1375.13	703.98

Source: Ministry of Commerce of the People's Republic of China.

gradually "tame" processing trade and to prevent criminals from making use of processing trade as a vehicle for smuggling.

Evaluation of measures for coping with the Asian financial crisis

Proof that the measures taken by China in reaction to the Asian financial crisis were effective includes the ongoing surplus (and expansion) in international trade, the fact that realized foreign direct investment remained at the high point of US$40 billion a year, and the continued surplus of international income and expenditure while the RMB Yuan exchange rate remained stable.

Some short-term measures designed to cope with the crisis turned into long-term measures and were not adjusted in time, contributing to the subsequent economic imbalance. For example, the policy of not depreciating the RMB Yuan exchange rate objectively caused the system to change from one of manageable floating rates into a de facto system pegged to the US dollar. After the crisis, the changes to the exchange-rate mechanism prevented the RMB Yuan from reaching equilibrium under the supply-demand effect of the foreign-exchange market. The prolonged accumulation of imbalance sowed the seeds for an unfortunate appreciation of the

Table 4.2 Imports and Exports

Year	Total export and import		Exports		Imports		Difference (exports minus imports), in US$bns
	US$bns	Year-on-year %	US$bns	Year-on-year %	US$bns	Year-on-year %	US$bns
1993	195.7	18.23	91.74	8.01	103.96	29.01	-12.22
1994	236.62	20.91	121.01	31.9	115.61	11.21	5.4
1995	280.86	18.7	148.78	22.95	132.08	14.25	16.7
1996	289.88	3.21	151.05	1.52	138.83	5.11	12.22
1997	325.16	12.17	182.79	21.02	142.37	2.55	40.42
1998	323.95	-0.37	183.71	0.5	140.24	-1.5	43.47
1999	360.63	11.32	194.93	6.11	165.7	18.16	29.23
2000	474.3	31.52	249.2	27.84	225.09	35.85	24.11
2001	509.65	7.45	266.1	6.78	243.55	8.2	22.55
2002	620.77	21.8	325.6	22.36	295.17	21.19	30.43
2003	850.99	37.09	438.23	34.59	412.76	39.84	25.47
2004	1,154.55	35.67	593.33	35.39	561.23	35.97	32.1
2005	1,422.12	23.17	762	28.43	660.12	17.62	101.88
2006	1,760.69	23.81	969.07	27.18	791.61	19.92	177.46

Source: General Administration of Customs.

RMB Yuan today. Besides, the policy of not lowering the exchange rate buoyed it toward the target of China's macro management rather than employing the exchange rate as a tool for regulating international balance of payments. This is also an important reason for the accumulating pressure for appreciation of the RMB Yuan today. In general, all remedial measures taken during the crisis should have been adjusted promptly after the crisis to prevent short-term policies from becoming long-term and to avoid accumulating pressures toward imbalances and reversals.

Accession to the WTO: radically opening up

Facing the turmoil that appeared in the external environment, the Chinese government further expanded its strategy of opening up and was unwavering in its resolve to push forward with this approach. Even when the Asian financial crisis was wreaking its worst havoc, China never abandoned efforts to join the WTO. After negotiations taking as long as 15 years, China finally became a member of the WTO at the end of 2001 and began a period of radically opening up. As the world's largest developing economy, China received extra care from leading trade partners in the negotiations and opened its market on an unprecedented scale.

After accession to the WTO, the Chinese government made comprehensive adjustments to its trade system and policies, in line with WTO rules. Even before accession, however, China had embarked on amendments to or formulations of many laws, regulations and rules related to trade, while the 30 ministries and commissions of the State Council streamline or clarified 2,300 departmental regulations concerning trade in goods and services, intellectual property, and investment. Of these regulations, 830 were abolished and 325 amended. Local governments took similar steps with more than 190,000 local regulations. Administrative authorities at all levels made a sweeping review of examination and approval items, including 4,159 items under the oversight of departments under the Central Government. These items involved trade rights, tariffs, import and export procedures, trade remedies, standards, inspection and quarantine of goods; investment measures, rules of origin, customs evaluation, and government procurement related to trade. They also involved the specific service sectors of banking, insurance, securities, telecommunications and distribution; trade-related intellectual property; and to matters such as transparency and implementation of the system. This has further improved China's legislation related to trade and pushed the trade system toward openness, transparency and fairness. The principles, rules and requirements of the WTO and the Protocol on China's Accession have been implemented effectively through complete domestic legislation.

Honoring its commitments, China lowered its average tariff level from 15.3 percent at the time of accession to 9.8 percent in 2006. Specifically, the average tariff of industrial products dropped from 14.8 percent before accession to 8.95 percent after, while that of agricultural products dropped from 23.2 percent to 15.2 percent (see Figure 4.1). China also completed tariff reductions for all products under the Information Technology Agreement by 2005, when they were reduced to zero. It is important to note that the bound tariff rate is 100 percent, equal to the applied tariff rate.

By January 1, 2005, China had cancelled the non-tariff measures that it had undertaken to cancel in Appendix 3 of the Protocol. Some of these cancellations were even done in batches ahead of schedule or turned into tariff quotas or replaced with automatic import licenses in line with WTO rules. China no longer has any import quantity restrictions that deviate from WTO rules. The licensing procedures of imports meet provisions in the WTO Agreement on Import Licensing Procedures. Restrictions on foreign trade rights were lifted.

Of the more than 160 service-trade departments classified by the WTO, China has opened more than 100 of them, or 62.5 percent, approaching levels typical of developed members. China has honored commitments to open its markets in service trade by revising and formulating domestic laws, rules and regulations. Market access for foreign service providers has increased greatly. In banking, for example, there were 14 wholly foreign-owned or Sino-foreign joint-venture institutions registered in China by September 2006, with 17 subordinate branches and affiliates. Seventy-three foreign banks of 22 countries and regions had set up 191 branches and 61 sub-branches in 24 Chinese cities, and 183 foreign banks of 41 countries and regions set up 242 representative offices also in 24 Chinese cities.

The total amount of deposits in the foreign banks in China reached US$33.4 billion, with an additional loan balance of US$54.9 billion. Foreign banks operate in more than 100 categories of business categories, and 111 foreign banking institutions received approval to do business in RMB Yuan. The RMB Yuan business of foreign banks developed rapidly and grew 4.6 times since the end of 2001, at an average annual rate of 92 percent.

Before and after accession to the WTO, the Chinese government revised laws and regulations related to foreign investment in line with WTO rules. For example, China cancelled foreign-investment companies' performance requirements for foreign-exchange balances, local content and export ratios in accordance with the WTO's "Trade-Related Investment Measures" and revised the country's "Development Policy of the Automobile Industry" in 2004.

To keep pace with new trends and requirements in foreign investment, China has continuously improved its laws and regulations. In 2006, through Order No. 10 of 2006, six commissions and ministries, including the Ministry of Commerce, promulgated the "Regulations on Mergers and Acquisitions of Domestic Enterprises by Foreign Investors," which established a legal framework for foreign investors to enter China through mergers and acquisitions.

China's government committed itself to the creation of a transparent and standardized investment climate, where domestic and foreign capital can compete fairly. The key to successfully absorbing foreign investment gradually shifted from a reliance on preferential treatments to an improvement in the overall investment climate. The government, at all levels, energetically improved the investment climate through reforms aimed at standardizing their actions, improving their services and efficiency, and simplifying examination and approval procedures. In 2007, China lowered corporate income tax rates further to unify taxation on domestic and foreign investment.

More transparency is a basic principle of the WTO and is an important aspect of reforms to China's administrative system. In 2002, the Ministry of Commerce established a WTO Notification and Enquiry Center to provide information on China's trade policies and to meet obligations for notifying the WTO about changes in the country's trade policies and measures. The Announcements of China on Foreign Economic Relations and Trade assemble the laws and regulations related to or influencing trade in goods and services and trade-related intellectual property. Official websites were launched by 96 percent of the departments of the Central Government and by 87 percent of the local governments. The Central Government's website, http://www.gov.cn, was commissioned on January 1, 2006 and immediately became an important resource to anyone interested in doing business in or with China.

The newly formulated "Legislation Law" expressly requires publicly soliciting input on legislation through symposiums, hearings, and the Internet, upholding the principle of transparency and participation by all interested parties. The new "Administrative Licensing Law" poses strict requirements for transparency in government transactions.

China has committed itself to the protection of intellectual property. This is not

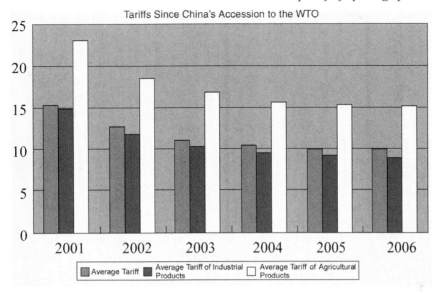

Figure 4.1 Tariffs since China's accession to the WTO.

only important for China's relations with other countries, but it is also a way to promote innovation. Seizing the opportunities that arose as a result of accession to WTO, China has made great strides in the legislation, law enforcement and public education associated with intellectual property. The Chinese government amended nearly all laws, regulations and judicial interpretations for the protection of intellectual property to align them with the WTO's "Agreement on Trade-Related Intellectual Properties" and other international rules. The Chinese government has highlighted law enforcement as the focus of intellectual property protection and has intensified the execution of intellectual property protection through administrative and judicial means. The long-term solution involves raising awareness about the need for and benefits of intellectual property protection. In 2004, the Chinese government designated April 20–26 every year as the Week of Intellectual Property Protection, when publicity and education activities about this issue are communicated throughout the society to promote respect for labor, knowledge, talent and creativity.

An evaluation of accession to the WTO

Accession to WTO was a major milestone in the China's efforts to integrate into the world economy. The impact on the country and on perceptions about change has been enormous.

First, accession provided the framework for China to move from a closed or insular economy to an open one. The commitments China made by joining the WTO were mainly about opening markets. But many commitments also entailed major system changes.

Changes of all types allowed China to introduce the funds, technology, products and services that were needed to not only become more integrated into the global economy, but also enhanced China's comparative advantages and promoted economic development. More importantly, the reform of China's economic system based on WTO rules greatly accelerated efforts to build and improve the socialist market economy system and will have a far-reaching influence on the establishment of an open market economy.

Second, accession to the WTO has liberated thinking about investment and the economy. Liberalization of trade and investment is bound to benefit some interest groups and result in losses to others. Even though advantages outweigh disadvantages, but the government must take steps to compensate for the losses of affected groups and to insure smooth progress in the opening up of the economy. Unlike most other countries, China greeted the WTO and the forces of globalization with much fanfare. Through its accession to the WTO, China has raised awareness about the merits of an open economy and raise consciousness about the need to respect new trade rules. China's campaign of enlightenment about economic change will have a lasting influence on the country's development.

Third, there was a sharp difference between expectations and results. The five years after the accession to the WTO were the most rapid and stable period of development of the Chinese economy. None of the negative effects of opening up that had been expected before accession to the WTO ever materialized, particularly in the automotive industry and in agriculture. Moreover, the growth in foreign trade exceeded most expectations. Did the disconnection between expectations and reality stem from an underestimation of China's development potential and the competitive force of its economy in negotiations? Is it that interest groups interfered with China's ability to accurately judge the competitive force in different fields? These and other questions should be reviewed.

A new situation in China's drive to open up

The opening-up strategy is integral to China's overall economic development strategy. Although the strategy is relatively independent, it must nevertheless revolve around the overall economic development strategy. Therefore, the formulation of any new opening-up strategy must take into account the needs of domestic economic development and the new changes in the relationship between the Chinese economy and the outside world and must keep track of new trends in globalization, new opportunities and new challenges, and must formulate measures that will maximize benefits and minimize harm.

The new situation in domestic economic development

After nearly three decades of rapid development, China has become the world's fourth-largest economy and undoubtedly has a bright future. Since the early 1990s, China has made fundamental changes to overcome many of the constraints to economic development. The most prominent constraints in the past were insufficient capital and foreign exchange. At present, however, China is witnessing a substantial oversupply of capital and foreign exchange. Today, the main constraints are related to resources, the environment, technical capabilities, unbalanced development, and an excessive gap in income. To meet these new challenges, the Central Government has put forward a series of new development ideas and strategies, such as its Scientific Development Approach, industrialization initiatives, the construction of an innovative society, and the "five harmonized arrangements," the essence of which is the realization of change in the mode of economic development – from an extensive development mode to an intensive one – through innovations in system and technology. Continued integration into the global economy will require an adjustment to the opening-up strategy to insure smooth implementation in an intensive-development mode in an open environment.

The new situation in foreign economic relations

China's foreign economic relations have entered a new dimension. On the one hand, globalization has gone so deep that it generates opportunities in areas such as outsourcing services and internationalizing the research and development of multinationals. In the past 20 or so years, China has grasped the opportunity for cross-border transfers in manufacturing to develop into a "world factory," which promoted China's industrialization and transformed the country into a large exporter of finished products. Seizing the new opportunities presented by globalization will allow China to promote the development of the service industry, increase competitiveness in exports by the services sector and strengthen capacities for research and development and for innovation. On the other hand, China is confronting many new challenges in its foreign economic relations.

The first is a constraint posed by globalized rules. Before its accession to the WTO, China had pursued a strategy that combined export orientation with import substitution. The strategy included measures that deviated from WTO rules. After the accession, however, China cancelled all measures and regulations that were not aligned with WTO rules.

The second is a worldwide trend toward regional integration. East Asia lags behind other regions in this regard. Regional integration has the dual effect of creating and transferring trade. Countries that avoid regional trade arrangements risk becoming marginalized and vulnerable to the negative impact of trade transfer. Regional integration essentially aims to actively promote trade and investment liberalization among some economies. If regional integration is pursued rashly, disadvantaged domestic industries may face severe challenges related to external impacts. Especially for an economy like China's, strategic industries (capital and technology intensive industries) are inadequately competitive overall, so there is a need for its regional integration strategy to be forward-looking, strategic and technical.

The third is the increasingly complicated international trade environment confronting China. On the one hand, exports are plagued by more and more trade frictions, and China has become the country involved in the largest number of disputes in areas such as anti-dumping, subsidies, and other protective measures. On the other hand, structural upgrading of Chinese exports are facing more and more restrictions through technical trade and intellectual property barriers, which cause China to miss out on export opportunities worth as much as US$100 billion and to suffer enormous direct economic losses each year. Trade frictions will likely persist in the years ahead.

The fourth is China's reliance on external natural resources. A large developing country relatively rich in human resources but relatively short on economic resources, China will rely more and more on natural resources from other countries. Finding ways to insure a reliable supply of overseas resources will be essential in any new opening-up strategy.

The fifth is that a mechanism of guarding against risks has not yet been established for the open economy, and the capacities for macro management are maladjusted. China is already the world's most open developing economy. Profound participation in the international division of labor meets national conditions. Besides, China is also one of the developing economies that have benefited most from globalization. Although China successfully shifted from a closed economic system to an open one, the country still needs to perfect risk-prevention mechanisms. In the future, China will inevitably implement the free conversion of the RMB Yuan under capital accounts. By then, cross-border capital flow will increase in scale and speed, meaning greater risks for the open economy. This has spurred new interest in increasing capacities for management of the macro economy. The imbalance in internal and external development, excessive reliance on exports, and the excessive fluidity and appreciation pressures on the RMB Yuan (caused by exploding foreign-exchange reserves) not only reflect problems in the development of the open economy, but also point to the inability of macro management of the economy remain in step with the development process.

The sixth is the heavier pressure brought on by the "China responsibility theory". Perceptions about China have change from the negative "collapse theory" and "threat theory" to the positive "opportunity theory" and "responsible stakeholder theory." But, the "responsibility theory" will also pose new challenges for China's future opening-up strategy. The international community now has expectations and requirements when dealing with China's economy, security and humanity, and with issues such as greenhouse-gas emissions, the appreciation of the RMB Yuan, the crisis in Darfur, and the controversy about nuclear power in North Korea.

Public opinion and ideology

Public opinion will influence the formulation of a new opening-up strategy. In recent years, changes in domestic and foreign circumstances have led to more and more discussion about strategy's future. Some of the discussion has been based on certain misconceptions, which must be addressed.

First, there is a need to combat China's sense of being a victim. China suffered nearly a century of humiliation after 1840. This unfortunate fact still influences the way China regards its relationship with the rest of the world. The hundred years of humiliation has led China to focus on its struggle, at the expense of its relationships with the rest of the world. But isolation will only result in backwardness and make China vulnerable to attack. Through persistent efforts to open up the country, China will be able to revitalize itself. As China emerges as a new power in the international arena, it is essential for the country to rise above feeling like a victim and rationally manage its profoundly changing relationship with the rest of the world with more confidence.

Second, China must address issues of nationalism. Although patriotism is embodied in the national spirit of contemporary China, it is necessary to prevent it from becoming "nationalism" and degenerating into xenophobia or anti-internationalization. In foreign economic relations, China should exhibit national pride and state honor but prevent nationalism from displacing rational thought. Special steps should be taken to prevent individual interest groups from blocking reforms and openness in the name of patriotism and national economic security to safeguard their vested interests.

Third, arrogance must be avoided. China was once the world's most developed country. This status was lost, in part, because ancient emperors mistakenly believed that China was so vast in territory and so abundant in produce that it was unnecessary to look beyond borders and build economic relations with the outside world. Such arrogance foretold the decline of China.

One of the reasons for China's rapid progress in the last 30 years is modesty, reflected in the careful observation of other countries' experiences and its adapting of approaches that lead to success while taking into account national conditions and goals. With today's rapid and impressive development, it is easy to become arrogant. For success to continue, the elite must always strive to remain modest. Instead of boasting about the miracle and soft power of China, it is better to ponder and address the shortcomings of the system.

The outlook for opening up

In the future, China's opening up should adhere to principles of mutual benefit and win-win arrangements in order to remain on a path to peaceful development. The state has required improvements to quality and level of the opening up. Specifically, the new opening-up strategy is about the full-scale merging into the world economy and heightening of China's position in the global production value chain. This strategy includes the following six core elements.

1   Promotion of the establishment of a more open, freer and more stable multilateral trade and investment system. China is a rising manufacturing giant with a rapidly increasing competitive edge. An open, free and stable multilateral trade and investment environment brings to China more advantages than disadvantages. Even if the new round of multilateral trade talks stall, China should still maintain authoritativeness of the multilateral trade system and strive for progress. Besides, China should also push ahead with trade liberalization and investment at the bilateral level and under the WTO framework.

2   Active promotion of regional economic cooperation. Some countries use regional integration as a second-best choice in lieu of multilateral trade liberalization and have turned to regional integration when multilateral talks got bogged down. China needs to both continue pushing liberalization of the multilateral trade system and strategically boosting regional economic integration, for the two are not mutually exclusive. The promotion of regional economic integration should be subject to the principle of giving priority to neighboring countries, to important markets and to regions rich in resources and energy. The limited negotiation resources should be concentrated first to enter into regional trade arrangements with the above three types of countries.

3   Expansion of foreign-investment utilization and improvement of utilization quality. In the strategy for an enhanced value chain, the focus of absorbing foreign investment should turn to capital- and technology-intensive projects, research and development projects and the services industry. Also, foreign investment should be channeled to underdeveloped regions for more inter-regional coordination.

4   The "beefing-up" of overseas investment. China's overseas investment may be only starting up, but the development so far has been rapid. In 2006, the amount of overseas investment reached US$16 billion. Overseas investment is the foundation for developing a country's multinationals, which are the leading actors for integrating global resources. Without a large number of competitive multinationals of its own, China would find it hard to really become a global economic power. In overseas investment, enterprises play a major role and will integrate global natural resources, energy, technology and market resources according to the national strategic interests and their own development strategy. The government should guide them in accordance with the national strategy. The development of overseas investment also improves foreign relations and will create a mutual-benefit and win-win situation for China in dealing with the countries that host the investment.

5   The enhancement of the value chain and the struggle to create a trade power. By taking part in the global production network, China realized a quantitative expansion of foreign trade and became the world's foremost manufacturer and exporter of low-end products. But, from the perspective of the global production value chain, China is still at the low end of the chain. The primary task of creating a trade power is to rise as soon as possible from the bottom of the "smile curve," that is, from activities involving assembly of low added-value. In the upstream direction, it is necessary to gradually unfold research, development and production of complicated components and industrial equipment. In the downstream direction, it is necessary to extend the value of the productive services industry to gradually form Chinese enterprises holding world famous brands. Outsourcing should be used as a breakthrough toward an energetic expansion of service exports. The policy orientation of "rewarding export and limiting import" should be discarded in favor of a balanced import and export trade policy.

6   The perfection of the risk-management mechanism of the open economy and

the enhancement of macro management. In-depth studies of risk-forming mechanisms of open economies are needed, as are studies of successful international experience in warding off risk, enabling lessons to be drawn from other countries, and allowing the perfection of China's risk-management mechanism to take place as soon as possible, the setting up of a risk-monitoring system, the improvement of the foreign-exchange rate mechanism, and achieving equilibrium of the RMB Yuan exchange rate based on the market. The conditions and process for the fully free conversion of the RMB Yuan should also be studied, and the mechanism for the prevention of financial risks by improving the domestic financial system and by stepping up international financial cooperation should be explored. And finally, the prospects for the evolution of the international financial system should be studied, and the possibility for, and strategic path toward, the RMB Yuan as an international currency should be assessed.

Part II

China's financial system and reform of state-owned enterprises after the Asian financial crisis

5 Reform of state-owned commercial banks

From disposing of non-performing assets to institutional reform

Liu Chunhang

Introduction

State-owned commercial banks (SOCBs) form the major part of China's financial system. Between 1998 and 2002, China's SOCBs undertook a series of reform measures focusing on resolving the problem of non-performing assets. After 2003, the Bank of China (BOC), China Construction Bank (CBC), China Bank of Communications (BOCOM), and Industrial and Commercial Bank of China (ICBC) were restructured into joint-stock banks with the objective of establishing modern financial institutions with a clear ownership structure and a good governance system. This has opened up the banking industry, developed banking regulation, and improved the financial infrastructure. Notable achievements have also been made in the reform and development of state-owned commercial banks. However, the banks still face formidable challenges in the current environment of increasing customer demands and intensified foreign competition. They will need to continue to improve corporate governance and strengthen their competitive capabilities in order to consolidate the achievements of reform.

Background to China's banking reform

From 1979 to 1984, four specialized banks, including ICBC, Agricultural Bank of China (ABC), BOC, and CBC, became independent from the People's Bank of China, separating commercial banking from the functions of the central bank. In 1994, the Law of the People's Republic of China on Commercial Banks was officially enacted. It specified that the four banks were wholly owned state commercial enterprises, which were to operate independently, conduct self-regulation, and assume sole responsibility for risks, profits, and losses. In the meantime, in order to separate finance policy from commercial banking, the government established three policy banks – the China Development Bank (CDB), the Agricultural Development Bank of China (ADBC), and the Export-Import Bank of China – to take over the policy function from the four commercial banks. In 1997, at the beginning of the Asian Financial Crisis, the assets of ICBC, ABC, BOC, CBC, and BOCOM[1] totaled RMB Yuan 8.6 trillion, accounting for 61 percent of the total assets in China's financial system. Currently, state-owned commercial banks still form the principal part of China's banking industry. The soundness and efficiency of their operations have always been crucial for China's financial security and stability.

From the beginning, the deposit and loan businesses of the SOCBs grew quickly, providing credit for the country's rapid economic development. However, during the process of China's economic reforms, the banks accumulated huge financial risks, which led to high levels of non-performing loans, poor profitability, and capital deficiency. After 1995, the proportion of non-performing assets of ICBC, ABC, BOC, and CBC increased rapidly. Based on the fourth-grade-loan classification, the average non-performing asset ratio at the four banks reached 21.4 percent in 1995, 24 percent in 1996, and 28.4 percent in 1997. Many viewed the SOCBs as technically bankrupt at that time, and the stability of the banking system was largely due to the huge deposits into Chinese household savings, and to explicit state support. China's financial system was largely unaffected by the Asian Financial Crisis of 1997 to 1998, not because its banking system was well managed and efficient, but because the country was protected by foreign exchange controls.[2]

Many factors contributed to the accumulation of non-performing loans in the SOCBs. First, with regard to external factors, many state-owned enterprises (SOEs) that borrowed heavily from the state-controlled banking system became insolvent during the process of enterprise restructuring and economic structural adjustment. Second, for a substantial period during China's economic reform the banks undertook certain policy functions and often suffered from government intervention, which seriously undermined the independence and prudence of commercial banking operations. Furthermore, it was difficult for the banks to enforce their rights as creditors due to deficiencies in the legal system, lack of a unified national credit registry system, and local protectionism. In addition, banking regulation was still relatively weak and insufficient to meet the needs of a rapidly developing banking industry.

With regard to internal factors, the lack of a well-defined ownership structure resulted in the institutional fragility of SOCBs. Similar to SOEs at that time, SOCBs were characterized by vague ownership boundaries, weak supervision and regulation, and multiple operational goals. At the same time, there was a serious problem of insider control, where management had significant decision-making power but received little effective supervision and regulation. Since the state assumed de facto unlimited liabilities and banks were protected from bankruptcy, risk awareness was inevitably low across the banks. The management structures of SOCBs corresponded to the governmental administrative structure, with multiple hierarchies and low management efficiency, further raising agency costs. While the selection and evaluation of bank employees deviated substantially from market norms, SOCBs suffered from a serious lack of skilled banking personnel, including technical personnel and management executives. Institutional deficiencies and a shortage of skills resulted in poor risk management, another important factor contributing to the accumulation of non-performing loans.

Reforming China's state-owned commercial banks

After the Asian Financial Crisis, the reform of SOCBs proceeded in two stages. In the first stage, which took place between 1998 and 2002, reform measures focused on the injection of capital and disposal of non-performing loans. In the second stage, beginning in 2003, ICBC, BOC, CBC, and BOCOM were restructured into joint-stock banks and listed on domestic and international capital markets. Reforms in the latter stage largely focused on diversifying ownership structure, improving corporate governance, and enhancing the overall competitiveness of SOCBs.

1998–2002: capital injection and disposal of non-performing loans

As the Asian Financial Crisis spread, the Chinese government became focused on the deterioration of the asset quality of SOCBs. The First National Financial Work Conference, convened in November 1997, determined a series of important policies for financial reform. The meeting emphasized the importance of SOCB reform, calling for the banks to strengthen credit risk management and reduce the proportion of non-performing loans. In 1998, the government started to implement reform measures in SOCBs, focusing on capital replenishment and the disposal of non-performing assets. There were four main aspects to this stage of reform.

1   In November 1998, the Ministry of Finance issued special government bonds totalling RMB Yuan 270 billion to replenish capital for ICBC, ABC, BOC, and CBC, raising their capital adequacy ratios to 4 percent.
2   After 1999, four asset management companies – China Huarong, Orient, Cinda, and Great Wall Asset Management – were established to purchase the non-performing assets of SOCBs. By the end of 2000, ICBC, ABC, BOC, and CBC had transferred RMB Yuan 1.3 trillion worth of non-performing assets to the asset management companies.
3   The four above-mentioned banks merged more than 110 second-tier branches at the municipal level into provincial branches, while abolishing or integrating a large number of third-tier branches at the county level. Between 1998 and 2002, the four banks reorganized and integrated a total of 45,000 branch organizations, reducing the workforce by a total of 250,000 people.
4   The four banks strengthened corporate governance and credit approval systems. Operational efficiency and asset quality were introduced as additional criteria in performance reviews of senior bank executives. At the same time, the government formally abolished the credit rationing system and the banks were asked to adopt the fifth-grade loan classification system.

Reforms at this stage centered on financial restructuring, reorganization, and management improvement. As a result, the risk awareness of banks was significantly enhanced, profit levels improved, and there were remarkable improvements in asset quality and capital adequacy. However, reforms at this stage did not address the fundamental issues caused by complete state ownership. The continuing accumulation of non-performing loans proved that mere financial restructuring and management improvement were insufficient to address the deficiencies in the banking system.

However, the experience obtained from the reforms between 1998 and 2002, and the progress made in financial and organizational conditions, laid the foundation for subsequent reforms. In February 2002, the Second National Financial Work Conference highlighted outdated management systems, backward operational mechanisms, and lax internal controls as the fundamental problems affecting SOCBs. The meeting pointed to SOCB reform as the most important task in China's financial reform, and determined that firm resolutions must be made to advance the reform process and resolve the institutional issues of SOCBs.

2003–present: ownership and institutional reforms

The Second National Financial Work Conference decided that qualified SOCBs could be reorganized into joint-stock commercial banks with majority state control and that the reorganized banks could subsequently seek stock market listing. The objective of the reform is to build SOCBs into internationally competitive, modern financial institutions with effective corporate governance, efficient operational systems, and sound financial positions.

The restructuring of ICBC, BOC, CBC, and BOCOM during this stage of reform underwent the following four stages.

1 Financial restructuring and establishment of joint-stock companies

ICBC, CBC, BOC, and BOCOM each adopted different organizational models based on their respective situations and development strategies. First, non-performing loans were written off against financial resources, including bank capital, reserves, and current-year profits. In the meantime, a total of RMB Yuan 1.1 trillion worth of non-performing assets were sold to asset management companies through open bidding processes. Second, the government adopted various approaches to increase the capital adequacy of the banks, including mobilizing foreign exchange reserves and allowing the banks to issue subordinated bonds. At the end of 2003, the Central Huijin Investment Co. injected US$22.5 billion into BOC and CBC. In 2004, the Ministry of Finance and Central Huijin Investment Co. injected, respectively, RMB Yuan 5 billion and RMB Yuan 3 billion into BOCOM. In 2005, Central Huijin Investment Co. injected US$15 billion into ICBC. Moreover, ICBC, BOC, CBC, and BOCOM issued subordinated debt of RMB Yuan 35 billion, RMB Yuan 26 billion, RMB Yuan 23.3 billion, and RMB Yuan 12 billion, respectively. As a result, capital adequacy in SOCBs was notably improved. The establishment of joint-stock banks followed. In August 2004, BOC was restructured into the Bank of China Ltd. with Central Huijin Investment Co. as the sole sponsor. In September 2004, CBC established China Jianyin Investment Ltd. and China Construction Bank Corp.[3] In October 2005, ICBC was restructured into Industrial and Commercial Bank of China Ltd., with Central Huijin Investment Co. and the Ministry of Finance each holding a 50 percent stake.

2 Establishing new corporate governance structures

Corporate governance reform was critical to the restructuring process. Improved corporate governance was the objective of the restructuring and was also deemed essential in establishing the competitiveness of modern financial institutions. The disposal of non-performing assets, capital injections, and the establishment of joint-stock banks formed the foundation for corporate governance reform, which was largely achieved through government action. However, establishing good corporate governance is a long-term and arduous task, requiring commercial banks to make substantial improvements in many areas, including business processes, management incentives, quality of human resources, and corporate culture.

ICBC, CBC, BOC, and BOCOM together formed the basic organizational structure required for effective corporate governance in a modern financial institution, establishing the institutions of shareholders' meeting, board of directors, board of supervisors, as well as special committees under the board of directors. The four banks each recruited well-known academics and overseas bankers as independent directors, who helped to improve the quality of corporate governance (Table 5.1). The banks also began to hire experienced overseas bankers as senior management executives.

In order to enhance corporate governance, the banks improved their decision-making processes, internal control and risk management systems, and began to adopt the concept of economic capital management. They also streamlined the number of hierarchies in management structures and adopted matrix management systems so as to enhance management efficiency and responsiveness to changes in the market. In human resource management, they began to adopt market practices and establish more effective incentives and behavioral constraints, abolishing the former quasi-governmental cadre management system. They established prudent financial and accounting policies according to international standards, while enforcing rigorous information disclosure protocols to increase transparency.

In order to provide guidance for the banks' efforts to improve corporate governance, the China Banking Regulatory Commission (CBRC) promulgated "Directives on Corporate Governance and Supervision of Bank of China and China Construction Bank" in 2004, announcing 10 requirements for corporate governance and internal control mechanisms for SOCBs. On the basis of the 2004 Directives, CBRC issued the "Directives on Corporate Governance and Relevant Supervision of State-Owned Commercial Banks" in April 2006. The 2006 directives outlined seven performance indicators to monitor the reform process through financial and operational benchmarks (Table 5.2).

3 Introducing overseas strategic investors

This is an important measure in the reform of SOCBs. Since HSBC invested in BOCOM in 2004, the other reforming banks have selected different international financial institutions as strategic investors (Table 5.3) based on their own needs and according to the guiding principles of long-term holdings, avoiding conflicts of interest, governance optimization, and business cooperation.[4]

Table 5.1 Independent directors of joint-stock banks

Name	Nationality	Academic background	Title	Years of employment
ICBC				
Liang Jinsong	China	PhD	Former Chairman of JP Morgan Chase, Asia Pacific	Over 20 years
John Thornton	USA	Master's degree	Former President of Goldman Sachs	Over 20 years
Qian Yingyi	China	PhD	President of the School of Economics and Management, Tsinghua University	Over 20 years
BOC				
Liang Dingbang	China	Bachelor's degree	Member of the International Advisory Board of China Securities Regulatory Commission	Over 30 years
William Peter Cooke	UK	Master's degree	Chairman of the Management and Supervisory Board of the Bank for International Settlements	Over 30 years
Patrick De Saint-Aignan	USA	Master's degree	Advisory Director of Morgan Stanley	Over 30 years
Alberto Togni	Switzerland	Bachelor's degree	Executive Deputy Chairman of UBS	Over 40 years
CBC				
Song Fengming	China	PhD	Head of Department of International Trade and Finance, Tsinghua University	Over 20 years
Masamoto Yashiro	Japan	Master's degree	Non-executive Chairman of the Board of Shinsei Bank	Over 40 years
Xie Xiaoyan	China	University graduate	Non-executive chairman of KPMG, China	Over 30 years
Elaine La Roche	USA	Master's degree	Former Managing Director of Morgan Stanley	27 years
BOCOM				
Xie Qingjian	China	Master's degree	Counsellor of the central bank	Over 30 years

continued

Name	Nationality	Academic background	Title	Years of employment
BOCOM *(continued)*				
Xu Haoming	China	Bachelor's degree	Deputy Chairman of Ocean Grand Holdings Limited	Over 30 years
Ian Ramsay Wilson	UK	Unknown	General Manager of Standard Chartered Bank, Middle East and South Asia	Over 30 years
Thomas J. Manning	USA	Master's degree	Chairman of China Board Directors LLC	Over 20 years
Chen Qingtai	China	Bachelor's degree	President of the School of Public Policy and Management, Tsinghua University	Over 40 years

Source: Annual reports of ICBC, BOC, CBC, and BOCOM.

Table 5.2 CBRC evaluation indicators of SOCB reform

CBRC assesses the reform of SOCBs according to seven indicators in three major categories – financial performance, asset quality, and prudential operation indicators. Financial performance indicators include net returns on total assets, net returns on equity, and cost ratios; asset quality indicators including non-performing loan ratios; and prudential operation indicators including capital adequacy ratios, concentration of large exposure, and the provisioning coverage ratio of non-performing loans. The specific requirements are as follows.

- The net returns on total assets should reach 0.6 percent in the second year following the completion of financial restructuring and reach leading international standards within three years.
- The net returns on equity should reach 11 percent in the second year following the completion of financial restructuring and thereafter increase annually to over 13 percent.
- From the second year following the financial restructuring, the cost-to-revenue ratio should be controlled at 35 to 45 percent.
- Asset classification must strictly follow the fifth-grade standard and non-performing loan ratios must be kept below five percent after financial restructuring.
- Capital management should be conducted strictly following the rules of the "Management Measures for Capital Adequacy Ratio of Commercial Banks" directive and the capital adequacy ratio should be maintained at over eight percent after financial reorganization.
- Banks must strictly control large exposure risks; the loan balance to the same borrower should not exceed 10 percent of the bank's capital.
- After financial restructuring, the provisioning coverage of non-performing loans should not fall below 60 percent. The banks should increase the coverage ratio annually and try to reach 100 percent coverage within five years.

Source: 2006 Annual Report, China Banking Regulatory Commission.

Table 5.3 Overseas strategic investors of four joint-stock banks

Financial institutions	Time of investment	Shareholding institutions	Percentage of shareholding
ICBC	March 2006	Goldman Sachs Group	6.05
		Allianz Group	2.36
		American Express	0.47
BOC	December 2005	The Royal Bank of Scotland	10
		UBS	1.61
		Asian Development Bank	0.24
		Asia Financial Holdings Pte Ltd.	5
CBC	August 2005	Bank of America	8.515
		Asia Financial Holdings Pte Ltd.	5.878
BOCOM	August 2004	HSBC	19.9

Source: 2006 Annual Report, China Banking Regulatory Commission.

The main purpose of introducing strategic investors was to optimize the owner-ship structure of the banks; introduce management best practices and technology; improve corporate governance, risk management, and internal control mechanisms; and to enhance product innovation capabilities. The ultimate goal was to strengthen the competitiveness of the banks.[5] Evidence shows that cooperation between Chinese banks and foreign banks has helped to improve corporate governance, management processes, employee training, and product innovation capabilities.

4 Capital market floatation

The banks' floatation on capital markets was a further step in this stage of the reform process. While maintaining state control, the banks were expected to further diversify their ownership structure and accept the supervision of market forces through floatation on domestic and international capital markets. After BOCOM and CBC were successfully listed on the Hong Kong Stock Exchange in 2005, BOC issued new H and A shares on the stock exchanges in Hong Kong and Shanghai in June and July 2006, respectively. On October 27, 2006, ICBC simultaneously floated on the stock markets in Shanghai and Hong Kong. ICBC's IPO was substantially over-subscribed and eventually raised a total of US$22 billion, setting a new record for IPOs on international capital markets. The international floatation of the four banks established a new milestone in China's financial reform process.

Improvements in the external environment

SOCB reform is not an isolated event but an integral part of the transformation of China's financial system. Since 2003, bank regulation in China has achieved substantial improvements, the banking sector has been opened up further to foreign financial institutions, and there have been notable improvements in financial infrastructure and in the market environment. These improvements in the banks' external operational environment effectively helped to advance the reform and development of SOCBs.

Improving bank supervision

Effective bank supervision and regulation form an important part of the financial infrastructure and are a prerequisite for maintaining a stable banking system. On April 28, 2003, the China Banking Regulatory Commission (CBRC) was established to supervise and regulate financial institutions in China's banking sector. The establishment of CBRC is a sign that bank regulation in China has entered a new stage of specialized development. CBRC adopted new supervision philosophies, emphasizing personal legal responsibility, risk management, internal control, and transparency. In accordance with the requirements of prudential regulation, CBRC formulated and issued more than 200 rules and regulations, including "Management Measures for Capital Adequacy Rate of Commercial Banks" and "Methods for Internal Control Assessment of Commercial Banks," which were urgently needed for the reform and development of the banking sector. The rules and regulations covered critical areas such as market access, corporate governance, and risk management, which laid the regulatory foundation for both banking operations and supervision.

In the process of reforming SOCBs, CBRC emphasized strengthening corporate governance and internal control, as well as enhancing risk management, while attaching great importance to the "dual reduction" of non-performing loans.[6] In order to implement the regulatory requirements of "accurate classification, adequate provisions, real profitability, (and) sufficient capital adequacy," CBRC enforced the fifth-grade loan classification system, established capital supervision, and urged the banks to substantially improve information disclosure and build up long-term risk management mechanisms. It also closely monitored loan migration and deviations in loan classification. As the pace of interest rate and exchange rate reforms quickened, CBRC organized on-site examinations of market risks and motivated commercial banks to pay greater attention to market risk management. CBRC has also launched campaigns against banking crimes and urged the banks to strengthen internal control systems so as to reduce operational risks.

Opening up the banking sector to foreign participation

As China increasingly integrates into the world economic and financial systems, the opening up of the banking sector has played a significant role in the reform and development of the sector. Opening-up policies include allowing overseas investors to invest in Chinese banks and granting foreign banks licenses to conduct banking business in the domestic market. By the end of December 2006, 29 overseas financial institutions had made equity investments totaling US$19 billion in 21 Chinese banks.

Since 1981 China has been gradually opening up its banking sector to the participation of foreign financial institutions. By the end of the 1990s there were already a large number of foreign banks operating in China, though their activities were largely confined to foreign currency and RMB transactions for foreign clients. Entry into the World Trade Organization (WTO) has significantly quickened the pace of opening up in the banking sector. In 2006, the Chinese government completely opened up RMB business to locally incorporated foreign banks. In November 2006, CBRC issued "Regulations on Foreign-invested Banks in People's Republic of China," which removed all non-prudential restrictions on the business activities of locally incorporated foreign banks. At the end of 2006, 74 foreign banks from 22 countries and regions operated 200 branches and 79 sub-branches in 25 cities in China. At the same time 14 wholly foreign-owned and joint-venture banking institutions had registered in China, and foreign banks offered over 100 types of financial services. Meanwhile, the total assets of foreign banks reached RMB Yuan 927.9 billion, which accounted for 2.1 percent of the total assets of China's banking sector.[7]

The opening-up policies have promoted competition and financial innovation in China's banking sector. Competition from foreign banks pressured Chinese banks to be more innovative, improve quality of service, and optimize business structures and processes. In addition, in the process of opening up, CBRC has enhanced its supervisory ability and regulatory standards by promoting international cooperation and drawing on international best practices.

The opening up of the banking sector has also created a favorable environment for Chinese banks to reach out to the international market. As an increasing portion of their domestic client base began to establish an international presence, China's commercial banks have expanded their overseas operations. By the end of 2006, China's SOCBs had established 47 branches, 31 subsidiaries, and 12 representative offices in 29 countries and regions, including the US, Japan, the UK, Germany, Hong Kong, Singapore, Italy, Russia, Australia, Brazil, and South Korea.

Improving the financial environment and infrastructure

In recent years, China has continuously deepened financial reforms and achieved important improvements in its financial infrastructure, which has created favorable conditions for the reform and development of SOCBs.

The last few years have seen substantial improvements in the legal system. In particular, the promulgation of the "Enterprise Bankruptcy Law" in August 2006 has not only laid the legal foundation for the market exit of high-risk banking institutions, but also strengthened the protection of creditor rights of banks in the bankruptcy process. In addition, the Property Law, promulgated in March

2007, has clarified ownership rights and strengthened the protection of property, effectively improving the judicial conditions for protecting the creditor rights of the banks.

In recent years, China's capital market has witnessed rapid development. From 1997 to the end of 2006, the aggregate value of China's stock market rose from RMB Yuan 1.75 trillion to RMB Yuan 8.94 trillion, and the issuance of enterprise bonds rose from RMB Yuan 25.5 billion to RMB Yuan 366.2 billion. The rapid development of direct financing has increased funding channels for enterprises, improved their capital structure, and, in turn, reduced banks' credit risks. Market development, especially the proliferation of financial derivative products, has allowed the banks to enhance their risk management capabilities. In addition, capital market development has provided another channel for commercial banks to raise capital to support future growth.

With regard to the macroeconomic environment, the Chinese economy has sustained rapid and steady growth in recent years. While SOE reform continues to enhance the efficiency of the state-owned sector, the private sector has achieved rapid growth and profitability has improved substantially. In the meantime, the construction of a corporate and individual credit history system has made substantial progress and the credit culture has been gradually improving across the country. China's macro-stabilization efforts have become more effective, gradually shifting from direct administrative intervention to a market-based approach emphasizing economic and legal measures. This has reduced the scale and frequency of economic fluctuations, providing a favorable macroeconomic environment for the reform and development of Chinese banks.

Policy results

With the deepening integration of the global economic and financial systems, the reform of SOCBs has been critical to China's financial stability and security. For China's policymakers, it was a must-win battle. After 1998, the quantity of resources mobilized, the decisiveness of government action and the speed of implementation during the process of SOCB reform have been unprecedented. What has been demonstrated is the government's resolute determination to advance financial reform, and to date the reform of SOCBs has achieved remarkable results.

During the course of reform, the overall financial position of China's banking sector improved substantially. The capital adequacy level increased considerably, and the number of banks with sufficient capital increased from eight in 2003, to 100 in 2006. Asset quality improved, and the non-performing loan ratio of major commercial banks[8] declined from 23.6 percent in 2002, to 7.5 percent in 2006. In 2006, the return on equity (ROE) of ICBC, CBC, BOC, and BOCOM all exceeded 13 percent, which was comparable to the average ROE of leading international banks. The capital adequacy ratio of the four banks all exceeded 10 percent. In the meantime, non-performing loan ratios declined and provisioning coverage rose substantially to the level of regulatory requirement (Table 5.4).

Table 5.4 Main financial indicators of ICBC, BOC, CBC, and BOCOM (2006)

	Return on assets (%)	Return on equity (%)	Non-performing loan ratio (%)	Provision coverage rate (%)	Capital adequacy ratio (%)
ICBC	0.71	15.16	3.79	70.56	14.05
BOC	0.94	13.86	4.04	96.00	13.59
CBC	0.92	15.00	3.29	82.24	12.11
BOCOM	0.78	14.15	2.01	N/A	10.83

Source: Annual reports of ICBC, BOC, CBC and BOCOM.

The SOCBs also began to change their operating philosophies, shifting away from focusing on scale only and towards pursuing risk-adjusted return and shareholder value. The four banks introduced indicators, such as economic value-added (EVA) and risk-adjusted return on capital (RAROC), as important criteria for resource allocation and management performance assessment. In addition, they introduced more market-based incentives in human resources management.

The floatation of the four SOCBs contributed enormously to improving the quality and investment value of China's stock market, and had a significant impact on the financial industry, both at home and abroad. This helped to promote the international status of China's banking sector. At the end of 2006, based on market capitalization, ICBC, BOC, and CBC were ranked second, sixth, and seventh, respectively, among the world's largest banks. International rating agencies, such as Standard & Poor, Moody's, and Fitch, subsequently raised the ratings of China's major commercial banks. Within just a few years, China's commercial banks, previously regarded as technically bankrupt, have become sought-after investment targets in the international capital market. This achievement would have been unimaginable without the reforms described above.

Future challenges

While the reform of China's SOCBs has achieved positive results, these banks still lag significantly behind leading international financial institutions. The overall competitiveness of China's SOCBs is still insufficient; major improvements are still needed in areas such as corporate governance, risk management, service differentiation, innovation, and human resources. In the meantime, the opening up of the banking sector means Chinese banks will face increasingly intense competition from foreign financial institutions, which have significant advantages in capital markets capabilities, international reach, technology, and management expertise. These institutions are therefore well positioned in terms of high value-added products and services, including trade finance, cash management, credit cards, on-line banking, and financial derivatives. In the near future, the battle for high-end clients, high-margin businesses, and high-quality management talents will intensify.

In January 2007, the Third National Financial Work Conference concluded that the country must deepen the reform of SOCBs (including advancing the reform of the Agricultural Bank of China), speed up the establishment of a modern banking system, improve the effectiveness of financial macro-adjustment efforts, steadily push forward the opening up of the financial industry, and improve financial regulatory ability. The meeting has clarified the future policy direction for financial reform in China.

The reform of the four SOCBs has now completed the journey from disposing of non-performing assets to establishing joint-stock banks. The reform has not only considerably improved the banks' financial position, but also fundamentally transformed the ownership structure and operating philosophies of the SOCBs. The subsequent reforms must increasingly focus on improving corporate governance and enhancing the international competitiveness of the banks. This transformation process will be even more arduous and complex. Central to this process is whether the banks can establish effective management processes and a risk culture that matches the standards of modern financial institutions, and whether they can attract, cultivate, and effectively employ, skills. While reforms in the previous stage have been mainly pushed forward by government policy, the driving force of subsequent reforms will increasingly have to come from bank management, regulators, and market forces. Whether the banks can successfully complete their transformation in the next stage will be crucial to the success of China's financial reforms.

Notes

1 The China Bank of Communications (BOCOM) was reorganized in 1987 and became the first joint-stock commercial bank in China. In 1990, the Ministry of Finance obtained a controlling stake in BOCOM. In 1994, BOCOM was restructured into a single legal-person entity. In this paper, the term "state-owned commercial banks" refers to five banks – ICBC, ABC, CBC, BOC, and BOCOM.

2 According to Yi Gang (2003), the Deputy Governor of PBOC, "China did not lose the game, because we did not take part in the competition."

3 China Jianyin Investment Ltd. inherited the non-banking assets and businesses of CBC. China Construction Bank Corporation inherited the commercial banking business of CBC.

4 CBRC has established rigorous standards for selecting overseas strategic investors in the banking sector. Specifically, there are five requirements: (1) the ownership represented by the acquired stake should not be below five percent; (2) based on the spirit of long-term cooperation, strategic investors should have a "lock up" period of at least three years; (3) strategic investors must have board representation to participate in the bank's corporate governance and management processes, and they are encouraged to send senior management talents to the banks and to participate in daily business management; (4) strategic investors must have ample experience in bank management; (5) in order to avoid conflict of interests, and according to anti-trust principles, strategic investors can, at most, invest in two banks in the same tier of the banking system.

5 At a press conference on December 5, 2005, Liu Mingkang, Chairman of the China Banking Regulatory Commission, pointed out that in order to solidify the achievements of the reform in SOCBs, and "to pay for getting the right system" in the banks, CBRC encouraged SOCBs to carefully choose qualified overseas strategic investors. The objectives are to achieve operational and institutional innovation, thus advancing

fundamental changes in the basic conditions for business operations, and, to rapidly enhance the competitiveness of the SOCBs.
6 "Dual reduction" means reductions of the balance of non-performing loans and of the non-performing loan ratio.
7 The proportion of the assets of foreign banks to that of Chinese banking institutions is not sufficiently representative of the position of the former in China's banking sector. Foreign banks have a much higher market share in the segments of high-end clients and high value-added products, especially in China's developed regions.
8 The major commercial banks include state-owned commercial banks and joint-stock commercial banks operating nationwide.

Reference

Gang, Yi (2003). *Process of China's Monetization*. Beijing: The Commercial Press.

6 System reform of China's capital market

Qin Bin and Huang Ming

The Asian financial crisis of 1997 had an impact on the regional and global econo-mies and also affected China's own economy. At that time, China's capital market had not yet opened to the outside market on a large scale. The crisis, therefore, did not wreak havoc on China's economy. The crisis did, however, take a limited direct toll on China's capital market by way of listed companies. The entire capital market was nevertheless affected indirectly.

Just prior to and after the crisis, when China ascribed risk in the capital market largely to non-standard practices in the domestic market, rather than to the impact of international capital. However, in view of China's opening up and of the irresistible tide of internationalization and globalization as a consequence of economic growth, China's capital market would have undoubtedly become involved in the global capital market sooner or later. Therefore, in order to lay a foundation for resisting risks arising from the international capital market in the future, China will first try to standardize practices in the domestic capital market. Assuming that risk is under control, China will then make efforts to open up its capital market to the outside. Since the onset of the Asian financial crisis, China has endeavored to ceaselessly facilitate the evolution of the system governing China's capital market. Against this backdrop, this chapter looks back on the reform and development of the capital market both during and after the Asian financial crisis and seeks to draw lessons from the past 10 years to further the standardization and positive evolution of the capital market.

Risk prevention and control before and after the Asian financial crisis

Endeavors to align the market and prevent and dissolve risks

Rectify and curb illegal stock transactions

In line with the decision under the "Notice of the Central Committee of the Communist Party of China and the State Council with Regard to Deepening the Financial Reform, Straightening Out the Financial Market, and Preventing Financial Risks," the China Securities Regulatory Commission (CSRC) has begun investigating and comprehensively studying ways to curb illegal stock transactions in all provinces and municipalities in the country since 1997. In addition, the authorities mobilized specialists in different parts of the country to study and present reorganization plans, and formulated a proposal in 1998 for straightening out and curbing illegal stock transactions and for allying with other departments for a similar purpose.

First, meticulous efforts were made across China to lay down reorganization plans. Indeed, such a reorganization effort is a highly sensitive task and an enormous undertaking that touches on the interests of numerous parties. The efforts must also help safeguard normal order in the financial market and maintain social stability. Therefore, it is critical for local authorities to lay down proper plans and guarantee that reorganization will proceed without a hitch. To insure success in this regard, CSRC held many seminars in several provinces and municipalities about rectifying and curbing illegal stock transactions. In these seminars, participants discussed the substance and detailed measures in their reorganization plans, described the reorganization itself, and examined and approved the reorganization plans of each province or municipality. CSRC also convened a special meeting of chairpersons to study the reorganization plans put forward by Shandong Province and Qingdao City (which were major players in this effort) and put forward concrete, feasible suggestions for consideration, with the aim of insuring success.

Second, integrated measures were presented for the disposal of listed companies' tradable shares. The hardest aspect of reorganization work is properly straightening out listed companies. It is especially important to dispose of de-listed companies' tradable shares taking into account their individual circumstances. Pursuant to reorganization plans, the following six major measures were adopted.

1   Companies that meet certain requirements are allowed to redeem their tradable shares according to market prices.
2   Others are encouraged to purchase the tradable shares of promising listed companies as long-term investments.
3   Companies that are to be listed in the stock market and that are engaged in identical or similar industries are encouraged to take over or merge with promising listed enterprises with a brilliant operating record, hence converting their tradable shares into shares of listed companies for trade on the Shanghai or Shenzhen stock exchanges.
4   A small number of well-performing listed enterprises that have relatively strong debt-repayment abilities and that have met requirements for corporate bond issues are allowed to convert their tradable shares into corporate bonds, after having been examined and approved by the National Development and Reform Commission, the People's Bank of China and the CSRC for compliance with applicable laws.
5   A small number of well-performing enterprises, which operate on a relatively large scale and which have satisfied listing requirements, are eligible to be recommended to go public in the stock market. A number of those enterprises that have posted good operating results and that have been engaged in identical or

similar industries, but have not operated on a large scale, can be recommended to go public in the stock market after undergoing asset reorganization.

6   The existing shareholders (intramural workers and especially staff members) of those listed enterprises that have not met the requirements, are mobilized to hold their respective shares continually, and enjoy stockholders' equity.

Among these six measures, the fifth (regarding enterprises' redemption of tradable shares) and the sixth (regarding original shareholders' continual holding of shares) have been adopted by most enterprises for reasons such as their relatively small operating scale, their inadequate ability to make a profit, and the limited value of stock shares.

Third, careful endeavors were made to dispose of de-listed companies and to close illegal stock exchanges. There have been a relatively large number of listed companies, and in some regions, certain companies are listed concurrently in different stock exchanges. Furthermore, in recent years these companies have witnessed a continued decrease in stock prices. Thus, investors have sustained relatively big losses, and many of the investors are laid-off workers and staff members who have not yet possessed a strong risk-resisting capability. Therefore, it is necessary to exercise prudence when de-listing any listed company from the stock market, and try every means to adopt disposal measures such as the redemption of stock shares and the augmentation of dividends to reduce the stockholding risks of stock investors. At the same time, during the course of de-listing, it is essential to patiently and meticulously reason with stock investors to avoid conflicts and not jeopardize social stability.

Sort out issues related to securities brokers

In 1998, after extensive surveys and research, the CSRC formulated a proposal for sorting out issues related to securities brokers. The proposal was later approved by the State Council.

First, during the process of survey and research, the CSRC requested that existing securities brokers re-register themselves, and at the same time guided securities supervision organs in different regions to probe into brokers' high-risk and non-securities assets, the amounts of the clients' paid-guarantee funds held by securities brokers for a long time, illegal securities brokers and service outlets, and providers of financial services dealing with securities.

Second, on a trial basis, the CSRC segregated non-securities assets. Based on information gathered during the survey, the CSRC chose different types of securities companies and brokers to manage this segregation. Meanwhile, the CSRC revoked authorization for illegal brokers and cancelled illegal securities service outlets whose risks had already been exposed, with the aim of guaranteeing the security of clients' funds and handing over responsibility for clients to competent authorities.

Third, the CSRC expanded the segregation of financial services and of businesses. It also created conditions for categorization-based management over securities companies. In addition, the securities service and trust service industries are subject to segregation from financial services and business segregation. Those securities services provided by trust companies are gradually being segregated from trust services. Under the arrangements that have been in place, all securities companies, regardless of their financing powers and management practices, are providing underwriting, brokerage and self-operation services. Plans are being made, however, to categorize securities companies into two types, general and brokerage, and to stipulate their respective scopes of business. Such categorization-based management will consolidate the market structure, leverage corporate strengths, expand the operating scales of general and brokerage securities service companies, provide more funds to the securities market, and insure the steady and healthy development of the securities market.

Sort out issues with securities trading centers

After conducting its survey and research, the CSRC formulated a plan for sorting out arrangements with securities trading centers and submitted it to the State Council for approval. After the release of the "Notice on the Plan of the China Securities Regulatory Commission in Regard to the Straightening out of Securities Trading Centres" forwarded by the General Office of the State Council (official document: 1998, number 135), the CSRC convened, on October 15, 1998, a workshop on addressing issues related to securities trading centers. Such work was carried out smoothly and methodically (step 1: take an accurate inventory of assets; step 2: branch off business services; and step 3: cancel related organizations).

Toward an accurate inventory of assets, local people's governments were requested to organize personnel, to make an inventory of the assets and debts of securities trading centers in their respective territories, appoint certified public accounting firms that were qualified to offer services in relation to securities businesses, to conduct audits, and to present audit reports. Under normal circumstances, securities trading centers must return any embezzled membership-seat fees. Or, in some instances, membership-seat fees could be converted into shares or long-term investments in new organizations as a consequence of reorganization undertaken by themselves.

After having been reorganized, securities trading centers are allowed to pass their originally registered businesses on to new organizations emerging as a result of reorganization or takeover, after having been examined by stock exchanges. With respect to securities trading centers that had been closed down, the registered businesses will be dealt with by the stock exchange. Before the securities trading centers are cancelled, they must still be held responsible for technical maintenance regarding online trading and management over membership seats. After being cancelled, securities trading centers must be handed over to stock exchanges in a timely and appropriate way. Stock exchanges must uniformly manage online seats or appoint organizations in charge of reorganization or takeovers to take charge of technical maintenance of online systems. In addition, it is necessary to coordinate the resolution of illegal trading, funds services and members, as well as illegal stock transactions and investment funds.

The last step is to cancel securities trading centers. Subject to the CSRC's approval, securities trading centers may be reorganized in the following ways: qualified securities companies may buy out securities trading centers and use them as their service outlets; qualified securities trading centers may be transformed into securities brokerages; and a galaxy of securities trading centers may ally themselves to purchase securities companies and reorganize new security brokerages on the basis of these companies. During the course of disposal, local governments will typically be the ones responsible for organizing personnel to close down securities trading centers, while stock exchanges will be responsible for dealing with online transactions and registered business services.

Straighten out and standardize the futures market

In early 1993, the CSRC adopted measures pursuant to the State Council's principles of "standard practices from the very start, reinforcement of law enforcement, putting into force and taking strict control of each and every link after experimenting necessarily." These measures were aimed at addressing issues in the futures market and yielded some positive results. Since the second half of 1998, the CSRC has intensified efforts in straightening out and standardizing the futures market in line with the Notice of the State Council in Regard to the Further Straightening out and Standardizing the Futures Market.

One of the first of these measures was the calling off of overseas transactions of futures brokerages. Since the early 1990s, some unscrupulous overseas businessmen had taken advantage of loopholes in the legal and supervisory systems in China, which had just initiated reforms and its opening-up policies, to rapidly enter the country and set up futures-transaction outlets, thus allowing their clients in China to conduct futures transactions outside the country. Overnight, a number of overseas futures-transaction organs emerged in China. According to statistics in 1994, China was hosting more than 500 brokerage companies engaged in futures transactions outside the country, with approval granted by local administrations for industry and commerce, and more than 200 similar brokerages approved by the State Administration for Industry and Commerce. There were also numerous other brokerage companies that had not been approved. These companies collected guarantee funds from clients in China and placed orders in futures exchanges outside the country through their overseas affiliates and through other intermediaries. Some companies even embezzled their clients' guarantee funds through private, direct offsetting or by absconding with the funds.

According to the findings from a sample survey of brokerage companies engaged in overseas futures transactions, more than 95 percent of their clients who were involved in overseas futures transactions incurred some loss, and a number of them even lost all their investments. Within only a few years, the total amount of those funds flown out of China has exceeded RMB Yuan 10 billion. CSRC reckoned that today's China is not an arena suited for conducting overseas futures transactions at all, and that ongoing overseas futures transactions incur nothing other than losses, and gravely jeopardize the social stability and due financial order, and hence must be prohibited. With an approval granted by the State Council, CSRC overcame a lot of setbacks and roadblocks, and finally managed to stop all overseas futures transactions of futures brokerage companies. They also worked with relevant organs to firmly crack down on various kinds of illegal overseas futures transactions. Over time, illegal overseas futures transactions have fallen into oblivion.

In the second half of 1996, there was resurgence in illegal overseas futures transactions. The CSRC allied with the State Administration for Industry and Commerce, the Ministry of Public Security, and the State Administration of Foreign Exchange to crack down on such transactions. In 1997, securities supervision departments handled 176 cases related to illegal overseas futures transactions. In September 1998, the CSRC and the State Administration for Industry and Commerce jointly released an official list of cases that involved illegal overseas futures transactions to be handled by the CSRC. Other organizations engaged in such overseas futures transactions were to be punished by the State Administration for Industry and Commerce in conjunction with the CSRC. Cooperation with and the division of labor between the CSRC and the State Administration for Industry and Commerce have helped reinforce the country's efforts to crack down on illegal overseas futures transactions.

A second measure was to subject futures exchanges to stricter supervision and management. By the end of 1993, the country had housed 33 futures exchanges that were already in operation after having been approved by their local governments or competent authorities, while 20 additional futures exchanges were slated to open after already having received the necessary approvals. The emergence of more futures exchanges resulted in an often-seen superimposition of trading items and caused exchanges to compete viciously to enhance their transaction volumes. Meanwhile, there was insufficient supervision and management of them. It costs a between RMB Yuan 10 million and RMB Yuan 100 million to build a futures exchange. Therefore, if no measures had been taken to stem the excessive emergence of futures exchanges, there would have been huge waste. Also, because futures trading is a special financial sector, it is exposed to a remarkable set of risks. Once a serious problem emerges in it, social stability may be in jeopardy.

At the end of 1998, the CSRC succeeded in compressing more than 50 futures exchanges into only three. This move not only met China's demand for economic growth, but it also adapted the country to the international futures market and laid a solid foundation for the positive evolution of the futures market. In the course of such compression, the CSRC relied on local governments, which played a leading role in taking comprehensive and reliable action and which helped realize the smooth transformation of the futures market. Such hard-earned achievements were reflected in competent market supervision and management and the high level of skills in these areas.

A third important measure was the ending of various types of futures transactions in medium and long-term contracts, thus eliminating risks before they emerged.

Lured by potential economic gains, local organizations demonstrated impressive initiative in embarking on futures exchanges. After the State Council unambiguously announced that it is forbidden to set up futures exchanges without authorization, some local organizations and departments, intent on evading these stipulations, launched a "medium and long-term contract market," which features "transactions based upon guarantee funds and treaties." In name, this market claims it hosts spot transactions; but in substance, it houses futures transactions. Futures transactions by nature involve the general public and therefore have a vast customer base. They are known for their wide coverage and high risks. Because such medium and long-term contract transactions are not yet regulated and are not subject to the basic rules of futures transactions (they are instead managed by practices that apply to the spot market), they are exposed to huge market – and financial – risks, and are vulnerable to a multitude of adverse effects.

Drawing on findings from its survey and research, the CSRC issued a report to the State Council on the "medium and long-term contract transactions," advising an end to such transactions. With approval from leaders in the State Council, the CSRC allied itself with competent departments to end transactions conducted in the name of medium and long-term contracts.

A fourth measure involved the streamlining of futures brokerages while standardizing their services. Futures brokerages have occupied an important position in the futures market and have served as a bridge between futures exchanges and their customers. As futures brokerages absorb guarantee funds, they discharge the duties of financial institutions. Statistics show that by the end of 1995, China was housing more than 2,000 organizations, in addition to 330 futures brokerage companies, as members of non-futures brokerage companies that were engaged in futures business (they dealt with futures concurrently, in addition to their principal businesses). These often-unqualified economic organs entered into vicious competition and fomented numerous disputes, causing huge risks and latent hazards. The CSRC spent three years suspending the auxiliary futures services of these organizations, completing the effort at the end of 1998.

Straighten out and standardize original investment funds

In order to further straighten out and standardize the securities market, prevent and dissolve financial risks, and insure the healthy and standard development of securities investment funds, the CSRC conducted studied the original investment funds in early 1998, before formulating a feasibility plan for straightening out and standardizing such funds.

The following measures were taken to straighten out and standardize the original investment funds. First, it was necessary to quickly liquidate the original investment funds that had reached maturity but that had not yet been liquidated. Second, in regard to the original investment funds that had not reached maturity, it was necessary to shorten the renewed term of the original investment funds to 10 years (in cases where the term was greater than 10 years); gradually convert assets from the original investment funds into tradable shares of listed companies, government bonds, cash and other high-fluidity assets; and, in the course of straightening-out and standardization, not allow original investment funds to increase in size, to renew the term, or to change trading mode or premise without authorization. Third, it was necessary to strictly standardize any remaining original investment funds resulting from efforts to straighten out the system. Specifically, this meant; (1) allowing the handover of original investment funds worth more than RMB Yuan 200 million (after adjustments to their terms and structure) to fund-management companies that had been established with approval by the CSRC or to fund custodians authorized by the CSRC and the People's Bank of China, with the goal of bringing them under normal supervision and management; (2) allowing further trade of those original investment funds that had already been brought under normal supervision and management, had been traded in stock exchanges, and had met related listing requirements of the concerned stock exchanges; (3) and allowing for those original investment funds, which had already met the listing requirements but that had not yet been traded in stock exchanges, to apply for permission to trade in stock exchanges. Suitable original investment funds whose debtors were main sponsors could be converted to financial securities. It was also required to liquidate those original investment funds that had failed to meet stipulated terms and conditions after having been standardized and which could not be converted to financial securities. This also applied to original investment funds that were requested to be liquidated in one year, in line with a resolution passed by their holders. In the course of liquidation, it was required to pay special heed to safeguard the rights and interests of small and medium-sized investors.

Formulation and implementation of the "Securities Law" and formation of a uniform supervision and management mechanism

Characteristics of the law

The "Securities Law" was passed at the sixth session of the Standing Committee of the Ninth National People's Congress on December 29, 1998 and has been in force since July 1, 1999. It has taken a relatively long time for the "Securities Law" to be formulated (in fact, this law took more time than any other legislation in the country's history) because of the amount of time it required to fully study practices in the securities market and to review other countries' laws and regulations to draw lessons for their application in China. It also took a long time because of the need to unify perceptions about the securities market and because the adjustments that were needed were in a very complicated area of economics and had to be made by experts. The law may have taken a long time, but it is now revered for being conceptually sound and for being a perfect fusion of pragmatism and far-sightedness. It is considered a milestone in the history of China's securities market.

The draft of the "Securities Law" was preliminarily examined at the third session of the Standing Commission of the Eighth National People's Congress in 1993 and discussed and passed at the sixth session of the Standing Committee of the Ninth National People's Congress on 29 December 1998. During those six years, this law was reviewed five times and is the product of joint efforts by theoreticians and pragmatic workers. In fact, the legislation process followed for this law, which embodies the interests of tens of millions of investors in China's securities market and also the principle of social stability, has displayed maximum stringency and meticulousness.

In view of the relatively large number of non-standard and highly speculative practices employed in China's securities market, the "Securities Law" specifies unambiguous stipulations about the responsibilities and obligations of securities supervision and management authorities, securities issuers and companies, listed companies, stock exchanges, securities registration and settlement organizations, as well as securities-transaction service organizations. In addition, the "Securities Law" includes detailed stipulations about legal liabilities of parties in breach.

The "Securities Law" was formulated taking into account China's own circumstances and current practices in the securities market. It affirmed several years of success in China's securities market. The law did not, however, include stipulations about issues that required further study or information and instead left these issues to be addressed at a later phase. Thus, the "Securities Law" showed the pragmatism suited to the present situation in the country. Meanwhile, the law served to digest the experience of more mature securities markets in the East and therefore consisted of internationally accepted practices and global trends. In brief, this law has not only been well suited for today's securities market but also allows for the market's evolution in the future.

The "Securities Law" was promulgated while the impact of the Asian financial crisis had not entirely dissipated. This crisis provides the basis for a memorable lesson about the potential harm from financial risks. After having experienced the after-effects of the crisis, China became aware of the need to remain vigilant in addressing financial risks, thus preventing, controlling and dissolving such risks. China also realized it was necessary to establish rigorous systems and stringent laws. The "Securities Law" particularly stressed control of risks. On the one hand, the "Securities Law" emphasized the necessity for standardization in issuing, listing and trading of securities (e.g., to restrict bank funds from flowing into the stock market without authorization; prohibit state-owned or controlled enterprises from making speculative investments in the stock market; stipulate securities transactions as spot transactions; remind investors about undertaking risks on their own; and not open the A-share stock market to foreign investors for now). On the other hand, the "Securities Law" dedicated itself to establishing a "risk control and prevention mechanism" from an institutional perspective (e.g., keeping a close watch on embezzlement of clients' settlement funds; requesting that clients deposit the entirety of their transaction settlement funds into designated commercial banks; and requesting securities companies, stock exchanges, securities registration, and settlement organizations set up risk reserves), thus showing a profound awareness of "risk prevention in advance."

Auxiliary stipulations and measures for the "Securities Law"

A committee liable for the examination of to-be-issued securities was set up and the system for examination of securities prior to issuance was reformed. An "approval system" regarding issuance of stock shares was put forth, resulting in noticeable differences between the "Securities Law," the "Management Regulations upon Issuance and Transaction of Stock Shares," and the "Company Law." In line with the approval system, it was necessary to set up a Committee for Examination and Approval of To-Be-Issued Securities, which would, on the one hand, absorb a number of governmental officials, experts, and scholars who would take part in the issuance stock shares (thus making more democratic decisions), and on the other hand, make the approval procedure public, accept supervision by all walks of life, and enhance the degree of transparency in the issuance of stock shares.

Venture capital management measures have been worked out for stock exchanges, securities companies and securities registration and settlement companies. The CSRC has allied itself with relevant departments to draft provisional measures for management of the venture capital of stock exchanges and securities companies and for the management of securities settlement venture capital. This alliance has also resulted in the formulation of detailed rules and management measures for the withdrawal and use of these three types of venture capital.

Existing securities companies were reorganized and subjected to categorization-based management. The "Securities Law" provides that "the country conducts categorization-based management over securities companies and categorizes securities companies into general service securities companies and brokerage service securities companies." This provision is one of the more significant reforms to China's securities company management system.

General-service securities companies separate their brokerage service from their self-operated service and comprehensively liquidate their customers' transaction settlement funds. The "Securities Law" provides for general service securities companies to "handle their brokerage service separately from their self-operated service, separate the working personnel in charge of their brokerage service from those in charge of self-operated service, separate the financial accounts in relation to their brokerage service from those in relation to their self-operated service, and never handle these two types of service in combination. Customers' transaction settlement funds must be deposited in full into designated commercial banks, and managed under separate accounts. It is strictly prohibited to embezzle customers' transaction settlement funds."

Bank funds are prohibited from flowing into the stock market without authorization; efforts were made to study the channels and methods of normal financing for securities companies. The unauthorized flow of bank funds into the stock market can cause huge bubbles in the stock market giving rise to intense ups and downs, which is inconsistent with the primary guiding principle of "segregation of financial services and business segregation" governing the banking and securities industries. Meanwhile, the "Securities Law" has left sufficient leeway in this regard, as it only prohibits bank funds from flowing into the stock market without authorization. It does not prohibit bank funds from entering the stock market through reasonable and lawful channels.

Regulations making buyouts of listed companies more feasible were formulated, resulting in significantly more opportunities.

The securities central clearing companies in Shanghai and Shenzhen were consolidated and a national uniform and centralized securities registration and settlement system was set up, guaranteeing that securities registration and settlement organizations could operate efficiently as requested under the "Securities Law." The consolidation also furnished the clearing companies with a full range of service facilities and a complete set of data security measures. It enabled them to establish high-quality business and financial management and control systems and a complete risk-control system.

Formation of a uniform supervision and management mechanism

The Securities Management Office of the People's Bank of China, founded in May 1992, is the earliest body liable for conducting uniform supervision and management over the securities market. In July of that same year, the State Council set up a "routine conference system" for the Securities Management Office, which represents the State Council in the management of the securities industry. However, a so-called "August 10 incident" further revealed the necessity of setting up a specific supervision and management organ for China's securities market in line with globally accepted practices. Therefore, the State Council set up the Securities Regulatory Commission of the State Council and the CSRC in October 1992. In December, the State Council released "The Notice with Regard to Further Intensification of Macro Management over the Securities Market," which clarified the uniform management mechanism, which the Central Government would apply to the securities market.

In November 1997, China's financial authority further clarified its principle of "segregation of financial services and business segregation among the banking industry, securities industry, and insurance industry." In April 1998, the State Council cancelled its securities committee and transferred its responsibilities (along with the responsibilities of the People's Bank of China for supervision and management of securities brokers) to the CSRC. Thus, the CSRC became the supervisory and regulatory authority for the country's securities and futures markets and began to take over securities-management offices at provincial and municipal levels. The CSRC put in force a supervisory and regulatory mechanism targeting main regions of the country, setting up 36 branches across China and building a uniform, centralized supervisory and regulatory mechanism for the securities and futures markets.

Standardization of the operating practices of listed companies

Policies and measures for improving the performance of listed companies

In 1998, the CSRC endeavored to improve the performance of listed companies by taking varied measures (e.g., taking stricter control of companies' entry into the market). Meanwhile, it put into force stricter requirements related to the issuance of new shares and the examination of share allotments. In 1998, the CSRC adopted concrete measures to improve the performance of listed companies. Specifically, the CSRC formulated and promulgated:

1 "Opinions Regarding Standardization of the General Meetings of Shareholders of Listed Companies," which laid out concrete provisions about how often meetings should be convened, the issues to be discussed at meetings, the relationship with the board of directors, resolutions to be reached, and the public notices to be issued about the meetings, thus standardizing behaviors of listed companies and insuring that listed companies' general meetings allow shareholders to exercise their powers and safeguard shareholders' interests according to the law;

2 the "Notice with Regard to Certain Issues of Replacement of Assets and Change of Principal Business Activities of Listed Companies" and laid out provisions for examination and approval, the scope of piloting initiatives, transparency, and procedures for replacing assets and changing principle business activities of listed companies;

3 the "Notice with Regard to Special Treatment of Stock Shares During Abnormal Operations of Listed Companies" requested special measures for stock exchanges to handle abnormal stock transactions, and laid out provisions for ceilings on the price increases for stocks on the date of their quotation;

4 the "Notice with Regard to Certain Issues of Listed Companies' Application for Allotment of Shares in 1998," and stipulated that "listed companies shall not be able to apply for allotment of shares until one full fiscal year after they get listed on the stock market"; and

5 the "Notice with Regard to Granting Prioritized Support to State-owned Medium and Large-sized Enterprises' Listing in the Stock Market," and requested local authorities to prioritize the 512 major state-owned enterprises under local and central governments to when selecting candidates to be listed on the stock market, thus supporting the reform and development of state-owned medium and large-sized enterprises;

6 the "Notice with Regard to Surveying the Restructuring of To-Be-Listed Enterprises," and stipulated that "the to-be-listed enterprises shall each render a written report upon their restructuring work, after accomplishment of such restructuring, to the CSRC," and that "after its receipt of such reports, CSRC will survey the restructuring of these enterprises (e.g., the independent operating capabilities of these enterprises, which have to keep their personnel independent, their assets complete, and their financial operations independent) how the principal underwriters have assisted these enterprises in such restructuring. Only those to-be-listed enterprises that have met the requirements, as indicated by the findings of such survey, will be allowed to render their applications officially to the CSRC."

In 1999, after summing up its supervision and management experience, the CSRC studied how to improve the examination and approval of stock share issues, adjusted the staffing for the examination and approval committee for such issues, further standardized the system for examination and approval of issues, amended and re-publicized procedures, intensified the social supervision in examination and approval, and upheld the principle of "putting operating performance above all other factors influencing judgment." The purpose of these actions was to select only promising and vibrant companies to go public in the stock market.

In addition to improving the examination and approval system for the issuance of stock shares, the CSRC further intensified supervision and management of listed companies, focused its efforts on reinforcing information disclosure, examined whether listed companies and their controlling shareholders had conducted a "separation" in assets, personnel and finance, standardized transaction behaviors of listed companies, and uncovered and meted out penalties for illegal behaviors, such as fraud, insider trading, and market manipulation.

Policies and measures to improve utilization effects of listed companies' funds raised through the stock market

In order to further normalize listed companies' use of their raised funds, CSRC stipulated on December 9, 1998 under its "Notice with Regard to Properly Handling Certain Matters of Listed Companies Mentioned in Their Annual Reports of 1998" that any listed companies that had not put the funds they raised to good use must provide an explanation in their annual reports and provide a similar explanation in a report to the CSRC. This stipulation somewhat mitigated the undesired effect of having some listed companies change, without authorization, the way they used the funds or fail to reveal information in this regard. On March 27, 1998, the CSRC issued its newly amended "Notice with Regard to Certain Issues of Listed Companies' Allotment of Shares," ameliorated stipulations laid out in 1996, stressed the reinforcement of responsibilities shouldered by boards of directors in companies and intermediary organs, and intensified efforts aimed at disclosure of corporate information, thus helping standardize practices in share allotment.

In view of the non-standard, legal, person-based corporate-governance structure and a the paucity of independence and prevalence of associated transactions, the new notice requested listed companies applying for share allotments to separate assets, staffing and finance and to maintain capabilities in conducting independent operations.

To reinforce supervision and management of formerly raised funds, the new notice requested those certified public accountants who presented audit reports for listed companies to provide specific reports about these funds. Such reports must state how listed companies' formerly raised funds had been used, point out the similarities to or differences from the wishes of their boards of directors, and disclose information related to the subscription or allotment of shares.

In order to allow investors to have a thorough understanding of the way in which the funds to be raised will be used, the new notice called on listed companies' boards of directors to make separate resolutions about the feasibility of funds' use with regard to the allotment of shares and stressed the importance of notifying shareholders about general meetings and disclosing any resolutions reached separately about the feasibility of funds' use. It also stressed that notices of general meetings include disclosure of investment of the funds to be raised and the feasibility of such investments.

When the assets for allotment of shares are to be used to purchase in-kind assets, it is necessary to evaluate the assets. The auditing and evaluation results must be disclosed in the notices of the general meetings of shareholders.

To insure that the use of funds raised by listed companies is effectively examined, the new notice extended the interval between the allotment of shares and the former issuance of stock shares to a full fiscal year, reinforced the responsibilities of listed companies' boards of directors, and called on boards of directors to make unambiguous decisions about whether companies have met the requirements for share allotments and for the investment of the funds they raised through share allotments. It also required boards of directors to state in detail, in the general meetings of shareholders, how formerly raised funds were used and how the funds to be raised would be invested in the future (and describe the feasibility of the planned investments). Whenever associated transactions are involved, it is necessary to confirm that such transactions will not jeopardize the interests of listed companies and non-associated shareholders.

To prevent securities companies from failing to perform due diligence merely because they wish to embark on more projects, the new notice provided that "the principal underwriters must conduct due diligence investigations into listed companies' efforts to carry out a separation in the aforesaid three respects and into the specifications for share allotments. In addition, reports on due diligence must be presented, helping to increase the responsibilities of securities dealers for the allotment of shares.

To insure fairness and equality in associated transactions, safeguard the interests of listed companies and their small and medium-sized shareholders, the new notice reiterated that, "when it comes to a vote on associated transactions in the general meetings of shareholders, associated shareholders must withdraw themselves from such voting, and apply their restrictive forces upon non associated transactions. In cases where the use of the funds raised via the allotment of shares involves associated transactions, the concerned board of directors is requested to necessarily express its opinion unambiguously on whether or not such associated transactions are fair to the concerned company and non-associated shareholders." The new notice also unambiguously provided that "in case the majority of shareholders appropriate funds or assets of a listed company and conduct any major associated transactions that jeopardize the concerned listed company's interests, the concerned listed company is then not allowed to allot shares within the ensuing year after its submission of the application for allotment of shares."

To reduce the operating risks of listed companies, the new notice particularly provided that "listed companies shall not render any guarantee, by use of their assets, for their shareholders or any individuals' debts."

The newly amended provisions have contained well-customized policies and measures, which were put forth in view of market-development trends and in view of issues in the former course of share allotments. These policies and measures also meet requirement for improving the structures of listed companies and ameliorating the performance of listed companies. They are conducive to optimizing the deployment of market resources, protecting investors' interests, and avoiding risks. They are bound to play a key role in enhancing the utilization efficiency of those funds raised by listed companies and standardizing their practices.

Policies and measures for standardizing listed companies' asset reorganization

Listed companies reorganize their assets with the goals of cleaning up property rights, optimizing the deployment of resources (such as assets in stock, human resources, and marketing), enhancing assets' operating efficiency, improving their performance, and bettering their structures. Through reorganization of their assets and through managerial and organizational integration, listed companies aim to reduce operating costs and maximize the holistic effects of their efforts.

In 1998, the CSRC adopted a policy to support a number of listed companies in their trial efforts in asset reorganization. To address the "emerging tide of asset reorganization" that occurred that year, the CSRC held a national conference on the supervision and management of the securities industry, during which it was made clear that "some listed companies engaged in the textiles industry are encouraged to play a leading role in conducting asset replacement and changing their principal business activities." Afterwards, the CSRC released the "Notice with Regard to Certain Issues of Listed Companies' Replacement of Assets and Change of Principal Business Activities" (official document [1998], number 26), which unambiguously laid out stipulations for the scope of trials in reorganizing assets and spelled out requirements for information disclosure and procedures. At the same time, the CSRC adopted a series of measures regarding listed companies' endeavors in asset reorganization.

First, rules and regulations were formulated and amended regarding matters subject to examination and approved by the securities supervisor and regulatory authorities (such as the issuance and allotment of shares). These rules and regulations were consistent with the latest requirements of the Central Government. Meanwhile, concrete requirements were clarified for matters such as the requirements for documentation in the issuance of new shares and allotments. Arrangements were also made for related departments to strictly conduct pre-examinations and appoint experts and others to jointly examine and approve these matters in line with established procedures.

Second, a patrolling examination department was established to reinforce on-site examination of enterprises that were to become listed and of companies that were already listed.

Third, efforts were made to properly handle relations between examination and approval, supervision and management, and guidance and coordination. Among the various modes of asset reorganizations, some had to be examined and approved by the CSRC according to laws and some correlated with listed companies' disclosure of significant information. The CSRC is liable for supervision and management of all these matters and for offering guidance. As for the piloting of asset reorganization in the textiles industry, the securities management authority must exercise its examination and approval authority and provide its insights into laws and regulations in the securities and capital markets, to guide organizations through this process. Besides, the CSRC guided more than 10 listed companies, which had incurred losses for three consecutive years (including Zhongyi in Hunan, Nantong Machine Tool, and Sichuan Changgang) in their asset replacement or debt displacement.

Fourth, listed companies' information disclosure behaviors were standardized. At the end of 1998, under the guidance and coordination of the CSRC, the Shanghai and Shenzen stock exchanges amended and made public their "Listing Rules," which included specific provisions for procedures for disclosure of information in regard to companies' issuance of new shares, allotment of shares, regular reporting, interim reporting, transfers of stock equity, sale and purchase of assets, and other significant matters.

Fifth, the "Company Law" and other related laws and regulations were strictly implemented, a "weeding-out" mechanism of the securities market went into effect, and unscrupulous speculative investments in junk shares were forbidden. On the one hand, a system for special treatment of stock transactions was implemented last year. Through this system, companies incurring losses for two consecutive years or experiencing deteriorating asset conditions are assigned an "ST" prefix to their stock names. These companies also have 5 percent limits imposed on both the increases and decreases of their stock prices, as a way of reminding investors of the risks. Meanwhile, these companies are pressured into adopting measures to turn losses into profits or carry out asset replacement within a specified period. For instance, Jiangsu Sanshan Industrial Co., Ltd. was suspected of incurring losses for three consecutive years. After the competent securities management authority surveyed and confirmed the losses, this company was suspended from the stock market in September, pursuant to the relevant stipulations under the "Company Law" and the State Council.

Post-crisis reform and development of China's capital markets

Standards development in the capital market

In November 2005, the "Securities Law" was amended, marking the further standardization of the capital market. The amendment also had a far-reaching influence on the establishment of the legal system that governs the capital market.

At that point, China was advancing reforms with the ultimate goals of improving the socialist market-oriented economy building a more prosperous society over all. With the continuation of economic reform, more and more state-owned and non-state-owned joint stock companies have entered the capital market. In December 2001, China gained entry into the World Trade Organization (WTO) and the economy was opened full-scale to the outside, while in-depth reforms in the financial sector were carried out and while the capital market expanded in size and substance.

Gradual improvement of the legal framework for governing the capital market

The "Securities Law", implemented in 1999, was China's first legal instrument designed to standardize behaviors of in securities issues and transactions. To aid the adaptation to further economic and financial reforms and to the development of the securities market since 2003, the National People's Congress set out to amend the "Securities Law" and the "Company Law." In 2006, the amended laws, together referred to as the "two laws," entered into force at the same time.

Subsequently, competent departments sorted out and amended relevant laws, regulations and normative documents. Since 1998, when the uniform, centralized supervision and management mechanism was set up, oversight of the securities and futures markets has been gradually improved and consolidated to meet the changing needs for market development. In 2004, the CSRC adjusted its "supervision and management mechanism based on partitioning into major regions" and set up supervisory and regulatory bureaus in different administrative regions. Meanwhile, the CSRC began to reinforce supervision and regulation of local securities supervision bureaus, and put into force a responsibility system featuring "supervision and management by local bureaus, clear-cut duties, delegation of responsibilities to individuals, and mutual coordination," and established a system of overall supervision and regulation in conjunction with local governments. In addition, the law-enforcement system was improved methodically. In 2002, the CSRC set up investigative branches in all parts of the country and established an organ particularly liable for investigation into market manipulation and insider trading. The State Ministry of Public Security set up a Securities Crime Investigation Office on the same premises as CSRC. This office is responsible for investigating securities crimes. Since the office's inception through late 2006, the CSRC investigated more than 760 cases and administered 506 penalties. Some cases were passed on to the judicial authority for criminal investigation, including major cases involving Minyuan in Hainan, Guangxia in Yinchuan, and Zhongke Venture, which had provided false information, committed fraud or insider trading or manipulated the market.

Standardization and development of the stock market

Since the "Securities Law" was promulgated in 1998, China's stock market has been evolving rapidly and positively. The number of listed companies rose quickly, stock-exchange transactions were enhanced, registration and settlement systems became more convenient, laws, regulations and accounting rules gradually improved, and the secondary market housed increasingly vibrant transactions. However, the historical problems remaining from the development of the capital market and the institutional defects and structural contradictions in the capital market have loomed large. In 2001, the capital market entered a phase of adjustment that lasted four years, during which stock indexes fell dramatically. It became more difficult and time-consuming to issue new shares and for listed companies to raise additional funds. Securities companies suffered huge operating hardships. By 2005, the entire securities industry had remained in the red for four consecutive years.

The root cause of these problems lies in the fact that China's capital market is a newly emerging one, which has gradually developed while the country shifted toward a market-oriented economic system based on pilot implementation of new policies. Since its beginning, this market had a very weak governing system, which lacked supportive reforms. Some problems that were not initially apparent gradually became obstacles to the further evolution and expansion of this market. Obstacles included the failure to thoroughly restructure listed companies, the incomplete governance structures of listed companies, the relative weaknesses of securities companies, the non-standard operating practices, the small size and limited variety of institutional investors, the irrational product mix in the market, the lack of quality blue-chip shares suitable for investment by major funds, the fixed-earning products and financial derivatives in relation to risk management, the singular trading system, and the lack of a trading system that would allow institutional investors to avoid risk.

To actively boost reforms, open up and insure stable development of the capital market, the State Council in January 2004 issued the "Certain Opinions with Regard to Boosting the Reform, Opening-up and Stable Development of the Capital Market," also referred to simply as "certain opinions." Afterwards, China's capital market adopted reforms to improve and consolidate the fundamental system governing the capital market. These reforms mainly included the separation of equity, the improvement of the performance of listed companies, the overall treatment of securities companies, the bold development of institutional investors, and the reform of the issuance system. After these reforms were adopted, investors regained their confidence, and the capital market reversed its downward trend, and the outlook brightened.

Efforts toward a multi-tiered market structure and a diversified product mix

For many years, China's capital market maintained a single-tiered structure and housed only two stock exchanges, in Shanghai and Shenzhen. In addition, the criteria to be met by companies seeking to be listed were singular and rigid and therefore out of range or unable to accommodate the diverse financing demands of enterprises in various stages of development and the different risk preferences of investors. In order to enrich the capital market, Shenzhen Stock Exchange embarked in 2001 on a growth enterprise market, and set up a board for small and medium-sized enterprises in May 2005. As of the end of 2006, 102 companies had been listed on the board for such small and medium-sized enterprises.

To properly resolve the issue of transfers of tradable shares of companies listed in the Securities Trading Automatic Quotation System (STAQ) and the National Electronic Trading System (NET), the Securities Association of China set up a commissioned stock equity transfer system in 2001, which undertook the transfer of tradable shares of those companies de-listed from the market. In January 2006, the joint stock enterprises in the High-Tech Park at Zhongguancun that had not yet been listed in the stock market began to enter the commissioned stock equity transfer system for trading, thus enriching the functions of this system. At the end of 2006, this commissioned system had hosted nine companies that were originally on the STAQ and NET systems, 36 companies that were de-listed from Shenzhen Stock Exchange and Shanghai Stock Exchange, and 10 companies from the High-Tech Park at Zhongguancun. The number of accounts involved in the transfer of stock equity reached 420,000. The number of stock shares transacted in the past years totaled 2.5 billion, with a combined total transaction value of RMB Yuan 5.9 billion.

The launch of the board for small and medium-sized enterprises and the emergence of the commissioned stock equity transfer system were important strides forward in the development of China's multi-tiered capital market system. In that period, China's capital market has witnessed the emergence of convertible corporate bonds, bonds of securities companies, bank credit assets securitization products, mortgage securitization products, corporate assets securitization products, bad bank asset securitization, integrated earning-plan products issued by enterprises or securities companies, and warrants, all helping meet the diverse needs of diverse investors. These products have greatly enriched the range of securities transactions.

Preliminary development of the bond market

In the past few years, China's bond market has expanded and its transaction rules have improved. The development of infrastructure such as the bond custodian and transaction systems has been accelerated ceaselessly. China's efforts have focused on three types of measures.

First, the inter-bank bond market was founded by the People's Bank of China in 1997. It is considered an intangible market established on the basis of the China Government Securities Depository Trust & Clearing Co. Ltd., and mainly features institutional investors and agreement-based transactions. Since 2000, the laws and regulations governing this market have been gradually improved, and the variety and scale of products have constantly expanded. Financial institutions' entry into the inter-bank market has been governed by a filing system instead of by the former examination and approval system. An approval system has governed financial bonds, a filing management system has been established for short-term financing bonds, and market participants have included overseas institutional investors and non-financial institutions. International institutions have been allowed to issue RMB Yuan bonds. New varieties of bonds, such as foreign currency financial bonds, commercial banks' overlying bonds, securities companies' short-term financing bonds, industrial and commercial enterprises' short-term financing bonds, commercial banks' ordinary financial bonds, commercial banks' mixed capital bonds, forward bond transactions, and credit asset backed securities, have been launched in succession. Corporate bonds are allowed to enter the inter-bank bond market for trading. In addition, this market's infrastructure, such as its transaction, registration and settlement systems, has gradually improved. The unencumbered treatment of delivery-versus-payment and bond transaction settlement has been achieved.

Second, the commercial bank over-the-counter market is an extension of the inter-bank market, which was founded in 2002. It mainly deals with retailing government securities and targets individual investors and small and medium-sized enterprises. In addition, the number of government securities trading outlets has increased quickly, and the number of individual investors and the value of transaction settlements have also risen.

Third, the number of product varieties in the stock exchange bond market and the size of this market have continued to increase, while trading modes have continuously improved. The net price trading mode implemented in 2002 enhanced the fluidity and vibrancy of transactions. In 2004, the buy-out trading mode of government securities was launched. In September 2005, the country's first asset-securitization product, the "linked earning plan," was placed for trade in the market. In 2006, regulations were launched for the convertibility of separated transactions into bonds, market registration, and trust and settlement businesses. In particular, the buyback of government securities has been streamlined. In addition, some corporate bonds were issued publicly (online) by stock exchanges on a trial basis, thus enhancing transparency and resulting in better information disclosure. However, because the market-oriented bond credit system had not yet been established and because a multi-headed management mechanism governed the bond market, the corporate bond market lagged behind for a while. What's more, the ongoing inter-bank, stock exchange and over-the-counter markets had not been inter-linked for the sake of communications among investors and across product varieties, impeding the positive evolution of the bond market.

The futures market's rebound and growth

Due to the implementation of the "Provisional Regulations upon Management over Futures Transactions" promulgated in 1999 and the subsequent relevant supporting management measures (with regard to futures exchanges, brokerage companies, qualifications of senior officials in brokerage companies and qualifications of brokerage specialists), a set of laws and regulations governing the futures market was established and the futures market thus stepped onto a path of standard operations. Meanwhile, endeavors toward straightening up the futures market also achieved positive results, and a group of futures brokerage companies, which have not met the qualification requirements or broken laws and regulations, have been revoked or were requested to suspend operations, thus preventing illegal futures transactions. In December 2000, the China Futures Association was founded in Beijing and became a national self-disciplinary, non-profit organization governing the futures industry.

In 2003, the futures market comprehensively put into force a system of confidentiality-based operations for futures transaction guarantees and strictly implemented futures transaction and settlement regulations, thus preventing and dissolving risks arising from the settlement and delivery of futures transactions. In 2004, China began successively launching new varieties of commodity futures such as cotton, fuel oil, corn, #2 soybean, white sugar, and purified terephthalic acid, or PTA. In the same period, "Guidance on Governance of Futures Brokerage Companies" and "Measures for Sealed Management over Futures Transaction Guarantee Funds" entered into force, and the net-capital-center system for risk supervision and management indicators of futures companies was implemented. Meanwhile a new futures guarantee fund depository system and the Investor Guarantee Fund were established. In May 2006, the China Futures Guarantee Fund Monitoring Center was founded, and a futures guarantee fund verification system and an investor inquiry service system were established. As a result of all these efforts, the operating quality and standardization of the futures market improved markedly, and the futures market has been more closely connected to the entity economy and cash market. In September 2006, China Financial Futures Exchange was established in Shanghai.

Thus far, China's futures market offers 13 varieties of trading and is gradually rolling out its hedging and price-discovering functions. The three commodity futures exchanges are unifying their trading rules step by step and are poised to allow online trading, thus reducing the cost of trading. Also, the "Futures Transaction Management Provisions" are being amended.

China's further opening up and its holistic fulfillment of commitments made upon entry to the WTO

Since China's entry into the WTO in December 2001, China's capital market has opened up to the outside at a faster pace. As of the end of 2006, China had fulfilled all its WTO obligations for opening capital markets. The opening up helped China's capital market expand, mature, and become internationalized and market-oriented. This transformation is manifested in four ways.

First, China set up joint-venture securities and futures organizations. In 2002, China issued its "Regulations upon Establishment of Securities Companies Using Foreign Investments" and the "Regulations upon Establishment of Fund Management Companies Using Foreign Investments." In the same year, the Shanghai and Shenzhen stock exchanges also released their respective "Provisional Regulations upon Management over Foreign Extraordinary Members." By the end of 2006, China had hosted eight Sino-foreign joint venture securities companies, and 25 Sino-foreign joint venture fund companies. Nine companies each had more than 40 percent of their total stock equities held by foreign investors. The China representative offices of four foreign-invested securities organizations have become extraordinary members of the Shanghai and Shenzhen stock exchanges and 39 foreign securities organizations and 19 foreign securities organizations have been dealing directly with B-share-related businesses in these exchanges.

In addition, China Galaxy Securities Co. Ltd., and ABN AMRO Bank made joint investments in 2006 to establish China's first-ever joint-venture futures company, which marked the official entry by foreign investors into China's futures market.

Second, the qualified foreign institutional investor (QFII) system and the qualified domestic institutional investor (QDII) system were built up. Because the RMB Yuan had not yet become freely convertible, China implemented a QFII system in December 2002 to allow approved overseas institutional investors to take part in transactions in the A-share secondary market, and in May 2006 put into force a QDII system to allow approved domestic institutional investors to invest in foreign securities markets. As of the end of 2006, up to 52 foreign institutions had qualified as QFIIs; 44 institutions had gained a total investment of US$9.045 billion, and 12 banks (including five foreign-invested ones) had been authorized to offer QFII custodian service. One securities investment and fund management company and six banks have qualified as QDIIs and made a total investment of US$8.3 billion. The continual development of QFIIs has reinforced the international influential power of China's securities market, and the introduction of QDIIs is not only helpful in straightening out supply-demand relationships in the foreign exchange market, but also enables Chinese investors to pour investments into the vast international capital market and have their assets deployed globally.

Third, foreign-funded joint stock companies are allowed to issue shares in China and get listed on China's stock market, and foreign investors may make strategic investments into listed companies. In November 2001, China unambiguously allowed foreign-funded joint stock companies that had not met certain requirements to apply to be listed in the Chinese stock market. In November 2002, China allowed foreign investors to accept state-owned stock equity and corporate stock equity to be transferred out by listed companies. In February 2006, China allowed foreign investors to obtain A-shares of listed companies that had already accomplished equity separation reforms through limited medium- and long-term strategic mergers and acquisitions and investments.

Fourth, international cooperation continued to progress in the supervision and management of the securities market. China's securities supervision and management organizations have entered into more intensive communications and cooperation with foreign securities and futures supervision and management organizations, international organizations of securities commissions (IOSCOs) and other international organizations. As of the end of 2006, the CSRC had signed 32 bilateral cooperation memorandums with securities and futures supervision and management institutions in 29 countries or regions. The signing of these memorandums enabled Chinese and foreign supervision and management institutions to exchange supervisory and regulatory information, provide cross-border investigation assistance to each other, compare information, and conduct cooperative research. In June 2006, Shang Fulin, Chairman of the CSRC, was elected Vice Chairman for the Executive Committee of the International Organization of Securities Commissions.

Reform measures adopted in the capital market in recent years

Release of "Certain Opinions with Regard to Facilitating the Reform, Opening-up And Steadfast Development of the Capital Market"

In only about a dozen years, China's capital market has traveled down the same path that other countries have sometimes taken hundreds of years to follow. However, holistically speaking, China's capital market is still embryonic and meanwhile must still address a number of deep-rooted problems. Starting in 2001, the stock market stagnated, and several structural contradictions began to loom large.

In order to help solve these problems, the State Council issued the "Certain Opinions with Regard to Facilitating the Reform, Opening-up and Steadfast Development of Capital Market" (also referred to as "certain opinions") on 31 January 2004 and defined a national strategy to develop China's capital market. The certain opinions were put forth on nine fronts, thus laying a foundation for the further reform and development.

The certain opinions pointed out that "it is a strategic task of significance to greatly tap the capital market, which is conducive to ameliorating the socialist market-oriented economic system, bringing into better play the function of the capital market in optimizing the deployment of resources, effectively converting social funds into long-term investments, adjusting and strategically restructuring the state-owned economy, accelerating the development of the non-state-owned economy sector, bettering the structure of the financial market, enhancing the efficiency of the financial market, and maintaining the security in the financial market."

> The certain opinions also pointed out that "the capital market shall be developed in adherence to the principle of 'openness, fairness and equitableness' and the creed of 'law-based administration, supervision and regulation, self-discipline and standardization'; it is necessary to manage the capital market according to laws, protect the lawful rights and interests of investors and in particular social public investors; stick to the market-oriented direction of the reform into the capital market, bring into full play the market-orientation mechanism, insist in solving those problems arising from the development course through pursuit of development, and persist in making progressive efforts, as well as constantly enhancing the scale of opening-up."

The "certain opinions" put forth tasks for the sake of reform, opening up and steadfast development of the capital market, all of which were intended to expand the scale of direct financing, bring into better play the basic function of the capital market in resources deployment, strike up an efficient, transparent, rationally structured, functionally complete, and safely operating capital market, and gradually establish a multi-tiered capital market structure that meets the financing demands of various kinds of enterprises.

Equity separation reform

The equity separation issue emerged chiefly because of the former disjointed perceptions about the joint stock system (specifically about the functions and positioning of the securities market at a time when the reform of the state-owned assets management system was still in a nascent stage and when the concept of state-owned assets operation was not yet entirely established). As a remnant institutional defect, equity separation impeded the standard development of China's capital market and the radical reform of the state-owned assets-management system. Besides, as more new shares were issued in the stock market, equity separation's adverse impact on reform, opening up, and steadfast development of the capital market, has been a major concern.

Before the certain opinions were released, China had tried to reduce state-owned shares. But because of the market's immaturity, such initiatives failed. As of the end of 2004, the total capital of listed companies in China amounted to 714.9 billion shares, including 454.3 billion (64 percent of the total) non-tradable shares. State-owned shares accounted for 74 percent of non-tradable shares.

The ultimate solution to the equity-separation problem was the transformation of the mechanism (i.e., eliminate institutional disparities in transferring of stocks in the A-share market, through an interest-balancing and coordinating mechanism between the holders of non-tradable shares and the holders of tradable shares). In course of reform, all parties in the market followed the principles of "uniform organizing and decentralized decision-making" and "implementation on a pilot basis, coordinated facilitation, and step-by-step settlement."

The equity reform proposals of listed companies must be determined by their shareholders and must be negotiated equitably and sincerely, with mutual understanding and independent decision-making. Because the implementation of equity separation will change expectations of price, "shares held by shareholders are not subject to trading for the period prior to listed companies' issuance of public shares," thereby generating significant changes to the pricing of the stock and altering the interests of two types of shareholders. Thus in the course of reform, holders of non-tradable shares and holders of tradable shares balanced their interests through parity pricing. Holders of non-tradable shares alienate a portion of the revenues earned from the trading of their shares in the stock market to holders of tradable shares. To keep an eye on the near- and long-term interests of the entirety of the shareholders and to facilitate the development of listed companies and support stability in the market, listed companies carrying out the equity separation reform may adopt stock-price stabilizing measures in light of their circumstances.

As of the end of 2006, 1,301 companies listed in the Shenzhen and Shanghai stock exchanges had already accomplished or launched equity separation reform (accounting for 97 percent of the total number of companies intending to undertake equity separation reform). Only 40 listed companies have not undertaken these reforms. The bulk of the reform occurred in less than two years.

Equity separation reform is considered an unprecedented innovation not only because it solved deep-seated problems but also because of the process of accumulating experience, meeting all the prerequisites for reforms in the capital market, and innovating the governance of the capital market.

China's experience with the reform underscores the need to adhere to the fundamental principles of "respecting the law of the market, boosting the stability and development of the market, and practically protecting the lawful rights and interests of investors, particularly public investors." When it comes to solving historically deep-rooted problems and adjusting complicated interest relations in the capital market, it is necessary to maintain a proper balance between the intensity of reform and the stability of the market and to focus on stabilizing market expectations. In the course of implementing reforms, it is necessary to properly handle the relations between the government and the market and coordinate the government's uniform organizational work with decision making, resulting in a win-win situation for all the parties involved.

Improving the performance of listed companies

Listed companies are the cornerstones in the development of the capital market. Over the course of about the past 10 years, China's listed companies have embraced constant business expansion and have already generated significant momentum toward corporate reform and industrial growth. However, quite a few listed companies have lacked a legal people-based governance structure and have not employed standard practices or achieved solid operating performance. These factors have diminished investor confidence and impeded the capital market's embracing of healthy and steady development. In the past few years, the CSRC launched successive reforms aimed at improving the performance of listed companies, protecting the lawful rights and interests of investors, and boosting the healthy and steady development of the capital market. In November 2005, the State Council approved and circulated the "Opinions of the CSRC with Regard to Improving the Performance of Listed Companies." Since March 2006, the competent supervision and management authority launched a campaign designed to further standardize the operating practices of listed companies, intensify the companies' governance, and improve their performance. The campaign featured six main actions.

First, the "responsibility system for supervision and management of listed companies by different regions," which came into force in 2004, was a significant reform for listed companies. This reform advanced the principles of "supervision and management by local bureaus, clear-cut duties, division of responsibilities to individuals, and mutual coordination." It further clarified roles and responsibilities for each branch organ, drew on the comparative advantages of each in the areas of supervision and management, made supervision more timely, accurate and effective, integrated the system's supervisory and regulatory forces, and broadened management's scope and substance. Following a "responsibility system of supervision and management by different regions," the securities supervisory and regulatory authority also quickened the building up and consolidating a comprehensive system for listed companies, in conjunction with multiple departments and all local governments, with the effect of enhancing the authoritativeness and effectiveness of supervision and management.

Second, supervision and management of listed companies since 1999 have emphasized information disclosure instead of administrative examination and approval. In view of the development practices of the capital market, the CSRC persistently pushed for standardizing listed companies' information disclosure practices. To meet the more stringent requirements for information disclosure by listed companies as spelled out in the "Company Law" and the "Securities Law", enhance transparency, meet newly arising requirements related to supervision and management of listed companies after equity separation reform, the competent securities supervisory and regulatory authority set out to formulate "Measures for Management of Listed Companies' Information Disclosure." The goal of these measures was the further improvement of rules and procedures regarding information disclosure in supervision and management.

Third, in recent years, to strengthen rules for corporate governance, the CSRC issued successive laws and regulations, including the "Guidance on Articles of Association of Listed Companies," the "Opinions on Standardization of the General Meeting of Shareholders," and the "Criteria for the Governance of Listed Companies." The CSRC also ushered in an Independent Director System. After the equity separation reform was launched, the CSRC amended the "Regulations on the General Meetings of Shareholders of Listed Companies" and the "Guidance upon Articles of Association of Listed Companies." Through these new laws and regulations, China established the framework and principles for the overall governance of listed companies and for putting listed companies on track for standardization.

Fourth, to solve problems related to majority shareholders and their associated parties' embezzlement of listed companies' funds, the CSRC restricted controlling shareholders and other associated parties from embezzling listed companies' funds, and put into force a practice of "offsetting of debts by relinquishment of shares." The CSCR worked with local governments and competent authorities to clear the embezzled funds of listed companies. Meanwhile, the CSRC focused on establishing a "long effect" mechanism and endeavored to prevent new cases of embezzlement. In addition, China's Criminal Law also contained new regulations dealing with embezzlement of listed companies' assets and established harsher penalties for majority shareholders and virtual controllers who embezzle assets. At the end of 2006, 399 companies had either completed the clearance of embezzled funds or had set out to clear them. This involved a total of RMB Yuan 39 billion. As a result, the number of listed companies suffering from embezzlement of funds and the total amount of such embezzled funds dropped 93 percent and 84 percent, respectively.

Fifth, since the "Company Law" and the "Securities Law" were amended, and since the equity separation reform was carried out, the legal environment and market environment for China's implementation of a stock-equity incentive mechanism have constantly improved. In January 2006, the CSRC issued the "Measures (for Trial Implementation) of Management of Stock Equity Incentives for Listed Companies." These measures aim to help listed companies establish and consolidate their respective incentive and restriction mechanisms. The measures stipulate that the main forms of stock equity incentives are restricted stock and stock options. They also standardize the stock equity incentive mechanism from the perspective of implementation procedures and information disclosure, which has a far-reaching influence on standard operations and sustainable development of listed companies.

Sixth, the CSRC amended the "Measures for Management of Purchase of Listed Companies" and the "Information Disclosure Rules" and launched the acquisition of assets, on a trial basis, for the sake of issuing shares to specific targets. This in turn was intended to help strengthen listed companies and allow them to become more competitive. It was also intended to encourage controlling shareholders to bring together their quality assets and their projects with competitive edges to allow a markedly larger number of listed companies to become market-oriented and listed. Since 2002, nearly 400 listed companies have undergone changes in their controlling interests. More than 250 listed companies have taken significant measures of asset reorganization. So far, the capital market has become a major arena for enterprise reorganization and industrial integration.

As reflected in a number of reforms aimed at improving listed companies' performance, the government's solid support for and the close attention to the development of the capital market together engendered a powerful guarantee. All measures to improve performance must facilitate sustainable and healthy development of the capital market, maintain equality among all subjects in the market, and bring fully into play the initiatives of all related parties. All measures must be market-oriented and adhere to a path of standardization and to widely accepted practices in the international capital market. A long-term effect mechanism must be established to solve problems that arise during the development of the capital market.

Comprehensive treatment of securities companies

Securities companies play a key role in boosting the healthy development of the securities market and serve as important intermediaries. Institutional and systemic defects have contributed to many problems during the rapid expansion of securities businesses. Some securities companies embezzled customers' transaction settlement funds and securities or engaged in transactions in breach of regulations. Some shareholders and their associated parties also embezzled funds on several occasions. Around the start of 2004 these problems were exposed and risks burgeoned. The survival and development of the entire securities industry faced daunting challenges. To address the symptoms and the causes of the problem, the securities supervisor and regulatory authority took comprehensive action. Deployed by the State Council, the authority launched concurrent efforts in the areas of risk disposal, routine supervision and management, and the facilitation of industrial management. Actions involved a combination of risk control and prevention and the formulation of a total solution and formation of a treatment mechanism.

In 2004, the CSRC worked out standards for securities companies and assisted well-performing companies pursuing business expansion based on controllable, measurable and bearable risks. The CSRC also conducted an in-depth survey into the risks encountered by securities companies, cleared embezzled guarantee funds paid by customers and the embezzled bonds of customers. It eliminated risks arising from the illegal provision of financial services and from operations outside of accounts. It proactively and smoothly disposed of 31 high-risk securities companies unable to rescue themselves or in violation of regulations, while maintaining market and social stability.

The CSRC explored a range of modes for mergers and acquisitions, put in place a "System for Depositing Customers' Transaction Settlement Funds into Third Parties," and reformed basic business systems such as buybacks of government securities, asset management, and self-operation. The CSRC established a "System for Securities Companies' Disclosure of Financial Information and Publicizing of Basic Information," carried out net-capital-based risk monitoring and warning system, intensified supervision and management of senior officials in securities companies and improved monitoring of shareholders. It standardized behaviors of senior managers and shareholders, changed the mode of withdrawal from the securities market to uphold the Investor Protection Mechanism, drew on international experience as a reference, and set up the China Securities Investors Protection Fund Co. Ltd.

After such comprehensive work, the long-accumulated risks and deep-rooted problems in securities companies have smoothly dissolved, and problems, such as false financial information, outside-of-account operations, and embezzlement, have been wholly resolved. A long-effect risk control and prevention mechanism was preliminarily established and various basic systems were formed and improved. Most securities companies have become more aware of the necessity of complying with laws and regulations, have initiated their respective innovations, and set out to optimize their industrial structuring. At the end of 2006, 104 companies in the securities industry had seen the total value of their assets reach RMB Yuan 620.3 billion and the total value of their net assets reach RMB Yuan 107.2 billion, up 27 percent and 73 percent, respectively, from levels recorded at the end of 2003. In 2006, the entire securities industry realized RMB Yuan 60 billion in sales revenue and a net profit of RMB Yuan 25.5 billion. Ninety-five companies in this industry made profits. The securities industry had thus ended a four-year pattern of losses and reached historically high levels, as reflected in all financial indicators for the industry.

The successful experience with the comprehensive approach to the strengthening of the securities industry reinforces the necessity to concurrently dissolve risk, establish supporting systems, and organically combine efforts to intensify supervision and management with efforts to promote innovation and pursue development. In the future, it will be necessary to formulate total solutions and solve all aspects of fundamental problems. When disposing of risks, it will be necessary to insure the stability of the industry, the market, and society. To sustain the health development of the securities industry in the long run, it will be necessary to improve and consolidate achievements in the basic system of operations, supervision and management of securities companies.

Reform of the share issuance system

After China's capital market was established, an examination and approval system was implemented to govern the issuance of stock shares. In March 2001, an examination and approval system was officially put into force and a responsibility system featuring "determination of responsibilities in advance, disclosure of information according to laws and investigation afterwards" was built up, along with a system focusing on compulsory disclosure of information. Laws and regulations for supervision and management in the issuance of securities were preliminarily written. The examination and approval procedures for the issuance of stock shares were further standardized. Meanwhile, the issuance-pricing system featured a "market-oriented pricing mode" instead of an "administrative-order-based pricing mode." However, much remains to be done to accomplish the goal of market-oriented reform in this area. Therefore, it is necessary to advance reform. There are three main tasks ahead.

First, the "Provisional Measures for the Sponsor System with Regard to the Issuance of Securities" went into force in February 2004. The Main Underwriter Recommendation System (which was subject to channel restrictions) officially gave way to the sponsor system. Meanwhile, an accountability system for sponsor organizations and representatives of sponsors was created. At the end of 2004, the "Provisional Measures of Examination and Approval Committees for Issuance of Stock Shares" was implemented. These measures included stipulations to eliminate secrecy about the capacities of members of the examination and approval committees. The voting mode gave way to the registration mode. Moreover, accountability and supervision systems were established, thereby making market participants under the examination and approval system take care of their respective tasks, follow the principle of "allowing each party to bear its own risks," and take the first step toward the goal of market-oriented reform of the share issuance system.

Second, market restrictions on the issuance of stock shares were strengthened. In 2006, the "Measures for Management over Listed Companies' Issuance of Securities," the "Measures for Management over Initial Public Offerings," and the "Measures for Management over Issuance And Underwriting of Securities" and supporting rules and regulations were launched in succession, forming a new share issuance mechanism under a "100 percent negotiability" mode. This mode included ushering in the "Listed Companies' Issuance of Addition Shares at Market Prices" system and a "System of Countermeasures for Failure in Allotment of Shares and Issuance of Shares." The sponsor system was strictly implemented and the requirement for a year of guidance was cancelled. Enterprises were allowed to decide when to issue shares and efforts were made to facilitate innovation of financing modes and tools. Convertible corporate bonds (which could be transacted separately) were launched. Institutional arrangements, such as inquiries into stock prices for new shares, allotments and sale of shares to specified strategic investors, concurrent issuance of shares in domestic and foreign markets, implementation of an over-allotment option on a trial basis, non-public offerings, and equity warrants, were put into force. Besides, market restrictions were further strengthened and the issuance efficiency was enhanced. Well-performing enterprises were assisted in issuing shares and going public.

Third, since the pricing capabilities of institutional investors had become increasingly strong, the CSRC issued the "Notice with Regard to Certain Issues about Trial Implementation of The Price Inquiry System for Initial Public Offerings" at the end of 2004. The CSRC replaced the examination and approval system for stock issue prices and adopted a price-inquiry system. The price-inquiry system strengthens the market's restrictions of share issuers. The "Measures for Management over Issuance and Underwriting of Securities," promulgated in September 2006, have further standardized links such as price inquiries, pricing and allotment of shares in regard to initial public offerings, and consolidation of the price-inquiry system. The measures reinforced the supervision and management over the behavior of share issuers, securities companies, securities service organs and investors in participating in the issuance of securities.

Reforms in the securities issuance mechanism have shown that the institutional arrangements for the securities market must conform to the principle of market orientation instead of the principle of "governmental predomination." Endeavors shall be made to reinforce the market restriction mechanism, enhance the transparency of market operations, and allow market participants to decide on the pricing process in relation to the issuance of shares. In this way, the accuracy of stock share pricing will be enhanced and the securities market will develop smoothly. Market participants will bear their respective responsibilities and risks in addition to gaining their respective interests, all of which are conducive to the enhancement of securities brokers' capabilities in risk control and prevention and the strengthening of their core competitiveness.

Propelling a market-oriented reform of the fund industry

Since its inception, the fund industry has remained immature, and because of the highly speculative market in the late 1990s, the "fund scandal" erupted, causing the industry to bottom out. In 2000, the CSRC put forth the concept of "extraordinary efforts in fostering institutional investors" and took steps to ameliorate the investor mix in the capital market.

First, market-oriented reform unleashed the fund industry's potential for development and innovation. In 2002, under the CSRC's guidance, progressive market-oriented reform in the fund examination and approval system was initiated. The competent supervisory and regulatory authority simplified the examination and approval procedures, ushered in a system of examination and approval by experts, and therefore increasingly institutionalized the examination and approval process of fund products and made the process more transparent, professional, and standardized. After 2003, the examination and approval system was further simplified and means to usher in an internationally prevalent registration system into China's fund industry were studied.

Second, in July 2002, the "Regulations upon Establishment of Foreign-invested Fund Management Companies" went into effect. At the end of 2006, among the 58 fund management companies in the country, 25 were joint ventures. So far, Chinese-funded companies, joint-venture companies, and QFIIs together pose effective competition among institutional investors, which has not only enriched the variety of investment products and the style of investment, but has also enabled the entire industry to foster standard practices and enhance holistic, professional management. It achieved this through communications and competition among market players and by allowing the entire fund industry to become somewhat internationally competitive. Meanwhile, the fund industry trained local financial specialists who are now of internationally acknowledged practices and understand the characteristics of China's capital market.

Third, with the development of the capital market, institutional investors dealing with insurance funds, the social security fund, and corporate annuities have methodically entered the capital market. The entry has helped mitigate imbalances between the mix of institutional investors and the degree to which various institutional investors have developed in the same market.

The most visible characteristics of the fund industry's reform are its market orientation, standardization and internationalization. The reform has enabled institutional investors to rapidly gain strength and has largely improved the investor mix. The mainstream investment mode in the securities market has radically changed from one of speculative investment and market manipulation to one "analysis of the overall market climate and long-term investment."

The legal system governing the capital market

First, the "Company Law" and "Securities Law" were initiatives to standardize the capital market. The "Company Law," which entered into force in 1994, has actively helped standardize the organization and behavior of companies, protect the rights and interests of companies, their shareholders, and financial creditors, propel the restructuring of state-owned enterprises, reform into economic system, and boosting the development of the socialist market-oriented economy. The "Securities Law," which entered into force in 1999, was China's first law formulated to adjust behavior in securities issuance and transaction. It has played a significant role in standardizing the behavior of parties involved in the securities market, protecting the rights and interests of investors, boosting the healthy development of China's securities market, maintaining the socio-economic order, and propelling the development of the socialist market-oriented economy. With the continuation of reforms to the economic and financial systems and the continual development of the socialist market-oriented economy, relatively large changes have taken place in the market. These two laws were unable to meet the pragmatic needs that arose because of new circumstances and were therefore in urgent need of amendment. In October 2005, the National People's Congress amended the "Company Law" and the "Securities Law." The amendments have been in effect since 1 January 2006.

Second, to cope with the amendments to the two laws, the National People's Congress and all the departments and commissions under the State Council rationalized related laws, rules and regulations and departmental bylaws. The National People's Congress passed the "Amendment VI of the Criminal Law," which clarified the responsibilities of listed companies and securities and futures organizations that violate laws and spell out harsher penalties for manipulating markets. Meanwhile, the "Enterprise Bankruptcy Law" was amended, aiming to standardize bankruptcy behaviors of operating entities in the capital market and to protect the interests of all parties. The CSRC facilitated the compilation and formulation of administrative decrees, sorted out and integrated rules and regulations, normative documents, self-discipline rules, and successively promulgated initiatives such as the "Enforcement Measures of Freezing up and Sealing up Assets," the "Regulations upon Governance of Listed Companies," the "Rules for the General Meetings of Shareholders of Listed Companies," the "Guidance on the Articles of Association of Listed Companies" (amended in 2006), the "Measures for Supervision and Management of Qualifications of Directors, Supervisors and Senior Management Personnel of Securities Companies," and the "Measures for Management of Securities Settlement Venture Funds."

Amendments to the "Company Law" and the "Securities Law" and the consolidation of rules and regulations in the capital market were important measures for reinforcing the operating mechanism of the capital market and consolidating the market-oriented economic system. The amendments created a legal guarantee for facilitating strategic decision making, had a far-reaching influence on the enhancement of legislation, and accelerated reform and development of the capital market.

Today's capital market and major measures to boost its development

Main problems

China's emerging securities and futures markets have lagged behind such markets in other countries even though the demands on it have grown as a result of the country's rapid economic growth. China has therefore taken steps to develop and strengthen these important markets.

A relatively small share of financing

From 2001 to 2006, the ratio of funds directly raised in China to increments in bank loans were 10.63 percent, 6.04 percent, 4.92 percent, 7.61 percent, 9.81 percent, and 19.40 percent, respectively. The small share of funds directly raised not only impeded enterprises' financing and capital formation endeavors, but also resulted in an imbalance in the structure of the financial system. This situation had a negative effect on the deployment of resources deployment in financial system and on the ability to meet the requirements for a modern financial system and improve the socialist market-oriented economy.

Delayed formation of a multi-tiered structure in the stock market

China's stock market comprises the Shenzhen Main Board, the Shanghai Main Board, the Small and Medium-sized Enterprises Board and Commissioned Stock

Share Transfer System. It has employed higher standards for the listing of candidate enterprises. The Small and Medium-sized Enterprises Board has been unable to meet all the financing demands of fast-growing enterprises. The over-the-counter market has also lagged behind in its pace of development. The ongoing Commissioned Stock Share Transfer System is merely a provisional tool intended to tackle only residual problems and to handle the transfer of stock shares of de-listed companies. The scope of its services must be expanded and its trading system consolidated (although it has started to host high-tech enterprises from the Sci-Tech Park at Zhongguancun for listing). In general, China has not yet formed a multi-tiered market structure that meets the demands of diverse investors with varying tolerance for risk and of those who raise funds.

Underdevelopment of the corporate bond market

China's corporate bond market is small and plays a minor role in direct financing. China has not yet set up a market-oriented bond-credit system and intermediary organs have not yet brought their functions into play in the market. China has also not yet set up consolidated effective systems for bond credit ratings, public disclosure of information, bond depository management, financial creditor meetings, supervision and regulation, and for administrative, civil, and criminal investigations. China has not yet integrated bond-transaction market segmentation, the inter-bank market, the stock exchange market and the over-the-counter market. Some investors and transactions are also not yet interlinked, increasing the risks of operating in the market and failing to meet the needs of developing the corporate bond market. In addition, there were diverse market management mechanisms, which had not been uniformly planned, thus contributing to impediments to the growth of the bond market.

A need to improve overall performance of listed companies

Listed companies must hone their corporate governance. The boards of directors of some companies lack powerful decision-making capabilities and have often had corporate matters controlled by certain individuals. Some controlling shareholders misused association transactions and other tools to jeopardize minority shareholders' interests and this has caused listed companies to deviate from operations targets and to become unable to sustain profits. This situation has harmed companies' long-term interests and interfered with the achievement of their holistic objectives. Non-standard information-disclosure practices persist, and the quality of information is sometimes incomplete, inaccurate or in violation of laws and regulations. Because of incomplete laws and regulations and because there have been too few management professionals, only a handful of listed companies have recruited their senior managers from the open market. Meanwhile, directors and senior management specialists in some companies have not yet been guided by well-structured incentives programs and restrictions mechanisms.

Difficulties in the development of securities companies

Securities companies have made a lot of progress in consolidating their governance and intensifying internal controls, but many still need to lay solid foundations for innovation and development. Besides, securities companies have entirely abandoned their "singular profit-making mode." Homogeneous competition in the industry remains prevalent. Most companies have lacked core competitive forces in their business and have not yet gained sufficient capacities for innovation. Securities companies still lack a reliable risk control system and an adequate capacity for internal control. The securities industry is bearing increasing pressure to open up, but how to go about this remains unclear.

Development of institutional investors

The fund market has made large strides forward in the past few years. However, relative to South Korea and other countries with emerging fund markets, China lags behind. Today's fund management companies in China have a singular operating mode, offer a limited range of products, and are unable to provide customers with more personalized products. In addition, these companies do not generally meet the various demands for financial management services sought after by high-end customers. The rapid growth of the fund industry has generated a huge demand for fund management specialists, who are in short supply. There has not yet been a balanced development of institutional investors. So far, the actual amount of investments made by insurance companies in the securities market has been low. The development of the retirement pension scheme has largely fallen behind. There exist a number of supervisory and regulatory organs in charge of products related to investment portfolio plans, but rules have been complicated and generally uncoordinated.

The legislative system has not been able to meet requirements for the development of the security futures market

The legal and law-enforcement systems have not been able to meet the demands of the fast-evolving securities and futures markets. The legal system must be further improved. Some administrative laws and regulations consistent with the newly amended "Securities Law" and the "Company Law" have not yet been promulgated. Laws specific to the adjustment and standardization of the futures market have not yet been worked out, and the country has not yet formulated laws specific to the protection of investors.

The law-enforcement system must be improved and the efficiency of law enforcement increased. At the moment, there have been too few actors involved in law enforcement and efforts must therefore be made to establish a uniform law-enforcement mechanism. The "Securities Law" laid unambiguously stipulated the duties of securities supervisory and regulatory organs but has not arranged supporting systems regarding the means and mode of law enforcement. Thus, the benefits of law enforcement cannot be assured. So far, branch organs have lacked power to administer penalties, which is to the overall detriment of law enforcement.

The law-enforcement environment must be further improved. In investigations into securities and futures cases, judicial departments have not yet applied accurate and uniform rules and have deviated from the accepted interpretations of laws and policies. They have therefore been unable to adopt the degree of professionalism required in securities and futures markets. Standards for prosecuting securities and futures crimes have shown themselves not to be feasible. Some violations of the law have interfered with market order but have not been prosecuted in a timely way. Some criminal cases have ended up with relatively soft penalties, weakening overall efforts to crack down on crime.

The legal system for investor protection must be improved. Investors have few means for safeguarding their rights and the means that do exist are inefficient and yield unsatisfactory results. Litigation and means, such as mediation, arbitration and amicable settlement, must also be developed, improved and systemized.

The futures market's small size and the impediments to its evolution

The futures market must be developed further. The range of products is limited, and there are few new products in development. So far, this market has hosted only commodities futures and only 13 varieties of products for trading. Petroleum, steel, coal, and precious metals are closely related to the national economy but have been available neither for trading in the futures market nor for financial and options futures. At the moment, coordinating new products in the futures market arising from innovation and development is difficult. Also, financial institutions and enterprises using credit funds for the collection, stocking, and processing of agricultural products are not allowed to enter the futures market. The current futures market is a closed one with little influence in the global arena.

Main measures for boosting the development of the capital market

Acceleration of securities issuance pace and enhancement of the ratio of direct financing

Actions are needed to encourage enterprises to become listed, help H-share companies issue A shares, continue to study the feasibility of allowing red-chip companies return to the A-share market for listing and issuance of shares, create necessary conditions for red-chip companies' return to the domestic market for fund-raising purposes, and to continue to support giant enterprises in becoming listed at home and abroad at the same time.

Actions are also needed to strengthen market-oriented reforms to issuance mechanisms. Actions are also necessary to formulate "Measures for Management of Securities Issuance Sponsor Business," the "Operating Criteria upon Non-public Issuance of Shares by Listed Companies," and the "Internal Control Guidance on Sponsors' Investment in Banking Business," and to consolidate the "Criteria on Due Diligence Investigation by Lawyers," improve the price inquiry system, standardize behaviors of intermediary organs in the price inquiring process, gradually letting the market determine the time and occasion for issuance of stock shares and bring fully into play the market's restrictive forces based on an initial allowance for re-financers to arrange their times of issuance on their own. "Over-allotment Option Criteria" must also be formulated, based on the Industrial and Commercial Bank of China's trial issuance of A shares.

Boosting of the construction of a multi-tiered stock market structure

Expanding the scale of the main board market, requires consolidating systems governing small and medium-sized enterprises, seeking methods to develop the growth enterprise market, propelling the development of the over-the-counter market, enriching the functions of the commissioned stock share transfer market, providing transfer and circulation channels for non-listed public companies to transfer their shares, and forming a platform for non-listed public companies' quotation and transfer of stock shares under uniform supervision and management.

Consolidating the board-jumping mechanism among different market tiers requires clarifying conditions and procedures for listed companies to jump from one board to another, establishing a mechanism for fostering, screening and washing out enterprises, helping the securities market bring its resource-deployment function into play, and gradually forming a stock market structure featuring organic links among different market tiers.

Consolidating the registration, custodian and settlement systems of the securities market requires bolstering the drafting of laws, regulations and systems, clarifying rights and obligations with a focus on protecting the rights and interests of investors, solidifying the risk control mechanism, safeguarding the safe operations of the market, enhancing the efficiency of market operations, drawing on international experience for reference, and striving to meet or match global standards for control, efficiency, and innovation.

Development of the corporate bond market

Reforming the corporate bond-management mechanism requires gradually setting up a market-oriented system for the supervision and management of bond issues, formulating supervisory and regulatory rules governing issuance, transactions and information disclosure related to corporate bonds, and developing supporting rules and regulations.

Setting up a credit-responsibility mechanism requires further rationalization and standardization of intermediaries participating in corporate bond market operations, enhancing transparency of entities that issue corporate bonds in the market, expanding the size of institutional investors capacities for identifying and undertaking risk, reducing the percentage of direct investments by non-professionals, opening up bond market investments to overseas investors to an appropriate degree, ushering in a bond depository management system and financial creditors' meeting system, and studying and formulating a corresponding investor-protection system.

Building a safe, efficient, uniform, and inter-connected bond market requires breaking down restrictions on bond investments by various types of institutional investors, boosting the coordinated developments of the exchange and inter-bank markets, propelling the renovation of related technical systems, increasing the efficiency of fund transfers, store-keeping and management among different securities registration and settlement entities, realizing the full competitive edge of the stock exchange and over-the-counter systems, enhancing the efficiency of securities issuance and transactions, enriching the variety of transactions, developing corporate bonds with options that meet various demands, and launching bond forward transactions, bond option futures transactions, and other bond-derived product transactions.

Promotion of the healthy development of listed companies

Promoting the healthy development of listed companies requires reinforcing listed companies' efforts in the areas of information disclosure, improving the content, format and procedures for information disclosure, improving supervision and management in information disclosure, increasing the effectiveness and authoritativeness of supervision and management in information disclosure, administering harsher penalties for violating rules for information disclosure, enhancing the quality of the information that is disclosed, drawing on international experience, consolidating the electronic platform for information disclosure, and increasing the timeliness of information disclosure.

Ameliorating the governance structure of listed companies requires enhancing the level of listed companies' skills in corporate governance, disseminating the cumulative stock certificate system and the voting right-collection system, improving the independent director system, setting up an appraisal system to monitor the performance of independent directors, urging listed companies to strive harder to build internal control systems, helping listed companies intensify their self-appraisal and external audits, enhancing risk control and prevention capabilities, establishing an effective restriction and incentive system, and encouraging institutional investors to take part in the treatment of listed companies.

Boosting the standardized development of the mergers and acquisitions market requires establishing a vibrant and standard market for mergers and acquisitions of listed companies, forming an effective mechanism for external restrictions on listed companies, improving laws and regulations governing mergers and acquisitions of listed companies, intensifying supervision after a merger or acquisition occurs, helping listed companies enhance the level of their corporate governance skills, and putting in place a market-oriented mechanism for weeding out poor performers.

Consolidating the system for listed companies' withdrawal from the market requires setting up a system for prosecuting senior managers of companies that have withdrawn from the market who have violated laws and regulations, setting up an effective compensation system, protecting the interests of investors and relevant financial creditors of listed companies that have withdrawn from the market, and setting up an effective bankrupt company-takeover system in line with the new Bankruptcy Law.

Propelling the standardization, innovation, and development of securities companies

Accelerating the disposal of risk requires intensifying coordination and cooperation with local governments, judicial organs and competent authorities, solving difficulties encountered by banks and juridical entities in facing frozen customer transactions or settlement funds or regarding identification and purchase of individuals' financial claims, and coordinating with local governments to maintain social stability.

Completing rationalization, reorganization and verification requires auditing dissolution of residual risks, restructuring and reorganizing securities companies in conjunction with the audits of the annual reports of securities companies and their supervision and management of information disclosure, investigating securities companies as needed, solidifying effects of rationalization, clarifying responsibilities, and laying down a foundation to prevent the recurrence of problems.

Putting in place basic systems requires coordinating with commercial banks to make arrangements for the implementation of the system for depositing customers' guarantee funds with third parties, urging securities companies and commercial banks to excel at renovating business flows and technical systems, and striving for the comprehensive implementation of the deposit-with-third-party system.

Boosting the standardized development of the securities industry requires helping securities companies become more competitive and gain corporate strengths, assisting qualified securities companies in increasing their capital funds by becoming listed, increasing share capital from specified sources, ushering in strategic investors, increasing public accumulation of funds and risk reserves, and consolidating the capital replenishment mechanism. Boosting the development also requires encouraging a galaxy of qualified well-performing companies to grow stronger, larger and more competitive, helping securities companies improve their corporate governance and internal control mechanisms, standardize shareholders' behaviors, put in place an independent shareholder system, and reinforce the creditworthiness responsibilities of directors and senior managers. It also requires urging securities companies to become aware of how to conduct business operations in compliance with rules and regulations and to constantly increase their risk control and prevention capabilities, while transforming their operating mechanisms and reinforcing and upgrading core business activities. It requires providing securities companies the assistance they need, based on risk measurability, controllability, and affordability, in presenting innovative products, services and business items and in exploring new profit-making modes actively. Finally, boosting the standardized development of securities companies requires coordinating with competent departments to address issues including taxation policies, financing channels, business expansion, and governing laws and regulations; and improving the external environment for the development of securities companies.

Continuation of full-scale development of institutional investors

Continuously increasing the ratios of investments by insurance companies or the use of investments by social security funds and corporate annuities in the securities market requires consolidating the pension and social security system, reinforcing individual accounts for old-age security, broadening the channels for use of funds in individual accounts, improving the system for establishing voluntary pension accounts for individuals, accelerating the accumulation of social pension funds, exploring, on the basis of proactive control and risk prevention, new means for pouring pension funds into the securities market for investment purposes (through, for example, securities investment funds), and guiding the amounts of such investments into the securities market, thus enabling pension funds to retain and even increase value.

Developing the finance-pooling plans of securities companies and tapping investment funds with a private placement nature requires forming a multi-tiered team of professional institutional investors.

Steadfast development of the futures market

Consolidating varieties of futures and properly developing transactions requires serving the country's demand for economic development, launching a galaxy of the bulk commodities that have a major influence on the national economy, such as petroleum, steel, gold and plastics, thereby meeting enterprises' increasing demand for risk management, and consolidating commodity varieties in the futures market, including energy, metals and agricultural products. Consolidating futures also requires launching financial futures, especially stock-index futures, before launching interest-rate and exchange-rate futures. It also requires developing option transactions and selecting the commodity varieties that have operated maturely have been transacted vibrantly to launch option transactions. It requires fully realizing the functions of the options market.

Consolidating the futures and derivatives transaction mechanism requires establishing and improving the futures guarantee fund monitoring mechanism and the monitoring system for the security of futures companies' net capital funds, facilitating the establishment of futures exchanges, consolidating futures transaction and settlement systems, enhancing the depth and elasticity of the market through construction of necessary systems, and insuring the orderly and stable operations of the market.

Optimizing the investor mix and fully realizing the functions of the market requires fostering institutional investors and enabling them to become key players in the futures market, allowing various types of financial institutions to lawfully use financial futures to conduct risk management on basis of risk controllability, allowing commercial banks and securities companies to take part in financial futures operations and to provide a wider range of financial services to customers, encouraging related enterprises to conduct hedging transactions on the basis of risk control and standard operations, intensifying the education of investors, stressing guidance for the multitude through the media, and guiding market entities in gaining a scientific understanding and in making proper use of the futures market.

Further consolidation of laws and regulations governing the securities and futures markets

Consolidating the legal system governing the securities and futures markets requires facilitating the formulation of and amendments to laws regarding the development, supervision, and management of the securities and futures markets and the protection of investors. Consolidating the legal system also requires boosting the formulation of laws specific to the protection of investors (such as the "Futures Transaction Law"), promulgating administrative decrees such as the "Regulations on Supervision and Management of Listed Companies," the "Regulations upon Supervision and Management of Securities Companies," the "Regulations on Disposal of Risks Arising from Securities Companies," the "Regulations on Independent Directors of Listed Companies," and "Management Regulations on Securities Investor Protection Funds," all of which are consistent with the newly amended "Securities Law" and the "Company Law." Consolidating the legal system requires amending and consolidating the prosecution standards for securities and futures crimes, clarifying the procedures for the handover of suspected crimes involving securities and futures, facilitating the formulation and consolidation of judicial interpretations of illegal behaviors such as insider trading, market manipulation, failure to disclose information, breach of loyalty obligations, and damaged interests of listed companies. It also requires clarifying legal issues regarding bankruptcies.

Consolidating law enforcement in the securities and futures markets requires improving the futures market, improving coordination and supervision in administration and law enforcement, strengthening the cadre of law-enforcement officials, enhancing the level of law-enforcement skills and efficiency, endowing branch entities with the right to administer penalties, ameliorating the system of administrative judges, studying the feasibility of establishing a system for administration, law enforcement and amicable settlements, and stepping up efforts to penalize illegal practices.

Intensifying coordination in law enforcement requires establishing an effective mechanism and platform for tackling disputes arising from the futures market (such as non-litigation alternatives, including arbitration, amicable settlement and mediation), helping competent authorities consolidate civil compensation and litigation systems, and boosting the development of marketing.

Expansion of opening up and intensification of cooperation with other countries in supervision and management

Facilitating the opening up of the futures market to the outside in a stable way requires allowing qualified foreign futures organizations to set up joint venture futures companies in China, establish a QFII system and a "ceiling amount of shares held by foreign investors" system for the futures market, opening up relatively mature varieties of futures transactions, opening up China's futures investment market, and allowing more qualified enterprises to conduct hedging for use by foreign futures markets.

Implementing the QFII system on a trial basis requires expanding the scale of the system's implementation, enabling the participation by more varieties of institutions, establishing a linkage mechanism between the QFII investment scale and the development of the securities market.

Improving the coordination mechanism between mainland China and Hong Kong requires improving their cooperation in supervision and management and their coordination of securities transactions, registration and settlement systems. Improving coordination also requires studying how to improve the cross-border investment mechanism based on the trial implementation of the QFII and QDII systems. It also requires intensifying the proactive feasibility study on the establishment of a linkage mechanism between A shares and H shares.

Intensifying cooperation with other countries requires reinforcing China's ability to crack down on cross-border crimes in securities and futures operations.

Reference

[General Office of the State Council] (1998). Notice on the Plan of the China Securities Regulatory Commission in Regard to the Straightening out of Securities Trading Centres. Official document: number 135.
[National People's Congress] 1998. 'Securities Law'. Beijing.
[State Council of China] (2004) 'Certain Options with Regard to Facilitating the Reform, Opening-up and Steadfast Development of the Capital Market'. Beijing.

7 Reform of state-owned enterprises

A three-year disconnect from difficulties leads to system innovation

Zhang Delin

The reform of China's state-owned enterprises (herein referred to as SOEs) is central to the entire process of Chinese economic restructuring – from its orientation, momentum, and smooth development, to its progress and achievements. Up until now, Chinese SOEs have been number one in the world for their large quantity, extensive distribution, enormous assets value, strong functions, and deep historic roots. Naturally, therefore, the future and destiny of Chinese SOEs has attracted a great deal of attention worldwide. In the 10 years since the Asian Financial Crisis, what changes have taken place in Chinese SOEs and what are the future trends? This paper seeks to review, analyze, and explore these questions.

Means and policies adopted by the reform of Chinese SOEs since 1997

The Asian Financial Crisis that erupted in Thailand on July 2, 1997 naturally impacted Chinese SOEs. As is well known, Chinese SOE reform began from the "milestone" of 1978.[1] In terms of the historical evolution of the reform process, different people will use different standards to review and analyze it.[2] How many phases has the SOE reform been through? From the author's point of view, this is not only an issue of logical narration, but also of institutional innovation and essential change. From this perspective the reform of SOEs experienced two phases before the 1997 Asian Financial Crisis and another two after 1997.

Path and policy orientation of China's SOE reform before 1997

Phase 1 (1978–1992) main theme: decentralization and interest concessions

During this period, the main thrust of the reform was on decentralization and interest concessions along with the expansion of independent operation rights and the contract system of enterprises, based on the successful experiences of the "Contract System" in Chinese rural reform and the introduction of the reform methods in the former Soviet Union. In the initial stage of the reform, state-owned enterprises were actually called state-run enterprises in the planned economic system, and they were attached to the government with neither economic assets nor legal independence. Thus, the government decided to expand the independent operational and managerial rights of the enterprises in order to mobilize the enterprise initiative. Several policies were put in place during this time.[3] In order to effectively implement the enterprise autonomy system, two steps were adopted consecutively: the substitution of profit delivery to the state with tax payments by state enterprises, and various forms of contract systems. By the end of 1988, most state enterprises had implemented the contract system. Up until July 1992, the State Council promulgated the "Regulations on Transforming the Business Management Mechanism of Industrial Enterprises Owned by All the People" ("Transformation Regulations"), which contained 14 administrative rules regarding management autonomy in state enterprises. Compared to the former planned system, the contract system achieved great improvements, but it never resolved the inherent problems in the state enterprise system, which led to much analysis and self-questioning from all quarters. The Central Government then put forward its own reform measures. For example, the experimental introduction of the stock-holding system in some state enterprises and allowing small state enterprises to try out paid transfer of assets. Accompanying this reform process, China's legislature promulgated two important laws – the "Enterprise Bankruptcy Law" (for trial implementation) in December 1986, and the "Law of Industrial Enterprises Owned by All the People" in April 1988 – which were the first two basic laws concerning state enterprises since the establishment of the People's Republic of China. Though these laws played an important role during this period, they showed more and more limitations later on. The main problem was that the legislative thinking around ownership produced different laws and regulations applying to enterprises with different ownerships, that is, the state enterprise law (on Chinese-foreign equity joint ventures), the collective enterprise law (on Chinese-foreign contractual joint ventures), and the "three types of foreign funded enterprises" laws (on foreign-capital enterprises). In short, the basic means and pattern of SOE reform during this period was making decentralization the main theme, the contract system the form, and the enterprise laws the guarantee.

Phase 2 (1993–1996) Main theme: establishment of a modern enterprise system

At this time, with the determination of China's market-oriented reform objectives, SOE reform turned from "institutional improvement" to "institutional innovation," the goal being establishment of a modern enterprise system, with "corporate system" enterprises as the typical form. One point needs to be explained: China's reform of SOEs is always confined by the selection and orientation of the overall economic reform objective (Zhang 1990), which ranges from "taking the planned economy as the mainstay and market regulation as the auxiliary"[4] at the beginning to "the planned commodity economy" after 1984 to "a mechanism that combines planned economy and market regulation"[5] after the market weakened at the end of the 1980s due to the dual inflation of consumption and investment. Up until 1992, the Fourteenth National Congress decided to establish a socialist market economy as the goal of reform. In November of the next year, the Third Plenary Session of the Fourteenth Central Committee passed "Decisions on Some Issues concerning the Establishment of the Socialist Market Economy," which, for the first time, set the goal and direction of SOE reform as the establishment of a modern enterprise system with "clearly established property-rights ownership, well defined rights and responsibilities, separating enterprises from government, and managing enterprises scientifically." China's reform of SOEs then turned from decentralization and interest concessions to marketized institutional innovation. Two things happened at this time, which were closely related to SOE reform. First, the restructuring of government departments in 1993 caused the establishment of the State Economic and Trade Commission (SETC), the former Production Office of the State Council, which was responsible for macro-economy regulation and SOE reform. Second, the "Company Law" enacted in December 1993 (the first such law since the establishment of the PRC) broke through the legislative thinking that had taken ownership as the main line, and specified two forms of Chinese companies – limited liability and joint stock. At the same time, the building of stock exchanges in Shanghai and Shenzhen was started, which propelled the restructuring and listing of many state enterprises. Thus the corporate system reform of SOEs was introduced through the rule of law.

Path and policy orientation of SOE reform after the Asian Financial Crisis

Phase 1 (1997–2002): the goal of "extrication from difficulties in three years"

The proposal on the establishment of a modern enterprise system as the goal of China's SOE reform aroused extensive discussions in academic circles. Many experts and scholars in economics and jurisprudence began to explain what a modern enterprise system was from different angles and disciplines, so that it seemed everyone had his/her own unique opinions.[6] In practice, this proposal generated further enthusiasm and confidence in the wisdom of the reform within the society. In order to carry out the SOE reform principle decided by the Central Government, the SETC took the lead in the preparation of the concrete implementation plan after 1993. The State Council then selected 100 state-owned enterprises to conduct the pilot project of establishing a modern enterprise system. Before the Asian Financial Crisis erupted, the reform of SOEs aimed at the establishment of a modern enterprise system was carried out robustly. However, the difficulties faced by SOE reform and development were far more serious than first imagined. Though the 1997 Asian Financial Crisis had little impact on China's SOEs at this time,[7] the historical problems, accumulated over decades, had not been addressed. This caused difficulties to SOEs particularly regarding the generally very high debts owed to banks, the excess of labor in enterprises, and the fact that enterprises were not separated from government. The result of the SOE operation was that one third of all the state-owned enterprises suffered clear losses, one third suffered latent losses, and only one third achieved profits. Facing a severe micro situation, and in order to tackle the Asian Financial Crisis from a better position, the newly inaugurated Central Government, based on the suggestion of Premier Zhu Rongji, determined to insure that most large or medium-sized SOEs could overcome their difficulties (6,599 of all large or medium-sized SOEs suffered losses in 1997) and reverse losses into profits, or reduced losses, within three years. This was called the Three-year Extrication from Difficulties Policy.

In September 1999, the Fourth Plenary Session of the Fifteenth Central Committee adopted the "Decisions on Some Issues Concerning the Reform and Development of State-owned Enterprises," which was the first systematic guideline document issued by the CPC since the initiation of the reform and opening-up process. In order to shake off difficulties, detailed policies and measures were put in place. With regard to the heavy enterprise burden, especially the bank debt burden and high rate of debts, a policy of turning creditor's right into stock right (or what became known as debt-to-stock conversion) was implemented for some SOEs. China decided to carry out the debt-to-stock conversion measure in those large or medium-sized SOEs with good product markets, development prospects, advanced technical levels, a good management foundation, and capable leadership, but which suffered difficulties only because of heavy debt burdens. In other words, China turned the creditor's rights of the banks against some SOEs into the stock rights of some financial assets management companies (four such companies had been established at that time, including the Great Wall and Huarong companies). After processing, 580 SOEs were approved to have their creditor's rights turned into stock rights. The total value of conversion was RMB Yuan 405 billion. The result was a fall in the rate of debts from above 70 percent to less than 50 percent, representing a saving of about RMB Yuan 20 billion in enterprise expenditure on debt interest.

In terms of the weak technical experiences and core competitiveness of SOEs, a discount was given on interest for technological upgrading during the implementation of a proactive fiscal policy. In order to counter the Asian Financial Crisis, the Central Government implemented an expansionary fiscal policy by issuing treasury bonds. In 1999, China decided to draw down RMB Yuan 9 billion from the newly issued treasury bonds to pay the interest on loans for technological upgrading, which exceeded the total paid for loan interests of SOE technological upgrading in the previous 10 years. In the next four years, about RMB Yuan 35.54 billion of discount interest funds for technological upgrading were arranged out of treasury bonds. Some 2,175 projects received a total investment of RMB Yuan 435.4 billion. This measure eased the contradictions of unreasonable product structures. Some important industrial products that China had been unable to produce, and thus had had to import, could now be supplied domestically and the market competitiveness of some key enterprises was improved greatly.

For the persistent problem of enterprises not being separated from government, the government both emphasized and speeded up transformation of its functions and the restructuring of its departments. Since the beginning of reform and opening up, the Chinese government had carried out institutional reform four times, in 1983, 1988, 1993, and 1998. In order to further transform government functions and achieve the required separation with the enterprises, in 1998 the newly inaugurated government cut down the number of ministries and commissions of the State

Council from over 40 to 29. Most professional economic management departments (which managed not only the investor's rights but also the public administrative management rights of SOEs) such as those covering internal trade, coal, machinery, metallurgy, petrochemical, light industry, textiles, building materials, and non-ferrous metals, were changed into state bureaus under the SETC. More than 200 functions were transferred to enterprises, intermediary organizations, and local authorities by various departments of the State Council. At the same time, all for-profit enterprises run by the army, the police, and political and/or legal organs were transferred to local governments while party and government organs were disconnected from their economic entities. For example, SETC state bureaus transferred 168 higher education colleges under the management of the Education Ministry or local authorities and 242 scientific research institutions into enterprises. Towards the end of 2000, another nine SETC state bureaus were dismissed. In the second half of 2001, the reform of the administrative examination and approval system was started, with the priority being the reduction of administrative examination and approval. Sixty-five State Council administrative licensing departments cancelled a total of 4,147 items requiring administrative approval. All levels of local governments also began putting in place institutional reform and administrative examination and approval system reform. It is safe to say that the strength and expansive scope of institutional reform and administrative licensing reform was unprecedented. At this time, China also put in place special inspectors, who were later replaced by externally appointed supervisory panels. In February 2002, the State Council promulgated the "Interim Regulations on Supervisory Panels of State-Owned Enterprises."[8] Through the application of the above-mentioned policies and measures, and the self-reform and development of enterprises, the 6,599 large and medium-sized SOEs suffering losses were reduced to only 4,391 by the end of 2000, and the goal of a "three-year extrication from difficulties" was basically realized. These policies were continued over the next two years to further promote the reform and development of SOEs.

Phase 2 (2003–present): the state-owned assets management system reform as the basic structure

In the 10 years of reform since 1993, the theory and practice of economic reform achieved important progress and the socialist market economy framework initially took shape. However, it was undeniable that many systemic impediments still restricted the rapid development of China's productive forces. Though SOE reform at this stage was carried out robustly and achieved great progress in completing the task of a "three-year extrication from difficulties," the state-owned assets management system at the macro-level, and the management structure on the micro-level still had defects in many aspects, some more conspicuous than others. The inherent requirement for institutional innovation and the rise of public opinion on policies highlighted each other. Thus a new round of SOE reform was started at this point. The promulgated policies and obvious signals included the new systematic structure for state-owned assets management set out by the Sixteenth

CPC National Congress in 2002. This called for the government to adhere to the basic rule that the country owns all the state-owned assets and establish a state property management system under which the Central Government and local governments perform the responsibilities of investor on behalf of the state, enjoying owner's equity, combining rights with obligations and duties, integrating managing assets with managing personnel, and other important affairs.

The Central Government and the provincial and municipal (prefecture) governments were also required to set up state property management organizations. On March 24, 2003, the state-owned Assets Supervision and Administration Commission of the State Council (SASAC) was founded to perform the responsibilities of investor on behalf of the State Council. Until June 2004, all provincial and municipal governments around the country established similar institutions to try to resolve the issue of investor vacancy, or existence in name only, which had troubled the SOE reform for many years. The aim was to insure a level-by-level responsibility for state-owned assets. Second, on May 27, 2003, the State Council promulgated the "Interim Regulations for the Supervision and Administration of State-Owned Assets of the Enterprises" (Decree No. 378 of the State Council),[9] which is the basic law for the supervision of state-owned assets for business purposes and clearly defines the investor representative and its rights, obligations, and duties, for the first time, in the form of an administrative regulation. Third, on October 14 of the same year, the "Decisions of the Central Committee of the Communist Party of China on Some Issues Concerning the Improvement of the Socialist Market Economy," was adopted. This document clearly called for the acceleration of SOE reform, and improvements in the strategic deployment and overall requirements on the state-owned assets supervision and management system. After another four years of implementation and perfecting, a new state-owned assets management system (Figure 7.1) has already taken shape. The reform and development of SOEs, especially the central enterprises, have also achieved conspicuous progress.[10] Because of the reasons outlined above, a few people began referring to the new round of SOE reform as the "post-SOE era."[11]

Policy effect and evaluations on China's SOE reform since 1997

If the above content deals mainly with the background introduction and general description of the policies and measures implemented in the past 10 years of SOE reform and development from a historical point of view, the following deals mainly with the rational analysis and evaluations on the policy effect.

In terms of the systematic configuration, there were many departments that were nominally responsible for the state-owned assets, but in fact, there was no one department in charge of state-owned assets. This situation has gradually changed, with specially established authorities now taking responsibility.

Though a series of policies and measures had been enacted between 1997 and 2003 in order to accelerate the SOE reform, the issue concerning who was really responsible for state-owned assets was not really addressed systematically. The main features and problems are as follows:

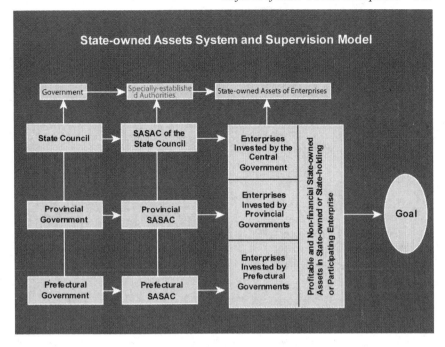

Figure 7.1 State-owned assets system and supervision model.

Departmental responsibility system

State-owned assets at this time were still distributed among the state-owned enterprises invested by the government and various departments. Nominally the government and various departments were all responsible for the state-owned assets of the enterprises invested. Some scholars call this phenomenon "nine dragons control the water."

No responsibility for either losses or profits

Regardless of whether the enterprise invested by the department achieved profits or suffered losses, neither the department nor the person responsible for the department were held accountable.

Policies out of many doors

All departments issued different policies or measures against the system and operation status of the SOEs attached to them. These policies or measures often conflicted with one another in content. The so-called "fight among papers" often confused the enterprises.

Confusion between administration and investment

Government departments assume two functions at the same time. On the one hand they are the investor representative of the invested SOE and enjoy rights as stockholders, while on the other hand, they are also the public management departments of the government that exercise administrative power over public management. They assume two jobs at the same time but the confusion between the two functions makes it difficult for them to do well in both jobs. Naturally they are unable to realize their responsibilities for state-owned assets based on the existing system. Therefore, the popular belief in the academic world during this period was that state-owned property rights "existed in name only" and the investor of state-owned assets was "vacant."

From 2000, the Central Government began to dissolve some professional industrial management departments. This move was meaningful because it accelerated the reform of the administrative management system, enhanced the macroeconomic regulation departments, and improved further the macro-management system, meeting the needs of the socialist market economy. It was also efficient in promoting the separation of government functions from enterprise management, and establishing a macro foundation for further reform of SOEs. The establishment of the state-owned Assets Supervision and Administration Commission of the State Council indicated that China was beginning to address, institutionally, the problems of the so-called "nine dragons control water" syndrome and "governmental functions and asset management functions mix-ups."[12] This measure not only deepened the reform of the administrative management system but also recreated a state-owned assets management system.[13] It was a very meaningful and important institutional innovation, not only from the perspective of China's reform practices, but also from the perspective of theoretical exploration. It built a necessary systematic structure on the basis of the macro-system for the SOE reform that followed and established an efficient guarantee system preventing the loss of state-owned assets.[14]

In terms of the micro enterprise structure, the nominal establishment of a modern enterprise system was, in essence, a kind of institutional improvement. Now this situation gradually changed in favor of corporate governance, with the corporate system as the typical form.

The SOE reform, starting from 1993, based its modernizing efforts on the Company Law and some SOEs were selected by governments at various levels to take part in this pilot project. According to relevant statistics and investigation, by 1996 2,343 SOEs had tried the corporate system restructuring route and 71 percent of these restructured companies had established a board of directors, 63 percent had supervisory panels, and 33 percent had held stockholders' conferences. Of the 520 state-owned or state-holding enterprises selected by the State Council, 430 (83.7 percent) had conducted corporate system restructuring, and 282 were entirely or partially transformed into limited liability companies or stock companies. In the next few years, the reform process continued to march forward. However, this reform, with the establishment of a modern enterprise system as the goal and direction, did not achieve the expected results. The problems were as follows.

The conception of the modern enterprise system created and described in theory aroused disputes from its beginning

People had different views about the modern enterprise system; even high-level decision-makers were not unified. The actual operators seemed more like "a blind man feeling an elephant."

The problem of "similar in shape, different in spirit" occurred in practice.

Though the image of a corporate system enterprise, which was the typical form of the modern enterprise system, was deeply rooted in people's hearts, most people in practical situations only copied the "imported one." It was rather like drawing a tiger with a cat as a model; they were not able to fathom the true meaning of the principle and structure of corporate governance – that is, the principle of separation and balance of power – or to adapt it to the enterprises that they were reforming. They did not resolve the problem of the "Chinese localization" of the governance structure principle. Whenever it was announced that an enterprise had established the modern enterprise system, people only wanted to know whether the enterprise had established the "new three parties" – the stockholder's conference, the board of directors, and the supervisory panel. But some "corporatized" enterprises with the "new three parties" were merely similar in shape and quite different in spirit when compared to the real meaning of corporate governance.

The problems in the governance structure of some state-owned listed companies were becoming increasingly obvious

These problems (of related transactions, information disclosure, etc.) not only represented administrative defects but also restricted the further improvement of these companies. This was closely related to the initial design of the policy restricting the flow of state-held stocks after coming into the market.

Most enterprise groups or parent companies invested again to establish sub-enterprises or sub-sub-enterprises across many levels

According to some research, a number of enterprises had more than 10 levels of subsidiaries. Some so-called titanic enterprise groups were like "aircraft carriers" composed of small junks. The results would be predictable. First, the investors were either in chaos or vague, which would result in the severe loss of state-owned assets, and second, management efficiency would be weakened and the risks would be increased. Some state-owned enterprises that were prominent worldwide were forced into restructuring, including the Three-nine and Huayuan groups.

In order to resolve the above-mentioned problems, the Central Government and some of its departments had been trying to improve the policies and measures for the restructuring of SOEs since 1997. Securities, banking, and other institutions continued to improve their administration and implemented the share-trading measure to resolve the circulation problem of state-held stocks. By the end of 2006, 98.5

percent of the 194 state-holding enterprises carried out the share-trading reform. The SASAC also accelerated improvements to the governance structure of central enterprises. Since 2003, 33 central enterprises covering the oil and petrochemical, communication, traffic and transportation, metallurgy, and construction sectors had made public offerings and were listed within or outside the territory of China. The ratio of central enterprises and their affiliated subsidiaries that had implemented the corporate system reform increased from 30.4 percent in 2002 to 64.2 percent. In order to make the governance structure of central enterprises conform to requirements, both in shape and in spirit, the government selected 19 enterprises, including the Shanghai Bao Steel Group, to conduct the trial work of the board of directors, with external directors exceeding one half of the total members (Li 2007). These policies and measures had played an unprecedented role in the reform and development of SOEs, contributing to the establishment of the stock-holding system and the improvement of corporate governance.

In terms of the macro-level, the state-owned economy had previously had a long front line, loose layout, and low efficiency. Now this situation began to change gradually to the strategic adjustment of the structure and layout of the state economy. The role that the SOEs and the state economy play for China's reform and social development is incomparable to that of any other country.[15]

The layout and structure of the state economy had been a long-standing problem and was not ideally addressed after 1997. This resulted partly from the planned economic system before 1978 and the difficulty in trying to move the "three-line" projects built in the 1960s in rural and mountain areas and partly from the dissolution of some departments in the 1990s, which were rebuilt into enterprise groups or parent companies. Though the Central Government suggested in 1999 that the state economy and SOEs "get some things done while leaving others undone" and split and reorganized some SOEs in the electrical power and telecommunications industries, the problems were not resolved. After 2003, in order to solve these problems, the state-owned Assets Supervision and Administration Commission of the State Council checked and ratified each of the core businesses among its 141 central SOEs for the sixth successive time. This pushed forward the combination and reorganization of central enterprises, the separation of the main body from auxiliary facilities, the restructuring of auxiliary facilities, and the separation of enterprises from performing social functions.[16]

These measures promoted the centralization of state capital towards important industries and crucial fields that have a vital bearing on the lifeline of the national economy and state security. By this time 73 central SOEs had participated in 38 reorganization activities, which reduced the number of central enterprises from 196 in 2003 to 158 at the end of June 2007 (Li 2007). According to finance department statistics, the number of China's SOEs was reduced from 254,000 in 1997 to 127,000 at the end of 2005, an average decrease of 8.3 percent per year. Meanwhile, studies were conducted of the plan for the strategic adjustment of the structure and layout of central enterprises covering 21 industries including metallurgy, automobile, telecommunications, large equipment, and trading. In order to realize the efficient flow of state capital and the reasonable and legal transfer of state-owned property rights, the SASACs, at all levels, required the transfer of state-owned property rights to be carried out inside those property-rights-transaction institutions with complete certification and standard management (according to statistics, at present 64 such institutions above the provincial level have been selected around the country). This is favorable not only for the efficient allocation of state-owned assets and the preservation and increment of the value of state-owned assets but also to avoid the loss of state-owned assets. Generally speaking, the above-mentioned policies and measures, adopted by the Central Government since 1997, have pushed forward the rational layout of the state economy and the gradual resolution of historical structural problems.

In terms of the operating effect, the SOEs often ran low-efficiency operations or even non-effective "idle running." This situation is now gradually shifting to efficient operations and large increases in profits and competitiveness.

Since the beginning of the reform and opening up exercise, particularly since 1997, massive changes have taken place in China. Not only has the national economy maintained a rapid growth of nine percent on average and accelerated industrialization, but the income per capita and people's living standards have also reached new highs and China's overall national strength has risen by a large margin. One of the important factors contributing to these achievements is the reform and development of SOEs. The various policies and measures promoting the reform and development of SOEs, as mentioned above, have finally paid off, increasing efficiency, enhancing competitiveness, creating new levels of wealth, and making the role they are playing more conspicuous.

In 1997, the total quantity of SOEs was 254,000 and their gross state-owned assets amounted to RMB Yuan 12.5 trillion.[17] Their net assets stood at RMB Yuan 4.6 trillion, sales income was RMB Yuan 6.8 trillion, profit achieved was RMB Yuan 79.13 billion, and return on net assets was 0.3 percent. At the end of 2005, these indicators changed, respectively, to the following: 127,000, 25.4 trillion, 10.6 trillion, 14.2 trillion, 968.29 billion, and six percent. The respective increase of the above indicators from 1997 to 2005 was -50 percent, 103 percent, 129.6 percent, 109.1 percent, 1123.7 percent, and 1903.7 percent, and the annual growth rate, respectively, was -8.3 percent, 9.3 percent, 10.9 percent, 9.7 percent, 36.8 percent, and 45.5 percent.

In terms of the central SOEs, by the end of 2003 (as the SASAC was established in 2003, the base period for those indicators reflecting the change of central enterprise can only be 2003) 196 of them had gross state-owned assets of RMB Yuan 8.3 trillion, net assets of RMB Yuan 2.9 trillion, sales income of RMB Yuan 4.5 trillion, profits of RMB Yuan 300.59 billion, and return on net assets of only five percent. Up to the end of 2006, these indicators changed, respectively, to 12.3 trillion, 5.3 trillion, 8.1 trillion, 754.69 billion, and 10 percent. The respective increase of the above indicators from 2003 to 2006 was 47.4 percent, 83.9 percent, 81.8 percent, 151.1 percent, and 100 percent, and the annual growth rate, respectively, was 13.8 percent, 22.5 percent, 22.1 percent, 35.9 percent, and 26 percent. During the three years from 2004 to 2006, which was the first term of the performance contracts for the responsible persons of these central SOEs, the average increase per year for gross assets was RMB Yuan 1.3 trillion, for sales income RMB Yuan 1.2 trillion, for profit RMB Yuan 150 billion, for tax paid RMB Yuan 100 billion, and for rate of preserved and increased value of state-owned assets 144.4 percent. Up to 2006, 19 out of all the central SOEs (an increase of 13 over 2002) had achieved a sales income exceeding RMB Yuan 100 billion, 13 (up by 7 over 2002) achieved a profit exceeding RMB Yuan 10 billion and entered the Fortune 500 club.

In all, the above mentioned aspects and relative statistics show that great changes have taken place in China's SOEs in the last 10 years, ranging from reform to development, from the institution to the operation, from the macro-level to the micro-level, from theory to strategy, and from policy to regulations. All these changes indicate not only the important position and functions of the SOEs in the national economy and for social development, but also the effectiveness and reasonableness of the policies and measures enacted and implemented.[18] These fruitful changes also represent the wisdom and courage of the Chinese people, especially the large number of theoretical workers, policy researchers, and decision-makers, as well as the operation implementers for SOE reform and development. These changes have also led people to the view that the so-called "Washington Consensus" must reflect China's experiences and history to form a "Beijing Consensus."

Current problems and countermeasures and the future outlook for SOEs

Based on the experiences, achievements, and problems of the last 10 years of SOE reform and development, it is expected that future SOE reform and development, the micro-level, will continue in the direction of diversification and improvement of the governance structure. It is also likely that the reform and development process will continue with the strategic adjustment and optimization of SOE layout and structure in terms of the macro-level, and will continue the improvement of the state property supervision system in the direction of separation between the government and the enterprise and between the government and the assets management. Finally, better and faster development and growth of state-owned enterprises will be realized (Figure 7.2).

In terms of the micro-level, the percentage of solely state-owned SOEs among all China's SOEs is heavy, and corporate governance in the corporate system enterprises is not so satisfactory, resulting in the need for a rapid increase in the efficiency and competitiveness of SOE operations. Therefore, future SOE reform and development will continue with the corporate system reform of the enterprises exclusively funded by state investment, the improvement of the governance structure of corporate system enterprises, and the increase of capital operation efficiency and core competitiveness of enterprises in the direction of diversification of investors.

Though great achievements have been made after decades of reform, it is an indisputable fact that some Chinese SOEs still operate at low operational

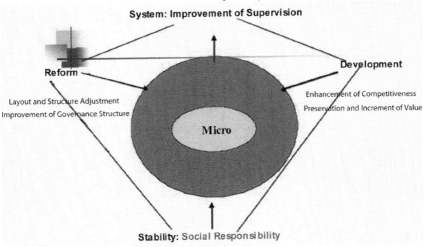

Figure 7.2 System: improvement of supervision.

efficiency and weak core competitiveness.[19] The causes, from the perspective of the micro-level, are due to two structural imbalances. First, the number of solely state-owned enterprises among all SOEs is still too high. Most of the current 158 central enterprises at the level of enterprise group or parent company are registered according to the "Enterprise Law" of 1988. The enterprises with this status are sometimes called "factory system" enterprises. From the perspective of the law, these enterprises are actually implementing the "factory director and manager responsibility" system and have not established the modern enterprise mechanism characterized by Separation of Power Balance Supervision. Second, some of the SOEs adopting the corporate system still have many of the above-mentioned administration problems, which are "similar in shape while different in spirit." Proposed countermeasures corresponding to the two problems and their causes are as follows.

Continue to actively push forward the corporate system, particularly the share-holding system reform of large and medium-sized SOEs

From the perspective of history, the enterprises selected for the governance structure are very different from one another because of the variations in investment contribution, responsibility form, and organization structure among all types of enterprises. The governance structure of classical enterprises (including proprietor enterprises, solely-owned enterprises, and partnership enterprises) is very different from that of a modern corporate system enterprise. In China, people have used the concept of state-owned enterprises for a long time. However, this is a very broad concept covering not only the solely state-owned enterprises[20] registered according to the "Enterprise Law," but also those solely state-owned companies registered according to the "Company Law," as well as state holding and joint stock companies. This confusion between different SOE organizations was finally clarified by an administrative regulation, the "Interim Regulations on the Supervision and Administration of State-Owned Assets of the Enterprises" promulgated by the State Council in 2003. This provided the legal basis and guarantee for the selection and improvement of the governance structure. In future, the development of the mixed-ownership economy, containing state capital, collective capital, and private capital, will be greatly emphasized. Large and medium-sized SOEs, after acceptable preparation, will be encouraged and supported to conduct stock system reform and to diversify investors through reorganization and being listed, through Chinese-foreign joint ventures, or through other forms of diversification. This is aimed at helping the stock system to become the main form of achieving public ownership. But surely the view that SOE reform is coming to the end will conflict with the reality?[21] On the contrary, the author agrees with the judgment of Professor Wu Jinglian. In recent years, the reform process has met many obstructions and achieved little progress in some crucial areas, including, among others, the stock system reform of large SOEs, the reform of the management system and property system of monopoly industries, and the market allocation of basic economic resources.[22] The SOE diversification reform relates not only to the results and success of SOE reform itself, but also to the foundation stone of China's socialist market economy. From the perspective of SOE functions, all SOEs, except those obliged to be solely state-owned, shall, in future, adopt diversified investors. Without this premise, it is impossible for SOEs to establish perfect corporate governance. As to the fields or industries in which SOEs will take the shape of sole investment or diversified organization, this shall be decided in line with the reform development and social progress. The principle is to obtain gradual and orderly progress while maintaining stability.

Continue to improve the governance structure of those state-owned companies that have completed the restructuring work

What is governance? Why do the enterprises need to be governed? How to select the governance structure for an enterprise? People did not see clear answers to all these problems in the past. Since the mid-1990s, many domestic scholars have translated or edited a large number of governance theories and case studies of companies in foreign, mainly Western, countries. This movement promoted domestic research and practice on this issue so well that people would refer to "governance structure" no matter what they wanted to say. Such information became so widespread that it even caused "overflow and pollution." However, as corporate scandals were exposed in the early 2000s in the US and other countries with so-called "matured" company governance, this problem again became vague. In addition, the "Lang-Gu Dispute"[23] between two economists, Lang Xianping and Gu Chujun, took place several years ago. Thus it is rare to see positive articles on this issue in recent times. In another words, the "Chinese localization" of the corporate governance structure in the market economy has actually not been resolved. This offers a new study task for us in future. As far as the author is concerned, the following questions need to be further discussed:

Governance is necessary for all enterprises

Any enterprise in the world needs to be governed. Without governance, it is not possible for an enterprise to insure its long-term existence and development. There are no exceptions, whether it is a family enterprise that has been famous for a long time worldwide, a state-owned enterprise, or a corporate system enterprise set up by the country after the Second World War.

Governance is the allocation of power and institutional arrangements

Power is a strong force, a rare resource[24] that should be used righteously and not misused. The right use of power is more important than the acquisition of power. There are always a large number of latent or explicit power problems in the enterprise that need to be resolved, such as the shareholder rights of investors, the management rights of operators, the democratic rights of employees, the public's right to transparency, and so on. At this point, it is safe to say the production and operation activities of an enterprise are actually the occupation, allocation, application, balance, and supervision among all kinds of powers or rights. The entrepreneurs often occupy the top of the power pyramid and enjoy a sublime position in their enterprises. Any problems they experience might herald a drop in the share index and even lead to the bankruptcy of the specific entrepreneur. The eternal question remains; how to arrange the enterprise's power in favor of its long-term existence and flourishing business, while insuring it remains favorable for entrepreneurs to do their duty and bring their talents fully into play.

Governance structure is dynamic and variable

Nowadays, nobody would imagine that corporate governance is a good governance structure. This is because the systematic arrangement of the corporate system turns absolute rights into relative rights; that is, power decentralization, which creates balance among various rights. Economists and jurists give an obscure term to this kind of systematic arrangement, that is, "governance structure." In Japan this translates as "ruling structure" and in Hong Kong, China, "supervision structure" or "corporate administration." Governance structure means power sharing between the three entities that run modern enterprises, formed in accordance with the principle of "power decentralization and equilibrium" of corporate rights. First there is the shareholders' meeting, which is a forum for all shareholders to express their opinions and make decisions for the company and also an organ of supreme rights. Second, the board of directors, elected by the shareholders' meeting, is expected to implement corporate decisions, offer advice on implementation of corporate business in accordance with relevant laws and decisions of shareholders, and select and recruit the general manager of the company in accordance with the articles of the corporation. Generally speaking, the chairman of the board is the public representative of the company. Third, the panel of supervisors, as the supervisory entity of a company, supervises the board of directors to implement corporate and accounting business. In the UK, the US, and some other countries, there are auditors who play a similar role to that of the panel of supervisors. This, then, is the so-called "corporate power hierarchy theory" or "organization separation." Therefore, the company is actually a "reappearance of the thought of autonomy of three rights politically on enterprise constitution."

Governance structure is selectable and continuously in need of upgrading

In the sense of districts and regions, the governance structure of one country is different from another. There is no uniform pattern or ideal for all countries and regions in the world. The governance structure model of the US is different from that of Germany, Japan, and other countries. Even governance structures among developed market economies cannot be regarded as perfectly safe, as revealed recently by the corporate scandals and subsequent meltdown of the US corporations, WorldCom and Enron. However, the core of governance structures of different countries is roughly the same, though they may vary due to differences in national conditions and other factors. Some Chinese scholars summed up this universality of the corporate system like this: improved corporate governance structures and sound corporate property rights are the most essential aspects of modern enterprise, as well as offering sufficient and necessary conditions for the existence and development of modern enterprises (Mei 2002). It is not difficult to see the defects that currently exist in the governance structures of China's SOEs. As a matter of fact, the corporate governance structure cannot settle all problems that occur in the process of production and operating activities of one company, even those in mature market economies. A good example is the issuance of the "Sarbanes-Oxley Act" in the United States.[25]

As to the progress of the pilot program setting up boards of directors of solely state-owned enterprises, relations with the CPC entities must be well handled

They must continuously select appropriate members of the board of directors and establish a good interior committee for the board of directors in accordance with the "Corporation Law." It is also necessary to further regulate the rights and obligations of the shareholders' meeting, board of directors, board of supervisors, and the operator/manager of each company to achieve effects of manifesting rights and liabilities, fulfilling one's own responsibilities by oneself, creating a power equilibrium, and bringing out the best in each other. This problem rests exclusively with governance structures in China, which need careful design and elaborate construction for settlement.

In terms of macroeconomics, the structure of the national economy is not yet reasonable; from the perspective of investors, it is necessary to further define the rights and obligations of investors, along with the principle and direction of consistent rights and obligations and systematic management, to accelerate the adjustment of the layout and structure. Because China is still in the process of industrialization, and the national economy is in the process of transferring from an extensive economy to an intensive economy, the entire national economy urgently needs to be enhanced, to say nothing of the state-owned economy. In a more meaningful sense, accelerating the strategic adjustment of the layout and structure of the state-owned economy is more urgent and more significant. The following three considerations may be selected as future countermeasures:

Optimize layout and structure, strengthen integration of resources, and regulate advance and retreat specifications

First, more increment state-owned capital should be invested in major industries and sectors related to national security and lifelines of the national economy in order to reinforce the controlling force of the state-owned economy. In this regard, effective measures used by other countries may be used for reference. The existing policies and measures may be reviewed in accordance with public product supply and system design. Second, the strategy of free advance and retreat and reasonable floatation of existing state assets should be carried out by way of capital merger, acquisition and asset reconstruction, structural readjustment, and so on, for existing state assets to retain the superior ones and weed out inferior ones through fair competition. Furthermore, adjustment of the layout and structure of the state-owned economy is not only a reform step but also a step for development. For a country with a large population in the process of industrialization, with a per capita income of just over US$1,000, this adjustment must be coordinated with the strategy of development of the western regions and that of revitalization of the old industrial base in northeast China, in order to step forward in harmony.

Improve the relevant laws and regulations necessary for the adjustment of the layout and structure of the state-owned economy[26]

This adjustment will be a long and rough process, and it won't end in a single operation. This is not only because its progress is actually linked to the overall progress of reform or that of each SOE, but also because relevant laws and regulations still need to be formulated and perfected. From the angle of both theory and practice, merger and acquisition is one of the major modes for adjustment of the layout and structure. Therefore, laws and regulations in this regard need to be further improved. In addition, anti-monopoly law should be formulated urgently,[27] in accordance with commitments made by China when it entered the WTO. This law is expected to play an important role in accelerating the adjustment of the layout and structure of the state-owned economy and in further advancing fair competition among enterprises at home and abroad.

Accelerate the establishment of the management budget system of state-owned capital

In the early 1990s SOEs were universally faced with the problem of insufficient stamina for development. This was due to a weak technical force, insufficient renovation and reformation funds, and the policy alteration from "changing allocation of funds into loans" to "changing loans into allocation of funds." The then Central Government, therefore, decided to allocate after-tax profit and earnings to enterprises for technical innovation and redevelopment. This policy has been continued to today. In other words, the country has not exerted the right to tax the earnings of enterprises it invested in, and the SOEs have not handed over any dividends to the country for more than 10 years. With the establishment of state assets supervision authorities, and increased economic returns from SOEs, there is an urgent need to accelerate the establishment of the management budget system of state-owned capital. Relevant departments and scholars carried out research and augmentation work on this issue from 2003, and a decision to initiate this system was taken in the executive meeting of the State Department on May 30, 2007. To be brief, a management budget of state-owned capital means the country obtains state-owned capital revenue (budgetary revenue) from enterprises it invested in and uses these funds for industrial development, structural adjustment, SOE reform cost compensation, social security supplement, and so on (budgetary expenditure). The State Department meeting made it clear that the budget will be implemented in Central Government-owned enterprises in accordance with the principle of "overall consideration and moderate centralization, relatively independent and interconnected with each other, compiling from one level to another and step-by-step implementation," while that of local enterprises will be decided by the local governments. It should be noted that the problems that can be settled by this system, co-exist with new problems arising out of this same system. For example, how should the relationship between the public budget and the management budget be dealt with? How is the revenue for the management budget to be effectively expended? How is the effect of budgetary expenditure to be reviewed and effectively supervised? These and other problems must be continuously explored and resolved in practice. The great significance of the creation of this system should not, however, be ignored.

In terms of the system aspect, the aim is to further perfect the managerial system of state-owned assets along the principle and direction of the separation of governmental functions from enterprise management, and from assets management and legality of power (rights).

With the establishment of state-owned assets supervision and administration commissions at different levels, the reform task of the managerial system of state-owned assets appears to be nearing completion. But this is not the case. There are still many problems regarding the supervisory and managerial system of state-owned assets, which urgently need to be resolved. First of all, the problem of separation of governmental functions from enterprise management, and that of separation of governmental functions from assets management, still cause trouble from time to time. First, from the aspect of the entire profitable state-owned assets, there are still 5,949 enterprises belonging to 81 government departments with total assets amounting to RMB Yuan 2,341.57 billion, major business revenue of RMB Yuan 1,469.57 billion, profits of RMB Yuan 112.06 billion, and a workforce of 5.1795 million. This portion of capital is not included in a relatively centralized and effective managerial system of state-owned assets.

Second, from the aspect of configuration of dual functions of the government, some public administration departments of the government are still acting as investors of state assets. Some old problems, like displaced functions, unclear obligations, and obscure power, are still not completely resolved. Third, from the aspect of state assets supervision authorities, the originally established system framework of "combining assets management with personnel management and business management and integration of rights, obligations, and liabilities" by state-owned assets supervision and management commissions has not been realized. In practice, the employee in charge of personnel management is not concerned about business management; the one in charge of business management is not concerned about assets management; and the one in charge of assets management is unable to be concerned about human resources and business management. The three rights (power) endowed to investors by the company law are scattered across many departments. In the past, a number of departments were in charge of many SOEs, but nowadays many departments are in charge of a single SOE. The *modus operandi* is actually unchanged. Fourth, there is a strong administrative sentiment towards provider organizations exerting rights and safeguarding benefits. There are even some who hold the opinion that the supervisory management of state-owned assets has been changed from "water control by nine (external) dragons" of the past, into "water control by many small (internal) dragons" today, which results in high-cost and low efficiency of assets supervisory management. The following issues should be considered and resolved in the future:

Implement the system in which the state assets supervision authority takes responsibility for administrating profitable state-owned assets in a relatively centralized way

Different countries have different measures in administration. Some distribute supervision responsibly to one, or a few special organizations on behalf of corresponding levels of government, while some have many governmental organizations to manage SOEs. Both measures are ongoing according to the author's overseas observations.[28] Some scholars in China labeled these measures as patterns from Northern Europe, North America, and Singapore. Whether this assessment is right or not requires further examination, but this author is of the view that completely copying other countries is absolutely harmful. The main difference between China and other countries is that the proportion of the state-owned economy and SOEs is higher in China than elsewhere and their legal status is sacred and inviolable. The purpose and task of the reform, therefore, is to establish and perfect the managerial system of state-owned assets adapted to the national conditions of China. From this point of view, it will be more effective for China when state assets supervision authorities manage state-owned assets in a centralized way. This measure may be implemented step-by-step. For example, unprofitable state-owned assets may be first brought into centralized supervisory management incrementally, and then integration of state-owned financial capital and industrial capital can be carried out when the time is ripe.

Realize real separation of governmental functions from assets management, with both types of organizations taking on their own responsibilities and obligations

The implication of this separation of governmental functions and assets management is that the departments in charge of social public administration are not allowed to take on the role of investor of state-owned assets, while the state-owned assets supervision and administration organizations are not allowed to conduct social public management. This issue concerns not only the above-mentioned managerial system to state-owned assets, but also the legal administration of governmental departments and organizations. As to the separation of governmental functions from assets management, the supervisory management regulations issued in 2003 by the State Department are clear and correct, but they have not been implemented in reality. Phenomena like rights without legality, implementation without regulation, obligations without investigation, and salvation without methodology are common occurrences. In this sense, the reform of state-owned assets management and SOEs is more like a political or an administrative issue than an economic one.

Put the rights and obligations of supervisory management organizations of state-owned assets into effect, improve the quality of personnel, and establish a sound accountability system

As has been said before, for each state-owned "assets supervisory management" organization authorized by corresponding level government, its rights and benefits are prescribed by law. Its rights and benefits should be organically integrated but not dispersed. The current situation in which its rights and benefits are dispersed is due to both historical and institutional factors. Settlement of this problem needs time and appropriate opportunity (primarily the progress of administrative-managerial system reform and of juristic construction). Nowadays, it is necessary to provide conditions to establish foundations. At the same time, function preparation and optimizing supervisory managerial organization of state-owned capital should be strengthened and the phenomenon of "water control by internal small dragons" should be avoided. In addition, the professional accomplishments and capabilities of personnel in specially established organizations should be improved faster to insure they use their power and enjoy their rights correctly, precisely, and legally, as opposed to incorrectly, obscurely, or randomly. Moreover, the liabilities ascertainment system should be established to investigate the liabilities of those who fail to meet their obligations and those who cause loss to state-owned assets, in accordance with the law.

Accelerate formulation and fine-tuning of the system of laws and regulations on supervisory management of state-owned assets

The progress of the Chinese market economy runs parallel to the progress made in establishing a sound legal system. The notion that the market economy is in some sense ruled by law is universally accepted and considered by the public (Zhang 1998). The reform of SOEs and the excellence of the managerial system of state-owned assets follow the same rule. The slow and unsupported progress of this process is not due to an absence of the necessary laws but, rather, to weak enforcement mechanisms and ineffective supervision. In other words, we must see to it that there are laws, the laws are observed and strictly enforced and law-breakers are prosecuted. As to lawmaking, there is a need to formulate a state-owned assets law in accordance with the Constitution and the recently enacted "Property Law."

Notes

1 China's famous economist, Professor Wu Jinglian (2003), says: "I call it a 'milestone,' which does not mean that it has given forth some concrete reform proposals and has adopted some concrete reform measures, but that it has broken through the ideological shackles of 'the two whatevers' and started the mind emancipation movement to encourage theoretical innovation."
2 Many scholars believe China's SOE reform has passed through three phases: the initial phase (1978–1984), the exploration phase (1984–1991), and the standardized development phase (1992–present). See Making the people rich and the country strong, revitalizing the enterprises and rejuvenating the state (2003), in *Think Tank*, No. 11.
3 Yuan Baohua, one of the main leaders of the former State Economic Commission at that time, recalls that after the Third Plenary Session of the Eleventh Central Committee, the State Economic Commission began to consider expanding enterprise autonomy. In the Central Work Conference in April 1979, 10 proposals on the expansion of enterprise autonomy power were put forward. In the National Public Transportation Conference held at Chengdu in July 1979, the State Council produced five documents, including "Several provisions on the expansion of the state enterprises' decision-making power with regard to their own operation and management." Expansion of enterprise power at that time was highly successful in bringing order to chaos. Finance ministerial authorities called it "Decentralization and interest concessions." But for enterprises, the aim was not only about making order out of chaos but, just as important, the reform of enterprises. See Decentralization and interest concessions: The breakthrough of SOEs – Interviewing Mr. Yuan Baohua (2005), in *Reform Fluctuation – [100 Years of Waves] Series*, December, Shanghai Lexicographical Publishing House.
4 At that time, many Chinese economists referred to this reform goal as a "bird cage economy," which means that the planned economy was the "cage" for the whole economy, while the market regulation was only a "small bird" locked in the cage of the planned economy.
5 When summarizing this part of the history, Professor Wu Jinglian (2003) was of the view that the Chinese economic theorists at that time were familiar with some conclusions of the Western "neo-classical synthesis" theory, while often neglectful of its hypotheses. If these conclusions were directly used to analyze practical issues, important errors could result. One such error was to "regard the planning and the market as amorphous resource allocation means and to think that the two can be combined without conflicts…"Another defect of this thought is to regard the planning and the market as two resource allocation methods irrelevant to the social system based on the simple assumptions of the new classical model. And people thought that no matter what the social system foundation was the planning or market could be selected at liberty and

some even thought that the market economy could be established on the property right foundation with the state ownership playing the dominant role. Thus people naturally neglected the necessity of the reform of SOE property rights, or thought that state enterprises would be revitalized only if "untying" or "decentralization" were carried out for state enterprises. Though the issue of SOE shareholding system was proposed during the medium and later stage of 1980s, the property right foundation of stock companies and related company management problems were not clarified for a long time. Naturally it was difficult to insure the efficiency of the companies established after the reform." At this time, many foreign experts, such as Minoru Kobayashi from Japan, started to study issues concerning China's reform of SOEs and put forward some profound opinions. This phenomenon also propelled the discussion of Chinese theories on SOE reform. Chinese economists began to pay attention to the comparison study of SOE systems in different countries, including the well-known and now deceased economist, Dong Furen.

6 The author has a detailed statistical analysis of such theses published in main domestic periodicals and newspapers between 1993 and 1994, with scholars providing more than 100 explanations about what a modern enterprise system looks like.

7 Fan Gang (2007) thinks that China's 1997–1998 financial crisis was not mainly due to the impact of the Asian Financial Crisis, but because China's financial system was rather closed at that time, although there were some relationships with the international financial world.

8 See *Compilation of policies and regulations on state-owned assets supervision and administration* (second edition), SASAC (2007), Beijing: China Economic Publishing House.

9 The author organized and participated in the drafting of this regulation. See Explanations for *Interim measures for the supervision and administration of state-owned assets of the enterprises* (2003), China Legal Publishing House.

10 According to the administrative attachment regulations, China's SOEs are classified into central enterprises attached to the Central Government, and departments and local enterprises attached to local governments and relative departments. In 2003, the Central Government authorized the newly established SASAC as the investor representative of 196 (a total of 15,546 legal person enterprises above third-class) central enterprises with investor rights. But there were still more than 5,000 attached to the State Council and relative departments, which the central enterprise, in the broadest sense, should include. But since 2003, people usually refer to the 196 enterprises (the number has decreased due to reform and restructuring) as central enterprises.

11 See 'SOE reform enters a "post-SOE Era"' (2003), in *Information for leader's decision-making*, No.25.

12 Prior to this period, some experts and scholars, such as the well-known and now deceased economist Jiang Yiwei, suggested that the key to SOE reform was not only the separation of government functions from enterprise management but also included the separation of government functions from asset management. To a degree, for if the "government" were not separated from the "assets" the separation of government functions from enterprise management would also be hard to realize.

13 Though a state-owned Assets Management Bureau had once been in place, it was only a vice-ministerial institution under the Ministry of Finance and an administrative management department of state-owned assets, not the ownership representative of state-owned assets in the enterprises. In 1998, this institution was dissolved and its functions were allocated to finance authorities.

14 After 1997, local enterprises, especially those at China's prefecture and county levels accelerated their pace of diversified reform. By the end of the 1990s, most SOEs had completed their restructuring work. As relative policies and laws were not improved at this time, the loss of state-owned assets was very severe under the double pressure of interest-driven privatization, restructuring, and "rent-seeking" – an economic theory of administrative power. Soon this issue became the focal point of the society. Thus, by

2003, how to efficiently avoid the loss of state-owned assets had become the important content of related policy-making departments of the government.

15 Article 6 of the Constitution of the People's Republic of China reads: "In the primary stage of socialism, the state upholds the basic economic system under which the public ownership is dominant and diverse forms of ownership develop side by side." Article 7 reads: "The state-owned economy, namely, the socialist economy under ownership by the whole people, is the leading force in the national economy. The state ensures the consolidation and growth of the state-owned economy."

16 China's SOEs not only carry out production activities, but also undertake the setting up of schools, hospitals, and even public security facilities. These tasks are auxiliary obligations of the enterprises and are not enterprise functions but social functions. So these functions had to be separated out from the enterprises. This action was called the "separation of main from auxiliary" or "separation of enterprises to perform social functions." By the end of 2006, the central enterprises had separated out 1,849 public schools and 345 public security organs, pro-curatorial organs, and people's courts, and transferred 148,000 employees and 63,000 retired teachers (Li 2007).

17 Non-profitable state-owned assets refer to the net assets and state funds in the form of capital that is invested, or funds allocated to all kinds of enterprise and administrative public institutions by all levels of government or departments and institutions authorized to represent the government. Its formula is as follows: non-profitable state-owned assets = state-owned assets occupied by administrative public institutions + state-owned assets occupied by infrastructure construction institutions + non-profitable state-owned assets.

18 In November 2006, the executive meeting of the State Council made the following evaluation: "In recent years, China has made important breakthroughs on the reform of the state-owned assets management system. The adjustment on the layout and structure of the national economy has made important progress. The reform of SOEs has been deepened continually. The economic benefits have been increased notably and all these have played an important role for the improvement of the socialist market economy and promotion of the sustained, rapid, and sound development of the national economy."

19 According to a study conducted by the China Enterprise Confederation in 2003, the sales income per capita of the top 500 enterprises in the world was US$295,300 and profit per capita US$2,900. At the same time, Chinese enterprises that have entered into the elite Fortune 500 club reached only 14.15 percent and 72.5 percent of the two indicators (Study group of the China Enterprise Confederation 2003).

20 The "Company Law" of the PRC has ruled that the investment institutions or departments authorized by the country have the right to build a solely state-owned enterprise, which is like the "one man" company in some countries. The solely state-owned company can be classified into two types: those with one stockholder and those with two or more stockholders coming out of the restructuring work.

21 Qiao Xinsheng is of the view that since most SOEs have already established the internal governance structure conforming to the provisions of the "Company Law," the SOE reform is naturally coming to the end stage, following the realization, in 1998, of the objective to extricate SOEs from their difficulties in three years. He thinks that if the dislocation status of SOE reform is not ended soon, the stock system of SOEs might be the transition to privatization and China's SOEs might gradually become private enterprises. See Study Report No. 1 (2007), Editorial Office of Study Reports.

22 See Wu Jinglian's professional spirit and ordinary feelings. Available online at www. Xinhuanet.com (accessed 29 May 2007).

23 The so-called Lang-Gu dispute was a rancorous public debate between economists Lang Xianping and Gu Chujun. Lang Xianping criticized the management-buy-out (MBO) in SOEs because he thought it caused loss of state-owned assets. On the contrary, Gu Chujun supported MBO in SOEs.

24 In terms of the expansiveness and applicability of power, there is not only a difference between public power and private power as addressed by Western laws, but also the

forcing of one person's will over others that exists everywhere in actual life. As Max Weber (1920), the famous social scientist said: "Power is the chance of a man or a number of men to realize their own will in communal action even against the resistance of others."

25 In July 2002, US President Bush signed into law the "Sarbanes-Oxley Act," which he characterized as "the most far reaching reform of American business practices since the time of Franklin Delano Roosevelt." The Act mandated a number of reforms to enhance corporate responsibility, improve financial disclosures, and combat corporate and accounting fraud. It also created the Public Company Accounting Oversight Board to oversee the activities of the auditing profession.

26 The author has conducted several investigations into the adjustment of Japan's coal industry. It has taken Japan many years to complete this adjustment work. For this purpose, the Japan government enacted the "Six Codes for Coal" and other preferential policies. In September 2003, the author conducted investigations into SOE reform in Thailand and Malaysia and found that both countries spent a long time on the adjustment of their national economies and on the privatization of their state-owned enterprises.

27 The author of this paper has organized and attended study and drafting sessions on this law, with authorization, since 1994 and is therefore aware of its extreme importance. The existing laws related to competition in China are limited to the anti-unfair competition act and such like, so it is urgent that the anti-monopoly law is quickly formulated and implemented.

28 The author has visited government departments and related institutions in Germany, Norway, Hungary, and Brazil, among other countries.

References

Economic Research Center of SASAC (2003), *Information for leader's decision-making.* No. 25.

Gang, Fan (2007). Revelations from the Asian financial crisis. *21st Century Economic Reports*, 4th edition, May 14.

Li, Rongrong (2007). Stress reform, adjustment, innovation, and management, and promote the healthy development of central enterprises. *Technological Development of Enterprise*, Issue no.3.

Making the people rich and the country strong, revitalizing the enterprises and rejuvenating the state (2003), in *Think Tank*, No. 11

Mei, Shenshi (2002). *Regulated Operation Theory on Governance Structure of Modern Enterprises*, revised edition. Beijing: Chinese Legality Press.

Renlin, G (2003) *Interim measures for the supervision and administration of state-owned assets of the enterprises.* Beijing: China Legal Publishing House.

SASAC (Policy Regulation Bureau of the State-owned Assets Supervision and Administration Commission of the State Council) (2007) *Compilation of policies nd regulations on state-owned assets supervision and administration.* Second edition, Beijing: China Economic Publishing House.

Study group of the China Enterprise Confederation (2003). Comparative analysis of top 500 enterprises of China and of the World in 2003. *Management Information*, Issue no. 18.

Weber, M. (1920). Class, status, party. In: H. H. Gerth and C. Wright Mills (eds.) (1958). *Max Weber: Essays in Sociology*, New York: Oxford University Press, p. 180.

Wu, J. (2003), Modern economics and China. *Comparison*, no.4.

Yuan, Baohua (2005). Decentralization and interest concessions: the breakthrough of SOEs – Interviewing Mr. Yuan Baohua. *Reform Fluctuation – (100 Years of Waves) Series*, December, Shanghai Lexicographical Publishing House.

Zhang, Delin (1998). *Law and the Market from the Perspectives of Economics and Jurisprudence.* Shandong: Shandong People's Press.

Zhang, Delin (1990). Reflections on theories of socialist economic reform. *Economic Research*, Issue no. 10, Economic Study Group of the Chinese Academy of Social Sciences.

8 China's rural reform and development after the Asian financial crisis

Han Jun

After Asia's financial crisis broke, the Central Committee of the Communist Party of China and the State Council aimed to increase demand in the domestic market over time. With the majority of the population living in rural areas, the rural market was the obvious key to expand domestic demand. In the 10 years that followed the 1997 Asian financial crisis, China developed and implemented policies to promote the growth of the rural economy in every way and specifically sought to raise farmers' incomes.

Basic policies to address issues related to the farmer, agriculture, and rural areas

Raising farmers' incomes: the primary goal

Since the Asian financial crisis, which erupted in 1997, China has experienced an adequate supply of agricultural products. In some years, even before the crisis, there was excess supply such as with grains. Starting in 1995, China reported five consecutive years of bumper crops, contributing to an over-supply of this commodity. Sufficient supplies of grains and other agricultural products contributed to market stability, higher living standards for rural and urban residents alike, and the rapid development of the national economy. Supplies, however, exceeded demand, making it difficult to sell these products, and because demand was lower than supply, prices were relatively low. The result for some farmers was a reduced growth rate in their incomes. In fact, after 1997, the per capita growth rate of farmers' incomes actually fell, 9 percent in 1996, 4.6 percent in 1997, 4.3 percent in 1998, 3.8 percent in 1999, and 2.1 percent in 2000. Many, particularly in major crop-producing areas, experienced stagnation or decreases in their incomes.

In the early 1990s, China's approach to rural development focused on "high yields, superior quality and high efficiency for agriculture" and sought above all to increase growth in agricultural production. By the late 1990s, China largely eliminated supply shortfalls. The slow growth of rural incomes, however, remained an impediment to the development of the national economy. It became apparent that China had to adjust the agricultural polices that had increased production.

In the mid-1990s, state government had dramatically elevated the purchasing price (with increases totaling as much as 102 percent). At that time, the prices of grain and most other agricultural products were actually higher than prices prevalent in the international market. This scenario shows that the former strategy of increasing farmers' incomes through enhanced production of agricultural products and raising prices of agricultural products had become infeasible. It was therefore necessary to seek alternative means to raise farmers' incomes. In response, in October 1998, the Third Plenary Session of the Fifteenth Central Committee of the Communist Party of China passed the "Decision on Certain Significant Issues with Regard to Agricultural and Rural Areas." Those involved of the formulation of this decision had observed the change from a situation of supply shortages to one of sufficient demand or surplus. Under this decision, it was unambiguously declared the need "to consider it a primary goal of agricultural development and rural economic development in the new era to increase the farmers' income."

Letting industry boost agriculture and letting urban areas help rural areas pursue development: new guiding principles for modernization and socialist rural construction

Since the beginning of the new millennium, China has adhered to the concept of the "Sannong issues" (farmer, agriculture, rural issues). The report of the Sixteenth National Congress of the Communist Party of China pointed out the need to "plan out socio-economic developments in rural and urban areas as a whole." The Secretary-General of the Communist Party of China, Hu Jintao, clearly stated at a rural-work conference in 2003 that "it is essential to make it the first and foremost task of the entirety of the members of the Communist Party of China to solve those issues in regard to agriculture, rural areas and farmers," thereby underscoring the importance of the "three-dimensional rural issues" in China's drive for modernization. Through scientific analysis of problems arising in the development of China's national economy, the Fouth Plenary Session of the Sixteenth Central Committee of the Communist Party of China further put forward an important judgment known as "Two Tendencies." (i.e., in the early stages of industrialization it is common to let agriculture feed industry, and it is a common trend in the middle and late stage of industrialization to let industry boost agriculture and let urban areas help rural areas pursue development). Later, the Central Committee rendered another important judgment about the need to allow industry to boost agriculture and to allow urban areas to help rural areas pursue development, indicating that this should be done to advance the three-dimensional rural issues. Meanwhile, the Fifth Plenary Session of the Sixteenth Central Committee of the Communist Party of China cited a need to "facilitate the construction of new rural areas with socialist features." From a policy perspective, the construction of new rural areas echoes requirements for multi-faceted rural development and is consistent with guidance from the Sixteenth Central Committee of the Communist Party of China about the resolution of contradictions between rural and urban areas. In addition, such construction is a concrete manifestation of the country's adoption of the concept of letting industry boost agriculture and letting urban areas help rural areas in pursuit of development. It is a significant strategic measure taken by the Central Government to follow the principles of scientific development and socialist harmony and to address the Sannong issues.

Policies and measures to address issues of the farmer, agriculture and rural areas since Asia's financial crisis

Comprehensive reforms in agricultural taxation

The heavy financial burdens of farmers have constituted a "persistent ailment" affecting rural China throughout the 1990s. To address this problem, the Central Government decided in 2000 to initiate agricultural tax reform in Anhui province. The reform, over the course of the following six years went through two phases: the first, from 2000 to 2003, started with the introduction of the reform and the extension across the country and the second, starting in 2004, mainly entailed the abatement and eventual cancellation of agricultural taxes in 2006.

Because of the reform, the financial burdens that had been borne by farmers for years were virtually alleviated. Compared to 1999, Chinese farmers together saw their financial burdens alleviated by about RMB Yuan 125 billion a year, with each farmer's burden reduced by more than RMB Yuan140. The reform ended 2,600 years of compulsory state tax on agriculture and succeeded in breaking the "payee-payer" relationship between the state government and farmers. The state government is now a provider, not a seeker.

The reform of agricultural taxation involved changes not only to the relations of production but also to the superstructure. Apart from alleviating the financial burdens of farmers, this reform also aided the in-depth transformation of state power at the grassroots level, facilitated reforms to the rural education management system, and insured social stability in rural areas.

Stabilizing and consolidating the land-contracting relationship and protecting the rights and interests of farmers

Since 1997, the Central Government has successively promulgated policies and other measures aiming to protect the rights and interests of farmers in the area of land contracts. Specifically, the Central Government vowed "to prolong the land-contracting term by another 30 years" (assuring farmers that they would have the right to use the land for a longer period) and to rationalize the "two kinds of farmland" system (one kind is the basic guaranteed land, which is evenly allocated among all farmers, and the other is called responsibility land, which is allocated on the basis of bidding), took strict control of reserve lands, and prohibited a willful increase of land-contracting charges. By the end of 2000, about 98 percent of China's rural villages had finished prolonging the land-contracting term and the amount of land subject to the two kinds of farmland system had dropped to 14 million hectares, from 40 million hectares in 1996, or by 15.8 percent and

42 percent of the total arable land, respectively. In 1998, the Third Plenary Session of the Fifteenth Central Committee of the Communist Party of China passed the "Decision of the Central Committee of the Communist Party of China on Certain Significant Issues with Regard to Agriculture and Rural Work," which officially put forth for a need to "formulate laws and regulations, as soon as possible, to insure the long-term stability of the land-contracting relationship in rural areas, and endow farmers with long-term and stable rights to use the land." The "Law on Contracting of Rural Lands" of August 2002 provided for a 30-year contracting term for arable lands and prohibited the awarders of the contracts from taking back the contracted land. The formulation and implementation of the "Law on Contracting of Rural Lands" demonstrate China's commitment to protect land contracts in line with the law.

Facilitating stable development of grain production and protecting the farmers' revenues from crop production

After 2000, China saw crop production fall for four consecutive years. In 2003, China's total grain production dropped to 430.65 billion kilograms. In order to retain a balance between grain supply and demand, the state government developed powerful supporting policies regarding production work.

One such policy reformed the grain-circulation mechanism. After 1998, at a time when grain supplies exceeded demand, the state government implemented a reform of the grain-circulation mechanism, which comprised "three policies and one reform" (purchasing as many residual grains as possible at protected prices, allowing grain collection and storage enterprises to sell grains at favorable prices, managing a sealed-bid grain-purchasing fund, and accelerating the reform of grain enterprises). Three years of experience with this reform have shown that as mass quantities of farmers' residual grains were purchased at protected prices, incentives were created for farmers to grow more grain, which resulted in large quantities of grain being held for long periods. This situation made it difficult for the state's finance department to sustain this policy. After 2001, new reforms were undertaken, including a market-based measure dealing with the purchase and sale of grains in major grain-selling regions. In May 2004, the State Council decided to open up the grain purchasing market as a whole, which was seen as a breakthrough in China's grain-circulation mechanism.

Another such policy dealt with subsidies. Starting in 2004, the state government began using a portion of its grain-risk fund as a direct subsidy to grain-producing farmers in major producer regions. From 2004 to 2006, China's direct grain subsidies reached RMB Yuan 39 billion. In 2003, the state government started to allocate a subsidy fund to promote use of high-quality varieties. From 2003 to 2006, the value of the subsidy fund reached RMB Yuan 11.2 billion. Because of a sharp increase in the price of fertilizers and pesticides in the past few years, the costs associated with growing grains rose and farmers' revenues resulting from crop production therefore fell. In 2006, the Central Government allocated another RMB Yuan 12 billion for the subsidy fund, which was directly distributed to farmers to help them finance their crop production. In addition, the state government offered subsidies to farmers for the purchase of farm machinery and conferred awards and subsidies to major grain-producing counties in the form of transfer payments.

A third such policy dealt with pricing. A major effort was made to set floors for the purchasing prices for the main varieties of grains. The implementation of these polices helped protect farmers' earnings and rehabilitate and enhance overall crop production capabilities. After 2004, China's grain output climbed for three consecutive years, with a growth in output totaling more than 130 billion catties. As a result, the "supply-demand situation" in grains improved, and the contradiction between supply and demand was alleviated.

Facilitating strategic adjustments to the structure of agriculture and enhancing overall benefits

After 1998, the Central Government deemed that strategic adjustments to the structure of agriculture were needed. Boosting agricultural development and the structural adjustment of the agricultural economy would improve the quality of agricultural products and enhance revenues from the sale of agricultural products while guaranteeing the growth of total grain output, insuring the safety of grains in all regions, giving prominence to the respective advantages of different regions, and reinforcing the market's role in the deployment of resources. The policy of facilitating strategic, structural adjustments has yielded significant results. First, the regionalized arrangement of crop production has gradually taken shape and the variety and quality of crops have improved. Second, while the crop-production sector is evolving positively, the animal-husbandry and aquaculture industries are developing at a faster pace, contributing more to the overall output value of agriculture. Different regions are tapping into the agro-processing industry, also increasing the overall value of agricultural production. Meanwhile, fisheries have transformed their mode of production to focus on breeding and oceanic breeding industry is also developing rapidly. Third, China carried out environmental projects to convert croplands into forests and grasslands, which has had great ecological benefits.

Facilitating the transfer of rural laborers across regions and protecting workers' rights and interests

Since 2000, the state government's policy regarding the transfer of rural laborers has undergone some positive change, including the cancellation of irrational restrictions on rural laborers' migration to urban areas to find work and the setting up of an employment system under which rural and urban laborers compete on an equal footing. After that, local governments began reforming social management systems with the goals of treating rural laborers equally, protecting their rights and interests, and providing public services. Such policy shifts have profoundly changed the employment structure of rural laborers. According to the "Survey Report on Rural Labourers in China" (2006), about 120 million rural laborers have left for urban areas. If the rural laborers employed by townships and village enterprises are also included, the total number of outgoing rural laborers would be closer to 200 million, accounting for more than 20 percent of China's total rural population. Such growth rural-to-urban migration has resulted in a new source of growth in the incomes of farmers and significant changes to the pattern of their incomes. In 1997, agriculture's share of total income dropped to 58 percent for the first time, while non-agricultural income rose to 42 percent. After 1997, however, with the decrease in grain output, the dramatic fall in prices for agricultural products, and the growth of wages earned by outgoing rural laborers, agriculture's share of total income began dropping rapidly. In 2000, the share of agricultural income fell to below 50 percent. Five years later, it dropped further, to 45 percent. From 1985 to 2005, wage income as a share of farmers' per capita net income rose from 19 percent to 36 percent. In 2005, farmers' per capita wage income reached RMB Yuan 1,000 for the first time, an increase of 17.6 percent from a year earlier. Wage income has been hovering at about 60 percent in recent years.

Increasing financial investments in agriculture and achieving progress in agricultural development

Propelled by the positive financial policies implemented by the state government over the past 10 years, China dramatically increased investments in agriculture, with the objective of bolstering the construction of agricultural infrastructure facilities, including the execution of water-conservation projects. Meanwhile, the state government also increased reserve funds under the financial budget to cover production expenditures in rural areas; administration charges levied by entities involved in agriculture, forestry, and water and gas supplies; costs associated with integrated agricultural development; and subsidies for impoverished groups. From 2000 to 2005, the state government's investment in agriculture grew from RMB Yuan 123.15 billion to RMB Yuan 245.03 billion. In the period of the Ninth Five-Year National Development Program, the state government's investment in agriculture amounted to RMB Yuan 784 billion, triple that in the Eighth Five-Year National Development Program. Particularly in the Ninth Five-Year National Development Program, the state government set up a water-conservation fund and risk funds for major agricultural products such as grain and cotton. In Ninth Five-Year National Development Program, the state government's financial investment in agriculture accounted for 13 percent of total investments. In the Tenth Five-Year National Development Program, the amount of the state government's investment in agriculture recorded an average annual growth rate of 15 percent. In 2006, the Central Government made it even clearer that "it is necessary to pour most infrastructure construction investments into rural areas and invest the majority of the state government's added capital construction funds into rural areas."

In the past decade, the scale of agricultural development and the construction of infrastructure in rural areas reached an unprecedented level. In 1998, the state government decided to invest RMB Yuan 290 billion over the course of five years to construct or rebuild rural power grids and make the rates for electricity consistent in rural and urban areas. In that five-year period, the State Power Grid Corporation invested a total of RMB Yuan 214.1 billion and the rates charged for electricity in rural areas plunged, reducing the burden on farmers by a total of RMB Yuan 40 billion a year. Efforts were made to facilitate the construction of agricultural infrastructure, with an emphasis on projects in areas such as water and soil conservation and forestry. The state government prioritized support for construction of small-sized infrastructure facilities in rural areas, including irritation systems, safe drinking water, rural roads and biomass pools, all of which had the potential to raise farmers' income.

Increasing investments in rural education and health sectors and promoting rural social development

In May 2001, the State Council promulgated the "Decision of the State Council in Regard to Reform and Development of Basic Education," which made it clear that "county governments shall be held chiefly responsible for offering compulsory education services in rural areas within their respective territories and are also requested to issue wages to teachers in a uniform way." In April 2002, the Central Government further stressed that it was necessary "to gradually have the costs of compulsory education in rural areas borne principally by county governments, instead of farmers and township governments." Having county governments take responsibility in this way has helped eliminate some of the obstacles to compulsory education in rural areas. A considerable number of counties and prefectures in Central China and West China are, however, economically underdeveloped, and therefore have financially weak local governments. Meanwhile, county governments have had difficulties in uniformly paying teachers and in covering operating expenses or the costs of reconstructing dilapidated facilities. Starting in 2005, the state government developed policies and measures to facilitate the reform and development of compulsory education in rural areas, gradually bringing rural education under the umbrella of the public finance system and setting up a financing security system in which the central and local governments undertake different but proportionate expenditures. In 2006, the state government exempted students in West China from paying tuition and incidental fees and offered textbooks to students from poverty-stricken families. The state government also granted living subsidies to boarder students. In 2007, the state government extended this policy to all of rural China. The main task in the reform of rural compulsory education is the constant reinforcement of the government's responsibility. In June 2006, the Standing Committee of the 10th National People's Congress passed the newly amended "Law of the People's Republic of China on Compulsory Education," which included stipulations for the development of compulsory education. Since these measures were carried out, farmers have borne less of a burden in accessing education.

According to the World Bank, China's rural cooperative medical system has "resulted in an evident improvement of China's health-care conditions and an apparent enhancement of Chinese residents' life expectancy" and has thus been considered a "health revolution." However after the 1980s, this system deteriorated rapidly and farmers soon began bearing greater financial responsibility for their health care. In 1997, China partially rehabilitated the rural cooperative medical system, in which 17 percent of the country's administrative villages and 9.6 percent of the country's rural residents have taken part. In October 2002, the "Decision of the Central Committee of the Communist Party of China and the State Council with Regard to Further Reinforcement of Rural Healthcare Work" stated clearly that it was "essential to gradually establish a new type of rural cooperative medical system featuring comprehensive arrangements for serious diseases." In the second half of 2003, the state government set out to implement a new rural cooperative medical system on a trial basis. By the end of 2005, 678 counties (prefectures) in China had adopted the new system, accounting for 23.7 percent of the total number of counties and prefectures and covering more than 236 million people. A total 178.8 million farmers (75.7 percent of all farmers) were covered by the new system. In 2005, China raised a total RMB Yuan 9.3 billion to finance the new system. Subsidies provided by local governments at all levels reached RMB Yuan 3.7 billion, and those provided by the Central Government totaled RMB Yuan 542 million. Local governments with more financial power granted more of the subsidies. Regions with especially well-developed collective economies were more successful with their support for the new rural cooperative medical system. Also in 2005, the Central Government decided to further increase the amount of funds to be provided by central and local governments to implement the new system and stated that the system would be implemented comprehensively throughout rural China by 2008. The new system has helped alleviate the financial burdens of farmers. In 2005, the state government spent RMB 6.175 billion on the system toward the equivalent of 5.85 million in-patient services and 95.31 million out-patient visits. In addition, 21.22 million physicals were carried out, enabling the diagnosis and early treatment of diseases. A survey of service-users in economically well-developed regions such as Beijing, Shanghai and Zhejiang, showed that farmers have earned relatively high incomes that local governments with comparatively strong financial power were better able to offer medical services to the rural poor and minimize their expenses in the treatment of serious illnesses.

New challenges in China's rural development

Agricultural development is entering a new phase of narrowing the balance between supply and demand and of stronger dependence on the international market

Since late 1990s, China's major agricultural products, such as grains, have experienced "a general balance between supply and demand, a surplus in years of bumper crops, and low prices for a long time." The price for grains in 2006 compared to 1996 increased only by 6 percent, while the price for meat and poultry increased 13 percent over the same period. As described earlier in this chapter, supplies of grains and other basic agricultural products were massive, providing a foundation for market stability and enhanced living standards for rural and urban residents and promoting continued rapid growth of the national economy. However, the incomes of farmers increased slowly. As the state government carries continues its structural adjustments to agriculture, the national economy continues to grow, China becomes more involved in the global economy, and important changes are taking place in the supply-demand relationship of agricultural products.

First, it has become harder to balance supply and demand with some agricultural products. For example, supplies of corn have exceeded demand. Supply and demand for wheat and rice, however, have been balanced. At the same time, soybeans, cotton, wool, edible vegetable oils, natural rubber, logs, sawn timber and wood pulp must be imported in mass quantities to satisfy the domestic demand. Imports account for more than 60 percent of the soybeans and edible oils consumed in China. With the growth of China's textiles exports, domestic demand for cotton has risen dramatically in the past few years and is resulting in a need to import more of this commodity. In 2006 alone, imported cotton was used for 54 percent of cotton goods produced domestically. Thus far, the volume of consumption and trade of key commodities has amounted to at least 50 percent of global totals. In 2006, for example, imports of wool, natural rubber, logs and wood pulp were equal to 70 percent, 300 percent, 53 percent and 205 percent, respectively, of domestic outputs.

Second, there are new patterns in the prices of agricultural products. Price increases since 2006 are due partly to cost enhancements and greater demand but mainly to the impact of revenue variations among different industries. In addition, competition for resources between producers of biological fuel products and grains has also affected prices. Taking these factors into account, it is likely that prices of agricultural products will rise constantly overall for some time, emerging from 10 years of stagnation.

At present, China's agricultural development has entered a new phase, with a narrowing of the balance between supply and demand, a strong dependence on international markets, and an overall rise in prices of agricultural products. The first and second aspects of this situation will encourage farmers to produce crops and will help increase farmers' income. Importing some agricultural and forestry-related products helps alleviate domestic shortages. Meanwhile, the rise in prices of agricultural products will have an important effect on the stability of China's macro-economy. Importing a huge quantity of agricultural products would, however, affect domestic agriculture, and fluctuations in global agricultural commodity prices could influence the healthy development of China's processing industry, which relies on raw materials. Soybeans and vegetable oil have become the two commodities that are most vulnerable to price fluctuations in the global market. The prices for animal feed and edible oil in China are already heavily affected by global market fluctuations, making it difficult to control and regulate these sectors.

Restrictions and institutional contradictions remain in agricultural and rural development

China has not yet adequately protected farmers' land tenure from a legal and institutional perspective. In fact, the scope of the country's land acquisition has expanded and resulted in the abuse of land tenure. Farmers whose land parcels had been expropriated received paltry compensation. Moreover, landless farmers were not properly resettled. The state government's expropriation of lands has led some construction sites to remain idle and resulted in lost incomes for an increasing number of farmers. Farmers have been ill equipped for China's entry into the global marketplace and for the new competition that resulted from it. Reforms in the rural financial system have failed to meet the constantly growing demand for financial services that emerged as a result of the rural economic transformation. Typical financial institutions have lacked adequate resources and have not yet been able to offer satisfactory services. Meanwhile the contradiction between supply of and demand for rural credit has still remained evident. The reform of the grassroots rural political system has not made any noticeable progress. Higher authorities have conferred the political power of township governments but there has been a lack of an effective restriction and supervision mechanism. All these factors create an environment that is not conducive for further grassroots development of democracy.

Rural-urban gaps have widened in incomes and access to public services

In 2005, the ratio of urban to rural incomes was 3.22 to 1, compared with 2.57 to 1 in 1978. For many years, China devoted a larger share of public investment to urban areas. Such practices have resulted in a larger gap between urban and rural access to public services. In the past few years, however, the state government launched six "minor projects" in rural areas to help improve farmers' living standards.

Governments at all levels have gradually stepped up their support for education and health care in rural areas. Nevertheless, many rural areas have not yet seen noteworthy improvements to facilities in these sectors or increases in the availability of services. In some areas, farmers have little or no access at all to health care. Moreover, the incidence of disease in rural areas is still disproportionately high. Generally speaking, China has a long way to go to consolidate and strengthen the social safety net, particularly for rural laborers whose land has been expropriated.

Resources necessary for agricultural development are scarce and infrastructure for agricultural production remains poorly developed. China has a large population and limited land resources. In per capita terms, arable land amounts to only 0.1 hectare, which is about 43 percent of the world's average. With the continued growth of the population, the per capita amount of arable land will inevitably decrease. In the next 20 to 30 years, an estimated 80 million acres of land will be needed for residential and industrial use, further reducing the amount of land available for agriculture and creating new challenges to produce sufficient amounts of food for the country. Even worse is China's already inadequate supply of water. In per capita terms, water supplies in China are only 25 percent of the world average. China is one of 13 countries considered to be suffering the worst shortage of water resources. Furthermore, water resources are unequally divided in geographical terms, with more than 80 percent lying south of the Yangtze River and less than 20 percent north of the Huai River. In some areas of the country, ground water is being tapped excessively, gradually shrinking the water table. Drought and water shortages have posed impediments to agricultural development in many regions.

Infrastructure for agricultural production remains poorly developed

In sum, China lagged behind other countries in the construction of water-con-servation facilities for use by farms. Meanwhile the total amount and the overall quality of arable acreage decreased from year to year. Water losses, soil erosion and desertification became increasingly problematic. The state government has failed to grant adequate support in agricultural sciences and technology, and the country has not yet established high-quality animal and plant disease control and prevention systems.

Future policies

Addressing the relationship between opening up the market for agricultural products to the outside and insuring stability in China's grain market while minimizing dependence on the global market

Since China's entry into the World Trade Organization, the volume of its agricultural exports has grown rapidly, while imports have accounted for a smaller share of the country's grains and the volume of imported oil-bearing crops (such as soybeans) and cotton has surged. Large-scale imports of agricultural products have helped meet domestic demand, preserve land resources and raise farmers' incomes. In view of the new challenges arising in agricultural development, however, it is essential to maintain a long-term perspective and work out medium and long-term countermeasures for different kinds of agricultural products. First, it is necessary to enhance overall crop productivity, realize a balance between supply of and demand for grains, and minimize dependence on the global market. Judging from the latest market scenario, it appears necessary to implement policies regarding price floors and subsidies for main foodstuffs, intensify the macro control over food imports and exports, maintain adequate inventories of food, and manage the development of corn-based ethanol. From a long-term perspective, the ultimate solution to stability in China's grains sector is the enhancement of overall productivity. Optimizing the fund investment portfolio is therefore recommended. Additional measures should include allocating more funds to support agricultural production; insuring stable provision of direct subsidies to farmers in major grain-producing areas (without increasing the amount or distribution of such subsidies too rapidly); increasing the government's investments in the development of high-quality grain varieties, water conservation, dissemination of agricultural technologies, and in the use of agricultural machinery. It is also necessary to further consolidate policies regarding the support for domestic production than would be affected by imported agricultural products' vulnerability to fluctuations in the global market. Because the macro control of agricultural imports and exports involves the interests of a multitude of actors and because different domestic departments often have different points of view, it is necessary to seize the best opportunities for establishing a uniform, highly efficient, and integrative control mechanism to reduce the domestic impact of the world market. In view of the volatility in domestic production and marketing of livestock products in the past few years, it is necessary to formulate policies to support stabilization of the livestock market. The main tasks are to foster the development of fine breeds; strengthen epidemic control and prevention; improve market-distribution infrastructure, facilities, and information services; disseminate policy-based insurance systems; and encourage the large-scale breeding.

Address the relationship between new rural construction and the progress of urbanization, while boosting economic prosperity in both urban and rural areas

China is industrializing and quickly urbanizing. This irreversible trend will lead to a an even greater demand for laborers and will allow rural residents to find jobs outside of the agricultural sector and take advantage of opportunities in urban areas. To narrow the urban-rural income gap in the long run, it will be necessary to reduce the number and share of farmers engaged in agriculture while enhancing the productivity of agricultural labor. To facilitate the construction of new rural villages, it will be necessary for urban areas to guide rural areas in the pursuit of development and to create more opportunities for farmers to access employment opportunities outside of the agricultural sector while protecting the rights and interests of farmers working in urban areas. It will also be necessary to help farmers move rationally and in an orderly manner into urban areas. Accelerating the establishment of a uniform labor market for urban and rural residents is needed too, as is the establishment of urban public services that will serve farmers who migrate to and work in cities. In addition to encouraging farmers to seek opportunities away from their home towns, China should also help township and village enterprises develop themselves fully and quickly, ceaselessly reinforce county-level economies, and help an increasing number of redundant rural laborers migrate to other regions to be able to earn a living.

Address the relationship between rural economic development and political stability and respect the democratic rights of farmers

When facilitating the construction of new rural villages with socialist features, it is necessary to guarantee the interests of farmers not only from an economic standpoint, but also from a democratic and a political standpoint. It is essential to take practical measures to promote democratic and political construction at the grassroots level, improve the structure of rural governance, enable farmers to become virtual owners and managers of their villages, and encourage local participation in propelling political development. It is essential to adhere to transparency in village affairs, encourage all populations to exercise their rights to vote and to pursue truth. All must also be assured of their democratic rights in line with established laws. It is also necessary to transform the social management and public service functions of government at the township level and establish a streamlined and highly efficient governance mechanism for government at the grassroots level.

Address the relationship between the government's provision of support, farmers' pursuit of development initiated by themselves, and the creation of a supportive environment for new rural villages

When boosting the development of new rural villages, it is necessary to set up an investment mechanism involving the government, society and farmers. Governments at all levels must discharge their respective responsibilities in making investments. Farmers are participants in – and beneficiaries of – the development of new rural villages. In propelling this development, the government shall not bear all the tasks on its own. Instead, it must respect the will of farmers, mobilize farmers and allow them to fully realize their own initiatives. It is required to organize and guide farmers to participate in policy making and setting exemplary roles. State government plays an important supportive role. Although the state government has provided generous financial support to address the three-dimensional rural issues, most of the investments in the past few years have mostly been used to repay debts. The government's support for agriculture has been insufficient. In reality, the imbalance between rural areas in general and the rural areas that receive financial resources from the state has not yet been fully rectified. Thus, it is necessary to decisively adjust the portfolio of state government's construction investments and use more of these investments in rural areas. The government must play a role as guide and pioneer in improving rural infrastructure and developing rural educational and health services. Encouraging the construction of new rural villages will require exploring additional means for providing financing and allocating more funds from the current financial budget of the agricultural sector. Besides, it is necessary to use a larger percentage of the government's revenues earned from the assignment of lands to support the construction of new rural villages.

Address the relations between the need to mitigate burdens, offer more support, liberate potential, and accelerate the establishment and consolidation of the planning system for rural and urban development

First, it is necessary to continually improve the practice of mitigating farmers' burdens and preventing them from recurring. In addition to actions that will foster economic empowerment, additional steps must be taken to establish a democratic decision-making mechanism that will allow farmers to express preferences and supervise the provision of public services. In general, it is necessary to create a safety net protecting farmers from their various burdens.

Second, it is necessary to offer more support to farmers and prioritize the provision of public services most urgently needed by them. It is also necessary to make practical steps to reinforce the construction of small and medium-sized infrastructure and facilities in rural areas, guarantee the balanced development of compulsory education in rural and urban areas, improve public health services in rural areas, enhance medical security for farmers, accelerate the start-up a social security network, protect the interests of the rural poor, establish and consolidate a system to insure a minimum standard of living for rural residents, create a new rural cooperative medical system, provide a basic insurance system for farmers, accelerate the offering of social security for rural laborers and farmers whose land parcels have been expropriated, and consolidate the aid and relief system for rural residents.

Third, it is required to accelerate the liberation of potential, establishing a system for changing the dual-standard for rural and urban areas; break down obstacles to employment in rural and urban areas; put in place an employment system under which rural and urban laborers are treated on an equal footing; bolster farmers' rights in land contracting and operation; allow farmers to request mortgages; set up a reliable and fair compensation system for farmers whose land parcels have been expropriated; make efforts to establish a trading and withdrawal system regarding farmers' housing sites, gradually endowing these sites with attributions of a commodity; set up a rural financial system that fits well with the circumstances of rural areas; eliminate unreasonable systems related to the domicile registry that have an adverse influence on employment, housing distribution and access to education; put recent rural-to-urban migrants on the same footing as long-term urban dwellers; gradually realize people's voluntary migration; and establish a uniform domicile registry and management system for rural and urban residents.

Part III

Restructuring China's social welfare system

9 Proactive employment policy and labor market development

Cai Fang and Wang Meiyan

The growth and structure of China's employment are the outcome of 30 years of reform, opening up, and development. Reviewing the journey of China's economic reform, we find that while it has been, by and large, gradual and incremental, it also takes relatively radical measures in certain areas and at certain stages. The choices of forms and measures in the reform process depend on the adaptability of different components of the economic system, and on how much the society is capable of adapting to the reform. After the 1997 Asian financial crisis, China's overall reform process sped up, as evidenced by the relatively radical measures taken to reform the employment system and develop the labor market on the basis of past growth in the non-publicly-owned economy. Thanks to government efforts and proficient functioning of the market mechanism, urban and rural employment has grown rapidly in China in the last decade.

Labor market shock

At the end of the 1990s, China's macro economy experienced a downturn as domestic demands on investment and consumption were seriously lacking, to the point where state-owned enterprises (SOEs) adopted reforms aimed at reducing staff and improving efficiency to extricate themselves from heavy losses. It was against this background that the Asia financial crisis hit the Chinese economy. At the time, tens of thousands of urban workers were laid off because their enterprises were doing badly, or even shutting down or going bankrupt. Some of those laid off were left unemployed or quit the labor market all together. Given that the social security system was yet to be perfected, laid-off and unemployed urban workers and their families received a violent shock due to the fall in their income and living standards. Meanwhile, the governments of many cities put in place measures to protect local workers, causing a negative impact on migrant laborers working in cities. According to National Bureau of Statistics (NBC) data on the unemployment rate in Chinese cities and towns during the past decade (Table 9.1), following the late 1990s reform, the unemployment rate rose to a relatively high level of 7.6 percent in 2000. The NBC also calculated the indicator of the labor force participation rate.[1] Since the indicator reflects the circumstances in which a section of the economically active population was forced to drop out of the labor

Table 9.1 Status quo of the urban labor market (%)

	Surveyed unemployment rate (%)	Registered unemployment rate (%)	Labour force participation rate (%)
1995	4.0	2.9	75.9
1996	3.9	3.0	72.9
1997	4.5	3.1	72.1
1998	6.3	3.1	71.2
1999	5.9	3.1	72.9
2000	7.6	3.1	66.1
2001	5.6	3.6	67.3
2002	6.1	4.0	66.5
2003	6.0	4.3	63.4
2004	5.8	4.2	64.0
2005	5.2	4.2	64.6

Sources: *China Population Statistical Yearbook*, National Bureau of Statistics; *China Labour Statistical Yearbook*, National Bureau of Statistics and Ministry of Labour and Social Security; and *China Statistical Yearbook*, National Bureau of Statistics (for all years).

force, due to the sluggish employment situation (i.e., the so-called "discouraged worker effect"), it can also help us observe labor market conditions.

The observation and comparison of several labor market indicators will elucidate further some characteristics of the employment situation in the period. In Figure 9.1, above, we use the surveyed unemployment rate as a benchmark to rank the provinces, autonomous regions, and municipalities directly under the Central Government, for a comparison with the regional distribution features of the laid-off rate and registered unemployment rate. The surveyed unemployment rate is based on the data of the Fifth Census in 2000 and is calculated according to the definition of unemployment given by the International Labour Organization (ILO), i.e., the proportion of unemployed people to the economically active population. The laid-off rate is the proportion of laid-off people to the economically active population at the end of 2000 and the registered unemployment rate is the figure published in the statistical yearbooks for the same year. An intuitive impression obtained from Figure 9.1 is that the three indicators reflecting labor market conditions differ in regional distribution. When we arrange the surveyed unemployment rate in a descending order, the laid-off rate also displays, to an extent, a tendency of descending distribution. The surveyed unemployment rate has a positive correlation with the laid-off rate in provincial, municipal, and regional distribution, showing a correlation coefficient of 0.53. Furthermore, both indicators have some differences in regional distribution. However, the registered unemployment rate has no correlation with the surveyed unemployment rate and laid-off rate, does

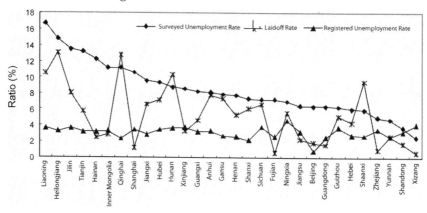

Figure 9.1 Regional distribution characteristics of three labor market indicators.

Sources: *China Labour Statistical Yearbook 2003*, National Bureau of Statistics and Ministry of Labour and Social Security; Fifth Census data.

not show a marked difference among provinces, and stays basically at the same level as indicated in the figure. If a standard deviation rate is used to express the range of regional differences of the three indicators, the laid-off rate is the highest in regional divergence degree, which is 3.54 percent compared with 3.27 percent for the surveyed unemployment rate, and only 0.71 percent for the registered unemployment rate, or equal to about one-fifth of the first two.

The relationship between the above three indicators is based on the several factors. First, the laid-off rate reflects a severe employment situation caused by the shock, and has a closer correlation with the changed employment demands of the public sector. Therefore, compared with the surveyed unemployment rate and registered unemployment rate, the laid-off rate is actually a phenomenon of economic transition. When the public sector gets stranded in difficulties during the course of transition, its employees bear the brunt of negative factors. Second, the registered unemployment rate is not an indicator that objectively reflects labor market conditions, for it can be manipulated, to some extent, by governments at all levels. Insofar as total registered unemployment is concerned, the government expands its scale and proportion progressively in keeping with the establishment process of the social security system. How high the registered unemployment rate can reach, is subject to the evaluation criteria of governments at all levels. Third, the surveyed unemployment rate follows the definition recommended by the ILO, and is equally credible and comparable. Since this indicator has not yet become a labor market indicator calculated and used by the Central Government, it receives minimal artificial intervention and can, therefore, mirror the actual conditions of China's labor market. According to the standard definition of the surveyed unemployment rate, the indicator also has limitations that prevent it from fully reflecting the regional situation and personnel status of the labor market. This is why we also need to base our observations on the phenomena of the "discouraged worker effect" and underemployment.

According to the estimates of government departments, about two-thirds of the cumulative number of laid-off workers were re-employed. When laid-off workers and unemployed persons got re-employed, they either changed their post types or industries, and, in most cases, the ownership of the work units also changed. This process of job change is known as employment informalization. For example, the survey,[2] carried out in five large Chinese cities, shows that before the change of posts 42.1 percent of people were concentrated in the manufacturing industry, but only 14.4 percent remained in the industry in their second or third change of job. In contrast the wholesale, retail, trade, and catering industries accounted for only 13.1 percent of first jobs and the proportion rises to 25.9 percent in the second and third jobs, while the community service industry accounted for only 8.4 percent of first jobs, compared with 18.9 percent after the change of jobs.

Overall, informal employment sectors have absorbed most of the displaced laborers. 33.1 percent of workers were in SOEs and 22.7 percent in private enterprises before the change of jobs, compared with 11.2 percent and 47.6 percent, respectively, after the change of jobs. The re-employment experience of former SOE workers is a typical example of such change of employment. Among the workers who left their original SOE employment, less than one-quarter found new jobs in SOEs, compared with about one-fifth in collective enterprises, and 40 percent in private enterprises.

As can be seen, besides those who are laid-off, or unemployed, or quit the labor market, the shock forced some laborers into informal employment, which features instability, low pay, and low social security coverage. This factor has also generated urban poverty. If we regard the labor contract signed with the employer, or the lack of it, as a division distinguishing between formal and informal employment, we can classify the following types of workers into informal employment on the basis of the survey data mentioned above: those who were employed after 1998 without signing a labor contract with the employer; those who work in private businesses without a labor contract; and those who are self-employed. According to the survey findings, the number of workers in informal employment accounts for 21.4 percent of the total number of employees.

The labor market statuses described above – namely being laid-off, unemployed, and out of the labor force – are all major factors causing shock-induced urban poverty. The policy establishing the minimum living standard guarantee program (*dibao* in Chinese) in cities aims to screen out the residents whose livelihood is lower than the minimum living standard and provides them with subsidies. Therefore the population enjoying *dibao* can roughly reflect the size of the urban population that is poverty-stricken. The total number of those in the urban population receiving traditional relief and *dibao* subsidies was only 879,000 in 1997, but jumped to 1.841 million in 1998. In 2004, over 40 percent of the 22.05 million urban *dibao* recipients were laid-off workers and unemployed persons (Ministry of Civil Affairs 2005).

A proactive employment policy

Since the late 1990s large numbers of urban workers have been laid off and, as a result, the urban unemployment rate climbed for a few years. To address the situation, the Central Government implemented a series of policies and many measures aimed at easing the labor market pressure and involving different stakeholders, including governments at various levels, communities, enterprises, and laborers. In the process of promoting employment and re-employment, the government obviously plays an irreplaceable role. The Central Government has borne principal responsibilities in the decision-making and implementation of all major policies related to employment and re-employment, institutional construction, and the establishment of important employment service systems.

In May 1998, the CPC Central Committee and the State Council held a working conference on the basic living standard guarantee and the re-employment of laid-off SOE workers. At that conference plans were drawn up for implementation of a proactive employment policy, with the re-employment project as the main focus. This was revealed in the Circular on Making a Good Job of the Basic Living Standard Guarantee and Re-employment for Laid-off Workers of State-owned Enterprises, which was subsequently promulgated. In September 2002, the CPC Central Committee and the State Council called a national working conference on re-employment and formulated and issued the "Circular of the CPC Central Committee and State Council on Further Improving the Re-employment of Laid-off and Unemployed Workers." Focusing on resolving the re-employment of laid-off and unemployed workers, the CPC Central Committee, the State Council, and related government departments, jointly formulated 25 policy documents. Local governments developed specific implementation methods and operational measures in combination with their concrete conditions, which enriched and improved the content of the proactive employment policy, and was the basis for a proactive employment policy system with Chinese characteristics.

The content of the framework of the proactive employment policy can be summarized into five pillars, six fields, and 10 policies. The five pillars refer to the five basic aspects of the proactive employment policy. The first pillar is the macroeconomic policy that aims to boost employment through increased economic growth. The second is the support policy that focuses on promoting the re-employment of laid-off and unemployed workers, while the third is the labor market policy that aims to realize the rational matching of labor force and employment needs. The fourth pillar is the macro regulation policy that aims to reduce unemployment, and the fifth is the social security policy that aims to effectively assure the basic living standards of laid-off and unemployed workers, and actively promote re-employment. The six fields refer to the directions for exploiting job opportunities, including development of non-public-owned sectors, tertiary industries, small and medium-sized enterprises, labor intensive enterprises, encouragement of flexible employment, and the export of labor services. The 10 policies refer to measures aimed at advancing the five pillars and six fields aspects, and include policies on tax exemption, micro loans, social security subsidy, employment aid, fiscal investment, establishment of the social security system, enterprise job displacement, community platform, and so on (Ye 2002).

Since the late 1990s, governments at all levels have made marked progress in helping laborers get employed and re-employed by taking a wide range of measures. These policy measures, and the form and effect of their implementation, require full discussion, as they need to be improved on the basis of an adequate scientific assessment. We will now briefly introduce the content of each to assess the effect of the policies.

Active fiscal policy

As an important part of the proactive employment promotion policy, the government put in place an active (expansionary) fiscal policy, issuing national bonds for infrastructure, technology, and construction of agricultural, forestry, and water conservancy facilities, as well as environmental protection, education, and social security. One of the major aspects of the monetary policy is to actively cooperate with the fiscal policy by increasing the credit investment in these fields while most of the fiscal investment, especially national bonds, is injected into infrastructure construction. The primary purposes of this active fiscal policy and the moderate monetary policy are to maintain the stable and rapid growth of the national economy, adjust the industrial structure, and boost economic growth to enhance employment. According to relevant information, the national bond project with its seed investment has led localities, departments, and enterprises to throw in matching funds and has allowed banks to arrange loans (CCTV Station 2002).

Although an important pillar of the employment policy is to incorporate the expansion of aggregate employment and creation of job opportunities into macroeconomic policy, other policy goals would sometimes conflict with employment targets, ostensibly during the business cycles. This was because the principle of employment taking precedence has not yet become the paramount basis, or even a major one, in the formulation of macroeconomic policy. Therefore, these goals often take precedence over the employment goal. For example, the major investment fields of national bond projects are industries that cannot effectively absorb employment, so that such expansionary government investment has an anti-employment tendency (Cai *et al.* 2004; Liu and Cai 2004). Furthermore, the role of investment in driving employment is mainly realized through the launching of large projects and the support given to large and key enterprises. Thus, as an integral part of the Central Government's proactive employment policy, the expansionary fiscal policy has not secured the expected employment boosting effect since being implemented. Instead, it has led to economic growth and employment increases being visibly out-of-step with each other.

Public and societal employment service

The Government has worked hard to step up the standardization and modernization of the labor market during the establishment of the public employment service system. After years of effort, comprehensive service sites with public employment agencies have been established at city and district levels, in medium and large cities as well as in some small cities with the right conditions. Neighborhood labor and social security platforms have been created in almost all prefecture-level cities, and labor market information networks are in place in nearly 100 medium and large cities across the country. The Central Government also encourages and formalizes the development of non-governmental job agencies. The public employment agencies, at all levels, provide easy access employment services, including job-seeking registration, vocational guidance, and handling of social insurance relations whereby public employment agencies help to connect social insurance between jobs. At the end of 2003, there were 26,000 employment agencies in China. Each year, public employment agencies provide employment services for nearly 20 million people and help 10 million people find jobs (Information Office of State Council 2004a).

An important function of the re-employment service centers established at enterprise level is to organize laid-off workers to take part in occupational coaching and re-employment training so as to guide and help them to get re-employed. In the period 1998 to 2000, more than 13 million laid-off workers and unemployed persons throughout the country took part in training, with 60 percent of them finding employment within six months after training (Information Office of State Council 2004b). These and other such government training programs are ongoing. In addition to the training organized by the re-employment service centers, the government also makes full use of existing education resources to carry out multi-level and multi-form re-employment training to improve the employment capacity of laid-off and unemployed workers. This includes skills training for laborers engaged in technical work, and business training and guidance for those with the necessary conditions to become entrepreneurs, thus creating more job opportunities for a wide range of laborers.

But employment has yet to be given a priority higher than economic growth, and the evaluation of the cadres at all levels is flabby in content. For these reasons the favorable policy and related services provided by the Central Government for re-employment are either an extra burden that needs resources for implementation, or represent a loss of vested interest, i.e., abandonment of the right to obtain rents for administrative departments of the government except the labor and social security department. This is why the favourable policy of the re-employment service cannot be perfectly carried out, and sometimes only lip service is paid to it. For example, the re-employment training implemented by the Government has failed to achieve any marked effect. A World Bank study, comparing the effect of re-employment training for laid-off workers in Wuhan and Shenyang, found that in Wuhan the training project implemented by the Government played a role in helping laid-off workers get re-employed, but the same training project produced a negative effect in Shenyang (World Bank 2002).

Establish and perfect three social safety nets

Since 1998, the Government has made efforts to establish and perfect three social safety nets, comprising a guarantee of basic living expenses for SOE laid-off workers, and unemployment insurance and *dibao* for urban residents. While under the umbrella of the re-employment service center, laid-off workers can receive the basic living allowance, which is jointly paid by the government, enterprises, and the society, and is issued by the re-employment center along with other employment services, including information and training. Those laid-off workers and other unemployed persons who fail to get re-employed after they leave the center, can, according to regulations, receive unemployment insurance compensation for up to two years if they have participated in the unemployment insurance program and paid the premium in full. Those laid-off and unemployed workers with a per capita family income lower than the local *dibao* line can enjoy the minimum living standard subsidy of urban residents according to regulations. Figure 9.2 shows the changes in the number of people who were laid-off, registered unemployed, and under *dibao* during the employment crisis that has taken place with the development of the labor market and the improvement of social security.

In the implementation of *dibao*, urban governments face a variety of constraints, especially concerning their financial capability. Therefore, judging from the level of assurance, the *dibao* program has not yet reached the stated goal of "assuring all who need." The data of a survey carried out in 14 cities by the Institute of Population and Labour Economics of the Chinese Academy of Social Sciences show that only 37.1 percent of the families eligible for *dibao* have actually received the subsidy, while it has been given to 5.5 percent of ineligible families. The targeting of social security remains in need of improvement.

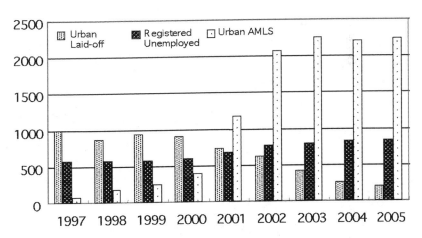

Figure 9.2 Urban residents laid-off, in registered unemployment, and under *dibao*.

Source: *China Labour Statistical Yearbook*, for all years, National Bureau of Statistics and Ministry of Labour and Social Security, China Statistical Press; *China Civil Affairs Statistical Yearbook*, for all years, Ministry of Civil Affairs, China Statistical Press.

In 1990, the proportion of retirees participating in the basic pension program was 40.6 percent, compared with 30.5 percent of urban employees. Because of the informalization of employment, the coverage of the basic pension program has not yet reached its goal. From 1997 the State Council decided to promote the basic pension program, combining social pooling and individual accounts. At that time, 73.4 percent of retirees participated in the program, compared with 41.7 percent of urban employees. Since then, the reform has gone through pilot experimentation, diffusion, and some revision. Although the coverage of retirees has been settled satisfactorily, a large part of the newly employed and re-employed people is not yet covered due to the fact they have not been included in the formal sector. For example, by 2004 the proportion of retirees participating in the basic pension program rose to 87.8 percent, whereas the coverage rate of urban employees only rose to 46.3 percent.

Implementing re-employment assistance

The government encourages laid-off and unemployed workers to start their own businesses and find employment in flexible and various ways, for example, in part-time, contingent, seasonable, and flexible employment. Those laid-off and unemployed workers who pursue the private business option can receive reduction and exemption of taxes and overhead fees. Loan guaranty funds and micro loans have also been established for those who are self-employed and/or start private businesses. Related formalities and procedures to initiate businesses have been simplified for laid-off and unemployed workers, to enhance service efficiency. Services and help are available for flexible employment through labor dispatching and employment bases. In addition, help is offered in different forms, for example instant post-job aid, to laid-off and unemployed workers aged over the age of 50 for men and 40 for women. These categories of workers are considered as primary objects of aid as they are able to work and desire to do so but face difficulties in finding employment. Former SOE employees who are advanced in age and have difficulty finding employment have been given priority in posts created by government investment and community arrangements. Governments at all levels provide such people with social insurance subsidies out of re-employment funds.

Although the Central Government has played an important role in helping with the employment of those having special difficulties, it is impossible for it to create the necessary amount of job opportunities. The Central Government may have a much greater effect in helping to eliminate the institutional barriers between urban and rural areas, between regions, between sectors, and between ownerships, and in getting the prices of production factors right so as to promote employment by leveraging the labor market. Therefore, among the measures of the proactive employment policy of the government, we can say that the one likely to produce the most visible effect is in the role of the labor market mechanism. Meanwhile, other measures for promoting employment should also accord with the direction of market forces.

Growth and structural changes in urban and rural employment

Although China has experienced a labor market crisis since the late 1990s, the government has protected the basic interests of laborers, defused the potential social conflicts that may have intensified, and completed the smooth transition from planned labor allocation to market-oriented employment. This can be attributed to two causes. First, the implementation of the proactive employment policy and the establishment and perfection of the social security system, have offset the pain of transition. Second, the unprecedented success of reform, opening up, and development have accelerated the maturity of the labor market and, therefore, promoted rural-to-urban labor migration and the process of urban re-employment. As a result, urban and rural employment has expanded at an ever-increasing pace.

Having failed to accurately grasp the particularity of Chinese statistical figures in a transition period[3] and to interpret the statistical data from the overall logic of China's reform and development, many domestic and foreign scholars and observers cannot understand the employment changes. Consequently, they have formed some common misunderstandings about China's labor market evolution and employment growth. They hold that China has witnessed zero growth in employment since late 1990s (Rawski 2001), and they attribute the serious level of lay offs and unemployment to the market-oriented reform (Solinger 2001). They also blame the difficulties in employment and re-employment, and the barriers in labor mobility, on neglect of the reforms (Solinger 1999), and invariably believe that China still has an inexhaustible surplus of rural laborers and redundant urban employees. We now attempt to describe the development process of the labor market and employment changes that have taken place since the financial crisis from the perspective of the overall logic of China's reform, opening, and development, through the collation and interpretation of existing statistical data, and in combination with other survey findings.

Transfer of the rural labor force

The expanded and ample level of rural employment has been realized through the transfer of the labor force from agriculture to the non-agricultural industries in the countryside and in cities and towns. Before the mid-1990s, township and village enterprises (TVEs) were the major contributors of non-agricultural employment in rural areas. But, if we limit the observation of the transfer of the rural labor force to TVEs only, we will find that the sector has been in a stagnant state since the mid-1990s, after absorbing a great deal of the labor force. However, in the same period, rural individual and private businesses have become more and more important avenues of employment, so it is not hard to understand why non-agricultural employment in rural areas has never stopped growing, even as the growth of employment in TVEs has slowed down. In the period 1995–2005, employment in TVEs grew by 11 percent, compared to 400 percent in private enterprises. Rural non-agricultural employment achieved a growth of 27.73 million people in the 10 years.

Now, we look at the allocation of the rural labor force beyond the scope of rural areas. As one of the important outcomes of urban and rural reform, and also the development process of the dual economy with the most distinctive Chinese characteristics, the cross-regional migration of the rural labor force has become a more and more important phenomenon and a major channel for the non-agricultural change of employment. Since the beginning of the 2000s, the central and local governments have created better conditions for the employment of the migrant labor force, in respect of residence, education opportunities for the children of migrant populations, and laborers' rights and interests, which have further pushed ahead the process. From the large-scale survey conducted by some administrative departments, we can get a relatively conservative estimate of the number of rural laborers who are seeking work, and changes to the figure over time. The number of migrant rural laborers increased rapidly from 38.9 million in 1997 to 103 million in 2004,[4] with about 40 percent of them having left their native provinces to find work. Currently, their proportion to the industry-specific total of employees is 52.6 percent for the catering and service industry, 57.6 percent for secondary industries, 68.2 percent for the manufacturing industry, and 79.8 percent for the construction industry (China Information Website 2004).

As a result of the transfer of the rural labor force from agriculture to non-agricultural industries, and its movement to cities and towns, urban and rural labor has formed a new pattern of distribution. The rural residual labor force has shrunk by a large margin in terms of both quantity and proportion. According to official statistics, in 2005 there were 485 million people in rural employment (National Bureau of Statistics 2006). The figure is based on the family location so it is actually a statistic of the rural labor force, irrespective of where the employment is and in which industry. Farmers, workers of township and village enterprises, non-agricultural employees, migrant workers and tradesmen, and even rural surplus (residual) laborers are all included in this figure. Below, we take a look at the distribution of this aggregate of the rural labor force to find out how much of the surplus labor force is left after nearly 30 years of reform and development in urban and rural areas.

The data provided by the Ministry of Agriculture show that the total number of rural migrant laborers was 108 million in 2005 (Ministry of Agriculture 2006). According to sources with the Ministry of Labour, to date about 200 million Chinese rural laborers have changed their employment, locally or further a field, from agriculture to non-agricultural sectors (Hu 2007) – that is 140 million in TVEs, 23.66 million in private enterprises, 21.23 million in individual business, and 108 million in cross-regional flow, minus the overlap between the two kinds of employments in rural and urban sectors. Therefore, in 2005 the number of rural laborers who transferred and did not transfer was 200 million and 285 million respectively. According to the present agricultural labor productivity, 180 million of the laborers remaining in rural areas need to pursue agricultural production (Zhang 2006),[5] which amounts to a surplus labor force of 105 million. That is to say, in 2005 the proportion of rural surplus labor force was 22 percent.

We now look at the age structure of the rural labor force in different categories of employment. First, we divide the working population of the 2005 agricultural population, i.e., divide 485 million rural laborers, into five groups on the basis of age. Second, on the basis of the data of a sample survey (Sheng and Peng 2006), we can also find out the age distribution of 108 million migrant rural laborers, and divide that figure into the same number of groups. Then we can see that, compared with all rural laborers, migrant laborers are more concentrated in the younger age groups. Third, we look at the age distribution of rural laborers who transferred locally, namely to rural non-agricultural sectors. According to past studies (Zhao 1999), the desire of rural laborers for a change is, in order of preference, employment in rural non-agricultural industries, employment as migrant laborers, and finally, farm work. Therefore, the human capital requirements for choosing employment categories can also be ranked in the same sequence. As an important factor, the demographic characteristic, which influences the ability of laborers to earn income, is also ranked in a similar sequence. Thus, we can, at least, assume that the age structure of laborers seeking employment in rural non-agricultural industries is the same as that of migrant laborers. Fourth, assuming that the age structure of the remaining laborers after transferring to rural and urban non-agricultural sectors is the difference between the total and transferred laborers, we deducted migrant laborers, and laborers who transformed locally, to obtain the age distributions of agricultural laborers and surplus laborers. We found that 50 percent of the residual rural laborers is over 40 years of age. That is to say, the absolute quantity of surplus rural laborers aged below 40 is only 52.12 million, accounting for only 10.7 percent (Table 9.2).

Growth and channeling of urban employment

Since the commencement of reform, China's strong economic growth has always gone along with the rapid expansion of urban employment. This trend has remained unchanged in spite of the financial crisis encountered in the late 1990s. In the 1995–2005 period, urban employment has grown by 43.5 percent, even disregarding

Table 9.2 Quantity and structure of the rural labor force (millions)

	All laborers	Transformed laborers	Agricultural laborers	Surplus laborers
Aged 16 or above	484.94	200.00	180.00	104.94
Aged 16–20	63.72	36.60	17.13	9.99
Aged 21–25	55.58	54.20	0.87	0.51
Aged 26–30	56.87	31.80	15.84	9.23
Aged 31–40	134.35	46.40	55.56	32.39
Aged 41 or above	174.42	31.00	90.60	52.82

Sources: The figure of rural employees is from *China Statistical Yearbook 2006*. The structure of migrant laborers is from Sheng and Peng 2006.

employed rural laborers in cities. In the meantime, employment structure and the driving force spurring employment growth have changed drastically. Insofar as the increments of urban employment are concerned, annual growth hovered around 3 million to 5 million people in most years before the financial crisis, i.e., from the late 1970s to the first half of the 1990s, but topped 8 million in 1996. Since then, growth has always remained much higher than it used to be, irrespective of mass lay offs and unemployment in cities, even though there was a slight decline. In the 1996–2005 period, urban employment expanded at an average of 8.29 million people annually and picked up speed after 2000. In the meantime, the state sector and the collective sector in cities and towns witnessed a decrease of employment at an annual average rate of 6.96 million people. Enterprises with new forms of ownership, including share-holding cooperative units, joint ownership units, limited liability corporations, share-holding corporations, units with funds from Hong Kong, Macao, and Taiwan, and foreign funded units, provided job opportunities for cities and towns at a rate of 2.98 million people a year. Employment in private enterprises and the number of self-employed individuals grew at a rate of 3.91 million people a year.

Comparing the above changes in employment, we find that the sectors where employment increased, including enterprises of new ownership, private enterprises, and self-employment, jointly created 6.88 million job opportunities a year on average in the 1996–2005 period. However, this is not enough to compensate for decreased employment in the state-owned and collective sectors, or to support the continued growth of urban employment. Where, then, is the new employment increase in cities and towns for the period?

After the employees of all registered units in cities and towns are added up, there are still a large number of employees who are not included. This means that there exists a difference between the real number of employees obtained through the household-based survey and the number of employees of units summed up on the basis of the statistical reporting system.[6] We call this employment residual. These employees accounted for only around 10 percent of all urban employees before 1997. Then, the proportion soared until it reached 36 percent in 2005, amounting to nearly 100 million people. Two reasons caused them to be missing from the employment reporting system. The first reason is that a number of employees are self-employed or work in private or individual enterprises that are not registered with the Bureau of Industrial and Commercial Administration. Therefore, these employees are not reflected in the statistics of the reporting system. The second reason is that some laborers are off the list. Many employers, including large state-owned enterprises, no longer include re-employed laborers and newly recruited employees in their headcount, but put them under the item of outsourced labor service, not to mention the migrant workers they hire. This has also caused omissions and underestimations. These workers make up the lion's share of all employees.

Through the above observations, we can conclude that if the urban employees under-reported in the statistics are included, the employment effect of economic growth is still optimistic. Such growth in employment was propelled mainly by the expansion of the non-public and informal sectors since the initiation of reform. In the late 1990s, SOEs had not yet completely broken their iron rice-bowl before they carried out the reform of the employment system with staff cuts and efficiency enhancement. So, although the non-publicly-owned sectors had achieved some development, their role in absorbing employment was marginal. After the radical reform of the urban employment system, the reform goal of realizing a market-led allocation of labor force resources has been finally reached. This is so in spite of the tide of layoffs and unemployment over a period of time, thanks to the re-employment policy and the reconstruction of the unemployment insurance system, basic pension insurance system, and *dibao* system, which basically insured a smooth transition. It is also due to the development of the labor market and sustained economic growth, which insured the expansion of employment.

Lessons learned

When forecasting the possible success of China's reform and development, most observers list the huge population and the employment pressure this causes as the number one challenge. Since the late 1990s, people have turned to the austere situation of urban lay offs and unemployment, as well as to rural underemployment reflected in the large-scale flow of rural labor to cities. A skin-deep observation of China's labor market situation after the financial crisis in the late 1990s often leads people to the view that the labor market shock at the time is an event that continues to adversely affect the expansion of employment. The reform of the employment system carried out by SOEs in the midst of the financial crisis to reduce staff and improve efficiency has only added fuel to the fire. However, the *de facto* expansion and structural change of urban and rural employment described above shows that, since the 1990s, an enormous breakthrough has been made in the reform of China's employment system and the development of its labor market in reaction to the shock, so that a fundamental change from increment to stock, and from marginal to all-round effect, has been realized in the market-led allocation of labor force resources.

Specifically, we can understand the achievements during the reform period from the following aspects. First, before China's labor market was hit by the shock, the economy of non-public ownership had developed considerably, which, to an extent, cushioned the austere situation of urban laid-off workers when the shock took full effect. Second, in the period, the development of the labor market was in synch with the construction of the social security system, thereby laying a foundation for the market-led allocation of the labor force. Third, because of the development of the urban and rural labor market, the rapid economic growth in the period created a large number of job opportunities. This not only eased the strong impact on the labor market caused by the shock, but also promoted employment, re-employment, business start-ups, and the flow of the labor force through the market, to realize a new bounce in the growth of urban and rural employment. Finally, to cope with the heavy pressure on the labor market, the government used all kinds of effective policy measures to expand employment and, in practice, gradually set forth the policy formulation and implementation principle of giving priority to employment. Therefore, government functions usually go in the same direction as market effects.

Labor market development prospects

Since 2004, a change has occurred in the supply and demand of the labor force in China. On the one hand, with the sustained rapid growth of the Chinese economy, the demand for labor is huge and has so far absorbed a large number of urban and rural laborers. This strong demand will continue. On the other hand, the growth rate of the working age population is going downhill and will remain at around only 0.7 percent in the decade to come. This is not only lower than the average growth rate of developing countries and the rest of the world, but also even lower than that of North American countries. The supply-demand pattern, which has been in existence for a long time, has begun to change, as shown by increasing shortages of migrant laborers and the rise of labor costs.

According to the view of development economics, the complete absorption of surplus labor means that the characteristics of a dual economic structure begin to disappear, and that the "Lewis turning point" has arrived (Cai 2007). While it is a concept for economic development, the judgment of the turning point itself has to do with the changes in the prolonged supply-demand pattern of labor. Meanwhile, the arrival of the turning point also suggests implications related to the labor market policy. If the reaction to the labor market shock has stimulated the development of the labor market, namely the transition of the employment system from planned mechanism to market-led mechanism and elimination of institutional obstacles deterring labor mobility, the reaction to the arrival of the "Lewis turning point" involves more labor market regulations.

First, the marketization of the labor force allocation has resulted in employment informalization, and posed challenges to the establishment of a network of social security and social protection that covers all laborers. To some extent, we can regard the employment left out by the employment reporting system in urban China as informal employment. The laborers who can be included in the ranks of such informal employment are mainly the rural to urban migrant laborers, re-employed workers who were laid off, registered unemployed persons in concealed employment, and a large number of young employees who got into the labor market only recently. On the one hand, it is an outcome of labor market development at a certain stage. On the other hand, it has, to a great extent, reduced the coverage of social security. Therefore, the construction of the network of social security and social protection should take into full account such change in the mode of employment.

Second, unemployment, especially the natural unemployment caused by frictional and structural factors, will exist long into the future, thus requiring continued development of the labor market, improved efficiency in governments' proactive employment policy, and adoption of comprehensive means for consolidation. A large part of the existing unemployment rate is the result of labor market imperfections, adjustment of industrial structures, and the existence of regulations unfavourable for access to employment opportunities. So knowledge about the causes and composition of present Chinese urban unemployment can help formulate and implement pertinent rectifying measures to, on the one hand, change the pure GDP orientation of macroeconomic policy, regard expanded employment as the paramount goal, and address the cyclical unemployment. On the other hand, it can also address natural unemployment from the angle of lowering the cost of economic activities.

Third, the shortage of labor makes it necessary to set up the principle of maximized employment and to tap the institutional potentials for the supply of labor. The change from an unlimited supply of labor to the arrival of the "Lewis turning point," as a sign of deficiency in the labor force, by no means implies that we can treat lightly the efforts to expand employment. The shortage of labor does not mean that existing labor force resources have been fully leveraged and left without any potential to tap. Insofar as cities are concerned, the supply of labor can be increased, even under existing patterns, by improving the policy environment for employment, re-employment and business start-ups, and strengthening the safeguards and protection of laborers in the informal sector. At this turning point, special attention should be paid to the use of policy instruments. For example, the minimum wage system should be used to protect the rights and interests of laborers, not as a tool to artificially enhance wage levels, but to avoid becoming a distorting force of market wage determination. Insofar as the flow of rural labor is concerned, a series of measures – for example further reform of the household registration system, increasing the transformability of contracted land within agricultural utilization, deepening compulsory education, and stepping up the training of migrant laborers – can be effective in expanding the supply of labor and in keeping down the excessive rise of labor costs, to slow down the loss of the comparative advantages of labor intensive industries and buy time for a change in the growth pattern.

Notes

1 For more about the definition of the surveyed unemployment rate, labor force participation rate, and data source and calculation methods, see Cai 2004.
2 The Institute of Population and Labour Economics and Chinese Academy of Social Sciences conducted this survey in the five cities of Shanghai, Shenyang, Wuhan, Xi'an, and Fuzhou in 2001.
3 For example, World Bank experts think that the reform and improvement of China's statistical system falls behind its economic development and reform. See Ravallion and Chen 1999.
4 For more information on the figures reflecting the scale of migrant rural laborers in the 1997–2004 period, see Cai 2006. There are also different surveys that show an even larger scale of migrant rural laborers. For example, one survey shows that, in 2004, the number of migrant rural laborers was 118 million. See Agricultural Survey Corps 2005.
5 To answer the question about how many laborers are needed for agriculture, we calculated the workdays needed for rural crop production and livestock breeding in a year, i.e., 57 billion workdays, according to the data provided in the National Bureau

of Statistics' China Rural Statistical Yearbook 2006, which were then converted to 190 million laborers on the basis of 300 workdays a year, and to 178 million laborers on the basis of 320 workdays a year.

6 For interpretations and explanations of the two statistical plans, see Cai 2004.

References

Agricultural Survey Corps (2005). Continued increase of national migrant rural labourers in 2004. 24 March. Available online at http://www.sannong.gov.cn/qwfb/ncjj/200503300220.htm (accessed March 30, 2005). National Bureau of Statistics.

Cai, Fang (2004). The consistency of China's statistics on employment: stylized facts and implications for public policies. *The Chinese Economy*, vol. 37, no. 5 (September–October), pp. 74–89.

Cai, Fang (2006). *Scientific Philosophy of Development and Sustainability of Growth*. Beijing: Social Science Academic Press.

Cai, Fang (2007). Approaching a triumphal span: how far is China towards its Lewisian turning point? *Social Sciences in China*, Issue no. 3.

Cai, Fang, Yang, D., Gao, W. (2004). Employment elasticity, natural unemployment and macroeconomic policy: why has economic growth failed to bring visible employment? *Economic Research*, no. 9.

CCTV Station (2002). Marked role of national bonds in boosting economic growth. Available online at http://www.cctv.com/lm/415/1.html (accessed 10 December 2002).

China Information Website (2004). One-third of rural labourers became workers of non-agricultural industries. Available online at http://www.china.org.cn/chinese/2004/Jan/484152.htm (accessed 21 June 2004).

Hu, X. (2007). China now has 200 million migrant labourers – a complicated issue. Available online at http://www.gov.cn/zwhd/ft3/20070126/content_509539.htm (accessed 26 January 2007).

Information Office of the State Council (2004a). *White Book on Employment State and Policy of China*. Beijing: State Council of China.

Information Office of the State Council (2004b). *White Book on Labour and Social Security*. Beijing: State Council of China.

Liu, Xuejun and Cai, Fang (2004), Institutional transition, technological choice, and employment growth. *China Labour Economics*, vol. 1, no. 2.

Ministry of Agriculture People's Republic of China. (2006). Migrant rural labourers to reach 114.9 million this year. Available online at http://www.gov.cn/jrzg/2006-11/22/content_450473.html. (accessed 22 November 2006).

Ministry of Civil Affairs People's Republic of China. (2005). *China Civil Affairs Statistical Yearbook 2005*. Bejing: China Statistical Press.

National Bureau of Statistics People's Republic of China. (2006). *China Statistical Yearbook 2006*. Bejing: China Statistical Press.

Ravallion, M. and Chen S. (1999). When economic reform is faster than statistical reform: measuring and explaining income inequality in rural China. *Oxford Bulletin of Economics and Statistics*, vol. 61, no.1, pp. 33–56.

Rawski, T. G. (2001), What's happening to China's GDP statistics? *China Economic Review*, vol. 12, no.4 (December), pp. 298–302.

Solinger, D. J. (1999). Citizenship issues in China's internal migration: comparisons with Germany and Japan. *Political Science Quarterly*, vol. 114, no.3, pp. 455–478.

Solinger, D. J. (2001). Economic informalization by Fiat: China's new growth strategy as solution or crisis? In L. Tomba (ed.) (2002). Vol. 36 of *On the roots of growth and crisis: Capitalism, state and society in East Asia*. Rome: Annali Della Fondazione Giangiacomo Feltrinelli, pp. 373–417.

Sheng, L. and Peng, L. (2006). Current situation of rural migrant labourers: quantity, components and individual characteristics. In F. Cai (ed.). *Green book of population and labour: demographic transition and its social and economic consequences.* Beijing: Social Sciences Academic Press.

World Bank (2002). *Has Training Helped Chinese Laid-off Workers Get Employed? Conditions of Two Cities.* World Bank Report Series no. 24161-CHA. Washington DC: World Bank, May 8.

Ye, Z. (2002) Proactive employment policy introduced by China will benefit six fields. *People's Daily.* Overseas edition. 15 October.

Zhang, Z. (2006). Employment of middle-aged and procreated females: new development of rural labour transfer. Available online at http://news1.jrj.com.cn/news/2006-12-01/000001817819.html (accessed 01 December 2006).

Zhao, Y. (1999). Migration and earnings difference: the case of rural China. *Economic Development and Cultural Change*, vol. 47, no.4, pp. 767–782.

10 Social security policy

Wang Yanzhong

Since the financial crisis in Asia in 1997, China's social security system has undergone continual reform and readjustment and has been integral to efforts to perfect the socialist market economy and a harmonious socialist society. Although building of the social security system has yielded tremendous results, it has also left a number of problems in its wake. As China's economy and revenues grow rapidly, a larger cross-section of the population is imposing greater demands on the social security system. Finding ways to perfect the system so that it conforms to current circumstances is an arduous task. This chapter begins with a brief retrospective of the development of China's social security system between 1997 and 2007, and then evaluates the role and effects of the system in meeting its own challenges, improving the socialist market economy, and analyzing problems and challenges in the system. The chapter concludes with suggestions for improving the present system.

Reforms explored before the crisis: realizing the dual transition of China's social security system

As early as the mid-1980s, China had begun social security reform as part of its overall economic structural reform and the reform of the recruitment system in urban state-owned enterprises. Traditional employment security, including pensions, medical care, collective welfare, including in-kind subsidies, such as housing, had gradually been transformed into the social security system, which was highly socialized and independent of employment. The main objective of the reform at that time was to establish the social-pooling system for endowment and medical insurance.

The social security system in the planned economy mainly covered regular unit employees with registered permanent urban residences. Most of these individuals were among the 100 million employees in enterprises with state or collective ownership or among the 40 million government employees. The social security system for government employees was never the focus of reform because the source of its funds (from budgetary appropriations) and the labor fluidity of this group had always been quite low. However, for the employees of state-owned and collectively owned enterprises and of non-public enterprises, it has been a different story. With the gradual deepening of enterprise reform, the proportion of employees in state-owned and collectively owned enterprises to overall employees in urban areas had fallen continuously. The number of these enterprises decreased steadily, resulting in massive lay-offs. As a result, the security they once enjoyed withered or disappeared. In the meantime, large numbers of employees in the non-public sector lacked appropriate social security. So finding ways to provide socialized (rather than traditional unit-based) social security for these two groups while meeting the needs of the changing labor force and responding to enterprise reform had become a vital goal.

A number of external factors influenced the course of reform and future design of China's social security system. These include the overall aging of the population, the initial success of the privatization of the social security system in other countries, namely Chile, the development of the publicly funded system in the name of individual accounts in Singapore, and the "three-pillar endowment insurance system" upheld by the World Bank.[1]

To equip itself for the aging of its population, China embedded an individual-account funded system in the basic social security system. In 1993 at the Third Plenary Session of the Fourteenth Central Committee of the Communist Party of China, a programmatic document, the "Decision on Some Major Issues Related to the Establishment of the Socialist Market Economy," was adopted. The document clarified the objective, pattern and path of social security reform. It proposed the principle of combining the social-pooling system with an individual account system for the construction of two major social security items: basic endowment insurance and basic medical insurance for employees. Therefore, the reform aimed neither for the pay-as-you-go system found in developed countries nor the funded system of countries like Chile. Instead, it aimed for a mix of the two.

In the following few years, related government departments at central and local levels conducted a series of pilot projects. The projects proceeded despite considerable controversy and results were not very successful on the whole. It was difficult to realize the dual transitions from employment security to social security, and from a pay-as-you-go plan to a mixed arrangement. Today, because the task is not yet completed, an overall evaluation has therefore not been carried out.

Originally, the focus of China's social security reform was employees' basic endowment and medical insurance. However, with the gradual deepening of economic restructuring as well as the impact of the financial crisis in Asia, the focus had to be readjusted to the new circumstances. After the 1997 crisis, the reform of economic structure intensified, exacerbating problems with unemployment and urban poverty. All of these factors resulted in huge pressure on the newly established social security system. The government responded with temporary measures, some of which went beyond the goals of the reform and had a lasting influence on the construction of social security later on.

Origins and effects of the policy of Three Social Security Lines and Two Protective Guarantees

Since the 1990s, China has been confronted with ever-worsening unemployment and urban poverty. Statistics in Table 10.1 show that between 1992 and 2006, despite the steady increase of employees in urban areas, the number of regular employees in traditional units dwindled continuously. The number of regular employees in units fell to its lowest point in 2003, with a decrease of 44.16 million, compared with a peak in 1995. Mainly responsible for this was the sharp drop in the number of state-owned and collectively owned enterprises involved in economic restructuring. Since 1992 the number of regular employees in collectively owned enterprises declined steadily and there was an overall decrease of 28.11 million until 2006 (with the largest year-to-year drop taking place between 1997 and 1998). In state-owned enterprises, the number of overall employees (regular and irregular employees) and the number of regular employees both showed a continuous downward trend since 1995. By 2006, the numbers fell by 49.73 million and 47.23 million, respectively (21.86 million and 21.40 million occurring between 1997 and 1998). In merely a dozen years, there was an overall combined decrease of 77.84 million in the overall number of employees in state-owned and collectively owned enterprises (75.34 million for regular employees alone). These numbers perhaps reflect the largest economic and employment restructuring in human history since the Industrial Revolution. China's economic and employment structure experienced the most dramatic fluctuation between 1997 and 1998, when there were 32.39 million fewer overall employees in state-owned and collectively owned enterprises (31.93 million for the regular employees alone). How to handle such an unemployment peak became a daunting challenge for China's government.

It is important to note that this daunting challenge occurred when the government had just started to establish the new social security system. In the planned economy, employees in urban areas were covered through the unit security system, and nearly all of their welfare came from the units that employed them. This process was referred to as the "setting up of a little society within an enterprise or a unit." Such a unit security system could manage to operate with full employment in cities in the planned economy. But with the continuous deepening of the market orientation of the economy, fiercer competition caused large numbers of state-owned and collectively owned enterprises to go out of business. So their former employees lost not only their jobs but also their social welfare. Many retirees of enterprises at the edge of bankruptcy did not receive timely pension payments, and current employees or ones who had been laid off, were considered fortunate if they any of their living expenses were covered or if they were reimbursed for medical expenses.

The Chinese government had made some reforms to the traditional unit security system during the course of economic restructuring. For example, the "Interim Regulations on Unemployment Insurance for Job-waiting Employees in State-run Enterprises" was formulated in 1986. It directed state-owned enterprises to pay 1 percent of their total payroll as an insurance premium to cover unemployment benefits for jobless personnel. Because of the limited scale of this arrangement, only some of the unemployed benefited from it and the amount of relief was quite low (equal to about 25 percent of average wages). In the same year, the "Interim Regulations on Practicing Labour Contract System in State-run Enterprises" was formulated, which specified that pensions of contracted workers (who accounted for a minor share of the labor force) be put under the social-pooling system. In the 1990s, China kicked off reforms to the unit security system to gradually establish a socialized social security system. In 1991, the "Decision on Reforming the Endowment Insurance System for Enterprise Employees" was promulgated, initiating the reform of the endowment insurance system for employees in state-owned enterprises. Since 1993, the system for insuring a minimum standard of living for urban residents has been gradually established in some cities. This system has wider coverage and higher standards than the guarantees system for the disabled. In the 1993 "Decision on Some Issues Related to the Establishment of a Socialist Market Economy," these attempts at reform were clarified so they would aim to establish a multi-level social security system suited to the socialist market economy. That system would have to include a social insurance system and a social relief system. To reach this goal, the Chinese government carried out pilot projects in the early 1990s to reform systems for basic endowment and medical insurance for employees in urban areas, while gradually establishing unemployment insurance (since 1994 "job-waiting" has been changed to "unemployed," and it was not until 1999 that the unemployment insurance system officially came into being), industrial injury insurance, maternity insurance, and the system for insuring urban residents' minimum standard of living. However, because of the limited scale of these newly established systems, they were temporarily unable to meet the needs of all the retirees and workers laid off by state-owned and collectively owned enterprises. For instance, in 1996, among the 5.53 million registered unemployed and the 8.15 million laid-off workers, only 3.31 million (24 percent of the total) could access unemployment benefits. In 1997, the number was 3.19 million (26 percent of the total). For the poverty relief system, only 850,000 rural residents in total 866.37 millions and 88,000 urban residents in 369.89 millions were covered by the system that insured the minimum standard of living in 1996 and 1997, respectively. The number of people covered by the system was much lower than the actual number of impoverished people (about 20 million). For those enterprises that did not take part in basic endowment insurance, their retirees either received no pensions or incomplete ones. The social security systems mentioned above, in their early existence, could only partially solve problems of unemployment, urban poverty and timely and complete pension payments.

These problems had an impact on the quality of life and interests of millions of people and had to be resolved to ensure social stability and success in economic structural transformation in the wake of the Asian financial crisis. Special times called for special policies. It is against this backdrop that the policy of the "Three Social Security Lines" was introduced.

"Three Social Security Lines" refers to the unemployment insurance system, the system for insuring a minimum standard of living for workers laid off from state-owned enterprises, and the system for insuring a minimum standard of living for urban residents. There was no consensus, however, on the way to launch these systems after China had decided on the goal to establish a socialist market economy. The process was therefore slow. To handle the sudden surge in lay-offs and unemployment, China adopted a "three-in-one approach" to establish the Three Social Security Lines.

China coined the term, "laid-off workers," in the 1990s, to refer to employees who lost jobs in state-owned enterprises (and later, in collectively owned enterprises) but who maintained an employment relationship with their enterprises and were thus eligible for re-employment training or other services. The terms also referred to employees of state-owned and collectively owned enterprises who lost their posts but who maintained an employment relationship with the original enterprises and who accessed re-employment service centers created by the government. Although workers were already being laid off in the early 1990s, China began reporting statistics on them only in 1997. From 1996 to 2000, the number of laid-off workers totaled nearly 10 million each year, many more than the official ranks of the "registered unemployed." Workers laid off from state-owned enterprises accounted for the lion's share, and their numbers annually exceeded those of the registered unemployed (see Table 10.2). Essentially, then, providing a security system for workers laid off from state-owned enterprises was equivalent to establishing another, separate unemployment security system.

The "laid-off phenomenon" refers to a type of unemployment with Chinese characteristics and also to a special unemployment phenomenon during a special period that required urgent action to insure laid-off workers' minimum standard of living. To accommodate downsizing and improving the efficiency of state-owned enterprises, the government provided support for workers laid off from state-owned enterprises through policies that included basic subsistence allowances for laid-off workers; obligations for enterprises to pay the premiums on all types of social insurance; and tax cuts, exemptions, or preferential treatment in industrial or commercial registration for those who were re-employed or who chose to strike out on their own. For laid-off workers to receive these types of support, they were required to access the re-employment service center (or simply, "the Center"), which was the custodian institution for laid-off workers that was funded through financial appropriations, enterprises, and society (unemployment insurance). The Central Government provided about RMB Yuan 10 billion in subsidies annually. The policies that made this support possible required laid-off workers to sign an agreement for accessing the Center, where they were allowed to remain for a maximum of three years. At the end of that period, the labor relationship with their enterprises had to be dissolved, and those who still could not be re-employed were placed on unemployment insurance. The stable sources of funds were credited with the assurance of the basic standard of living for laid-off workers. Nationally, about 95 percent of workers laid off from state-owned enterprises were covered through this arrangement.[2] The Center not only insures the security of workers laid off from state-owned enterprises, but it also actively carries out re-employment training and job introduction, enabling between one-third and one-half of all laid-off workers to become re-employed.

Table 10.1 Employees in urban areas 1992–2006 (in millions)

	Urban employed persons		Number of staff and workers		Number of staff and workers in state-owned units		Urban employed persons in state-owned units		Urban employed persons in urban collective-owned units	
	Number	Change from previous year	Number	Change from previous year	Number	Change from previous year	Number	Change from previous year	Number	Change from previous year
1992	172.41	2.64	147.92	2.84	108.89	2.25	108.89	2.25	36.21	-0.7
1993	175.85	3.44	148.49	0.57	109.20	0.31	109.20	0.31	33.93	-2.28
1994	184.13	8.28	148.49	0	108.90	-0.30	112.14	2.94	32.85	-1.08
1995	190.93	6.80	149.08	0.59	109.55	0.65	112.61	0.47	31.47	-1.38
1996	198.15	7.22	148.45	-0.63	109.49	-0.06	112.44	-0.17	30.16	-1.31
1997	202.07	3.92	146.68	-1.77	107.66	-1.83	110.44	-2.00	28.83	-1.33
1998	206.78	4.71	123.77	-22.91	88.09	-19.57	90.58	-19.86	19.63	-9.20
1999	210.14	3.36	117.73	-6.04	83.36	0.27	85.72	-4.86	17.12	-6.2
2000	212.74	11.60	112.59	-5.14	78.78	-4.58	81.02	-4.70	14.99	-2.13
2001	239.40	26.66	107.92	-4.67	74.09	-4.69	76.40	-4.62	12.91	-2.08
2002	247.80	8.40	105.58	-2.34	69.24	-4.85	71.63	-4.77	11.22	-1.69
2003	256.39	8.59	104.92	-0.66	66.21	-3.03	68.76	-2.87	10.00	-1.22
2004	264.76	8.37	105.76	0.84	64.38	-1.83	67.10	-1.66	8.97	-1.03
2005	273.31	8.55	108.50	3.58	62.32	-2.06	64.88	-2.22	8.10	-0.87
2006	283.10	9.79	111.61	3.11	61.70	-1.62	6430	-0.58	7.64	0.46

Sources: *Statistics Yearbook of China* (1993, 1996, 2001, 2006, 2007); *Social Insurance Yearbook of China* (1997); China Personnel Press, 1997; Ministry of Labour and Social Security: *Labour and Social Security Yearbook of China* (2001, 2002, 2003, 2004, 2005, 2006); Ministry of Labour and Social Security, State Statistics Bureau: 2006 Statistics Communiqué on the Development of Labour and Social Security Undertakings, website of the Ministry of Labour and Social Security (http://www.molss.gov. cn/gb/news/2007-05/18/content_178167.htm).

While establishing the system for insuring laid-off workers' minimum standard of living, China accelerated improvements in the unemployment insurance system and in the system for insuring urban residents' minimum standard of living, as a priority for building a socialized social security system. In January 1999, the State Council promulgated the "Regulations on Unemployment Insurance," which changed "job-waiting insurance" to "unemployment insurance," and the "job-waiting relief fund" to an "unemployment insurance benefit." The new regulations also expanded coverage from state-owned enterprises to all kinds of urban enterprises and institutions, raised the contribution ratio of the unemployment insurance premium (from 1 percent to 2 percent of payroll for organizations), added a personal contribution (1 percent of personal wages), and set forth the standard and duration for payment of unemployment insurance benefits. The standard for unemployment insurance benefits was lower than the lowest local wages and higher than the assured minimum living standard of local urban residents. The maximum duration of the benefit was 24 months. Meanwhile, the "Interim Regulations on Collection of the Unemployment Insurance Premium" were promulgated, further clarifying coverage and payment of unemployment insurance. The "Regulations on Unemployment Insurance" provided system and monetary support to enable laid-off workers to leave the Center.

The traditional relief system for people with "Three Nos" (no labor capability, no work unit, and no legal supporter) during the period of the planned economy was narrow in its coverage. In 1992, only 190,000 urban residents experiencing difficulties across the country received regular, fixed-amounts of relief, while many other poverty-stricken urban residents, such as laid-off workers, the unemployed, and senior citizens who retired a long time ago, did not receive life assistance because of limited relief funds and too strict a standard for relief. To help overcome the difficulties of these groups, Shanghai began to establish a system to insure a minimum standard of living for its residents in 1993. In 1994, the Ministry of Civil Affairs encouraged other cities to draw on Shanghai's experience and follow suit. In August 1997, the State Council issued the "Circular on Establishing the System for Ensuring Urban Residents' Minimum Standard of Living in All Places," requiring that a system be set up in all cities and towns where a county government is located by the end of 1999. On the basis of the experience of all places in establishing this system, the State Council promulgated the "Regulations on the System for Ensuring Urban Residents' Minimum Standard of Living" in September 1999, which clarified the relief principle of the system. For people with the Three Nos, full relief was provided according to the assured minimum living standard. For urban residents with some income, relief was provided to make up the part of the per capita family income that was below the locally assured minimum living standard. To effectively help overcome the difficulties of poor residents, the state lifted the assured minimum living standard and stepped up financial support. By March 2000, 3.01 million poverty-stricken urban residents throughout the country were put under this coverage, including 2.36 million enterprise employees, unemployed persons and retirees, accounting for 78 percent of the total (Zheng *et al.* 2002, 22).

To make the Three Social Security Lines more effective, the State Council promulgated a number of policies and regulations for establishing and improving the social security system between 1997 and 1999. For example, the "Decision on Establishing a Unified System of Basic Endowment Insurance for Enterprise Employees," which was promulgated in 1997, stressed the implementation of a unified system of basic endowment insurance system for enterprise employees from three aspects: a unified proportion for contributions by enterprises and individuals, a unified scale of individual accounts and unified measure for calculation, and the payment of old-age pensions. In addition, the government promulgated the "Decision on Establishing the System of Basic Medical Insurance for Urban Employees" in 1998 and the "Regulations on Collection and Payment of Social Insurance Premium" in 1999. Together with the Three Social Security Lines, these systems became important measures designed to ward off the impact of the 1997 Asian financial crisis, expand domestic demand, curb the deflationary trend, and help with the reform of state-owned enterprises.[3] To increase the likelihood that the above measures would be effective, the government further clarified the "Two Assurances" policy: assuring laid-off workers of state-owned enterprises who accessed the Center that they would receive timely subsistence allowances (with the Center paying their social insurance premiums), and assuring that enterprise retirees who participated in endowment insurance would receive full and timely basic old-age pensions.[4]

The Three Social Security Lines and the Two Assurances have contributed significantly to the success of China's handling of the peak in lay offs and unemployment in mid and late 1990s. In 2000, for example, 3.3 million unemployed persons received unemployment insurance benefits, about 6.5 million workers laid off from state-owned enterprises received subsistence allowances, and over 3 million poverty-stricken urban residents benefited from the assured minimum living standard. Together, these beneficiaries accounted for about 6 percent of the total urban work force that year. The number of people who received unemployment insurance benefits or subsistence allowances for laid-off workers approached 10 million, accounting for more than 60 percent of the total number of urban laid-off workers and unemployed persons. This satisfactorily insured the basic living standard, maintained stability, facilitated progress with economic reforms and restructuring, and laid the foundation for China's success in confronting plummeting exports and sluggish economic growth and for China's accession to the World Trade Organization.

Work hard to build a new social security system: progress and effects

Combining the systems for insuring a minimum standard of living and unemployment insurance

The system for insuring a minimum standard of living for laid-off workers was a transitory measure intended to play only a limited role when it was established. The

Table 10.2 Unemployed and laid-off workers, retirees and resignations 1992–2006 (in tens of thousands)

Year	Registered unemployed		Number of people receiving unemployment benefits	Year-end number of workers laid-off from state-owned enterprises		Retirees	Number of people who retired from enterprises	Change from previous year
	Number	Change from previous year		Number	Change from previous year	Total (all kinds of retirees including enterprises' retired people)		
1992	364	12	30			2,598	1,681	595
1993	420	56	103	300[b]		2,780	1,839	158
1994	476	56	197	360[b]		2,929	2,079	240
1995	520	44	261	563[b]		3,094	2,241	162
1996	553	33	331	815[b]		3,212	2,358	117
1997	577	27	319	634	-181	3,351	2,533	59
1998	571	-6	158	610	-24	3,594	2,767	234
1999	575	4	271	653	53	3,730	2,864	97
2000	595	20	330	657	4	3,876	2,978	114
2001	681	86	469	515	-142	4,018	3,072	94
2002	770	89	657	410	-105	4,223	3,261	189
2003	800	30	742	260	-150	4,523	3,486	225
2004	827	27	754	153	-107	4,675	3,775	289
2005	839	12	679	61	-92	5,088	3,842	67

Year	Registered unemployed		Number of people receiving unemployment benefits	Year-end number of workers laid-off from state-owned enterprises		Retirees		
	Number	Change from previous year		Number	Change from previous year	Total (all kinds of retirees including enterprises' retired people)	Number of people who retired from enterprises	Change from previous year
2006	847	8	327	0	-61		3,966	124

Notes:

a. There have never been complete statistics for laid-off workers in China. According to Lu Ming (2002, 196), laid-off workers totaled 9.95 million in 1997, 8.77 million in 1998, and 9.37 million in 1999. These figures include the laid-off workers from non-state-owned enterprises. Alternatively, according to Zheng Gongcheng et al. (2002, 419), laid-off workers at the beginning of 1998, 1999, and 2000, respectively, totaled 9.95 million, 8.71 million, and 9.42 million, including 6.92 million, 5.92 million, and 6.53 million from state-owned enterprises. The end-year numbers for those same three years were 8.77 million, 9.37 million, and 9.11 million respectively, including 5.95 million, 6.53 million, and 6.57 million from state-owned enterprises. Year-end statistics, on page 276 of Chinese Economy in Sub-rapid Growth Stage, by Liu Yingqiu, et al., show that urban laid-off workers in 1993, 1994, 1995, 1996, 1997, 1998, and 1999 totaled 3 million, 3.6 million, 5.64 million, 8.91 million, 11.51 million, 10.8 million, and 11.74 million, respectively.

b. The data for 1993–1996 show the total number of laid-off workers.

Sources: As for Table 10.1.

1998 "Circular on Doing Well the System for Ensuring the Minimum Standard of Living for Laid-off Workers of State-owned Enterprises," allowed laid-off workers to remain in the Center for a maximum of three years. How this subsistence-allowance system for laid-off workers could be phased out smoothly after 2000 and how the normal social security system could assume its designated role were questions for which China sought answers. Under the "Plan for Pilot Projects to Improve Urban Social Security System" promulgated by the State Council, a pilot project was launched in Liaoning Province in 2001 that included the following regulations: no new Center may be set up by state-owned enterprises as of January 1, 2001; employees trimmed by enterprises may no longer enter the Center; and unemployment will be combined, step by step, within about three years. Other places also gradually began to move laid-off workers out of the Center and transfer employees who were experiencing difficulties and were unable to be re-employed to the unemployment insurance system. Because of the large number of laid-off workers, this process lasted intermittently for more than five years. By the end of 2005, the number of employees who still found themselves in the Center dropped to about 250,000. In 14 regions, including Beijing, the combining of the systems was mostly complete. According to the "2006 Statistics Communiqué on the Development of Labour and Social Security Undertakings," the integration of the subsistence-allowance system for laid-off workers of state-owned enterprises into the unemployment insurance system had been essentially accomplished. For laid-off and unemployed workers, the transition of the Three Social Security Lines into Two Social Security Lines" (unemployment insurance system and the system for insuring the urban residents' minimum standard of living) had been realized (Ming *et al.* 2005), taking a great stride away from traditional enterprise security to social security.

Improve the basic insurance and individual account system for urban employees

While vigorously promoting the improvement of the Three Social Security Lines, the Chinese government did not neglect its fundamental goal in building the social security system: the establishment of a fairly perfect social security system that fits within the socialist market economy and the current level of economic development. The "Plan for Pilot Projects to Improve the Urban Social Security System" promulgated by the State Council in 2000, not only prescribes the integration of systems for dealing with layoffs and unemployment, but also sets targets and means for adjusting and perfecting the system of basic endowment insurance. As the most important part of social security, endowment insurance had been the focus of China's reform of its social security system since the 1990s. The large scale layoffs in state-owned and collectively owned enterprises in the mid-1990s caused a decrease in the number of employees paying insurance premiums and increased the number of people retiring ahead of time to receive an old-age pension. In 1998 and 1999, socially pooled funds for basic endowment insurance were not enough to pay pensions, making diversions from individual accounts inevitable, thus aggravating existing delays in payments of old-age pensions. This problem led people to challenge the combining of the social-pooling system with individual accounts in the basic endowment insurance system. The "Plan for Pilot Projects to Improve Urban Social Security System" called for persistence but nevertheless corrected and improved specific implementation methodology.

First, the Plan called for a reduction in the scale of individual accounts. The contribution by enterprises would no longer be allocated into individual accounts, and the rate of individual contributions would ultimately be raised to 8 percent and completely charged to individual accounts. Second, individual accounts would be placed under real account operations; the funds for social pooling and those of individual accounts would be managed in separate accounts; and the separate accounts would be placed under the centralized management of provincial-level social insurance institutions and could only be used to buy national bonds within a fixed time-frame. Third, the level of the basic old-age pension would be lifted, with a pro rata increase for every full year for those who had made contributions for more than 15 years (subject to a ceiling equal to 30 percent of the local average wage of the previous year). Fourth, enterprises would be encouraged to establish enterprise annuities, for which a 4 percent tax discount would be available.

To fulfill the tasks set out in the "Plan for Pilot Projects to Improve the Urban Social Security System," the State Council selected Liaoning Province for piloting in July 2001. To insure the smooth running of the pilot, the Central Government provided pro rata subsidies for materializing individual accounts for basic endowment insurance. The pilot ended in 2003 and a year later pilots were launched in Jilin and Heilongjiang provinces, but the proportion of materialized individual accounts was reduced.[5] By 2005, the three provinces materialized the individual accounts of 1.789 million people, 1.3 million people and 1.825 million people, respectively, involving RMB Yuan 20.1 billion, RMB Yuan 2.73 billion, and RMB Yuan 3.74 billion, respectively, in individual accounts (Cai 2007, 185). On the basis of the tests done in the three northeastern provinces, the State Council issued the "Decision on Improving the Basic Endowment Insurance System for Enterprise Employees" at the end of 2005. This essence of this decision may be boiled down to three points. First, gradually materialize personal accounts. Second, unify the insurance participation and contribution policy for urban self-employed laborers and workers in flexible employment (i.e., 20 percent of the local average wage in the previous year, with 8 percent of it going toward individual accounts). Third, adjust the individual accounts of the basic endowment insurance of urban employees of the whole country to 8 percent of local average wages and exclusively pay for them through individual contributions. In 2006, eight provinces, including Tianjin, Shanghai and Shanxi, started to materialize individual accounts in line with this decision and the Central Government provided the central and western regions with subsidies as it did to those in the northeast. In 2007, other provinces that needed no central financial subsidies were allowed to carry out similar tests.

Improve the system of guarantees for minimum living standards and build the social relief system for urban residents

The "Regulations on the Minimum Living Standard Guarantee System promulgated in September 1999 laid the foundation for the urban subsistence-allowance system. During the implementation of the "Plan for Pilot Projects to Improve the Urban Social Security System," "coverage for all with eligibility" was further realized for the subsistence-allowance system. Under the constant support of national finance, the urban subsistence-allowance system has been improved continuously and the assured minimum standard of living rose to RMB Yuan 156 on average by the end of 2005. In that year, the financial departments at all levels allocated a total of RMB Yuan 19.19 billion as subsistence-allowance funds. The coverage has expanded continuously, basically realizing the goal of coverage for all with eligibility (see Table 10.3).

Simultaneously, with the expansion of the coverage of the urban subsistence-allowance system, the major social relief system was gradually formed the basic framework for the social relief system. In 2003, China abolished the "detention and repatriation" system applied to beggars lacking support systems in cities and promulgated the "Administration Measures for Relief to Vagrant Beggars with No Life Support in Cities." In the promotion and perfection of the subsistence-allowance system for urban residents, further efforts were made to establish and improve the disaster-relief system, the rural "Five Guarantees" support system, and the relief systems for rural households in exceptional poverty and for vagrant beggars. Further efforts were also made to push ahead the building of rural relief systems for subsistence allowances, medical care, education, housing and legal assistance, leading to continuous perfection of social relief system.

Actively build the medical security system, focusing on basic medical insurance for urban employees

Pursuant to the "Decision on Establishing a Basic Medical Insurance System for Urban Employees" promulgated in 1998, the Chinese government strongly pushed for a basic medical insurance system that combined social pooling and the individual accounts of employees. But, because of the inconspicuous effect of the individual account system for basic medical insurance and the excessive rise of medical expenses, people were disgruntled with the medical security system, especially the medical and public health system. The crisis with the severe acute respiratory syndrome, or SARS, that erupted in 2003 pointed the spotlight onto the public health sector and the medical security system. It is against such a backdrop that the Government increasingly values the building of a medical security system. The coverage of the basic medical insurance system for urban employees widened. In 2006, the number of employees participating in the insurance reached 157.37 million, with an increase of nearly 100 million since 2000. Also in 2006, the Chinese Government advanced the notion of a basic medical insurance system for urban residents focusing on social pooling for serious diseases. A pilot effort was scheduled to begin in 2007. Initiated in 2003, the experiment of building a new cooperative medical system in rural areas had brought 410 million rural residents under coverage by 2006 and is scheduled to cover all rural residents by 2010 (Wen 2007).[6] The building of the public health system and the development of the medical relief system became important additions to the efforts to build the medical security system.

Actively promote the building of the rural social security system

Rural social security has always been a weak link in China's social security system. Since the Sixteenth Communist Party of China Congress, the party and the Government have paid great attention to rural social security, regarding it as an important measure for realizing rational development, narrowing urban-rural differences, speeding up the construction of new socialist rural areas, and building a harmonious society. Investment was increased in building systems to insure rural residents' minimum standard of living, new cooperative medical care and rural social relief, and promoting the rapid development of the rural social security system. What is praiseworthy is the development of the system for insuring rural residents' minimum standard of living. By 2006, 27 provinces had established this system, covering 18.15 million rural residents. In 2007, China was set to promulgate and implement a policy establishing a nationwide system for insuring rural residents' minimum standard of living. The system would lay a solid foundation for a social relief system covering urban and rural residents across the country as a "last safety network." The experimental new cooperative medical system launched in 2003 is currently a high-intensity project to build rural social security and has brought nearly 50 percent of farmers under its coverage. The concomitant rural medical relief system is also under continuous development and has provided a degree of medical security to the masses of farmers. In the process of industrialization and urbanization, more and more rural laborers ("farmer workers") and rural residents ("land-requisitioned farmers") have found their way into cities to work and live. The establishment of some degree of social security for these people has been put on the agenda. In some places, this is already available for farmer workers (for example, industrial injury insurance and medical insurance). In some regions, land-requisitioned farmers have been gradually incorporated into the urban social security system. Generally, these efforts are still in the experimental stage.

Continuously expand coverage of social insurance system

The social insurance system is the principal component of the social security system and is the focus of reform of the entire social security system. As the backbones of urban social insurance, the systems of endowment insurance, medical insurance, and unemployment insurance formed a fundamental framework by the end of the twentieth century (after nearly 20 years of exploration of reforms), and their coverage is constantly expanding. After the "Regulations on Industrial Injury Insurance" was promulgated, farmer workers were included in the industrial injury insurance system, which quickly expanded its coverage. By 2006, it had become the fourth-largest social insurance program, with more than 100 million participants. In recent years, the progress of establishing maternity insurance has quickened noticeably and the coverage of the social insurance system has broadened continuously (see Table 10.4).

Future development of China's social security system: problems and suggestions

Problems and challenges of China's social security system

In the recent decade, China has achieved great results in building its social security system. The continuously developing and improving social security system has become an important vehicle for China to perfect its socialist market economy and build a socialist harmonious society. But, the establishment of a perfect social security system is by no means something that can be done in one stroke in any developing country with a large population, the majority of which is rural, or in a rapidly industrializing and urbanizing country, with an aging population and with huge urban-rural and inter-regional differences.

At present, the social security system of China is far from perfect. It has many problems and faces many challenges. The narrow coverage of social security, especially social insurance, still looms large, leaving a long way to go before reaching the goal of universal enjoyment of the system. In the five major social insurance systems of China, the basic endowment insurance system has the largest coverage. Still, there are only 200 million people participating in it, including incumbent employees and staff members of government agencies and institutions. For nearly 280 million urban workers, 420 million workers of secondary and tertiary industries, and society's total 760 million workers, the coverage of endowment insurance is about 70 percent, 45 percent, and 25 percent, respectively. Large numbers of rural laborers have little or no endowment insurance and more than 100 million rural senior citizens enjoy no socialized old-age support. The coverage of other varieties of social insurance is even narrower, neutralizing social security's effect and triggering social tensions. Huge costs are involved in reforming and modernizing social security. When designing the new system, China paid insufficient attention to this, thus overlooking many historical problems. The old security system mainly covered employees of urban state-owned and collectively owned enterprises. During the market-oriented economic structural reform and the establishment of a social insurance system, large numbers of people experiencing difficulties encountered problems finding employment. Enterprises that had closed down or gone bankrupt left behind problems with employee resettlement and system combination. In different industries, the gaps in incomes and retirement benefits between employees have widened, resulting in many contradictions. One such contradiction is the differences in retirement benefits offered by government agencies and institutions, whose retired employees enjoy benefits that are about double those of enterprise employees. Presently, more than 50 million retired employees (over 10 million of them had retired before the

Table 10.3 Urban residents covered by the minimum living standard guarantee system

Year	1996	1997	1998	1999	2000	2001	2002	2003	2004	2005	2006
People covered (in tens of thousands)	84.9	87.9	184.1	265.9	402.6	1,170.7	2,064.7	2,246.8	2,205	2,234.2	2,240.9

Source: Ministry of Civil Affairs: *Statistics Report on Development of Civil Affairs in 2005*. The data for 2006 is from the website of the Ministry of Civil Affairs.

statutory retirement age) require an annual RMB Yuan 100 billion expenditure on endowment insurance, which is the transformation cost that the current system must pay. The failure to properly solve residual problems will cause new and old systems to coexist for a long time, and it will be an arduous task to straighten out social insurance's management system, the fund-collection and payment system, and the investment system. Greatly influenced by huge urban-rural and inter-regional differences, the China's social security system will suffer from inter-regional inconsistency and difficult urban-rural linkages for a considerable period of time to come. This not only makes it hard to narrow the differences between social security benefits but is also antagonistic to the flow of the labor force. Rural social security remains the bottleneck in building China's system over all. It is very difficult for large numbers of urban workers in flexible employment to participate in social insurance, while the army of farmer workers and land-requisitioned farmers find it very hard to integrate into the current urban social relief and social insurance systems that are based on urban census registries. To perfect the social security system, these thorny issues must be addressed. The rapidly aggravating pressure on the payment of social security funds is something to guard against. With the expansion of endowment insurance coverage, the amount of collected social insurance funds, especially endowment insurance funds, has been rising. In 2006, the total amount of collected social insurance funds topped RMB Yuan 600 billion. Payments, however, are also increasing rapidly. If accumulation is based on individual accounts alone, it will be hard to meet the payment needs of any given year. Therefore, the failure to materialize individual accounts remains an apparent problem, and no effective solution has been found through trials carried out in various locations. One of the original purposes of the reform of the social security system was to alleviate the burden on enterprises, especially state-owned ones. However, the rapidly increasing expenditures of social insurance have not only failed to reduce the burden on enterprises, but have also made it impossible to reach the target of "partial accumulation" of the new endowment insurance mode. As the aging of the population continues, social security funds will come under heavier pressure for "additional payment." This will be an austere test on whether the new social security system of China is sustainable. The social security system visibly lags behind in legislation. In the past dozen years, the plan for reforming China's social security was primarily based on "decisions" or "regulations" of the State Council and local governments. There is not yet a national "Social Insurance Law," "Social Relief Law," or "Social Security Law." Such a state of affairs makes the new social security system less authoritative and also reflects the non-legal nature of China's reforms to and construction of its social security system. Under such circumstances, many reform measures cannot be implemented effectively.

Suggestions for promoting the reform and development of the social security system

The current zeal for promoting the development of China's social security system is accompanied by higher and higher targets and requirements. From a long-term perspective, China's social security system will inevitably improve continuously in step with economic development. But, China must still confront the paramount challenge of successfully managing the relationship between economic development and the building of the social security system. Social security has a complicated influence on economic and social development. To establish a sustainable social security system, it is imperative to balance the relations between efficiency and fairness and between the level of social security and the level of economic and social development. This is a significant issue that tests the wisdom of the Chinese. China should pay attention to the following principles in the future development of its social security system. First, it should persist in considering the realities of the country. Lessons drawn from the experience of other countries should better serve the formulation of policies for China's social security but should not be blindly or mechanically copied. Second, China must correctly handle the relationship between long-term goals and short-term measures. The former are the foundation, but they must be met step by step. The principle of a "great leap forward" should not be applied to the building of social security. Otherwise, the drive will be short-lived. Likewise, the latter must facilitate the realization of long-term goals and must not be allowed to be consolidated or to be obstacles to future development. On the one hand, the major problems blocking the development of social security need to be solved and, on the other hand, the cause of social security should be championed as a whole. These principles can be summarized as: wide in coverage, multiple-layered (pillars), and a foundation insuring sustainability. In relation to these targets, it is necessary to deepen the reform of the social security system and actively and reliably promote its development. To this end, the following suggestions are made.

1   Work hard to expand the coverage of the social security system and accelerate the building of a multi-pillared and multi-layered old-age support system. The expanded coverage of social security is a long-term trend that cannot be avoided. While improving the basic endowment insurance system for employees, China should earnestly study the expansion of the coverage of old-age support. From a long-term perspective, the high threshold of urban social insurance must be lowered to accommodate laborers who transfer to cities. Subject to a lowered threshold, urban social insurance should be fairly flexible. No attempt should be made to use a social insurance system of high threshold to cover social groups at all levels. It is necessary to establish a sustainable, low-threshold and multi-form social insurance system that involves the participation of urban laborers. That is the only system that will appeal to laborers who have not yet participated in social insurance. To reflect the principle of matching rights to obligations of endowment insurance, it is necessary to speed up the reform for the employees of government agencies and institutions to participate in the basic endowment insurance system. This can broaden the coverage, provide stable fund sources for endowment insurance and better embody the redistribution function of social security. While perfecting the endowment insurance system, China should establish the

Table 10.4 Participants of major social insurance varieties (in tens of thousands)

Year	2000	2001	2002	2003	2004	2005	2006
Basic endowment insurance for urban employees	13,617.4	14,183	14,736.6	15,506.7	16,353	17,487	18,649
Basic medical insurance for urban employees	3,787.0	7285.9	9,401.2	10,901.7	12,404	13,783	15,737
Unemployment insurance	10,408.4	10,354.6	10,181.6	10,372.4	10,584	10,648	11,187
Industrial injury insurance	4,350.3	4,345.3	4,405.6	4,574.8	6,845	8,478	10,235
Maternity insurance	3,001.6	3,455.1	3,488.2	3,655.4	4,384	5,408	6,446

Source: Annual Statistics Communiqué of the Ministry of Labour and Social Security (2000, 2001, 2002, 2003, 2004, 2005, 2006).

annuity system for its nationals with the progress of its industrialization and urbanization and the enhancement of national fiscal power. The primary aim is to provide support for the poor, the elderly, and the disabled. The funds may be sourced from the social security expenditure items from general taxation. Consideration can also be given to collecting social security tax at a low level for financing. Only by launching national annuities based on age will it be possible for the old-age support system to cover all elderly people.

2   Take active measures to improve the systems to address unemployment, industrial injury and disease. The present dreaded disease insurance for rural and urban residents is a measure taken because there were no other alternatives available. As the economy develops, it is necessary to increase the investment in basic medical care, especially disease prevention. The prevention of diseases, education, and the transformation of environmental sanitation aim to make people less susceptible to disease. This way, money invested will generate greater benefits. The coverage of unemployment insurance also needs to be broadened. Meanwhile, it is necessary to strengthen control over the use of unemployment insurance funds to devote a portion to training, job introduction and implementation of a proactive labor market policy.

3   Continuously perfect the social relief system on the basis of establishing the system for insuring the minimum standard of living that covers urban and rural residents. The focus is on expanding this system in rural areas. Some economically developed regions have already established the system in rural areas. In regions with relatively poor economic conditions, the Central Government and higher-level governments can make transfer payments to help establish a system that meets local conditions. With the establishment of this system in rural areas as the focus, efforts should be made to gradually

improve the social relief system, including medical relief, education relief and housing relief, to provide the poor with the fundamental life support and a defense against social risks.

4   Strengthen the management of social insurance funds, straighten out the collection system of social insurance premiums, improve social security management capabilities, and enhance legislation. Without a complete and sound management system for the collection of social insurance premiums, it will be very difficult or even impossible to establish complete and sound social insurance or social security systems. The flow from collection to payments of social insurance premiums involves many links. The collection link involves participation registration, payment declaration, base verification, criterion verification, and premium collection. The link of fund management involves the delivery of collected funds to the treasury, account splitting of funds, value preservation of funds, cumulative fund investment, distribution of fund proceeds, make-up of fund losses, and the inter-regional flow of funds. The link of payment involves equity recording, decision of treatment criteria, determination of equity payment channels and form, treatment adjustment, payment of funds, disposal of residual equity, and the handling of equity under a special policy and termination of equity. The link of fund safety and supervision involves supervision of the bases declared by participating persons and units, supervision of collection departments and staff, supervision of the fund flow of all links from collection to payment, supervision of fund trustee-ship management institutions, investment institutions and related personnel, supervision of the distribution of fund proceeds, and the implementation link of related taxation policy. A sound collection management system of social insurance premiums should have some basic targets, including: a good connection between all links and departments, and smooth operations, which are the foundations for the positive operation of the system; a low operating cost (including short-term and long-term costs), relative high gains of participants and the entire society, and highly efficient operations, which would enable the system to last for the long-term; a rational division of work for all links and "sunlit" operations, which facilitates mutual support and constraint to assist supervision. The supervisory system is fairly sound and can prevent risks related to fund operation, management and investment, to insure the safety of funds. From the perspective of fund management, the establishment of the mechanism for repayment of historical debts should be studied so as to perfect the basic system of social security. The Chinese government wants neither assets nor tax revenues and does not have many explicit debts. What form (current form, normal account and subscribed liabilities) is used for a solution has a direct bearing on the mode of the old-age pension system and the long-term operational mechanism of China. The most fundamental measure for strengthening the management of social security funds is to improve related laws and regulations. It is necessary to accelerate the legislation of social security, especially social insurance, to gradually realize legalized management.

Take reliable measures to complete the two-fold transition in the modes of China's basic endowment insurance and basic medical insurance system

By building its social security system, China does not merely aim to expand its coverage. Rather, it needs to accomplish a two-fold transition as soon as possible. The first transition – the change from employment security to social security – has not yet been completed. Overall, however, the steps of reform have been quick and the effect conspicuous. What is more difficult is the second transition – changing from the pay-as-you-go system to a partially funded system. For the individual account system of the basic endowment insurance for employees, the financing mode and fund management system are still being adjusted. In academia, there are still debates about whether individual accounts should be materialized. Most provinces are unwilling to materialize them. The fund management system, especially the investment supervision element, is still far from being complete. According to initial design, from 1997, when this system was first founded, to the present, individual accounts should have accumulated nearly RMB Yuan 1 trillion of funds, but the actual amount is much smaller. In time, this "implicit" debt will gradually become explicit, leading to a greater and greater impact on the healthy operation of the whole system. In fact, this is also one of the core issues in improving the social security system. It is essential to pay a high degree of attention to it and come up with relevant solutions. The "Social Insurance Law," which is being legislated, may satisfactorily address the issue.

The individual account system is the basic medical insurance system for employees, which has been embroiled in controversy since its inception. The principal reason for supporting the system is that the addition of a fund regulation mechanism would help discourage individual employees' unnecessary consumption demand while leading to reserves in the medical fund. The opposing argument is that the complicated management and high cost make it difficult to control the actions of medical service providers. Also, the ratio of socially pooled funds and the effect of regulation are impaired, the initiative deviates from the just principle of medical insurance, the accumulated funds are absolutely incapable of meeting the swelling expenses entailed in addressing dreaded diseases, and the investment of accumulated funds is drowning in a sea of difficulties. In accordance with the "Document" adopted at the Third Plenary Session of the Fourteenth Communist Party of China Central Committee in 1993 and the "Regulations" promulgated by the State Council in 1998, the individual account system of the basic medical insurance for employees has been generally established in all places and has accumulated a certain scale of funds (about RMB Yuan 100 billion over 10 years). However, as the problems described above are worsening, people tend more and more to negate this system. Its cancellation means the return of the basic medical insurance system from the partially funded system to a pay-as-you-go system. Given the determination to solve the problem and the support of appropriately increased financial capital, the difficulty should not be very high. Of course, this depends on the choice made by the politicians.

Notes

1 The World Bank publication, *Averting the Old Age Crisis*: *Policies to Protect the Old and Promote Growth*, introduced and recommended the "three-pillar system" to the governments of many countries. The three pillars are: (1) a publicly managed system with mandatory participation and the limited goal of reducing poverty among the old; (2) a privately managed, mandatory savings system; and (3) voluntary savings.
2 According to relevant survey information, in June 2001, there were 6.32 million laid-off workers of state-owned enterprises. 91.6 percent of which accessed the re-employment service center, which covered basic subsistence costs for 99.9 percent and paid social insurance premiums for 99.6 percent. See Zheng, *et al.*, 2002, p. 177.
3 In 1997, the Chinese government set a goal for lifting large and medium-sized state-owned enterprises out of poverty within three years. Achieving this goal would require diverting a large number of redundant personnel for purposes of staff cuts and efficiency improvements. This would in turn require establishing a complete social security system. At that time, the understanding of social security system was limited to providing auxiliary services for the reform of state-owned enterprises.
4 The social-pooling system for the endowment insurance of urban enterprise employees, which came into existence in the early 1990s, primarily covers employees of state-owned enterprise. But, because some state-owned enterprises mired in operating difficulties could not fully pay the endowment insurance premium, their employees could not receive full pensions.
5 In Liaoning, individual accounts were materialized at the rate of 8 percent. The Central Government financed 75 percent of the first 5 percent, d the remaining 25 percent of the first 5 percent, with the other 3 percent being made up by collected funds. In Jilin and Heilongjiang, individual accounts were materialized at the rate of 5 percent.
6 By March 31, 2007, the number of counties (cities, districts) in China that had launched new rural cooperative medical care reached 2,319, accounting for 81.03 percent of the total and reaching the target set in a 2007 government work report delivered by Premier Wen: "New rural cooperative medical care should reach the goal of covering 80 percent of the counties (cities, districts) in 2007." The agricultural population receiving coverage is 799 million, accounting for 91.93 percent of the national total, and the population participating in the cooperative medical care is 685 million, accounting for 78.78 percent of the total agricultural population of China, reflecting a participation rate of 85.70 percent.

References

Cai, Fang (ed.). 2007. *China's Population and Sustainable Development*. Beijing: Science Press.
Lu, Ming. 2002. *Labour Economics*. Shanghai: Fudan University Press.
Liu, Yingqiu *et al.* 2002. *Chinese Economy in Sub-rapid Growth Stage*. Beijing: Social Science Literature Press.
Ming, Chun; Liang, Liqun; Gao, Peng. 2005. Linkage Between "Three Assurances" and Reemployment Policy – Investigations and Research. *Monthly of Budget Management and Accounting*: 11.
Ministry of Civil Affairs. People's Republic of China. 2005. *Statistical Report on Development of Civil Affairs in 2005*. Available online at http://admin.mca.gov.cn/.
Ministry of Labour. People's Republic of China. 1997. Administration of Social Insurance Undertakings. *China Social Insurance Yearbook* 2007. China Personnel Press.
Ministry of Labour and Social Security. People's Republic of China. 2000, 2001, 2002, 2003, 2004, 2005, 2006. Beijing: Annual Statistics Communiqué of the Ministry of Labour and Social Security.

Ministry of Labour and Social Security. People's Republic of China. 2001, 2002, 2003, 2004, 2005, 2006. *Labour and Social Security Yearbook of China.*

Ministry of Labour and Social Security. People's Republic of China. 2007. Available online at http://www.molss.gov.cn/gb/news/2007-05/18/content_178167.htm.

State Statistics Bureau. People's Republic of China. (1993, 1996, 2001, 2006, 2007). *Statistics Yearbook of China.*

Wen, Premier Jiabao (2007). New rural cooperative medical care should reach the goal of covering 80 percent of the counties (cities, districts) in 2007. Available online at http://news.sina.com.cn/c/2007-06-11/110013201975.shtml.

Word Bank. 1994. *Averting the Old Age Crisis: Policies to Protect the Old and Promote Growth.* China Financial & Economic Publishing House.

Wang, Yanzhong. 2004. Issues on Labour and Social Security of China. Beijing: Economic Management Press.

Zheng, Gongcheng 2002. *Evolution and Evaluation of China's Social Security System.* Beijing: Renmin University Press.

11 Reform and development of the public health system

Zhang Zhenzhong and Wu Huazhang

Since 1997, when the Asian financial crisis erupted, the Chinese government has adopted countermeasures to foster and enlarge domestic demands, and effect a significant "package reform" of the country's economic and social systems. The aim has been to mitigate the impact of stagnant external demands and a slump in domestic demand, and to insure China's national economy continues to grow in a fast and healthy way. The implementation of such macroeconomic policies and reform measures has enabled China's economy to keep growing rapidly during the past decade, fortified the country's overall strengths, and boosted the development of the health service. These policies and measures have also laid the foundation for carrying forward a deep and comprehensive reform of the country's health care system.

Development of the health service constitutes an important component in the construction of a harmonious socialist society. This chapter seeks to summarize and review the evolution of the reform of China's public health system in the past decade. We include the development of related laws and the pace of change in constructing the system for urban and rural residents, to enable Chinese citizens to share the positive results of the reform and allow the health service to attain harmonious development featuring "sharing positive results through joint construction, joint construction through sharing" (Zhao 2007).

Macro policies and economic development: growth of the health service since 1998

Active fiscal policies accelerate public health system for urban and rural residents

Since 1998, China's macro fiscal policies have boosted the development of its public health system. This boost has been mainly manifested in terms of the organization and implementation of public health projects financed by government bonds, and demonstrates different characteristics at different stages.

From 1998 to 1999, funds raised by the State Council through the issuance of additional government bonds were largely used to finance construction of infrastructure facilities in agriculture, forestry, water conservancy, transportation, urban public facilities, communications, and environmental protection, as well as reconstruction of power grids in both urban and rural areas. After 2000, these funds were poured into the social sector, scientific and technological development, construction of educational facilities, harnessing of the natural environment, and ecological environment construction. Since 2001 the Chinese government has begun to pour these funds into the fortification of certain weak links in the health sector.

Efforts were made to construct more blood stations and to set up China's blood transfusion network for the purpose of clinical application. In 2001, in order to control the spread of AIDS and other diseases through blood transfusions and insure the safety of blood for clinical application, the State built a number of city/prefecture-level central blood stations to stipulated standards. These were located in west and central China in areas where there had been no blood stations before. These new blood stations were fully equipped and resourced. The investment in this project was RMB Yuan 1.25 billion of which RMB Yuan 1.01 billion was invested in west and central China. These funds were raised through the issuance of government bonds and RMB Yuan one billion allocated by local governments. The project involved construction and reconstruction of 319 blood stations and centers, as well as 141 county-level blood banks in west China. Since this blood station project was completed, China has been able to guarantee the supply of blood for clinical application purposes in 85 percent of the country, and the other 15 percent is advised to guarantee the safety of blood for clinical transfusion by means of conducting stricter blood tests.

Efforts were made to intensify the construction of the disease prevention and control systems and medical rescue and treatment systems, so as to enhance capabilities in coping with significant diseases and public health emergencies. After 2002, the Chinese government further increased its investment in those public health projects financed through the issuance of government bonds, spending most of this investment on fortifying the disease prevention and control system and the medical rescue and treatment system. From 2002 to 2003, the Central Government allocated RMB Yuan 2.92 billion of these funds (RMB Yuan 2.86 billion of which was poured into west and central China) to initiate the construction of a three-layered (province, region, and county) disease prevention and control mechanism. The funds were used to finance 1,589 projects, thus enabling this disease prevention and control mechanism to cover all the provinces, regions, and counties in the target areas. In 2003, the State Government allocated funds raised through the issuance of government bonds to initiate the construction of a medical rescue and treatment system for emergent public health incidents. From 2003 to 2005, the total investment in this project was RMB Yuan 11.4 billion, of which RMB Yuan 5.7 billion came from funds raised through the issuance of government bonds. These funds were allocated to 2,306 construction projects. In 2006, the State Government allocated RMB Yuan 480 million of those funds raised through the issuance of government bonds to finance the construction of 43 state-level and provincial-level chemical poisoning and nuclear radiation rescue bases.

Efforts were made to construct a public health system in more rural areas in an effort to mitigate peasants' inconvenience in accessing medical services.

The Central Government allocated RMB Yuan 394 million in 2003 and 2005 to buy 1,771 fully furnished patrolling medical vehicles for use in poverty-stricken counties in west and central China, thus mitigating the inconvenience suffered by peasants in these areas of the country. In 2004 and 2005, the Chinese government allocated another RMB Yuan 4 billion to develop the public health system in more rural bases, financing 7,537 projects. In 2006, the State Government continued to strengthen the capability of the health service in rural areas, allocating a total of RMB Yuan 2.7 billion from funds raised through the issuance of government bonds. These funds were used to ameliorate the medical service conditions in 5,436 town-level health stations, and 672 county-level hospitals, county-level Traditional Chinese Medicine (TCM) hospitals and county-level hospitals for women and children, hence fortifying the three-layered public health network in rural areas.

Improving living conditions and the environment has enhanced the health status of Chinese citizens

The changes in the health conditions of Chinese citizens are largely derived from the decade-long betterment of living conditions and the environment of the Chinese people. As demonstrated by the World Health Organisation (WHO), way of living, living environment, genetics, and medical care are the four primary elements influencing human health, contributing 60 percent, 15 percent, 15 percent and 10 percent respectively to the total. The Central Government has implemented active fiscal policies, fostered and enlarged domestic demands, and gradually improved infrastructure and facilities in regard to transportation, communications, energy, water conservancy, and education. In doing so it has enhanced the incomes of rural and urban residents, and achieved huge changes in the lifestyles and living environment of the Chinese people. All these factors, together with improved medical care, have brought active changes in terms of the key indicators of people's health, such as average life expectancy, and maternal and infant mortality rates (Table 11.1).

Socio-economic advancement boosts the all-around development of the health service

Since 1997, the rapid and constant growth of China's national economy, the robust evolution of China's educational, scientific and technological research, and positive cultural changes have all boosted the all-round development of the health service.

The total volume of health resources was increased, the country's capability in meeting the people's demand for basic health services was improved to a certain degree, and the traditional inconvenience in accessing medical services was radically mitigated. Since 1997, the total volume of health resources in China has increased (Table 11.2), while a health system covering both urban and rural areas has been formed. By the end of 2006, the country had 19,200 hospitals, up by

Table 11.1 Changes in the main health indicators of Chinese citizens (1995–2005)

	1995	2000	2005
Average life expectancy (years)	70.5	71.5	72.5
Infant mortality rate (%)	36.4	32.2	19.00
Maternal mortality rate in surveillance regions (1/100,000)	61.9	53.0	47.7

Sources: *China Health Statistics 2006,* China Health Economy Study and Training Network 2007.

20.75 percent from 1997, and 2.56 million ward beds, up by 20.82 percent. As for large-scale medical equipment, according to rough statistics in 2004, China had 4,752 CT machines, 1,110 NMR machines, and 98 PET machines. On average, every one million Chinese people have access to 3.65 CT machines and 0.85 NMR machines. In 2005, the country's health expenditure amounted to RMB Yuan 866.819 billion, or 4.73 percent GDP.

Medical technologies made great progress and medical service skills were improved rapidly too. In recent years, the development and application of state-of-the-art technologies, such as genetic engineering, molecular biotechnology, remote-sensing information technology, interventional imaging, microsurgery, visceral organ transplants, man-made organs, and reproduction engineering, have advanced medical services in Chinese hospitals. The advancement of the medical technologies in China's health sector has demonstrated three basic trends. First, an increasing number of large-scale, automatic and informal diagnostic and therapeutic devices have been introduced. Second, those medical technologies intended to prolong life expectancy and reduce the probability of disability have been rapidly distributed. Third, many new and specialized drugs have been developed, introduced, and applied in clinical treatments.

There have been many positive results from the advancement of medical technologies in hospitals. The level of diagnostic and therapeutic skills has been enhanced, the life expectancy of patients has been prolonged, and the quality of patient care has been improved. In addition, patients have suffered fewer difficul-

Table 11.2 Development of medical and health-care resources (1997–2006)

Health resources	1997	2000	2002	2004	2006
Number of hospitals	15,944	16,318	17,844	18,703	19,246
Number of ward beds (10,000 beds)	211.92	216.67	222.18	244.50	256.04
Number of medium/ high-grade health specialists (persons)	1,046,774*	1,139,664	1,182,449	1,283,060	–

Source: *2006 China Health Statistical Yearbook*

* Posted in 1998

ties in the diagnostic and therapeutic areas, and the quality of medical service has also been improved. Moreover, therapeutic procedures have been streamlined so that the number of days spent in hospital by patients with certain diseases has been cut, thus reducing medical costs and mitigating the difficulties low-income patients experience in paying their expenses for the use of modern medical technologies.

A basic framework of the health security system for urban and rural residents has been established. After reviewing China's health system reform over the past 20-odd years, the fastest and most visible progress was achieved in the reform of the health security system for urban and rural residents. To date, the introduction of a basic medical insurance scheme for urban employees has proceeded smoothly and now covers more than 160 million workers and staff members in urban areas. The basic health insurance system for urban residents will be put into trial operation in the second half of 2007. In 2008, efforts will be made to sum up the experience in implementing this system on a trial basis, and to work out new methods to disseminate this system in other parts of the country. It is expected that this system will be implemented nationwide in 2009 (Wang and Sun 2007). The new rural cooperative medical scheme (NCMS) has proceeded smoothly too, covering more and more parts of the country at a fast rate. At the same time the sum insured for each person in west and central China has climbed to about RMB Yuan 50 from RMB Yuan 30. As of the end of 2006, the NCMS covered 14,551 counties (cities, districts) in the country, with a total population of 508,199,400 persons. The total population covered by this cooperative medical system amounted to 409,895,800 persons, and the coverage ratio of this system reached 80.66 percent. This system has benefited 272,150,812 person-times. Up to 27.8 percent of those peasants covered by the NCMS have already had their hospital expenses reimbursed under the same system.

The medical assistance system for urban and rural areas has been disseminated consistently. As of the end of 2006, medical assistance work has been carried out in 1,119 cities and districts in the country on a trial basis, and benefited 1.63 million person-times, at a total cost of RMB Yuan 520 million (Minimum Living Subsidy Department of the Ministry of Civil Affairs 2006).

Since 2005, the rural medical assistance system has covered all the rural counties (prefectures and districts) in the country. As of the end of 2006, a total of 12.712 million poverty-stricken peasants in the country had been rescued (among others, 9.844 million poverty-stricken peasants were given financial support to gain coverage by the NCMS), at a total cost of RMB Yuan 890 million (General Office of the State Council 2007).

Health laws and systems have been improved on a daily basis. In recent years, China has made breakthroughs in formulating health laws. So far, China has enacted eight national laws on health, 22 statutes regarding health administration, 423 rules/regulations governing health departments, and many local health provisions, rules, and regulations. Thus, China has formed a law-governed health framework comprising three elements overall – social and public health, health-related products, supervision and management by health institutions and professionals –

and gradually subjected various types of health work to management, according to the legal system.

Discussions on significant issues in China's health-care reform since 1997

Since 1997 in-depth discussions have been initiated in all walks of life on the purpose, direction, and objective of China's health-care reform. The government is faced with a number of complicated issues and cannot solve them all at the same time, but in the prevailing social environment, when an issue is raised sensitive media and policy researchers are able, more often than not, to make responses. Due to the endeavors of media and policy researchers, this issue will be gradually become a widespread debate and the force of public opinion will follow. In the event of some public attention-grabbing event the issue in question will be quickly transformed into a common understanding of the public. At this point, the importance and urgency of the issue will be reflected by policy and decision makers and given political priority.

In the historical course of China's reform of the health system, three milestone events that drew much public attention have rapidly turned the reform of the health system from a topic of mild discussion within health circles, into a hot topic attracting huge attention from across the society. In 2003, the outbreak of SARS exposed all the problems that existed in the country's health system. In 2004, the Ministry of Health issued the "Main Finding of the Third National Health Survey." This report exposed the challenging situation in health services used by urban and rural Chinese, with concrete and solid data. In 2005, some scholars with the Development Research Centre of the State Council released the "Evaluation and Recommendations on China's Health System Reform," which "united" a range of critical voices on the health status quo. These voices have stimulated both government and public discussions into the depth, purpose, direction, and mode of China's health-care reform, accelerating the pace of reform as well.

Purpose and direction of the reform

The year 1997 is a dividing line in the history of China's health-care reform. By that year, the first round of China's reform, which was started in the mid-1980s, had largely achieved its mission to enhance the supply volume of health services, reinforce the vigor and vitality of health organs, and mitigate the difficulties in seeing doctors, getting hospitalized, and receiving operations. By the end of 1996, the total number of ward beds in China had grown to 2.0965 million from 1.4124 million at the end of 1984, an increase of 48.44 percent, and the total number of health specialists in China had climbed to 5.419 million from 4.214 million, a 28.6 percent increase. Within 10 years, the health sector had largely alleviated the short supply of basic health resources, and greatly mitigated those difficulties suffered by the Chinese people in getting proper hospital care and receiving operations.

However, the reform is a dialectic one featuring old defects being removed, while new ones are being born. The reform of the early 1990s, which was intended to enhance the supply capabilities and efficiency of medical institutions, has worked out some preliminary results. In the meantime, the diagnostic and therapeutic technologies of Chinese medical institutions have been quickly enhanced and the quality of medical services has been gradually improved. Rapid improvements also took place in market supply capabilities and the prices of medical services soared as well. From 1991 to 1996, the outpatient/emergent treatment expenses per time and hospital expenses per time posted by general hospitals at county level or above were 30.82 percent and 31.13 percent, respectively, on an annual basis. Hence, complaints from all those sectors bearing such medical costs, that is from government, enterprises and public institutions, and those people not covered by the traditional health security system. Meanwhile, as the policy of reform and opening up is carried forward, the national economy has been growing rapidly and the general public has demanded better quality medical services. Furthermore, an increasing number of people have begun to seek high-end medical services, while difficulties in accessing superior health resources have emerged. Great changes have taken place in terms of the challenges and major tasks that the reform faces, and there has been a radical change in the purpose of the reform. This change is largely manifest in the "Decision of the Central Committee of the Communist Party of China and the State Council with Regard to Reform and Development of Health System." This edict has made it clear that the reform aims to enhance the vigor and vitality of the health services, mobilize the initiatives of health institutions and specialists, improve quality and increase efficiency, serve the Chinese people's need for better health care, and serve the country's need for realizing modernization with socialist features.

After the purpose of the reform is determined, the key issue determining whether the direction of such a reform is correct is how to deal with the relationship between the market and the government. According to a report by scholars with the Development Research Centre of the State Council, the root cause of the failure of the health-care reform is that "the model of commercialization and market operation went against common rules of health development," and the next-step of the reform must "focus on reinforcing government obligations" (Topical Research Team of the Development Research Centre of the State Council 2005, Development Research Centre of the State Council 2005). However, according to those who hold opposite opinions, "there was never an excessive "market operation" in health reform. In fact, market forces only touched upon a tiny fraction of the health industry in China. Only by gradually removing systemic barriers and encouraging social resources to enter the health sector, can we make success in the health reform" (Zhou 2007).

At the Sixteenth Central Committee of the Communist Party of China (CPC) Conference in October 2006, the Central Government shaped the direction of health reform with the following goals: to safeguard public interest in public health; reinforce government obligations; tighten regulation and administration; establish an essential health-care system covering both urban and rural residents;

and to deliver safe, effective, convenient, and inexpensive public health and essential medical services to all. This is the first time in China's health development history that the direction was clearly set at the highest level. Not long after the conference, on 23 October 2006, President Hu Jintao delivered an important speech at the Thirty-fifth Plenary of the CPC Political Bureau, in which he reiterated the direction of health reform, re-emphasizing the public-interest nature of the health services. Throughout the year, the top leadership has continued to restate the public interest nature of the health system, thus putting an end to the debate over direction. As noted by one officer of the Ministry of Health, the health reform direction set in 1997 was correct and the reform failure was due to operational problems (Qian 2007).

Purpose, mode, and proposal of the reform

Since 1997, the promulgation of every significant policy for health-care reform has been accompanied by an in-depth study into the main contradictions in the particular domain under review. Such a course of action features not only a step-by-step clarification of the objectives, steps, means, and methods of various measures of health-care reform, but also a systematization, consummation, clarification, and formation of common understanding of the objective, mode, system, and framework of the reform into the entire health system.

In 2000, based on the reform into the basic health insurance system for workers and staff members in urban areas, all local governments in China initiated local reforms for rural and urban residents, and pledged "to offer relatively satisfactory medical services at relatively low costs, and endeavour to meet the multitudes' demands for basic medical service" (Wang 2000). This local policy stated, for the first time and in a systematic way, that the reform of the health system must always be combined with governmental supervision and adoption of a market-oriented mechanism. It added, "It is necessary to separate political affairs from other affairs, separate management from business operations, separate prescribing from dispensing, and conduct classified management over profit-oriented and non-profit medical organizations" (The Decision of the CPC on Key Issues Related to Establishing Socialist Harmonious Society 2006).

After 2001, the country initiated its reform of the health system for rural areas, the new rural cooperative medical scheme (NCMS), and the reform of the medical assistance system for rural areas, in succession. It also accelerated its pace in implementing the disease prevention and control system and health supervision system, and in reforming the health service for communities in urban areas on a trial basis. The adjustments into and reform of medical service charges, and endeavors to straighten out drug production and distribution, were carried forward more gradually. Unfortunately, the above stated reforms have not been able to mitigate the difficulties in accessing medical services, partly due to their faulty design, poor organization and implementation, or failure in generating due social benefits. After 2004, there were increasing outcries from all sections of the society about exorbitant medical charges and the State Council addressed the issue as a prominent problem in China's socio-economic scene. Since then, both the government and the public at large began to review and evaluate China's health system reform over the past two decades in a systematic and objective manner. This debate revealed the institutional and structural contradictions of the country's health system, explored from new angles the controversial objective of the reform, and thus shed more light on the purpose, mode, system, and framework of China's reform. In June 2006, the China Network for Training and Research in Health Economics and Financing put forward, for the first time, a reform blueprint featuring "universal essential health services," and designed, in a systematic way, an institutional framework consisting of three basic systems – health service, health security, and essential drugs. "The Decision of the CPC on Key Issues Related to Establishing Socialist Harmonious Society," passed by the Sixth Plenary Session of the Sixteenth Central Committee of the Communist Party of China, pointed out that "providing better medical and health care and enhancing the people's health level are major tasks in regard to construction of a harmonious society." It also stated that "the objective of the reform into the health system is to strike up an essential health-care system covering urban and rural residents." (The Decision of the CPC on Key Issues Related to Establishing Socialist Harmonious Society. Available online at http://www.china.com.cn/policy/txt/2006 10/18/content_7252336. htm (accessed October 18, 2006).)

After the objective and mode of the reform were clarified, the debate then turned to the proposal for the reform. Some have opted for the UK model, some for the German Model. The Ministry of Health (MOH), National Development and Reform Commission (NDRC), Ministry of Finance (MOF), and Ministry of Labour and Social Security (MOLSS) held different viewpoints on how to organize and implement this strategy as a whole. In the national health conference held in 2007, the MOH took the lead in putting forward a package of reform proposals, which was hailed by the media as the "blueprint" for the next phase of the reform. After this proposal was put forward, arguments were immediately triggered between the Ministry of Health, Ministry of Finance, and Ministry of Labour and Social Security.[1] The debate focused mainly on three aspects, namely financial input for the essential health-care system, supply side or demand side, and how to define essential medical care. According to preliminary estimates by the health reform task force of the MOH, government needs to spend RMB Yuan 260 billion to finance free delivery of essential medical services to all. The MOF challenged this assessment, arguing that it might open a can of worms. On the second aspect, of whether government spending on community services should go to the demand side or the supply side, the MOH scheme advocated for subsidies to the supply side as the government offers free essential services, but MOLSS stated that such a practice may have serious quality concerns. As for who would and how they might, define essential medical services, the MOH called for the most essential medical drugs and treatment to be delivered free of charge to all. MOH also proposed to draw up a list of essential medical services and drugs to be offered and disease types to be treated free of charge. However, MOLSS argued that there would be many technical difficulties in defining essential medical care and that system loopholes would be inevitable in deciding who should be recipients.

However, as we can see from its track record on reform, China has to step onto a path of reform with its own characteristics, instead of copying any foreign mode. This is because China has a population of 1.3 billion people, with a per capita GDP of only just over US$2,000. The health system of China shall not follow the UK model (the governmental budget covers the entire costs of health services to citizens), the German model (rural and urban residents are forced to take up social health insurance in a uniform way), or the US model (residents take up commercial insurance in order to have access to health services).

Design and implementation of the reform

The reform and development of the health-care system involves a number of functional departments of the government. Only when Central Government and local governments, at all levels, play designer, organizer and implementer roles in taking care of and boosting the health cause, will it be possible to insure that the predetermined objective of the reform is accomplished. Since China's initial adoption of its policy of reform and opening up, the design and implementation of the health reform have undergone three important stages of development. The first stage, from the mid-1980s to 1996, featured learning and imitation. In this stage, China conducted its health reform by copying its experience in reforming the economic system, focusing on reform of the operating mechanism of health institutions, while neglecting the reform into the management mechanism governing the entire health industry. The second stage, from 1997 to 2005, featured tentative explorations. In this stage, health reform was not planned in a comprehensive, creative, and innovative way. Since 2006, the design and train of thought for implementation have undergone a change from "reform of single departments" to "reform through multi-departmental coordination." Moreover, increasing prominence has been given to the necessity for government supervision of overall design, organization, and implementation, while, from the very start of the design of the reform, attention has been paid to the purpose, completeness, creativity, and dependence of this reform. In September of 2006, under the direct leadership of the State Council, the Ministry of Health and over 10 commissions and ministries, including the National Development and Reform Commission, the Ministry of Finance and the Ministry of Labour and Social Security, formed a health-care reform coordination team, which manifests this change to a certain degree.

Practical evolution of China's health reform since 1997

Reform of basic medical insurance for urban employees

In 1997, the State Council announced that it would spend about three years in enabling a majority of state-owned middle/large-sized enterprises that were not making profits to step out of their financial plight and strike up a modern enterprise system. In order to realize this objective, it is necessary to provide laid-off workers and staff members with a guarantee of a minimum living standard, including basic medical services. However, in relative terms the then medical insurance system for urban employees lagged behind the needs. As of the end of 1997, only 3.6 million of those workers, staff members, and retired employees of state-owned enterprises, or 2.5 percent of the entire labor force in China, had taken part in the reform. Even if we take into account those workers, staff members, and retired employees of enterprises who were covered by the social pool for major diseases, the reform had included only 11.3 percent of those workers and staff members in urban areas. Therefore, at that time, the reform of the basic medical insurance system for urban employees was an urgent task. Meanwhile, the traditional free medical service system and Medicare system were unable to perform as well as they used to. According to statistics, in 1997 the total medical expenses of workers and staff members in China was RMB Yuan 77.37 billion, being 29 times that allocated in 1978 (when China initially put into force her policy of reform and opening up), registering an annual growth rate of 19 percent. However, in the same period, China's financial revenue had an annual growth rate of only 11 percent. On top of that, unreasonable medical expenses had taken up about 20 to 30 percent of the medical expenses of workers and staff members, indicating an excessive waste of money. Therefore, after having conducted trial work for several years, the Chinese government launched a basic medical insurance system for urban employees in 1998.

Compared to the traditional labor protection and Medicare system, the basic medical insurance system for urban employees emphasized fund raising and fee management. First, the cost of basic medical insurance premiums is shared by employers and workers and staff members (specifically, the amount of those premiums payable by employers is about six percent of the total wages and salaries to workers and staff members, while the amount of those premiums paid by workers and staff members is usually two percent of their wages and salaries). The rates were mainly based on the actual circumstances at that time. According to the statistical data for 1996 and 1997, workers and staff members in China spent nearly 10 percent of their wages and salaries on their medical expenses. Among others, the total amount of those medical expenses covered by the financial departments and enterprises was about 7.8 percent of the total amount of wages and salaries to workers and staff members. If we exclude those medical expenses incurred by retired employees who do not fall within the coverage of basic medical insurance and those incurred by industrial injuries and childbirth, this percentage would be reduced to about six percent. That portion of medical expenses to be undertaken by workers and staff members is set at two percent of their wages and salaries, after considering the economic capabilities and psychological thinking of most workers and staff members. Second, the basic medical insurance system for urban employees requires the insurance premiums to be paid jointly by social funds and individual funds; a social fund and individual accounts must be established in order for employers and workers and staff members to pay basic medical insurance premiums. In this way, it is possible to realize mutual benefits and overall planning of medical insurance funds, mitigate risks, and balance out the financial burdens so as to contribute to social equality.

In recent years, the basic medical insurance system for urban employees has been proceeding smoothly. By March 2007, this system had already covered up to 162 million workers and staff members in urban areas. Other types of social insurance directly related to the people's health have been expanding coverage too. For instance, the total number of persons to have taken up work-related injury insurance and that of persons taking up childbirth insurance, reached 104.07 million and 66.32 million, respectively.

Reform of medical care and the drug system for urban areas

In 2000, the reform into medical care and the drug system made breakthroughs. In February, the General Office of the State Council handed down the Guiding Opinion with Regard to Reform of the Medical Care and Medicine System, which was drafted by the eight commissions and ministries, listed above. This clarified the objective and guiding principle of the next stage of health reform for urban areas. From 24–26 July, the State Council held a national working conference on the basic medical insurance system for urban employees and the reform to the medical care and drug system in Shanghai. In this conference, participants emphasized the necessity of carrying out, in a well-rounded way, the reform of the basic medical insurance system for urban employees, the reform of the medical care and drug system for urban areas, and the reform of the drug production and distribution system. This was to be carried out by means of establishing a sharing mechanism and ushering in a competition mechanism, with the aim of setting up, within two or three years, a medical care and drug system for urban areas that meets the requirements of a socialist market-oriented economy. Following the Shanghai conference, the Ministry of Health worked with the relevant departments to jointly publish relevant documents outlining stipulations on classification-based management over medical institutions in urban areas, policy for subsidizing the health cause, and control of hospital revenues from the sale of medicines apart from control of hospital expenditure on medicines. There were also guidelines on taxation policy governing medical care and health organizations; management of medical service charges; control of drug prices; and centralized purchase of medicine by medical organizations through public bidding; identification of and supervision and management over qualifications of medicine bidding agencies, patients' selection of doctors, standardization of chargeable medical service items, and methods for estimation of medical service costs. In this way, a relatively complete framework of policies for reform of the medical care and medicine system for urban areas has been established, providing concrete guidance and policies for local governments in their reform processes.

The train of thought governing the reform into the medical care and medicine system for urban areas is "summarization of proven experience." The primary purpose of the reform into the basic medical insurance system is to enable residents to bear the costs of medical treatment. The purpose of the reform into the medicine production and distribution system is to standardize the drugs market, and enable patients to obtain quality medicines at affordable prices. The purpose of the reform of the medical service system is to prevent medical expenses from escalating and to enable the general public to bear medical expenses.

The direction of the reform into the medical care and medicine system for urban areas is correct. However, inadequate efforts have been made to address the coordination, interaction, and implementation issues. When designing the reforms for the medical care and medicine system, health security system, and medicine system, the commonalities between them were not well balanced, giving rise to poor interaction. As for the health security system, efforts are made to use the government's powers and limited resources to balance out the relations among hospitals, patients, and medicine dealers. In terms of the hospitals, they do not maintain smooth information exchanges with the other parties and are thus unable to develop mutual trust. Regarding medicine dealers, due to a poor legal system, it is hardly possible for them to employ standard market-oriented practices. For instance, kickbacks given by sales representatives to doctors have been a headache for years. As a matter of fact, these three reforms involve the interests of multiple parties and the competent authorities have not worked out specific policies to balance out their interests, or established a mechanism to coordinate relations among the parties. If the contradictions among these interest groups cannot be solved effectively, the final "victim" will definitely be the majority of citizens. According to the findings of a 2002 survey by the Chinese Consumers' Association, the most dissatisfying aspect in the eyes of the general public is poor transparency in relation to medical expenses, and the most dissatisfying commodity was medicine (Jin and Zhang 2005).

The reform measures implemented since 1998 have, to a certain degree, checked the excessive growth of medical expenses and allowed for some preliminary results. As per statistics of the medical industry, from 1990 to 1998 the annual growth rate of the average cost of each person-time in the outpatient department, and that of the average medical expense of each in-patient in general hospitals, were 25.9 percent and 23.7 percent respectively. In 1999, these two indicators were lowered to 14.8 percent and 11.3 percent respectively, and in 2000 they were reduced to 8.6 percent and 6.7 percent respectively. Before the reform, the annual growth rate of the average medicine cost of each person-time in the outpatient department, and that of the average medicine cost of each patient leaving the hospital, were 24.5 percent and 22.0 percent respectively. In 1999, these two indicators fell to 11.2 percent and 6.6 percent respectively, and in 2000, the same two indicators dropped to 6.1 percent and 4.3 percent respectively.

Reform of the health system for rural areas

At the end of the last century, the main problems in China's agriculture sector and its development of an agricultural economy were the then slow growth of peasants' income and the unstable yield of crops. To solve these problems local governments made bold efforts to readjust their agricultural structures, speed up modernization, and initiate a reform of agricultural taxes and charges, in order to mitigate peasants' burdens and increase their income. Amelioration of the medical care and health of peasants, allowing disease-afflicted peasants (especially those suffering severe diseases) to receive timely medical treatment, has had a significant impact in accelerating the ability of peasants to get rid of poverty and embrace wealth, and on stabilizing agricultural production. The health scenario in China's rural areas has already made great progress, which has been widely acknowledged by the rest of the world. From 1949 to 2001, the country saw the mortality rate of rural infants drop to 33.8 percent from 200 percent, and the mortality rate of rural pregnant and lying-in women dropped to 61.9/100,000 from 1500/100,000, while the average life expectancy of the rural population climbed to 69.55 years in 2000 from 35 years in 1949. On the other hand, the health reform in rural areas has also encountered difficulties and problems in the course of its evolution. These problems and difficulties include: the slow improvement of main health indicators of rural residents, a widening gap between urban residents and rural residents in terms of the level of accessible medical care, lack of an effective medical security system for peasants, lack of resistance to severe diseases, and vulnerability in terms of getting thrown into, or stuck in, poverty due to sickness. In certain places, these difficulties and problems have prevailed (Table 11.3). These problems have affected the development of the rural economy and social stability in rural areas, impeded peasants from shedding poverty and pursuing a higher standard of standard. In short, it is imperative to reform the health system for rural areas.

In order to further intensify and improve the health work in rural areas on the basis of the 1997 "Decision of the Central Committee of the CPC and the State Council with Regard to the Reform and Development of the Health System" and the "Guiding Opinion on the Reform and Development of the Health Cause for Rural Areas," approved by the State Council in 2001, the National Working Conference on Rural Health Work was held in October 2002. It was the first conference of its kind convened in the name of the State Council since 1949 when the People's Republic of China was founded. In this conference, the "Decision of the Central Committee of the CPA and the State Council with Regard to Further Intensifying the Health Work for Rural Areas" was passed. In order to better carry out the policies and measures put forward under the Decision of 2002, the General Office of the State Council finalized seven auxiliary documents covering the development

Table 11.3 Analysis of reasons for poverty of rural residents (%)

	1998	*2003*	*Change*
Lack of labor force	23.1	27.1	+4.0
Disease or injury	21.6	33.4	+11.8
Poor natural conditions	16.9	17.2	+0.3
Artificial factor	10.6	8.5	-2.1
Other factors	27.7	13.8	-13.9

Source: Report on the Second National Investigation and Survey of Health Service 2007.

of the primary health service in rural areas, management of rural doctors, urban forces' medical support to rural areas, policy of subsidizing the health service in rural areas, fostering of health specialists for rural areas and construction of health teams, reform and management of health organs in rural areas, and establishment of the new rural cooperative medical scheme (NCMS).

Since 2003, 31 provinces, autonomous regions, and municipalities in China have selected some counties under their respective jurisdiction to conduct the NCMS on a trial basis. On a volunteer basis, peasants may take part in these trials which are jointly financed by the finance authorities of the Central Government and local governments, as well as the peasants themselves. This system is principally intended to offer subsidies to those peasants stricken by severe diseases. In December 2005, the "Certain Opinions of the Central Committee of the CPC and the State Council with Regard to Boosting the Construction of Socialist New Rural Areas" was issued. Since then, the new rural cooperative medical system has been implemented at an accelerated pace on a trial basis in selected regions. In 2006, the Central Government decided that its finance authorities, and those of local governments, would allocate more subsidies to those peasants covered by this system. The Central Government also determined to put this system in place throughout the rural areas of China by 2008.

Over the past few years, in terms of rural areas, the above policies have boosted the construction of health infrastructure and level of equipment, increased the number of health specialists, constructed the new rural cooperative medical system, and improved the medical assistance system. Since 2003, the new rural cooperative medical system has achieved marked results. Holistically speaking, the country has seen the new rural cooperative medical system standardized and operating smoothly on a day-to-day basis, while the level of health service available in rural areas has been increased. In particular, the new rural cooperative medical system has been linked effectively with the rural medical assistance system, in order to mitigate peasants' medical burdens and alleviate the possibility of peasants getting stuck in poverty due to sickness.

Major contradictions and problems of health-care reform and development

Contradictions between the objective requirements of health development and the health system present fundamental inconsistencies in the health sector that shape the nature and content of major contradictions in this field. The major contradiction in China's health sector is that of ever increasing health needs and insufficient health service delivery, which results in the following main problems:

There is a growing gap in health services between urban and rural China, and among different regions and different population groups

During the period of China's Tenth Five-Year National Development Program (from 2001 to 2005), with its accelerated urbanization process, reorganization of rural townships and towns, and expansion of migrant movement, big urban hospitals began to grow rapidly, with the number of hospitals with more than 800 beds, up from 149 to 284. In contrast, the number of rural township health centers (THCs), beds, health professionals, and visits in rural China kept declining, with beds reduced by 57,000, and outpatient visits by 140 million persons over the period. In 2004, cities contributed 65.1 percent of total health expenditure and the countryside contributed 34.9 percent. By the end of 2005, eastern, central, and western China had, respectively, 1.74, 1.37, and 1.39 practicing doctors per 1000 people, and 2.81, 2.23, and 2.24 beds per 1000 people, revealing more resources in eastern China. Such disparity also exists in terms of quality, as is indicated by the concentration of large equipment in eastern regions. In this context, difficulties in getting health services are most in evidence in big urban hospitals and remote rural areas.

The overall supply of quality health resources is inadequate, and the health service system at grassroots level remains weak

Currently, the major contradictions in the health sector are between insufficient resources supply and ever increasing health demands, and between diversified needs and single-channel supply. Severe shortages of quality health resources, remains a chronic challenge. Despite huge government efforts in promoting urban community health services, consolidating the rural health service network, and launching the NCMS pilot, urban community health services and rural THCs remain vulnerable – in terms of human resources, housing, and equipment as well as the service delivery model – and thus fail to function effectively as grassroots health institutions. At present, only one-quarter of the staff in urban community health centers have a bachelor's or higher degree. In rural THCs, only 17 percent of the staff received junior college or higher education and there is a serious shortage of general practitioners (GPs). In 2006, total visits to health institutions in China numbered 2.447 billion, of which 83 million were to community health centers and 701 million to rural THCs, representing only 32.04 percent of the national total.

Medical expenses have been skyrocketing

From 1980 to 2005 health expenditure in China grew to RMB Yuan 866 billion from RMB Yuan 14.3 billion with the out-of-pocket proportion increasing to 52.2 percent from 21.2 percent. From 1997 to 2005, the annual average growth rate of medical expenses in terms of per-time access to outpatient and emergency medical service in hospitals at county and above-county levels, and that of average medical expenses in terms of per-time access to in-patient medical service in hospitals at county and above-county levels, was 8.07 percent and 6.20 percent respectively. Both rates where slightly lower than the growth rate of per capita disposable income of urban residents (9.28 percent) in the same period, but higher than the growth rate of the average net income of rural residents per annum (5.69 percent) in the same period. In reality, the general public feels that medical services are getting more and more expensive (Figure 11.1).

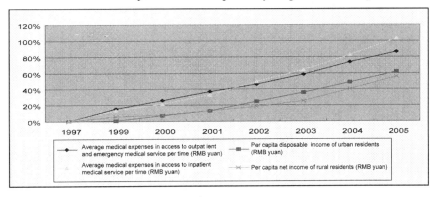

Figure 11.1 Cost increase in comprehensive hospitals administered by the Health Department.

Source: *Health Statistics Yearbook of China* 2006.

An incomplete medical protection system leaves many people covering their own medical expense

In the absence of a universal primary health-care system, development of social medical insurance is stumbling, and coverage of NCMS is still shallow. To date, the medical insurance system has covered less than 200 million urban employees, leaving urban laid-off workers, the unemployed, minimum wage earners, migrant workers, and children with no insurance having to pay out of their own pockets to see doctors. Even for insured employees, out-of-pocket payment is still the majority of their medical expenditures. In rural China, 685 million farmers enrolled in NCMS, but the coverage is still low and farmers can only get a small proportion of their medical costs reimbursed. Health insurance organizations, the supposed "agents for patients" that regulate inappropriate behavior on the part of providers, do not have effective constraint measures in place.

The government has not poured enough funds into health

Medical institutions have to rely largely on the proceeds of medicine sales to survive, and have even become profit-oriented, striving to make huge profits out of the sale of medicine. In 2005, the Chinese government budgeted RMB Yuan 155.253 billion for health (or 17.93 percent of the country's total medical expenses), which was far below (more than 30 percent) the level recorded in the early 1980s. Pursuant to the statistical data of WHO, based on two indicators – the percentage taken up by the public health expenditure in GDP and the percentage taken up by the public health expenditure in the total health expenditure – the Chinese government's investment in health is far below the average level of the international community (Table 11.4). In 2004, the financial allocation made by the Chinese government was only seven percent of the total revenue of hospitals, and the other 93 percent

Table 11.4 International comparisons in public health spending (2003)

Item	China	Low-income countries	Lower-income countries	Higher-income income countries	High-income countries
Public health spending/ GDP (%)	2.0	1.3	2.5	3.7	6.7
Public health spending/ total health expenditure (%)	36.2	29.1	43.7	57.2	63.9

Source: Development and Research Centre of the State Council 2005.

of the revenue was earned by hospitals on their own. Profit orientation as such is the root cause of the exorbitant medical expenses.

There is disorder in drug approval, production, and distribution

In 2005 China approved 11,086 applications for drug registration, for both clinical experiment and production. Among them were 1,113 applications for new drugs, 1,198 for change of dosage or form, and 8075 for reproduction of similar drugs, demonstrating the weak link as abuse of the approval system. In this context, many "new" drugs appear that merely have different names. In fact, to escape regulations on price reduction, many pharmaceutical companies create "new" drugs by changing the name, dosage, or form of existing drugs and charge the patients more.

The country has not yet achieved a multilateral setting for its health cause, or realized the objective of its health reform "to usher in a competition mechanism into the health domain."

In 2005, for-profit health institutions (mainly small ones like clinics, outpatient offices, and nursing stations) accounted for 54 percent of the total. The number of beds, outpatient visits, and in-patient episodes, were, respectively, 4 percent, 3.3 percent, and 2.5 percent of the national total. The number of for-profit hospitals was 1,477, or 16 percent of the national total. Even in Zhejiang Province, where the private sector is developed, there were only a few large for-profit hospitals. As for-profit hospitals are mostly private, and non-profit ones mostly public, it is clear that public hospitals remain dominant in China.

Inventory resources have been utilized at a low efficiency level, and residents' access to medical services has appeared unreasonable

Despite a rapid increase in the overall total, health resources are not efficiently utilized. The number of outpatient and emergency visits nationwide declined from

2.55 billion in 1980 to 2.3 billion in 2005. In the absence of adequate patient-loads, township health centers and community health services are under-utilized. In large or medium cities, most patients are crowded into tertiary hospitals; the primary and secondary hospitals encounter hardship in surviving since their resources are idling. In large and medium hospitals, haphazard procurement of large equipment has also led to inefficient utilization.

Doctor-patient tension and increasing disputes created major concerns for social harmony. Only 2.7 percent of doctors and nurses and 13.2 percent of patients and their relatives are satisfied with the current level of doctor-patient relations, and 62.3 percent of doctors and nurses are dissatisfied with the current relationship. According to the statistical data for 100 hospitals in a survey conducted by the Chinese Doctors Association, over the past three years hospitals witnessed 66 disputes per year on average, and on average there were 5.42 incidents of patients damaging hospitals, and five incidents of doctors being injured by patients (Yao 2007).

The reform into the management and administration of the health sector has lagged behind

Too often multiple managerial authorities give orders concurrently while failing to coordinate well with each other. This has become an important institutional factor impeding the reform and development of the health system. At present, China's management and administration mechanism is a multi-department-led one, and has been a second-to-none option globally, under which a dozen governmental authorities are jointly responsible for managing and administering the health sector. The defects in this mechanism have been exposed on a daily basis. To be specific, under such a multi-department-led mechanism, it is impossible to effectively integrate the ongoing human, material, and financial resources for the sake of forming a unified force conducive to improving the people's health level. Neither is this mechanism favorable to setting up a complete, highly efficient health system nationwide. When it comes to design and selection of a reform proposal, more light has been shed on the defects existing in this mechanism. To be concrete, it is hard to coordinate the decisions made by these authorities, so decision-making with regard to health issues is often delayed. In this sense, the ongoing management and administration of the health sector has become an insurmountable barrier to the establishment of a new Medicare and health system for the benefit of the general public. Therefore an imperative task is that of reforming China's ongoing management and administration of the health service.

Policy orientation of China's health reform

It is necessary to clarify governments' function, and to fulfill governments' obligations. Further clarification is needed on the roles of central and local governments in leading health reform and development, and further enhancement of the three basic functions of government in developing plans, securing funding, and regulating the industry. Governments at all levels are expected to gradually fulfill their obligations in health development, particularly in regard to balancing several major obligations. These include the promotion of health reform and innovation, rationalization of the health administrative system, improvement of the public finance system to increase spending on health, and building healthy and harmonious doctor–patient relations.

It is essential to put in order the management and administration mechanism, optimize the functions of governing authorities, make timely adjustments in the management and administration mechanism, streamline the reform proposal, and put an end to the situation of having many leaders in multi-departments. Only one managerial body is necessary to exercise all the managerial functions necessary to reduce operating costs and to enhance operating efficiency significantly. This is determined by the coupling mechanism functioning both inside the health sector, and in relation to other sectors. Therefore, to enable the reform of the health system to maximize its functions it is necessary for a single entity to formulate the proposal for this reform. This requires a reform of the management and administration mechanism of the medical care and medicine system. It also requires bringing health security, medicine distribution, and supervision over medical services into a systematic design that optimizes all functions, thus allowing all the component parts to restrict, rely on, and boost one another. In this way, it is possible to establish a dynamic and balanced relationship, enable health reform to give equal regard to the quality and safety of medical services, control medical expenses, and ensure fairness in access to medical services in a well-balanced manner so as to maximize the overall functions of the system. Such practises are not only suitable for China's national circumstances and able to solve the core problems arising from China's reform of the health system, but have also been successful in the international arena.

It is advisable to consolidate the public health system and to reinforce the urban and rural health-service systems. Efforts in this regard should include the establishment and improvement of the public health emergency response mechanism and information surveillance network system, and the consolidation of the surveillance system for major communicable disease outbreak and public health emergencies, medical treatment information system, and command system for public health emergency response. These measures would serve to comprehensively build up capacity in the surveillance, response, treatment, supervision, command, and decision-making capabilities in case of a public health emergency. The urban and rural community health-care system serves as the basis of China's national health-service system, consisting mainly of community health centers and service stations in the cities, and township health centers and village clinics in the countryside. Construction of the community health-care system shall be guided by regional health plans, mainly through reorganization of existing health resources, and transformed from grassroots medical institutions such as government run primary and secondary hospitals and medical institutions affiliated to state-owned enterprises. Where existing health resources are insufficient, government can either finance the establishment of urban and rural community health service institutions, or encourage private capital to finance these services and then contract them in order to meet public needs.

It is essential to establish a multi-tiered health security system. Given the great disparity between urban and rural China, and among different population groups, any single health protection model would only meet the needs of certain groups. In this context, a multi-tiered and multi-form health protection system, covering all Chinese citizens, will be most compatible to Chinese conditions. This system will consist of four components: a rural basic health protection system centered around NCMS, which seeks to cover most rural residents, improve access to health services by rural farmers, and alleviate the social concerns of disease-induced poverty, mainly among rural people; an urban basic medical protection system based on BMI, which will be open to all urban employees; an urban basic medical protection system, open to urban residents without employment and delivering medical protection to them; and a medical assistance system that will effectively offer the poor access to basic medical services and cover all poor people left without coverage from the previous three-tiered system. The latter component seeks to reduce the financial burdens on the poor, ease social contradictions, and foster social equity (Figure 11.2).

NCMS will strive to meet the ambitious goal of covering all farmers before 2010, while at the same time continue deepening the benefit package, so that the financing gap between NCMS and BMI will gradually narrow, ultimately allowing a universal medical insurance system to become a reality.

It is necessary to establish a national essential drug system, strengthen medical service regulation, and rectify drug production and distribution with the aim of guaranteeing essential drugs to the general public. An essential drug category compatible with essential health care shall be developed following the principles of necessity, safety, effectiveness, reasonable prices, and convenience, which will serve as basis for the national essential drug system. To meet this goal, government initiatives will emphasize four aspects. First, develop an essential drug category that designates production, consistent prices, concentrated procurement, and unified delivery. All drugs used in rural medical institutions and CHS institutions

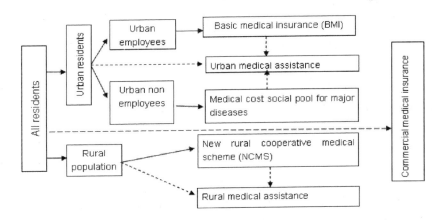

Figure 11.2 Urban and rural health security system.

must fall within the scope of this essential drug category, while hospitals must also fix a proportion of essential drugs on their drug lists to guarantee the availability of essential drugs to the general public. Second, rectify drug production and distribution orders with stricter controls on access, production, and distribution. In addition, reform drug price management to insure reasonable prices, and ban over-pricing. Third, consolidate the construction of drug supply and regulation networks[2] in rural China. A breakthrough will be made in expanding the regulatory system, thus streamlining supply channels, improving safeguard measures, and serving NCMS on the principles of "consolidation, intensification, expansion, and enhancement." Fourth, promote reform and innovation in the drug regulatory system, and establish and improve a long-term effective mechanism to protect drug use safety for the general public (Zhao 2007).

It is necessary to adjust the ownership structure of medical organs. This includes carrying forward the reform into state-run hospitals, actively boosting the adjustment of the ownership structure of medical care and health organs, and encouraging, supporting, and guiding the development of those medical organs that have not adopted a public ownership system. It is also necessary to break up the monopoly by state-run medical organs, usher in a competitive mechanism to check the excessive increase of medical expenses, quicken the pace in reforming state-run hospitals, and give state-run hospitals more social responsibilities and capabilities in serving the general public's need for health services. The overall objectives of the reform in state-run hospitals include boosting the reform of the management and administrative mechanism governing medical organs, allowing medical organs to be managed by local governments without being affiliated to the authorities, and reforming the operating mechanism of state-run medical organs. Others include reforming the "use of proceeds of medicine sales to cover hospitals'" shortage of operating funds' mechanism, separating the proceeds of medicine sales from hospitals' operating receipts, and preventing doctors from over prescribing, while enhancing the salaries of medical personnel commensurate with their skills and labor value. It is also necessary to reduce the charges on the use of large-sized examination devices in hospitals, standardize the income distribution mechanism governing medical specialists and the management over income and expenditure of state-run medical organs, and prevent state-run medical organs from being overly profit-oriented.

The history of reform and development of China's health system is a record of struggle against various difficulties in seeking medical service. When old problems are overcome, new ones arise. Over the past decade, China has achieved unprecedented results in mitigating the setbacks suffered by citizens in gaining access to health services and also encountered an unprecedented amount of challenges and opportunities. The basic tasks in the following stage of China's health reform are to keep up the good work, seize the opportunities, stand up to challenges, and gradually solve those practical, concrete difficulties in accessing medical services, as well as to realize sustainable and healthy development of China's health service. Indeed, ameliorating the medical care and health conditions of the people and enhancing their health levels is not only the ultimate goal of health reform, but also one of the ultimate goals of China's socio-economic reform. The experience of reform proves, that so long as we meticulously assess and learn the lessons, adhere to the correct direction of health reform, and formulate and put into force a broad proposal for reform that fits into the actual national conditions of China, our health-care reform process is bound to weather the storm and achieve success.

Notes

1 Wang *et al.* (2007).
2 The two networks are the Medicine Supervision Network in Rural Areas and Rural Medicine Supply Network.

References

China Health Economy Study and Training Network (2007). Training documents.

Economic News of The 21st Century. January 23, 2007. Available online at www.sina.com. cn (accessed January 23, 2007).

General Office of the State Council. Available online at http://www.gov.cu (accessed March 19, 2007).

Jin, Yonghong and Zhang, Peng. Hot and cold points of three reforms. Available online at http://health.people.com.cn/GB/14740/21474/3677767.html (accessed September 08, 2005).

Minimum Living Subsidy Department of the Ministry of Civil Affairs. People's Republic of China. (2006). *Analysis Report on Medical Succour Work Implemented on a Trial Basis in Urban Areas.* May.

Ministry of Health. People's Republic of China. (2006) China Health Statistics Yearbook 2006. Beijing: National Bureau of Statistics.

Qian, Haoping (2007). Health Minister Gao Qiang: the health reform direction set in 1997 was correct. *The Beijing News.* March 05, 2007.

Report on the Second National Investigation and Survey of Health Service. Available online at www.moh.gov.cn/open/statistics/ronhs98/ronhs21.doc (accessed May 05, 2007).

The Decision of the CPC on Key Issues Related to Establishing Socialist Harmonious Society. Available online at http://www.china.com.cn/policy/txt/2006-10/18/content_7252336. htm (accessed October 18, 2006).

Topical Research Team of the Development Research Centre of the State Council (2005). Evaluation of and suggestions on China's reform into her Medicare and health-care system. *China Development Review* supplement 1. Beijing

Wang, Shiling and Sun, Lei (2007). China's national medical security program to be launched on a trial basis: No more individual accounts will be set up. *Economic News of the 21st Century.* March 01, 2007.

Wang, Yantian (2000). The basic health insurance system for workers and staff members in urban areas and the medical and health system reform meeting. *Xinhua.* July 26, 2000. Available online at http://www.people.com.cn/GB/channel1/10/20000726/160509.html (accessed May 05, 2007).

Yao, Libo. (2007). *The government has to pay its due in helping to strike up a harmonious relationship between patients and doctors.* Online. Available at http://xinhuanet.com (accessed 09 March 2007).

Zhao, Hejuan (2007). The method for registration of new drugs to be promulgated by the end of this year, and redefine new drugs. *First Financial Daily.* February 09, 2007.

Zhao, Xuehua (2007). Hu Jintao: Building a harmonious society in co-construction and co-sharing. Available online at http://news.qq.com/a/20070307/003141.htm (accessed March 07, 2007).

Zhou, Qiren (2007). Expenditure medical expenses are not attributable to hospitals' market-oriented practices. *Shanghai Securities News*. February 05, 2007. Available online at http://news.china.com/zh_cn/finance/11009723/20070205/13921412.html (accessed May 05, 2007).

12 Educational policies

From expansion and equity to quality

Zhang Li

In the 1990s, at a time of rapid economic globalization, China had entered a new critical period of reform and opening up. China adapted its education policies to reflect the new era, in line with the Education for All (EFA) initiative promoted by international organizations.[1] A new enthusiasm for educational development arose in China. The 1997 Asian financial crisis had only an indirect effect on Chinese educational policies. China understood that to remain internationally competitive and nationally strong, human resources had to be developed through the development of the education sector. The financial crisis served to bolster the government's confidence in accelerating educational development. In the past 10 years, China pursued educational development, mobilized resources, and leaped forward, achieving remarkable results. Educational policies in the current century are different than those of the last: the government used to have unclear responsibilities in some aspects of the education sector but today has clear public service responsibilities. It moved away from its earlier emphasis on expanding the scale of educational services toward a new emphasis on equity and quality. China is marching toward the equalization of basic public education and toward the construction of a learning society that conforms to China's current situation. Educational development will provide strong support for sustainable development of the economy, politics, culture and society.

Review of concepts and impact of Chinese educational policies of the past 10 Years

Understanding Chinese educational policies of the past 10 years requires looking further back, to the "Guidelines for the Reform and Development of Education in China" issued in 1993. At that time, the Central Government's strategic educational goals for 2000 and beyond included universalizing nine years of compulsory education, eliminating illiteracy among youth and the middle-aged (sometimes referred to as the "two basics" approach), accelerating development of vocational education, enhancing key university disciplines, increasing public finance for education, and strengthening the construction of teaching contingents (State Education Commission 1994). In 1995 the National People's Congress adopted the unprecedented "Education Law" (Legislative Affairs Office of the Ministry of Education 2004) and the Central Government decided to pursue a strategy of invigorating the country through science and education (Jiang 2006, 1:428). This initiative opened the door for restructuring, popularizing and accelerating the development of the sector.

In 1997 the Fifteenth National Congress of the Communist Party of China laid out the overall arrangements for implementing the strategy (Jiang 2006, 2:25–26). In 1998, the State Council announced the strategy would be regarded as the primary task of the government, and established a leading group of scientific education with the premier as the group leader. In the same year, the Ministry of Education formulated the "Action Plan for Invigorating Education Towards the 21st Century and for 1998–2002." It was ratified by the State Council in 1999 (Ministry of Education. 1999). In June 1999, the Central Government held its third national conference on education since the reform and opening up and promulgated "Decisions on Deepening Educational Reform and Fully Promoting Quality-oriented Education," which promoted the new focus on quality-oriented education and proposed supportive measures such as reform of basic education, expansion of higher education, reform of the administrative system and the construction of teaching contingents (Ministry of Education 1999b).

In 2002, Sixteenth National Congress of the Communist Party of China included educational development among its four major targets in the overall construction of a prosperous society (Jiang 2006, 3:543). The documents from subsequent plenary sessions underscored the strategic position of education. The sixth plenary, in 2006, gave priority to developing education and promoting educational equity as important elements of a harmonious socialist society (Communist Party of China 2006). The State Council held conferences on basic education and rural education and two conferences on vocational education between 2001 and 2005 and approved the "2003–2007 Action Plan for Rejuvenating Education," formulated by the Ministry of Education (2004).[2] It put forth requirements for major policies aimed at resolving problems in educational development and at reforming the system. The educational progress made in China in the past 10 years was not only the result of constant improvement of state policies and laws but was also the result of a series of new policies issued by the Central Government at the turn of the century.

Developing education: a means for improving human resources

China used education policies to harness the power of the country's greatest resource – its people. Through educational development, China is transforming the world's largest population into an asset for progress. Table 12.1 shows that from 1997 to 2006, educational opportunities expanded remarkably as the total population grew from 1.236 billion to 1.314 billion (State Statistics Bureau 2007). As the population growth rate has dropped each year, the population of school-aged children eligible for, or subject to, compulsory education (primary school followed by junior middle school) decreased by 50 million. At the same time, however, the number of students receiving non-compulsory education has increased considerably. Therefore, the population receiving some type of educational services has increased from 311 million to 318 million. In 2006, there were 1.105 million doctoral and postgraduate students, 22.64 million undergraduate students, 42.96 million senior middle school students and secondary vocational school students, 60 million junior middle school students, 107 million primary school students, 22.60 million kindergarteners, and 58.17 million students receiving non-diploma education. Together, these statistics show that China has the world's largest scale education system (Ministry of Education 2007).[3] In the same period, 98 percent of the population was covered by the "two basics." Primary school enrollment rates reached nearly 100 percent, and the illiteracy rate among young and middle-aged people was less than 4 percent. The gross enrollment rate of junior and senior middle school students increased by about 20 percent over 1997, and reached 59.2 percent and 97 percent, respectively. The gross enrollment rate in higher education increased from 9.1 percent to 22 percent and entered a phase of mass education (Trow 1970).[4]

Other countries around the world have typically taken 20 to 30 years to universalize both primary school and junior middle school or to raise gross enrollment rates for higher education from 5 percent to 15 percent. For example, it took

Table 12.1 Survey of educational progress in China, 1997 and 2006

Indicator	1997	2006	Change between 1997 and 2006
Total enrollment in all levels and types of education*	311 million	318 million	+7 million
Illiteracy rate among youth and middle-aged people**	about 5.5%	<4%	-1.5 percentage point
Gross enrollment rate for pre-school education**	about 35%	42.5%	+7.5 percentage points
Net enrollment rate of primary schools	98.9%	99.3%	+0.4 percentage points
Gross enrollment rate of junior middle schools	87.1%	97.0%	+9.9 percentage points
Gross enrollment rate of senior middle schools	40.6%	59.2%	+18.6 percentage points
Gross enrollment rate of higher education	9.1%	22.0%	+12.9 percentage points

* Includes pre-school, primary, secondary, higher, and special education. These figures cover diploma and non-diploma programs.

** The illiteracy rate among young and middle-aged people and the enrollment rate of pre-school education in 1997 are estimates.

Sources: Department of Development and Planning of the Ministry of Education, *Education Statistical Report* (January 29, 2006); Department of Development and Planning of the Ministry of Education, *Educational Statistics Yearbook of China* (1997); Research Group, *Stride from a Country of Tremendous Population to a Country of Profound Human Resources* (2003), pp. 525, 535.

South Korea 15 years to achieve these goals. China, however, required only about 10 years. The forward leap in educational development in this period has made China the country with the largest labor force with at least a junior middle school level of education. The average amount of time the population spends in school rose from seven years in the mid-1990s to more than eight years today. The educational attainment of the labor force has improved remarkably, and the basic knowledge and skills levels of average citizens were enhanced considerably. In 2006, the per capita gross domestic product (GDP) in China was US$2,040. Meanwhile China's enrollment rates in primary, secondary and tertiary levels of education are equivalent to those in countries with a per capita GDP of at least US$3,000. Educational development laid a solid foundation for a prosperous Chinese society.

Deepening educational reform and promoting quality

Educational reform in the past 10 years has helped overcome the former rigidities of a highly centralized system. The centerpiece of reform has been adherence to multi-level administration by the government and the strengthening of the local government's responsibility for planning education as a whole. An amendment to a law in 2006 led to an administrative system in compulsory education where "under the leadership of the State Council, the provincial government plans and implements, and the county government takes chief responsibility."[5] In vocational education, the administrative system that has taken shape features "multi-level management, with chief responsibility of the local authorities, government planning and social participation." As a result, the partnership of government planning and market mechanisms has been somewhat enhanced. In the field of higher education, the "two-level management by the Central Government and provincial government, with provincial management in the lead" has been initially established. Through measures such as "joint construction, adjustment, cooperation and merging," the original 345 general universities subordinated to the various ministries or commissions under the State Council have been reduced to 111 and several comprehensive universities have been formed. This has promoted the construction of first-class research-oriented universities. Colleges and universities managed by provincial and local governments exceed 2,000, which has stimulated initiative among local governments and has helped meet the needs for regional development.

The direction of reforms to the input and operating systems of Chinese education reflects an attempt to tap the potential of the government and social forces. In the past 10 years, China established an educational input system that was based mainly on public financial support. Costs are shared and non-public funds are raised. The government takes the lead in running schools but various social forces also jointly run them. In 2006, there were 92,200 privately run across the country. Students enrolled in educational programs that award diplomas reached 23.13 million, accounting for 10 percent of government-run education. In some other countries, educational reforms and policies have aroused social unrest but this phenomenon has not occurred in China. Government-led reforms have generally been recognized and supported by schools and various interest groups. Through pilot efforts, China has identified effective ways for reducing costs and social risk while maintaining the stability of schools and society.

Quality has become the new focus of reform of Chinese education.[6] Much progress has already been achieved in this regard. Many regions have accumulated beneficial experience in pursuing comprehensive reforms for quality-oriented education. An orientation toward quality has also been promoted by the international community. A new round of reforms in curricula and teaching materials for basic education has raised scientific literacy, encouraged an innovative spirit, and promoted practical capabilities. In autumn 2005, all primary and junior middle schools in 30 provinces (autonomous regions and municipalities) began to implement new courses, and new courses were also rolled out in general senior middle schools in nine provinces (autonomous regions). Reform of the admissions system for colleges has been promoted. Reforms in examinations or evaluations, graduate employment, and logistics have also been carried out. More information and communications technologies are being used by the education system, and modern distance education for rural middle and primary schools is progressing smoothly. The quality of 13.25 million full-time teachers all over the country is steadily improving, and teachers' incomes have risen remarkably. Reforms are generally creating a more favorable environment for the development and implementation of quality-oriented education and are resulting in a larger cadre of well-rounded students.

Key points about policies for basic, vocational and higher education of the past 10 years

The education system in China is generally divided into four categories: basic education (nine years of compulsory education involving primary and junior middle schools as well as regular senior middle schools), vocational education (mainly secondary and advanced vocational education), higher education, and continuing education (adult education).[7]

Basic education: attaching great importance to popularizing compulsory education

The past 10 years were a watershed period for compulsory education in China. In the years leading up to 2000, China sought to accelerate the popularization of education popularization and promoted the "two basics." According to the United Nations Educational, Scientific and Cultural Organization's (UNESCO) *Education for All Global Monitoring Report 2005* (244–245), China ranked fifty-fourth on the Education for All Development Index and was second only to Mexico among the top nine countries with large populations. Compared to all 127 countries included in the index, China had a mid-level ranking.[8] After 2000, China sought to consolidate the "two basics" and tackle other key issues. Rural tax reform resulted in the abolishment of the educational surcharge, with the government now covering farmers' standard donation and bearing responsibility for raising funds for compulsory education. The government has stipulated that rural primary and middle schools may charge limited incidental and textbook fees and practise a "two exemptions and one subsidy" policy for poor students (exemption from incidental and textbook fees and subsidized boarding). On the basis of implementing the two-phase "State Compulsory Education Project in Poverty-Stricken Areas"[9] between 1995 and 2006, the State Council issued its 2003 "Breakthrough Program" of the "two basics" in Western China for 2004 to 2007. According to an amendment to the Law of Compulsory Education (including complete exemption of tuition fees and incidental fees) in 2006, the government commits to incorporating compulsory education into public finances. The process of free compulsory education in the rural areas has accelerated and it will be completely realized in 2007. The population benefiting from compulsory education in the western regions increased from 77 percent in 2002 to 96 percent in 2006 (Wen 2007).[10]

Compulsory education policies in rural areas achieved remarkable results. The finance guarantee mechanism has implemented in most regions, and the prohibitive cost of education for children from poor families is being alleviated. The gap in basic educational opportunities between urban and rural residents has been somewhat narrowed. The completion rate for farmers' children in junior middle school has risen from about 33 percent at the start of the 1990s to about 75 percent today. Conditions for basic education have been universally improved, and the higher-quality buildings in rural areas (especially in the middle and western areas) are usually primary and middle schools. Cities, towns, and developed rural areas have promoted balanced development of compulsory education: they have practised open admissions, transformed weak schools into quality ones, abolished establishment of key schools (classes),[11] and improved the quality of teachers. Meanwhile, now that compulsory education is almost completely popularized, general senior middle schools are rapidly developing, as demand for higher education expands. In 1997, there were altogether 8.5 million students enrolled in the first three grades of primary school. In 2006, the number of students in first grade alone amounted to 8.7 million, which met the increasing demand for education after nine-year compulsory education was completely popularized in urban areas and most rural areas. This shows that society's focus on education equity is still to narrow the gap between urban and rural areas and that there is a tendency to gradually change to senior middle schools.

Vocational education: an employment-oriented model

The past 10 years witnessed an adjustment to the model for vocational education in China. In the mid-1990s, vocational education developed rapidly. In 1995, students enrolled in secondary vocational education accounted for a maximum of 56.8 percent of all senior middle school enrollments, up slightly from the 56.2 percent reported for 1997. Later, some local governments lacked the resources to support more public vocational schools so they encouraged schools to charge tuition and to create a system for privately run institutions. The results, however, were mixed. In addition, the expansion of higher education after 1999 resulted in increased enrollment for regular senior secondary education. The share of students enrolled in secondary vocational education dropped to 38.6 percent in 2004.[12] Because vocational education is directly related to the employment market, and the proportion of vocational school students who come from middle- and low-income families is high, vocational schools, whether they are government-run or market-oriented, are difficult to align with social and economic development programs and objectives (this has been the case in many countries, not only in China). In the context of China's rapid economic development and the huge pressure on employment in the twenty-first century,[13] human resource-development will face serious challenges. While many countries of Southeast Asia were forced to readjust their industry structures as a result of the 1997 financial crisis, China managed to see a steady rise in foreign direct investment because foreign enterprises value China's highly skilled, high-quality labor force. The demand for skilled labor is rising in China. Vocational education is central to meeting that demand.

As required by the "Guidelines for the Reform and Development of Education in China" of 1993, the State Council convened two conferences on national vocational education in 2002 and 2005. Policies passed in 2002 were not completely implemented, but the policies passed at the 2005 conference were remarkably effective. The State Council's "Decision to Vigorously Develop Vocational Education" of October 28, 2005, called for an employment orientation in vocational education, capacity building, streamlined management, increased public and other expenditures from multiple sources, systems to cover students' costs, and completion of vocational education and training networks in urban and rural areas.

In recent years, the government has strengthened financial support for poor students and for the construction of schools. It also pushed for an arrangement whereby trades, enterprises and schools worked together, and through which industries helped run the schools. The new system helped vocational education recover from a difficult situation. The proportion of the students in middle vocational education rose to 41.1 percent in 2006 and the proportion of entrants rose to 45.6 percent (see Figure 12.1). Advanced vocational education has occupied half of the higher education system. A comparatively complete, separate system after junior and senior high school graduation has been formed. Each year, 5 million students from middle vocational schools and 2 million students from advanced higher vocational institutions graduated and went on to find jobs in the manufacturing and processing industries.

Higher education policies: expanding the scale and strengthening research and development

The recent decade was a period of expansion in higher education in China. In 1999, the Central Government decided to greatly increase enrollments in colleges. From 1997 to 2006, the number of students admitted into regular higher education (for two- to three-year courses and bachelor degrees, not including postgraduates,

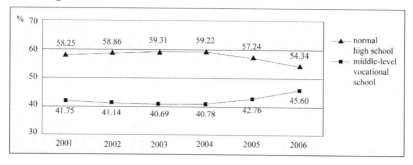

Figure 12.1 Share of all secondary students enrolled in regular high schools and vocational schools, 2001–2006.

Source: Ministry of Education, 2007.

adult higher education, e-learning, and other students) grew from 1 million to 5.4 million, and the number of students receiving higher education grew from 7 million to 25 million, making China the country with the world's largest higher-education system, surpassing Russia, India, and the United States. The policy of enrollment expansion was pursued at a time of economic globalization and the emergence of a knowledge-based economy. The policy was also pursued because of a need to upgrade the skills and expertise of the labor force while delaying young people's entry into the job market. Moreover, in expanding enrollments, China took many supportive measures, such as requesting public colleges to share tuition costs, improving the teachers' employment system, adopting a market orientation in the provision of college logistics, transferring the power and duty of management in advanced vocational education to the provincial government, and allowing the establishment of non-governmental (or private) colleges to create additional opportunities for enrollment. Table 12.2 indicates that the number of graduates who had at least a junior middle school diploma but did not continue their education and instead chose to enter the labor market increased by 1.564 million between 1998 and 2006. Meanwhile, the proportion of graduates with at least a two- to three-year higher education diploma grew by 17.51 percent, which has greatly affected the supply of people entering the labor force. In the same period, North America, Europe and Oceania entered the universal stage. If it had not been for the enrollment expansion at start of the new millennium, China would have lagged further behind industrialized countries in providing enrollment opportunities.

After the enrollment expansion, the layout and structure of colleges, the composition of students, and the management system all underwent significant changes. From 1997 to 2006, the average number of students including postgraduates in each university or college grew from 3,272 to 9,849. The amount of infrastructure built from 2001 to 2005 was double what was built during the five decades after the establishment of the People's Republic of China. Between 2000 and 2006, the amount of space used for dormitories rose from 190 million square meters to 600 million square meters. In the present freshmen classes of all

Table 12.2 Structural change of graduates as they enter the labor force

Year	1998	2006	Change: 1998–2006
Total number of students who entered the labor market directly after having completed at least junior middle school	14.184 million (100%)	15.748 million (100%)	+1.564 million
Share of all graduates with a junior middle school degree	49.86%	34.12%	-15.74 percentage points
Graduates with a senior middle school degree	44.47%	42.70%	-1.77 percentage points
Regular higher education for two- to three-year courses and bachelor degrees*	5.45%	21.12%	+15.67 percentage points
Postgraduate	0.16%	1.82%	+1.66 percentage points
Doctoral	0.06%	0.24%	+0.18 percentage points

* Statistics for higher education do not include adult colleges and in-service students because most of adult students have their own jobs.

Source: Ministry of Education, 2007.

universities and colleges, the share of rural students exceeds 50 percent. Women account for 48 percent of college freshmen.

To meet the need for a higher education system capable of turning out graduates ready for careers in professional fields and graduates with the skills to scientifically innovate and modernize social services, China simultaneously introduced two types of policies over the past decade. First, through the 211 and 985 projects,[14] the government attached great importance to constructing several world-class research universities and a large number of other high-quality universities, which have become famous in China and abroad and offer degrees in nearly 1,000 thousand subjects. During the Tenth Five-Year Plan (2001–2005), some research universities cumulatively won 55 percent of the national nature science awards, 64 percent of the national technology invention awards, and 54 percent of the national science and technology progress awards. In addition, the comprehensive universities made new achievements in the social science of philosophy and took on new roles as think tanks. The university system is becoming a significant part of the national system for innovation and its capacity for contributing to the development of social services and for participating in cultural construction is obviously increasing. Second, since 2006, the government has started to control enrollment expansion to the point where it has become relatively stable. It began attaching greater importance to the enhancement of quality, urged colleges to adjust the structure of their subjects and majors, offer superior courses, finish implementing a digital reference and documents system, build research facilities, and create a high-grade information-resource sharing system. China also strengthened the links between theory and practice. China attached importance to making advanced vocational institutions more responsive and adaptive to changes in the market, optimized full- and part-time teaching faculty in applied subjects, carried out the national quality evaluation for all colleges every five years, established an information periodic issuance system, and adopted measures aimed at improvements or reforms, including limiting enrollments or even suspending colleges that were unable to meet standard conditions for operation. Generally speaking, the Chinese government has greatly enhanced the quality of higher education, a key goal for 2010 (Guideline for the 11th Five-Year Plan for National Economic and Social Development of the People's Republic of China (2006–2010), *People's Daily*, March 16, 2006).

The Chinese government has been so successful with the development of its higher education system that 26 other countries, including Australia, the United Kingdom and the United States, have has signed mutual degree agreements with China's institutions. Academic exchanges and cooperation are constantly expanding. In 2006, 149,000 students from 179 other countries were studying in China. China has become one of the most desired destinations in Asia for foreign students.

Obstacles to educational development and the outlook for future policies

Generally speaking, China's educational policies over the past decade have had four prominent features. First, policies have always been positioned within the broader framework of the national economy and social development and have been adjusted along the way as circumstances changed. Second, when governments decrease direct economic investment, educational policies should place greater emphasis on government support for public education. Meanwhile, the problem of arrears in paying teachers' salaries in poor rural areas is expected to be fundamentally solved because total expenditures on compulsory education will be included in the government's budget. Third, educational policies are frequently issued and are being developed at an unprecedented rate. Government evaluations and inspections are also very frequent. Every one to five years, both national and local governments will arrange a series of educational policies, many of which are implemented by way of establishing a project for additional funds. Fourth, some emergency policies and measures will continue to have a long-term impact. For example, the decision to expand enrollments in higher education in 1999 to stimulate domestic demand for consumables (for example, millions of college students may pay more tuition and other living expenses), actually prevents a narrowing of the gap between the higher education enrollment rates in China and the developed countries. Compared with much of the developing world, China has obvious advantages in this field. Chinese education encountered many problems common to developing countries while facing some unique challenges.

Evaluation and analysis of the main obstacles to the development of Chinese education

When viewed as a whole, it is apparent that the great leap forward of the Chinese educational system occurred without major economic support and is attributable to the great efforts of government, schools and society. Unlike in many other developing countries, there is a strong demand from the public for education in China. The conditions for operating schools and financial support for them, however, are below the average level around the world. Only 21 percent of China's labor force, from ages 25 to 64, has at least a high school degree – about one-third the amount in industrialized countries. Only 6.5 percent of China's labor force has a junior college degree – about one-quarter the level in industrialized countries. Three major types of obstacles must be overcome to enable China to catch up to the rest of the world in their efforts to raise the overall value of human capital.

Obstacles in educational inputs and system operations

China set out in 1993 to allocate 4 percent of GDP to education by 2000, but this goal has not yet been achieved. Although the total amount of expenditures in the sector increased five-fold between 1997 and 2005, the percentage of GDP rose from 2.36 percent to 2.81 percent. As a percentage of GDP, China's educational expenditures are lower than 130 other countries.[15] In each year from 2002 through 2005, there were respectively 7, 17, 19, and 23 regions within provinces where the local budgets' shares spent on education were lower than in the previous year. This is an indication that some areas failed to assume the responsibility of educational outlays as required by law. It is also a sign that the educational system was operating at a low level, that there was insufficient supervision of budgets and financial accounts, and there was still a long way to go before the public finance system would be fully upgraded, efficient, and functioning smoothly. From 1997 to 2005, the government's share of expenditures on education fell short of expectations, but the share of household income and expenditures grew from 2 percent in the 1990s to 9 percent in 2005. At the same time, household savings grew as more families began setting aside money to pay for their children's future education.

In addition, educational development has varied from location to location. For example, per-student funding in some elementary schools is 10.7 times higher than it is in other areas. A similar gap exists among junior middle schools. In some areas, per-student funding is 9.3 times higher than in other areas. Funding in some regular senior middle schools is 7.7 times higher. Some vocational high schools receive 5.8 times more funding than others, while some ordinary colleges receive 8.2 times more per-student funding.[16] These gaps are likely to remain in the near future. Half of the compulsory education systems in China's counties are unable to meet national standards for per-student funding and for teaching. Some areas have resorted to very large class sizes and hiring temporary teachers to meet some of the burgeoning demand.

Obstacles in the educational system and socio-economic relationships

In many instances, quick expansion of educational services may satisfy need. But simply expanding the scale usually only benefits full-time, formal schooling. It often neglects the need to cultivate students' talents and lacks complexity and flexibility. Expansion also does not address the need to adapt to the industrializing economy and knowledge-based society. Some vocational schools and colleges sometimes blindly and slavishly adhere to standardized curricula and operations, often for the same of achieving higher status. Textbooks for some disciplines do not reflect the latest academic or technological developments or trends. There is inadequate attention paid to the need for informal education and flexible study arrangements to accommodate the changing work force. Formal schooling and "social education" remain isolated from each other, resulting in missed opportunities for sharing resources. In the course of constructing new rural areas, the relationships between education in the countryside, the spread of science and technology, and cultural construction must be further clarified. Solid regulations to insure the integration of industries, higher learning institutions, and research agencies are lacking, as are regulations to insure the integration of production and teaching in vocational schools. Colleges, independent scientific research academies, and the research and development sections of enterprises are separated from each other, while links between students' training and the practical application of their lessons are weak. At the same time, the reform of the economic system eliminated enterprises' obligations for human resource development, and this change resulted in less independent innovation. Guilds and the other social organizations play only a limited role. In some areas, there are structural problems with employment, reflecting an essential change in the relationship between the supply and demand for talent for large numbers of individuals with high-level degrees. Many foreign capital enterprises, joint ventures and private enterprises say there is still unmet demand for middle- and high-level professionals and managers who are familiar with the international rules for production and trade and who can adjust to the requirements of the modern service trade and high-tech industry, even though the number of postgraduates has exceeded 1 million.

Obstacles in studying methods and educational quality

Factors ranging from cultural traditions to the desire for good jobs combine to increase pressures on students to enter institutions of higher education after they complete their compulsory education. Many enterprises and social organizations prefer recruiting people with diplomas, while the private internal rates of return and the social expectations for graduates of vocational education remain inadequate. Competition for jobs leads to competition for degrees and diplomas and therefore in entrance examinations. This in turn encourages the educational system to follow curricula designed to help students excel on entrance examinations, often at the expense of enabling students to pursue their own interests and intellectual development. Schools and administrators often rely solely on grades and test scores in making decisions about admissions. They often neglect to evaluate students' interests, specialties, attitudes and social skills. This approach may result in education that focuses on a handful of subjects, with the aim of helping students pass their examinations. Many primary school teachers have been unable to adapt to new textbooks and continue to teach material that is no longer relevant or useful to China's new economy. In some areas, an over-emphasis on quality education has resulted in too much homework for students in elementary and middle schools, meaning less time is spent on recreation or physical activity. This, in turn, is leading to an increased incidence of obesity. What is lost in the process is the development of students' individuality and creativity.

The outlook for educational policies

Government reports by the premiers of the State Council in recent years show that Chinese educational policies have followed two main paths. First is the path toward equity, the responsibility for which has been taken by the government. The second path is the one toward quality, for which schools have taken responsibility. The planning and coordination of the relationship of the two types of policies are significant for long-term stability and harmonious development in China. China is striving to achieve an overall prosperous society by 2020 and is already becoming a great human-resource power. With this in mind, China will take four approaches to educational policies in the future.

Redefine the serviceability of education

"In the present world, knowledge is increasingly becoming the determining factor for the elevation of comprehensive national strength and international competitive strength. The human resource is increasingly becoming the strategic resource pushing economic and social development." President Hu said in 2006 (www.xinhuanet.com, August 30, 2006). Competition in talent and knowledge is increasingly propelling international competition in economics, science and technology in the twenty-first century, and social wealth is accruing daily to countries and regions with knowledge advantages. For China to construct a prosperous and innovative society, build the socialist new countryside, and industrialize, it has no choice but to make constant improvements in human resources. Education is central to the achievement of these goals. Thus, it is necessary to prioritize educational development and foster all-round human development for the modernization of the Chinese nation. The core of future educational policies in China will be a people-centered orientation and sustainable development (The Decision Made by the Central Committee of the Communist Party of China on Some Issues in Completing the System of Socialistic Market Economy, passed by the third session of the Sixteenth Central Committee, October 14, 2003). An emphasis will be placed on quality at every level and in every type of education. Also, more importance will be paid to organically integrating national modernization with human modernization and socio-economic development with human development. Thus, it is necessary to make a full-scale change in studying methods, reform the country's concept of education and the overall system and content. It is also necessary to stress applied education, encourage independent thinking and the pursuit of new knowledge, promote innovative thinking and creativity, cultivate a scientific spirit, and consider the diversity of individuals to allow them to develop their special interests and potentials, become better communicators, and be more socially adaptable. The aims should be to cultivate hundreds of millions of high-quality skilled workers, more than 100 million highly skilled professionals and technicians, and tens of millions innovators, and "to build our country's great human resource potential and to provide a strong foundation, from the talents and human resources, for the overall construction of a prosperous society and for the great rejuvenation of the Chinese nation" (www.xinhuanet.com, August 30, 2006).

Strengthen the government's promotion of equity in education

Experience in other countries indicates that it is generally progressive to promote equity in education. The first step in China toward this end is to provide as much education as possible. The second step is to insure that everyone receives at least a basic education. The third step is to allow everyone to receive as much education as possible. The needs and expectations for services vary across China and are not currently progressive. For example, in rural areas demand exceeds supply and quality is relatively low. In cities and towns, residents prefer high quality, publicly provided services, even though they are limited in quantity and access. Regardless of whether the services are public or not, however, all are dependent on the nation's public financial ability and regulatory framework.

Government intervention in public services falls under three main categories: monitoring, payment, and direct provision (Stiglitz 1988, 239). The line between basic and non-basic public education should be clearly drawn, as should the line between public and non-public education. The line between the government's power and its responsibility should be made clear, and different methods should be applied to different problems. Thus, according to the requirements of the Central Government to clarify the responsibility of government at each level to supply public education services,[17] future educational policies should lean more toward the promotion of equity of education, the gradual realization and equalization of basic public education, the constant broadening of non-basic public education, and the transparency and good supervision of services provided by non-governmental (or private) education.[18] In line with laws, the government should take overall responsibility for basic public education and should directly appropriate funds to support the state-run organizations. The government should also attach importance to some non-basic public education services (especially services which the market may not be able to adjust) and pay greater attention to appropriations, investments, funding sources or financial support for the sector. For some types of non-basic public education, the government's role should be limited to authorizations, permissions, commitments, or partial purchases. In the area of non-public education, the government should introduce market mechanisms, create rules for admission and competition, and provide supervision according to the laws (Yarrow 2005). The educational policies of China will try to strike a balance between the effective and restricted equity with the goals of making education "satisfactory to the people" (Hu 2006), especially for low-income groups, making non-basic public education satisfactory for those who are able to share the costs, providing financial support for qualified low-income groups, and making non-public education satisfactory for groups with special requirements and an ability to pay for the services.

Pay more attention to improving quality

The Guideline for the Eleventh Five-Year Plan for National Education Development (2006–2010), which the State Council passed and forwarded, says that China should focus on education as an engine for overall economic development and strive to complete the "three great tasks" of popularizing and consolidating compulsory education, speeding the development of vocational education, and improving the quality of the higher education. Table 12.3, on the state of educational development and the goals for 2010, shows rising indexes for gross enrollment rates in pre-school and senior secondary education, the number of students receiving middle vocational education, and students enrolled in higher education.[19] Other levels of education, particularly higher education for two- to three-year courses and bachelor degrees all show steady increases. The future educational policies in China will pay more attention to improving the quality of education at all levels.

Implementing quality-oriented education involves complex policies and must take a variety of environmental factors into consideration. To a large extent, the contradiction between supply and demand for educational resources also has an effect. Recent educational policies in China have relied on a temporary solution: reforming entrance examinations. In compulsory education, balanced local development should be realized and the phenomenon of selecting public schools should be eliminated. In non-compulsory education, the content and mode of examination should be reformed, tests and evaluations should be made more comprehensive, and an enrollment system for middle- and high-level vocational schools to recruit students through different methods and assorted exams should be explored. It is necessary to suitably expand the scope of colleges' independent recruitment and complete the management and supervision system. In the long run, China should build a learning society in which all citizens study throughout their lifetimes (Jiang 2006, 3:543).

China must build a flexible, open and diversified platform for study in cities and the countryside and a modernized system to provide a variety of study environments and opportunities. China must also form laws, regulations, policies and systems that benefit or facilitate studying for one's entire life and experiment with innovate approaches that give credit for life experiences and informal education, thus helping citizens gain acknowledgement from employers for their full range of personal development. Such changes will help make studying a basic right and need for every citizen (National Center for Education Development Research 2006; World Bank 2003).

Table 12.3 Status of educational development and goals for 2010

Year	2000	2005	2010	Increase from 2000 to 2005	Expected increase between 2005 and 2010
Pre-school education					
Gross enrollment rate of kindergarteners three years before school	37.7%	41.4%	55%	3.7%	13.6%
Compulsory education					
Gross enrollment rate of junior middle school	88.6%	95%	98%	6.4%	3%
Remained rate of junior middle school	90.1%	92.8%	95%	2.7%	2.2%
Senior secondary education					
Gross enrollment rate	42.8%	52.7%	80%	9.9%	27.3%
Students	25.18 million	40.31 million	45.10 million	15.13 million	4.79 million
• Regular high school	12.01 million	24.09 million	24.10 million	12.08 million	10,000
• Middle-level vocational school	12.84 million	16 million	21 million	3.16 million	5 million

continued

Year	2000	2005	2010	Increase from 2000 to 2005	Expected increase between 2005 and 2010
Higher education					
Gross enrollment rate	12.5%	21%	25%	8.5%	4%
Students	12.3 million	23 million	30 million	10.7 million	7 million
• 2–3 year courses and bachelor degree programs	5.56 million	15.62 million	20 million	10.06 million	4.38 million
• Postgraduates	0.30 million	0.98 million	1.3 million	0.68 million	0.32 million
• Adult higher education	3.54 million	4.36 million	6 million	0.82 million	1.64 million

Source: Guideline for the Eleventh Five-Year Plan for National Education Development, May 24, 2007.

Look for the keystones in system reforms

While system reforms over the past decade aimed to expand the scale of education, many obstacles to education's full development and evolution remain. The sustainable and long-term development of education will depend on further reform in areas such as school management, supportive laws and policies, and on social participation. A report from the Organization for Economic Cooperation and Development (2006) on the future of higher education deemed that even state-run colleges supported mainly by the public finance may introduce the so-called "new public management mode," which relies on market forces. In recent years, China has been researching the causes of problems in areas such as school management. One of the goals for the system in the future is to complete the laws and regulations for the modern school system. The government will manage, appropriately fund, and provide services in line with national laws. State-run schools are considered "corporate organizations" and operate according to relevant laws. Non-governmental (private) schools (or institutes) and the Chinese-foreign joint schools or projects should be run according to the specific laws.[20] In the event that financial support increases year by year, the power over and responsibilities for the distribution and use of funds by state-run schools should be further clarified, and schools should strictly enforce financial regulations and make the financial and school affairs more transparent. Audits of the educational administration and state-run schools should be periodically reported to the government and the People's Congress. Moreover, the results of audits should be made available to everyone, thereby encouraging public supervision of investment, distribution and use of funds for public education. It is also advisable to rebuild the relationships between schools, enterprises and society, to introduce additional elements of social supervision, and to establish a mechanism in which evaluations by the government, the schools themselves, and the public are combined to improve the quality-monitoring system. At the same time, the government should encourage the lawful development of the non-governmental education, bring it into the national plan for the development of education, implement separate management, and establish a public finance mechanism to benefit public welfare and non-profit privately run education.

Notes

1 The Education for All (EFA) movement had two phases. The first began in 1990, with the World Conference on Education for All. The conference, which took place in Thailand, was sponsored by international organizations such as UNESCO. At the Conference, countries were encouraged to reduce illiteracy and universalize primary education. The second phase began in 2000 with the World Education Forum in Senegal, where quality education for all was promoted. For more information, visit the UNESCO website at http://www.unesco.org.

2 Also see major documents from the State Council's conferences on education on the Ministry of Education website at http://www.moe.gov.cn.

3 Also see the Ministry of Education website at http://www.moc.gov.cn, which is the source for data on 2006 educational undertakings. Sources for statistical data on educational undertakings in 1997 are from the *Educational Statistics Yearbook of China 1997*.

4 According to Trow (1970), higher education is in the elite stage if the gross enrollment rate is less than 15 percent; higher education is in the mass stage if the gross enrollment rate is between 15 percent and 50 percent. It is in the universal stage when the gross enrollment rate is higher than 50 percent. From 1998 to 2002, the gross enrollment rate in higher education in the countries of North America, Europe and Oceania increased from less than 50 percent to more than 50 percent, but no such significant changes occurred in other regions.

5 The "Compulsory Education Law of the People's Republic of China" was adopted at the Fourth Session of the Sixth National People's Congress on April 12, 1986 and amended at the Twenty-second Conference of the Standing Committee of the Tenth National People's Congress on June 29, 2006

6 According to the Central Government, "Carrying out quality-oriented education is to fully implement the educational policies of the Communist Party of China, enhance the qualities of the people as the fundamental aim, cultivate students' innovative spirit and practical capability as the focal point and cultivate socialist builders and successors with ideal, morality, knowledge and discipline, and help them develop all around in moral, intellectual, physical, aesthetics and other aspects." To help achieve this goal, the educational system has carried out reforms in teaching ideology, methods and curricula, textbooks, and examinations, and has developed a model for cooperation among society, enterprises, and families. See: "Deepening Educational Reform and Fully Promoting Quality-oriented Education," Documents of the Third National Conference on Education Work. Beijing: Higher Education Press, 1999.

7 Basic education should also include pre-school and special education. In addition, according to the Vocational Education Law of China, there is also primary vocational education, which has been incorporated into compulsory education. In 2006 there were 335 vocational junior middle schools in China with a total of 205,700 students.

8 The Educational for All Development Index includes nine developing countries with large population. These "E-9" countries are Bangladesh, Brazil, China, Egypt, India, Indonesia, Mexico, Nigeria and Pakistan, The combined populations of these countries account for about one half of the world's total population. In the early 1990s, the combined illiterate populations of these countries accounted for 70 percent of the world's total illiterate population. The *Monterrey Declaration of the E-9 Countries* (2006) indicated "…primary school net enrolment ratios in E-9 countries range from under 60 percent to over 90 percent, and adult literacy rates from just 40 percent to over 90 percent (2000–2004). In some countries, there were increases in literacy rates, a narrowing of gender disparities, and an expansion of secondary education."

9 This project mainly involved the construction of schools and facilities and the training of teachers in poverty-stricken areas. The financial investment on this project from 1995 to 2000 totaled to RMB Yuan 11.6 billion, of which the central financial support amounted to RMB Yuan 3.9 billion. From 2001 to 2006, the Central Government provided RMB Yuan 5 billion in financial allocations, while local governments provided about RMB Yuan 3.83 billion for this project.

10 Wen Jiabao, Premier of the State Council, said in his government work report on March 5, 2007, "A total of RMB Yuan 184 billion was allocated by both central and local governments to fund rural compulsory education, enabling us to pay tuition and miscellaneous fees for the 52 million rural students receiving compulsory education throughout the western region and in some areas in the central region, provide free textbooks to 37.3 million students from poor families, and grant living allowances to 7.8 million students staying in dormitories" (*People's Daily* 2007).

11 From the 1980s, local governments have intended to provide more resources including high level teachers to a few public primary and junior middle schools, which are often called key schools (also some key classes select students who have higher learning achievement within a public school), especially in more urban areas of China. In 2006 the "Compulsory Education Law" was revised and its article 22 required that all

Zhang L.

key schools must be closed for the sake of balanced development among the public schools.

12 In 2004, there were 14.092 million students enrolled in secondary vocational education, a 29.3 percent increase since 1997. There were 1.6 times more students in general senior middle schools in 2004 than in 1997.

13 According to a communiqué from the State Statistics Bureau, there were 764 million employees across the country. Urban employees accounted for 283 million of that total. The urban unemployment rate was 4.1 percent.

14 Within China's macro educational policies, "211 projects" refers to building up about 100 top universities to equip them for the twenty-first century, while "985 projects" refers to enhancing about 39 top research universities among the 211 projects. Background documents are available from the Ministry of Education website at http://www.moe.gov.cn.

15 UNESCO estimates that between 1998 and 2002, the average percentage of public educational expenditure in GDP is 4.5 percent; 128 countries exceeded 3 percent, 88 countries exceeded 4 percent, and 56 countries exceeded 5 percent. http://www.unesco.org.

16 These statistics come from several sources, including the Statistics Bulletin of the Ministry of Education's Enforcement Condition of the National Educational Expenditure, the State Statistics Bureau, the Ministry of Finance, and from references in the *People's Daily*. An analysis of the gap in educational expenditures should take into account the variations in purchasing power in the eastern, middle and western areas. Some researches argue that the absolute purchasing power parity should be applied to determine the exchange rates among different areas. Owing to the fact that the economic conditions vary across different areas of a country, the prices of commodities are also obviously different. Prices in developed areas are obviously higher than that in undeveloped areas. Thus, the payout effects of educational expenditures in different areas may not be as strong as what is reflected in statistics. See "A New Research of the Exchange Rate Deciding Theory" at www.lunwencar.com/news/1000007645/.

17 Decision on Some Important Issues of Constructing a Socialist Harmonious Society (adopted at the sixth plenary session of the Sixteenth Central Committee of the Communist Party of China on October 11, 2006).

18 The Chinese National People's Congress enacted the "Law for Promotion of Non-governmental (or Private) Education" in 2002. The government signed the "World Trade Organization's General Agreement on Trade in Services Schedule for Education" in 2001, and issued the "Statutes for Chinese-foreign Joint Schools" in 2003. However, in the course of enforcement in recent years, many areas encountered problems with issues such as property and property delimitation education.

19 The forecast for an increase in the number of students enrolled in higher education during the eleventh five-year period compared to the tenth five-year period is not clear, possibly because the number of spaces reserved after the higher education growth rate slows.

20 For relevant educational laws and regulations, see the homepage of the Ministry of Education at http://www.moe.gov.cn.

References

China Central Government 2006. Guideline for the 11th Five-Year Plan for National Economic and Social Development of the People's Republic of China (2006–2010). *People's Daily*. March 16.

Communist Party of China. 2006. Decision on Some Important Issues of Constructing a Socialist Harmonious Society (Adopted at the Sixth Plenary of the Sixteenth Central Committee, October 11).

Department of Development and Planning. Ministry of Education. People's Republic of China. 2006. *Education Statistical Report*. January 29.

Department of Development and Planning. Ministry of Education. People's Republic of

China. 1997. *Educational Statistics Yearbook of China*. Beijing: Higher Education Press.

Hu, Jintao (President of the People's Republic of China). 2006. Available online at http://www.cnhubei.com/200608/ca1148037.html (accessed August 30, 2006).

Hu, Jintao (President of the People's Republic of China). 2006. Reported in the *People's Daily*. Available online at http://edu.people.com.cn/GB/4761850.html (accessed August 31, 2006).

Jiang, Zemin. 2006. *Jiang Zemin Selected Works*. Vols 1–3. Beijing: People's Press.

Legislative Affairs Office. Ministry of Education. People's Republic of China. 2004. *Laws and Regulations on Education*. Beijing: Educational Science Publishing House.

Ministry of Education. People's Republic of China. 1999b. *Deepening Educational Reform and Fully Promoting Quality-oriented Education – Documents of the Third National Conference on Education Work*. Beijing: Higher Education Press.

Ministry of Education. People's Republic of China. 2004. *Guidance to 2003–2007 Action Plan for Rejuvenating Education*. Beijing: Educational Science Publishing House.

Ministry of Education. People's Republic of China. 2007. Guideline for the Eleventh Five-Year Plan for National Education Development. May 24. Available online at http://www.chinanews.com.cn.

Ministry of Education. People's Republic of China. 1999a. *Reference Materials for the Action Plan for Invigorating Education towards the 21st Century*. Beijing: Normal University Press.

Ministry of Education. 2007. *Statistical Newsletter on 2006 Educational Undertakings*. March 7.

Ministry of Education Research Group. People's Republic of China. 2003. Stride from a Country of Tremendous Population to a Country of Profound Human Resources. Beijing: Higher Education Press.

National Bureau of Statistics. 2007. Statistical Communiqué of the People's Republic of China on the 2006 National Economy and Social Development. Beijing: National Bureau of Statistic.

National Center for Education Development Research. 2006. *Green Paper on Education in China*. Beijing: Educational Science Publishing House.

Organization for Economic Cooperation and Development. 2006. Four Futures Scenarios for Higher Education. Athens: Meeting of OECD Education Ministers, June 27–28.

State Education Commission 1998. *Educational Statistics Yearbook of China 1997*. Beijing: Higher Education Press.

State Education Commission. People's Republic of China. 1994. *New Milestone: Selected Documents of National Conference on Education*. Beijing: Educational Science Publishing House.

Stiglitz, Joseph E. 1988. *Economics of the Public Sector*. New York: W. W. Norton & Company.

Central Committee of the Communist Party of China. The Decision Made by the Central Committee of the Communist Party of China on Some Issues in Completing the System of Socialistic Market Economy, passed by the third session of the 16th Central Committee, October 14, 2003.

Trow, Martin. 1970. Reflections on the transition from mass to universal higher education. *Daedalus* 99 (Winter 1970): 1–42.

United Nations Educational, Scientific and Cultural Organization. 2005. *Education for All Global Monitoring Report 2005*. Paris: UNESCO Publishing.

United Nations Educational, Scientific and Cultural Organization. 2006. *Monterrey Declaration of the E-9 countries*. February 14. Mexico: UNESCO Publishing.

Wen, Jiabao (Premier of the State Council). 2007. Reported in the *People's Daily*. March 6.

World Bank. 2005. *Lifelong Learning in the Global Knowledge Economy: Challenges for Developing Countries*. Beijing: Higher Education Press.

Yarrow, George. 2005. Regulatory Framework and Tools for Public Service Delivery in China. In *Comparative Studies*. Wu Jinglian (ed.) 2005. Beijing: China International Trust and Investment Corporation Publishing House. 16: 141–154.

Part IV

Reflections on the Asian financial crisis and China's opening up to the outside world

13 The 1997 Asian financial crisis

Review and reflections

Bai Chong-En

On July 2, 1997, the central bank of Thailand announced that it would abandon its fixed exchange-rate regime, which had pegged Thai Baht to the US dollar for about 10 years. The change permitted free fluctuation of the exchange rate between the two currencies. On the same day, the exchange rate plunged 17 percent. The incident rippled through East Asia – and many other parts of the world – and triggered the Asian financial crisis, which lasted about two years and caused enormous losses to many countries, especially in Southeast Asia. Today, more than a decade later, it is possible to draw lessons from the crisis and better understand how to prevent such a crisis from happening again.

Review of the Asian financial crisis

Before the crisis erupted

In the few years prior to the crisis, the deficit of Thailand's current accounts rose continuously and accounted for 5.7 percent, 6.4 percent, and 8.4 percent of gross domestic product (GDP) in 1993, 1994, and 1995, respectively. In 1996, Thailand experienced a reduction in its GDP growth and a further rise in its current-account deficit, which accounted for as much as 8.5 percent of GDP. At the end of 1996, the basic conditions of Thailand's economy already looked precarious because of the huge foreign deficit and increasing short-term foreign debt. However the biggest problems lay in the financial institutions. Starting from early 1990s, real estate investments made by Thai financial institutions increased explosively, with most of the funds having been borrowed from foreign financial institutions. By 1993, real estate prices peaked and began a downturn. However, the bubble did not burst immediately; it took some time for problems associated with real estate to be reflected in non-performing loans. Besides, Thailand's banking supervision was far from perfect: there were no sound systems in place for credit examination and classification. By early 1997, bad debts of financial companies had accumulated to a dangerous level, pushing many of them to the brink of bankruptcy. The Thai Government intervened to prevent financial companies' bankruptcies from eroding market confidence and prompting a run on banks. In the first quarter of 1997, the Financial Institution Development Fund (FIDF) under the central bank loaned

US$8 billion to the financial companies, with the lion's share – 17.5 percent – going to the then-largest financial company, Finance One. On March 4, the Thai Government required 10 financial institutions to immediately increase their capital by THB8.25 billion (US$385 million) and raise the bad-debt reserve rate from 100 percent to between 115 and 120 percent to address problems in asset quality and shortage of liquid capital. However, the measure, designed to appease public sentiment, led the market to believe that this was a sign of profound problems in the Thai financial system, causing panic-stricken customers to withdraw THB15 billion from 10 financial institutions. On March 10, the government announced that it would purchase US$3.9 billion worth of debts from these companies, but the measure was far from enough to salvage them. In May, the Thai Government made a last-ditch attempt to bail out these companies through reorganizations, but soon gave up because it found that they had already exhausted their foreign-exchange reserves while resisting international financial speculators and had nothing left to support the government's rescue plan. Already in November and December 1996, the Thai Baht had already begun to be assaulted by international financial speculators, who launched another (tentative) attack in February 1997. This forced the central bank to dramatically lift the interest rate for short-term loans and spend a large part of its insufficient foreign exchange reserves defending the Thai Baht. On May 14, the Thai Baht fell to an 11-year low against the US dollar. Overwhelmed by massive panic selling by the public, Thailand was unable to single-handedly counter the new offensive of international financial speculators and had to turn to the central banks of Malaysia, Singapore and Hong Kong for help. Although the Thai Baht managed to stabilize, Thai foreign exchange reserves dried up and expectations for a depreciation of the Thai Baht continuously rose until July 2. Then the Thai Government finally abandoned attempts to defend the exchange rate of the Thai Baht against the US dollar, unleashing drastic currency depreciation.

In 1995, Indonesia's economy showed signs of overheating, with high inflation and a decrease in the balance of current accounts. The central bank adopted a mild austerity policy of raising interest rates, lifting the deposit reserve rate from 2 percent to 5 percent, and tightening control over bank credit. At this time, the Indonesian central bank faced a dilemma. On the one hand, it hoped to control overheating domestic demand and, on the other hand, it feared that a higher interest rate would attract the additional inflow of foreign capital and cause appreciation of the currency, the Rupiah. The measure taken by the central bank was a repeated widening of the band of exchange-rate volatility of the Rupiah, hoping to increase risks for possessing on the currency, thus making the higher domestic interest rate less appealing to overseas capital. But the effect was insignificant and foreign capital continued to surge into the country because of strong expectations for rising interest rates. Meanwhile, the government took measures to enhance efficiency and competitiveness in the export sector, but the market was skeptical about this and lacked confidence in the government's ability to solve problems in the macro economy. At the end of 1996, the economic overheating seemed to have abated somewhat. Therefore, the central bank lowered the interest rate by 0.5 percent in December and by another 0.5 percent in March 1997, in a bid to discourage the inflow of foreign capital and promote exports. However, Indonesian companies continued to borrow large amounts of foreign debt. At the end of 1996, Indonesia's official statistics showed that the balance of total debts was US$117 billion. However, a report for the same period holds that the official statistics overlooked the quantity of short-term offshore loans and underestimated the debts by about US$67 billion.

Malaysia faced a similar problem with a swelling deficit of current accounts, which already accounted for 8.8 percent of GDP in 1995. The amount of direct foreign investment in the same period was not enough to offset the deficit. Influenced by Mahathir's vision of an industrialized nation, the Malaysian Government increased its investment in infrastructure construction by 25 percent in 1995. Although the government did not think that the economy was noticeably overheating (because of a relatively low consumer price index, some observers did. They argued that the index was artificially low because the government controlled prices of major commodities included in the index. Meanwhile, overheating had already begun to be reflected in the trade deficit.

Since the government was unwilling to reduce the investment in infrastructure construction projects, the central bank took a number of restrictive measures to control economic overheating. In October 1995, the central bank relaxed restrictions on automobile and housing credit and raised the level of bank reserves. As was the case in Indonesia, the Malaysian central bank found itself in a dilemma and had to use every opportunity to raise interest rates. In 1996, economic growth in Malaysia slowed and the economic overheating also seemed to ease, but this was mainly due to a sharp fall in exports. Because of the high domestic interest rate, overseas large-scale, short-term capital began to flow in – a dramatic change from an outflow of US$8.4 billion in 1994 to an inflow of US$11.3 billion in 1996. Bank credit soared, and the main flow shifted from the manufacturing industry to the securities industry. In the meantime, asset prices skyrocketed.

South Korea already witnessed a serious deterioration of its macro economy in 1995 and 1996, when the current-account deficit jumped from 1.5 percent in 1994 to 4.8 percent in 1996, the balance of short-term foreign debts hit an all-time high, and export growth declined considerably. In 1996, the growth of industrial production fell by half, and the profitability rate of large enterprises, which was already very low, continued dropping, with a debt ratio reaching a dangerous level. The value of the stock market had dropped by 36 percent from 1994, and the currency, the Won, also began to weaken. By early 1997, a number of large business groups went bankrupt, causing a series of after-effects, including fleeing foreign capital and worsening liquidity in the banking sector. All of the economic problems began to surface.

Relatively speaking, the Philippine macro economy was basically stable. Under the supervision of the International Monetary Fund (IMF), some effect was achieved in the reform of the macro economy: the economy maintained a steady growth, the privatization of state-owned enterprises had been smooth, the government budget was in surplus, and the bad debts of banks were only 3.4 percent at the end of 1996. However, the current-account deficit remained large, the de facto appreciation of the currency was obvious, and the large amount of credits for the private sector flew to some high-risk projects, and a dense speculative atmosphere prevailed in the real estate industry.

Very few people would link Japan directly to the outbreak of the crisis. However, as the largest economic entity in Asia, Japan's influence cannot be denied. Just when it took a turn for the better in early 1996, the Japanese economy fell into another recession in 1997, which course caused a reduction in imports from other Asian countries. But the worst came in 1995. The prolonged trend of an appreciating Yen against the US dollar began to turn around. The depreciation of the Yen placed heavy pressure on other Asian countries. By 1997, all the currencies of Southeast Asia that were pegged to the US dollar experienced a sharp real appreciation. However, Japanese banks played a more important role in the crisis. After the Japanese economic bubble burst in 1991, Japan implemented a relaxed currency policy. Its nearly 0 percent interest rate stimulated many foreign investors to borrow money from Japan, which they invested in the assets of Southeast Asian countries for foreign exchange arbitrage transactions, for purchase of assets, or for direct investment. The overseas Yen loans that flew into Southeast Asia from 1995 to 1998 reached an estimated US$260 billion. In Thailand, 55 percent of the foreign debts were in Yen. However, in 1995, the problem of non-performing loans began to loom large in the Japanese banking industry, and the bankruptcy of small banks infected the large banks that had contact with them. Meanwhile, with the Japanese economy falling into recession and with the weakening of the Yen, foreign investors began to withdraw their investments and the value of loans in US dollars began to rise. Japanese banks had to recover overseas loans in order to meet capital adequacy ratio requirements. Some analysts even regarded that as a major fuse igniting the Asian financial crisis.

What is noteworthy is that before the occurrence of the Asian financial crisis, some omens had already appeared in a number of countries, including current-account deficits, slowdowns in exports, rapid increases and low-quality of credits in the financial sector, and latent troubles of dual mismatch (short-term loans and long-term investment, and investment in foreign exchange and returns in domestic currency). But the problems were not so serious as to foretell the upcoming crisis. In fact, market players and observers both made fairly optimistic forecasts before 1997. No credit-rating institutions, such as Standard & Poor, and Moody's, warned of risks, the forecasts by investment banks were all optimistic, and the IMF annual report still predicted a high economic growth rate.

Outbreak and proliferation of the crisis

The first economy that bore the brunt was Thailand, which had weaker economic foundations. When the Thai Baht began to depreciate in July 1997, the currencies of other economies, such as Malaysia, Indonesia and the Philippines, also fell prey to attacks from investors. By the end of July, the Thai Baht devalued by 25 percent, the Indonesian Rupiah by 9 percent, the Malaysian Ringgit by 4 percent, and the Philippine Peso by 14 percent from the beginning of the year. Then, the situation worsened. By the end of September, the Thai Baht devalued by 42 percent, the Indonesian Rupiah by 37 percent, the Malaysian Ringgit by 26 percent, and the Philippine Peso by 29 percent from the beginning of the year.

Faced with currency depreciation, the first response of these countries was to prevent monetary contraction and interest rate increases in the domestic market. Therefore, Thailand and other countries first intervened in the spot-exchange and forward-exchange markets. Finding that the strategy was futile, Thailand tried to restrict the flow of capital, but again failed. These countries faced double constraints: if they raised interest rates to maintain exchange rates, borrowers would be hurt and the vulnerability of banks would be exacerbated; if they did not raise interest rates, a large amount of foreign exchange reserves would be lost.

It was not until the crisis had spread far and wide that these economies resorted to contractile monetary policies and abandoned policies for maintaining low interest rates. The problem with earlier loose monetary policies is that it caused continuous currency devaluation and an upsurge in foreign debts, which threw many enterprises into financial difficulty, with the government having insufficient financial power to pull them out. Just as Radelet and Sachs (1998) describe, when the government finally adopted a credit-retrenchment policy, it created market panic through the transmitting mechanism and caused a further withdrawal of capital, thus finally producing a negative effect on the economies hit by the crisis. First, not only would the domestic nominal exchange rate fall because of the withdrawal of capital, but so would the real exchange rate, and the falling real exchange rate joined the high interest rate in pushing up the ratio of non-performing loans. Second, the losses caused by the rising non-performance ratio and currency depreciation depleted most bank assets as they had done in Indonesia, Taiwan, and South Korea. Third, the withdrawal of foreign capital itself produced the effect of credit contraction, which, together with the bankruptcy of native banks, directly resulted in restricted bank loans and the closure of many enterprises. Furthermore, before and during the crisis, South Korea, Thailand, Philippines and Indonesia all showed signs of political instability. The crisis of government reshuffling, along with doubts about the intentions of government, had a negative impact on investor confidence of investors.

When the Thai Baht devalued on July 2, 1997, Thailand already had no foreign exchange to sustain its currency and could not help but turn to the IMF for help on July 28 to combat the crisis. In August, the IMF raised US$17 billion as aid for Thailand, which, however, failed to thoroughly reverse the situation. Besides, the IMF's prescription before late 1997 included three requirements: keep a mandatory capital adequacy ratio, close banks lacking capital, and tighten controls over credit. But these requirements actually served to intensify the retrenchment and caused even larger scale panic.

After the crisis with the Thai Baht, many South Korean financial institutions went bankrupt. Foreign banks slashed credit for South Korea. Foreign banks that had provided large amount of loans for South Korean banks began to refuse requests for more loans, forcing South Korean conglomerates to raise funds within the country. The annual interest rate of short-term loans soared from 14 percent to 40 percent, and capital outflows increased. By the end of October 1997, the Won had devalued by 14 percent from the beginning of the year and then further devaluated 25 percent in November. At the same time, exports slumped, investment fell, and large conglomerates began to experience troubles. This forced South Korea to accept US$60 billion of aid from the IMF in early December. Given the important influence of South Korea in Asian economy, the move had an adverse influence on other countries suffering from the crisis, which devaluated their currencies one after another.

The speculative attack reached Taiwan in October 1997. Originally, Taiwan had sufficient foreign exchange reserves to resist currency devaluation. However, by mid-October, given how the above countries were too weak to resist currency devaluation, Taiwan authorities chose a floating exchange rate, which immediately triggered a currency devaluation of 5 percent.

On December 22, 1997, Moody's lowered the bond rating of crisis-stricken economies. The situation worsened further because financial institutions could no longer provide guarantees for domestic imports and exports, and the liquidity of debt shrank.

In early 1998, Indonesia again depreciated its currency by a large margin in its most serious economic recession so far. The IMF's prescription for the country failed to obtain the expected result. On February 11, the Indonesian Government announced that it would implement a fixed exchange-rate system that pegged the Rupiah to the US dollar to help stabilize the currency. The move was unanimously opposed by the IMF, the United States and Western Europe. The IMF threatened to withdraw aid to Indonesia, and the country fell into a political and economic crisis. On February 16 the exchange rate between the Rupiah and the US dollar dropped below 10,000 to one. Feeling the effects, the Southeast Asian foreign-exchange market again plunged into turbulence. The Singapore dollar, Malaysian Ringgit, Thai Baht and Philippine Peso all sagged in value. It was not until April 8, when Indonesia and the IMF reached an agreement on a new economic reform plan, that the Southeast Asian foreign-exchange market temporarily quieted down.

In the summer of 1998, the regional financial crisis in Asia began to spread across the globe, affecting the economic environment of India and Pakistan. Japan's economic situation deteriorated further, and the continuous downhill trend of the Yen put the currencies of China and Hong Kong under heavier pressure. In August, international financial speculators launched a new round of assault on the Hong Kong dollar, forcing Hong Kong Monetary Authority to intervene. But, Hong Kong boasts excellent supervision and sufficient capital. Its powerful banking system became a vital protective dam that prevented the Hong Kong economy from collapsing. Aware of the solid fundamentals of the economy, Hong Kong authorities focused most of the efforts on maintaining market confidence. Playing the role of lender of last resort, the monetary authority bought large numbers of blue chip shares to continuously infuse fluidity and succeeded in suppressing panic selling, ultimately restoring market confidence and tiding over the crisis.

On August 17, Russia's central bank announced its decision to widen the band of volatility of the exchange rate between Ruble and the US dollar, postpone the repayment of foreign debts and suspend treasury bond transactions. The Ruble began to depreciate, and the stock market fell drastically. Very soon, panic spread to Latin America and investors pulled their money out of the emerging market countries. The crisis in Russia and Latin America also took a toll on the American and European capital markets, directly causing the collapse of the Long Term Capital Management Company (LTCM) in the United States. The Asian financial crisis had resulted in global financial turbulence.

However, the measures taken began to work. These included the Federal Reserve's raising of interest rates twice, the US Congress' motion to increase the supply of capital to the IMF, and the efforts made to rescue the LTCM. In October 1998, the confidence of investors began to rebound, and interest rates began to fall in the crisis-stricken Asian countries. But, the banking system of these countries was so devastated by the crisis that it had yet to restore its financing functions, making it hard for many companies to raise funds to purchase raw materials. By mid 1998, exports still showed no signs of growth in the crisis-stricken countries. The economy began to recover, exchange rates began to rise, and interest rates returned to pre-crisis levels only in 1999, after consuming tremendous social wealth and prompting painful bank reorganizations and reforms. Except for Indonesia, all other countries had begun to rise from the financial crisis, signaling the crisis' end.

Causes of the Asian financial crisis

The Asian financial crisis involved a number of East Asian countries and was quite complicated. There are several theories about the causes: one attributes the crisis to the errors in the internal and external economic policies and institutional defects of East Asian countries, the other attributes the crisis to unnecessary financial panic. Observers who support this theory say that the crisis was inevitable and point to the crisis-stricken countries themselves as the root cause. Another theory would indicate that the crisis was not inevitable. Despite the differences between these two major theories, they are closely related. Even if policy errors and institutional defects did not necessarily result in the crisis, they were preconditions for financial panic. In addition to these two theories, there is perhaps another: changes in external factors were the fuse of the crisis. As the major source of foreign capital for the crisis-stricken countries of East Asia, Japan experienced economic changes, which caused the foreign capital that was originally heading for other East Asian countries to abruptly change direction, thereby triggering the financial crisis.

Errors in economic policy and institutional defects

Excessive speed of financial liberalization

In late 1980s and early 1990s, all the crisis-stricken countries implemented financial liberalization policies. Owing to lowered thresholds for entry, financial institutions faced fewer restrictions in extending loans. Meanwhile, the stock and bond markets grew rapidly. More importantly, financial institutions could raise funds through overseas markets. These measures led to a ballooning of internal credit and foreign borrowings. Regarding internal credit, the share of GDP in the aggregate investment in the private sector made by Thai, South Korean and Malaysian banks rose by 50 percent in seven years. Regarding foreign borrowings, the proportion of the foreign debt of Thai banks to GDP increased from 5 percent in 1990 to 28 percent in 1995; South Korean commercial banks provided loans to large enterprises through hefty borrowings from overseas, causing a rapid rise in the liability rate of large enterprises; Indonesian large enterprises raised money overseas directly. Because of overly rapid financial liberalization, the government could not monitor and supervise the financial institutions in a timely way, and the financial institutions could not develop their own capabilities in a timely way. Therefore, the quality of loans declined. Some financial institutions saw an inadequate capital adequacy ratio and a rise in the non-performing asset rate.

The problems resulting from excessive speed in financial liberalization (including excessive foreign debts, high expansion of investment, declining quality of investment, and the weakness of financial institutions) increased the risks of financial crisis. But these problems were not so serious as to inevitably cause the Asian financial crisis. As a matter of fact, from 1994 to 1996 the non-performing asset rate of Indonesian banks fell from 12 percent to 9 percent, while that of Malaysia fell from 8 percent to 4 percent. Moody's' bank-health indicators revealed no marked difference between crisis-stricken countries and other emerging economies.

Pegged exchange rates

In the early 1990s, every crisis-stricken economy maintained a fixed interest rate or just allowed exchange rates to change at predictable speeds. The advantage of this approach was that it could reduce the uncertainty arising from exchange-rate fluctuations. Such an approach may, however, result in a crisis if it cannot be maintained. Therefore, while an exchange rate policy of this type may reduce small risks, it may bring larger risks. There are three reasons why a fixed interest rate may increase the likelihood of a crisis. First, the fixed interest-rate system makes overseas investors believe that they face minimal exchange-rate risks, thus encouraging the inflow of short-term capital, which can sow the seeds for the risk of capital outflow and cause excessive investment together with financial liberalization. Second, under the fixed interest rate system, the prices of tradable products are fixed, while the prices of non-tradable products, especially in the construction and real estate industries, rise because of increased investment. In the end, the relative prices of tradable products fall, the local currency effectively appreciates, export enthusiasm is dampened, and the incentive for investment in non-tradable products increases. The appreciation of the US dollar against the Yen and European currencies after 1995 aggravated the over-evaluation of East Asian currencies that were pegged to the US dollar. Radelet and Sachs (1998) estimate that before the crisis, the currencies of Thailand, Indonesia, Malaysia, and the

Philippines were over-valued by about 20 percent, and that of South Korea by about 10 percent. In 1996, the export growth rate took a nosedive in South Korea, Malaysia and, especially, Thailand. Indonesian export growth began to slow down in 1993. Every crisis-stricken economy saw a rise of the shares of bank loans taken up by construction, real estate, finance and other service sectors. The third problem caused by fixed interest rates was that the success or failure of the system itself became the focus of attention of all investors. When a fixed interest rate cannot be maintained, it is likely to throw investors into panic and lead to a financial crisis. In fact, the landmark incident in the Asian financial crisis is exactly the failure of Thailand to defend its fixed interest rate policy.

Apart from the factor of the changing exchange rate, there are several other reasons for the export deceleration in crisis-stricken countries before the crisis. The first was the sharp rise in labor costs. In the textile industry, for example, workers' wages grew by over 12 percent between 1990 and 1995 in Indonesia and Thailand. In Malaysia, they rose 23 percent. The second was that overabundant production capacity brought about by excessive investment and dwindling demand caused a decline in the prices of export products. South Korea's semiconductor and steel industries are two examples of this phenomenon. The third reason was that the Japanese economic depression in the 1990s affected the exports of East Asian countries. In the months before the crisis the Japanese economy suddenly went downhill, smashing hopes for a recovery. The fourth reason was the escalating export competition among East Asian countries and other countries.

Similar to excessive speed in financial liberalization, pegging exchange rates can increase the risk of a financial crisis and cause problems, ranging from slower export growth to excessive short-term foreign debt. But these problems by themselves were not so serious that they were the main cause of the crisis in Asia in 1997.

Moral hazard

The moral hazard theory of financial crisis originates from Akerlof and Romer (1993). The theory holds that when bank deposits receive explicit or implicit government guarantee, the risks of bank investments do not greatly affect depositors, who therefore will not play a role in supervising bank investment. If, at the same time, banks are not under the effective monitoring of the government and their capital accounts form too low a proportion of their assets, banks are strongly motivated economically to invest in high-risk economic activities. Such high-risk investments may lead to financial crisis. The savings and loan crisis that hit the United States in the 1980s can be explained to a great extent by this moral hazard theory.

After the Asian financial crisis erupted, some analysts, such as Krugman (1998), blamed moral hazard. Corsetti, Pesenti and Roubini (1999) elaborated on this view, addressing enterprises, domestic finance, and international finance. Many large enterprises in East Asia had close relations with the government, and some even received the support of government industrial policy. These enterprises enjoyed many preferences in the acquisition of loans, and such preferential treatment often directly caused excessive investment of these enterprises. In the meantime, these enterprises could often count on a government rescue when they fell into mismanagement, and investors' expectations for such rescues also drove them into excessive investment. In area of domestic finance, the inadequacy of East Asian economies in terms of institutions and capabilities caused poor supervision. Meanwhile, banks were low in capital; credit allocation fell prey to non-market factors and was even influenced by serious corruption. These factors constituted strong economic incentives for financial institutions to invest in high-risk projects and caused low investment efficiency. In the area of international finance, international banks hoped that the governments of East Asian countries or the IMF would provide guarantees for their loans, directly or indirectly, and therefore issued large amounts of loans to the financial intermediary agencies of in the region. What is worse is that most of these loans were short term. In South Korea, Indonesia and Thailand, the level of short-term foreign debt exceeded foreign exchange reserves.

These factors combined to sow the seeds of a financial crisis. The factors related to enterprises and domestic finance caused low investment efficiency, high risk in investment, and excessive investment, while factors related to international finance caused two serious imbalances: between long-term investment and short-term loans and between domestic currency investment and foreign debt. With problems like these, a financial crisis will result when investors' confidence suddenly plummets because of worsening economic fundamentals.

East Asian countries witnessed a slowdown in export growth in 1996. The worsening economic fundamentals resulted in sliding real estate and stock markets in 1997, which in turn caused widespread losses and repayment difficulties for enterprises and financial institutions. In the subsequent investors' panic, foreign capital was pulled out, triggering a regional collapse in currency values.

It is an undeniable fact that nepotistic capitalism is a serious issue in East Asian countries. In the dozen years before the Hanbo Iron and Steel collapse of 1997, the South Korean Government did not let any large enterprise group go bankrupt. In Indonesia, it was a general belief that the enterprises owned by members of the Suharto family would receive a variety of preferences. However, corruption in the countries stricken by the Asian financial crisis did not worsen noticeably before the crisis in comparison with those emerging economies that were not directly affected by the crisis. It would be far-fetched to claim that moral hazard associated with nepotistic capitalism was a major cause of the crisis.

Financial panic

The theory of financial panic debuted in the bank-run theory advanced by Diamond and Dybvig (1983). According to the bank-run theory, even if a bank is in normal operation and its investment is profitable in the long run, it may collapse because of a run on it by panic-stricken depositors. Such a run is subject to three preconditions: first, the short-term assets of the bank are less than its short-term debts, while its long-term assets are hard to liquidate in short run, thus making the bank unable to meet all withdrawal requests during a run; second, the bank cannot find an investor with sufficient capital to rescue itself. Third, the government has not provided the bank with guarantees to insure that no depositor will suffer losses when the bank lapses into a payment crisis. Under these three conditions, if a bank run does occur, the last ones to attempt withdrawals may suffer losses because the bank has no money to pay. Therefore, when a run is suspected, depositors will vie with one another to withdraw money.

Some analysts, especially Jeffrey Sachs, point to financial panic similar to a bank run as a major cause of the Asian financial crisis. Before the financial crisis, the short-term foreign debts of many East Asian countries exceeded their foreign exchange reserves. This did not necessarily mean that these countries had poor investment efficiency or dim prospects for long-term development. However, panic in the international financial market started a chain reaction, thus causing the financial crisis. First of all, foreign investors took the lead in withdrawing their capital out of a fear that these countries might run into a payment crisis. When they did so, they caused a decline in foreign exchange reserves and a loss of ability to maintain the pegged exchange rate and currency depreciation in these countries. The currency depreciation produced a direct impact on the enterprises that owed foreign debts and increased their cost of repaying the debts. Many enterprises lost the ability to obtain new investment because of this. Some even could not repay debts and were liquidated. The withdrawal of foreign capital and depreciation of currency also exerted an immense negative impact on the domestic financial sector and further indirectly affected other domestic enterprises. The withdrawal of foreign capital reduced liquidity in the domestic financial market and increased the cost of capital. Meanwhile, financial institutions experienced a rise in losses and fall in capital, which greatly weakened their ability to issue credits. The increased losses of the financial institutions were derived from two sources. On the one hand, the financial institutions themselves were also neck-deep in foreign debt, and currency devaluation increased their cost of repayment. On the other hand, the problems encountered by other enterprises increased the bad debts of the financial institutions. When domestic financial and production sectors suffered heavy losses and were deprived of investment capability, panic escalated and pushed more foreign investors to pull out their funds. Such a chain reaction finally caused a currency collapse so that enterprises suffered heavy losses and their production shrank, leading to a highly destructive financial crisis.

Compared with the policy errors and institutional defects discussed above, financial panic is a more important cause of the Asian financial crisis. Several facts support the financial panic theory. First, the countries hit by the crisis were those with high short-term foreign debts versus their foreign exchange reserves, rather than countries with more serious corruption and more problems in their banking system; second, the crisis took only a short time to sweep several countries in the same region that had very different economic structures and fundamentals; third, in only a year after its occurrence, the crisis already began to let up, regardless of the absence of conspicuous improvements; and fourth, there was nearly no one who foresaw the Asian financial crisis.

Changes in external factors

The changes in external factors must also be considered in analyzing the Asian financial crisis. The common ground between this theory and the theory of financial panic is that before the crisis East Asian economies had no problems in their economic fundamentals that were serious enough to cause the financial crisis. The difference between the two theories is that the latter attributes the crisis to investors' loss of confidence, which does not necessarily have an inevitable relationship with economic fundamentals, while the former attributes the financial crisis to the unexpected, but material deterioration of the external economic environment of the crisis-stricken economies. For example, Shen (2007) argues that the sudden course change in the capital flow between Japan and Southeast Asian countries is the fuse that ignited the Asian financial crisis. In the mid-1990s, Japan implemented a policy of low interest rates and energetically promoted the outbound investment of the Yen to avoid its excessive appreciation. The result is that a large amount of Yen investments flew to Southeast Asia, including some US$260 billion worth of loans. Things began to change in 1995, when a large number of non-performing loans began to emerge in the Japanese banking sector. Then, as the economy slowed down and foreign investors pulled out their capital because of the Yen's depreciation, share prices slumped in 1996 and 1997, causing a further decline in value of banking capital, which included a large portfolio of equity shares. The depreciation of the Yen also raised the value of US dollar loans, which further lowered the capital adequacy ratio of Japanese banks. The only way to reach the required capital adequacy ratio was to reduce outbound loans. From 1996 to 1999, the loans provided by Japanese banks to the five crisis-stricken economies decreased by US$47.4 billion. The abrupt course change of the capital flow between Japan and Southeast Asian economies caused a strong impact on the latter, initiated a chain reaction, and aggravated the financial crisis. The theory of external factors complements those discussed earlier.

Lessons and policy implications

The Asian financial crisis caused enormous damage, and there are lessons to be drawn from it.

1   The development of the financial system must be compatible with the institutions and capabilities for supervision and prevention. Without sufficient supervision, the financial system will abound with moral hazard. Without necessary preventive measures, the risk of panic will be high. During the development of industrialized countries, financial crisis and panic took place more than once. Gradually, these countries set up financial supervision systems to prevent crises, e.g., the Federal Reserve system, deposit insurance institutions, the Securities and Exchange Commission, modern bankruptcy systems and more effective legal systems in the United States. These measures have greatly strengthened the stability of the financial system and reduced the likelihood of crisis. Even so, the savings and loan debacle still occurred in the

United States in 1980s. The savings and loan organizations took advantage of loosened supervision to provide a large number of loans for the high-risk commercial real estate industry, finally forming substantial non-performing loans. The problems that plagued Japanese banks in 1990s are still fresh in our minds. Therefore, it is a difficult and slow process to establish and improve the financial supervision system, which is a task that cannot possibly be fulfilled in one fell swoop. Before the financial supervision system is established and the necessary supervision capability is obtained, it is inadvisable to relax market access and investment control or go too fast in deregulating new products and the market.

2   Establish a sound enterprise financing system. First, enterprises should not be provided with excessive protection and preferences. Otherwise, moral hazard will result; enterprises will use the protection and preferences for excessive investment or investment in projects that are too risky, and financial institutions will also be more motivated to finance such investments. The experience of the large business groups of South Korea and the Indonesian enterprises connected to the Suharto family in the Asian financial crisis showed the importance of the lesson. Second, it is necessary to strengthen corporate governance and increase the transparency of enterprises to reduce the risks of investment in enterprises. Finally, the capital market should be developed to encourage direct investment, reduce over-reliance on banks, and improve risk sharing in the financial system.

3   One must be very cautious to open the cross-border flow of capital in emerging markets. In particular, great caution should be taken before abandoning the restrictions on short-term foreign debts. Compared with goods trade and direct investment, the liberalization of international capital flow poses even higher requirements for supervision capabilities. The flow of international capital is more unstable than the domestic financial system, for there are no international institutions that correspond to the bankruptcy law, deposit insurance and central bank within an economy. International flows of short-term capital are especially prone to panic and susceptible to external factors that cannot be controlled, hence the high volatility in international capital flow. Therefore, the control over international flows of short-term capital should not be relinquished easily.

4   Fixed or nearly fixed interest rates are risky. Although a fixed interest rate can reduce the conventional risks associated with exchange rate fluctuations, it may create risks that do not occur very frequently, but will cause a tremendous impact once they do occur. The impact on the economy will be strong if the fixed interest rate is suddenly changed because it can no longer be maintained. Before the Asian financial crisis, the pegged exchange rate of East Asian countries caused large-scale inflows of short-term capital, excessive investment, distortion of the relative prices of tradable and non-tradable products, over-valuation of exchange rates and lowered export competitiveness, foreshadowing the financial crisis.

Although the current conditions in East Asia very much differ from what they were before the crisis, fixed interest rates still have their risks. The currencies of many East Asian countries are undervalued, which has resulted in too strong a stimulation for exports and excessive trade surpluses. In the expectations for currency appreciation, huge amounts of capital have flowed in. To maintain a low exchange rate, the monetary authorities have to buy foreign exchanges in a major way, thus causing a sharp rise in foreign exchange reserves. To mitigate the rapid increase in the supply of local currency, the monetary authorities have to sterilize the increase of foreign exchange reserves. However, the extent of sterilization is limited, resulting in a large increase in the money supply and bank credit, which in turn increase pressure of inflation, especially the swelling of asset prices, and may also cause excessive investment. The capital that has flowed in may flow out, the bubble of asset prices may burst, and excessive investment may generate non-performing bank loans. All these make a financial crisis possible.

At present, the undervalued currencies of East Asian countries have resulted in a rapid growth of export and excessively high reliance of the economy on foreign countries, which expose the economy of these countries too much to the risks resulting from the changes in the external environment. Once fluctuations occur in the US economy, East Asian economies may suffer. Meanwhile, the imbalance of global current accounts may not be sustainable, which has increased the possibility of global economic fluctuations. This is another risk brought about by fixed exchange rates.

5   It is necessary to establish an international mechanism for debt mediation and for suppression of international financial panic. Developed industrialized countries have established mechanisms to prevent serious financial crisis. These mechanisms include lenders as a last resort, strict financial monitoring and supervision, deposit insurance institutions, modern bankruptcy systems, and a more effective legal system. Emerging economies are trying to set up such a system but do not have corresponding international institutions, whose establishment is of great significance for preventing the occurrence and proliferation of financial crisis.

Conclusion

The Asian financial crisis caused huge losses to crisis-stricken and other countries. The errors in economic policies and institutional defects of crisis-stricken countries paved the way for the crisis. The policy errors mainly included overly rapid financial liberalization and an exchange-rate system lacking flexibility. Another major cause is that some governments were hand-in-glove with enterprises and provided some enterprises with so much protection and preferences that investors formed expectations that the government would always come to the rescue and therefore made excessive high-risk investments in these enterprises. However, although the problems were serious, they were not enough to explain the severity of the Asian financial crisis. Financial panic is a major reason why the crisis was so serious. The deteriorating Japanese economy and the consequent repatriation of Japanese capital flows to East Asian countries are among the important factors that triggered the crisis.

Highly valuable lessons may be drawn from the Asian financial crisis. On the domestic financial market, it is necessary to strengthen institutions and capabilities for supervision and prevention. Only after these institutions are strengthened is it safe to practice financial liberalization. Meanwhile, an excellent enterprise financing system should be set up to reduce investment risks. With regard to international finance, one must be very cautious before lifting the control over cross-border capital flows. In particular, great care must be taken to lift the control over short-term foreign debts. As for the exchange rate system, full consideration should be given to the risks associated with fixed or nearly fixed interest rates. For the international community, there is the need to create an international mechanism for debt mediation and for suppression of international financial panic. This is the only way that it will be possible to effectively prevent crises in the future.

References

Akerlof, George A. and Romer, Paul M. Looting. 1993. The Economic Underworld of Bankruptcy for Profit. *Brookings Papers on Economic Activity*, 1993, no. 2:1–60.

Corsetti, Giancarlo; Pesenti, Paolo; and Roubini, Nouriel. 1999. What Caused the Asian Currency and Financial Crisis? *Japan and the World Economy* 11, no. 3 (October 1999): 305–373.

Diamond, Douglas W. and Dybvig, Philip H. 1983. Bank Runs, Deposit Insurance, and Liquidity. *Journal of Political Economy*. 91:401–419.

Krugman, Paul. 1998. What Happened to Asia? (Unpublished manuscript.)

Radelet, Steven and Sachs, Jeffrey. 1998. The East Asian Financial Crisis: Diagnosis, Remedies, Prospects. *Brookings Papers on Economic Activity*, 1998, no. 1:1–74.

Shen, Liantao. 2007. Ten Years after the Asian Financial Crisis. *Caijing Magazine* (Special Issue). June 25.

14 China in the realm of the world economy

Li Daokui (David D. Li)

China's experience in coping with the Asian financial crisis

The Asian financial crisis had a significant and negative impact on the Chinese economy, which was largely manifested in the evident decrease in demand for China's exports. Therefore, export-oriented enterprises, especially ones in the coastal regions, shouldered more of the burden brought on by the crisis. In fact, China experienced a marked drop in the growth rate in the value of exports for two consecutive years (1998 and 1999). This drop in turn affected China's economic growth (see Figures 14.1 and 14.2).

The impact of the crisis on China's economy was also reflected in the outflow of capital from China (see Figure 14.3). In fact, for the first time since China's reforms and opening-up policies, foreign direct investment (FDI) dropped from 1997 to 2000. Also, from 1998 to 2000, the number of errors and omissions in China's international revenue and expenditure account increased dramatically. In 1998, for example, the value of these errors and omissions reached US$20 billion, accounting for more than 50 percent of current-account balance (see Figure 14.1).

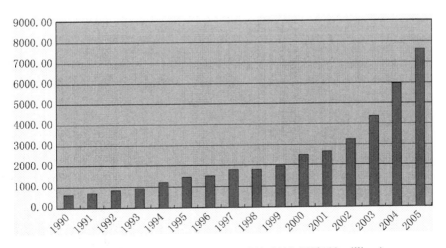

Figure 14.1 Variations in China's export value, 1990–2005 (US$100 millions).

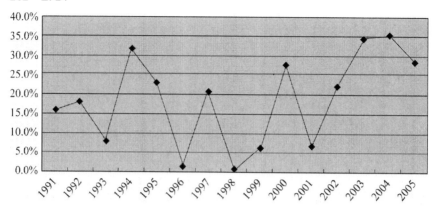

Figure 14.2 Growth Rate of China's Export Values, 1991–2005 (%).

Meanwhile, the capital account posted a US$6.3 billion deficit. Deficits have rarely occurred in China since the launch of economic reforms.

Measures adopted by the Chinese Government considerably mitigated the impact of the Asian financial crisis. Three of them, in particular, warrant analysis.

A flexible micro-market mechanism

By the time the crisis started sweeping across China's economy, the government had already been implementing economic reforms for nearly 20 years and had already established a market-oriented economic system by and large, Meanwhile, a stunningly flexible micro-market mechanism had also been fostered.

In China's economic environment between 1997 and 1999, the labor market was already considerably flexible and was actually better off in that regard than the labor markets of many other countries whose economies were undergoing change or becoming more market oriented. After having undergone reform for several years, state-owned enterprises in China had all adopted contract-based employment arrangements. In the course of reform, many state-owned enterprises also adopted relatively flexible systems for reducing payrolls by laying-off laborers and created new systems related to laying off workers. These arrangements and systems have on the one hand boosted reforms of state-owned enterprises and helped reinvigorate them, while on the other hand prevented any potential adverse impact of unemployment on social stability. At the same time, China's economic climate included a vast number of township and village enterprises, as well as non-governmental enterprises, most of whose employees were laborers flowing out of the agricultural sector. The employment system for these rural laborers has been rather flexible. Compared to China, other countries, such as India, have adopted employment systems with much less flexibility (Japan is particularly well-known for its inflexible employment system). A flexible employment system is one that allows enterprises to skillfully adjust their production scales and product mixes in response to the rapidly changing market.

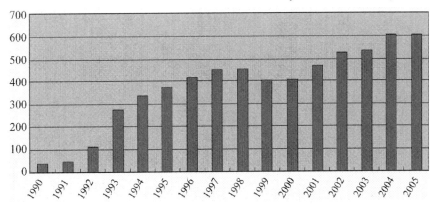

Figure 14.3 Absorption of foreign direct investment in China, 1990–2005 (US$100 millions).

Figures 14.5 and 14.6 show the estimated numbers of laid-off workers in China as a share of total workers in state-owned enterprises. Figure 14.7 illustrates the evolution of factual wages in the course of Asia's financial crisis. Though factual wages did not fall, the factual wage costs of enterprises did, due to the large scale of layoffs.

The flexible micro-market mechanism is also largely manifested in the formation of the "perfect competition scene" in China's product markets by 1997. In other

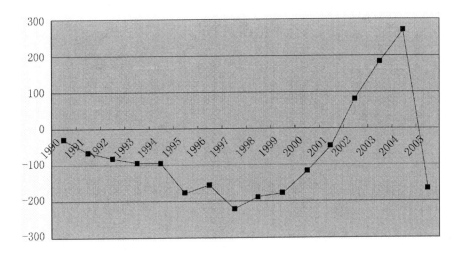

Figure 14.4 Errors and omissions in statistics on international revenues and expenditures (US$100 millions).

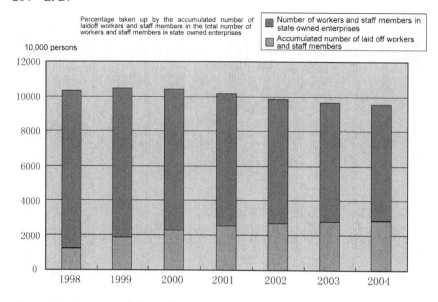

Figure 14.5 Employed and laid-off workers in state-owned enterprises.

words, most of the product markets in China had already opened up by then. The pricing mechanism dominated the market's supply and demand, and in the event that external demand dropped and domestic demand was adequate, the pricing mechanism has functioned well in alleviating the un-marketability of products.

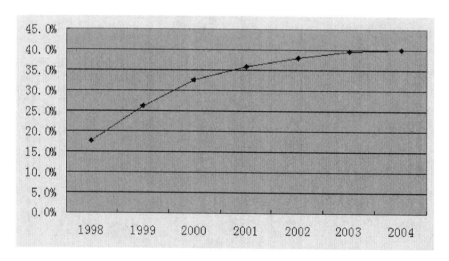

Figure 14.6 Percentage of accumulated laid-off workers and staff of state-owned enterprises, 1998–2004.

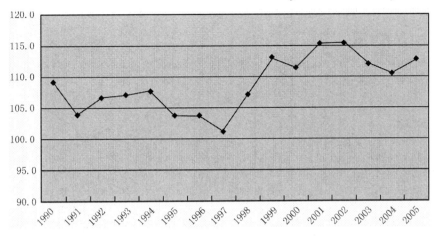

Figure 14.7 Factual wage index of workers and staff in China before and after the Asian financial crisis (last year = 100).

The flexible micro-market mechanism is most importantly manifested in the large-scale influx of new types of enterprises, which include not only those enterprises with a diversity of ownership systems in urban areas but also township and village enterprises in rural areas. Although the property-rights arrangements made by these enterprises have not seemed as clear as those made by wholly privately operated enterprises or state-owned enterprises, they have been well-acclimatized to the restrictions on the objective market environment. In addition, the degree of clarity in the property rights of these enterprises has matched the degree of market maturity and has enabled the operating efficiency of these enterprises to reach a rather high level.

Effective macro control measures

When Asia's financial crisis began to affect China's economy, the Chinese Government, compared to governments of other affected countries, adopted a more effective and potent macro control mechanism, principally comprising proactive financial policies. From 1998 to 2001, the Chinese government launched a series of government-guided investment projects, which stimulated a drive for large-scale urbanization and mostly targeted the infrastructure-construction sector. In fact, under the then economic scenario in China, infrastructure construction was seen as a particularly important precondition for China's development. Government investments helped boost the growth rate of China's gross domestic product by somewhere between 2 percent and 5 percent (see Figure 14.8).

At that time, monetary policy seemed comparatively ineffective because of the defects in the operating mechanism of commercial banks, which caused the Chinese government mainly to take financially oriented policy measures. China, however, also formulated a series of supporting social policies to help increase domestic demand. These policies included recruiting more students into colleges and universities, increasing investments in higher education, and augmenting wages and salaries for civil servants and others. Such social policies not only solved some longstanding social problems but also enhanced domestic demand by leaps and bounds.

In contrast, Indonesia, Malaysia, South Korea, and Thailand accepted conditional loans from the International Monetary Fund (IMF) and employed restrictive measures in relation to after Asia's financial crisis. These measures were based on the IMF's past experience in coping with financial crises and called on concerned national governments to swiftly reduce financial expenditures, consumption, and financial deficits. However, these IMF-driven measures undoubtedly fuelled the flames of the crisis, causing affected countries to experience even greater economic woes. Unlike the measures implemented in many countries in the region, the measures taken in China made a major difference in weathering the effects of the financial crisis and therefore merit review.

In fact, China's proactive financial policies are what prevented Asia's financial crisis from spreading its adverse impact on the country These policies have not only stabilized China's economic scene but have also given a strong boost to the growth of Asia's whole economy.

Meticulous treatment of capital flows and setting up an effective firewall

When Asia's financial crisis erupted, the weakest link in China's national economy was its financial system, which was far more vulnerable than those of Thailand, Malaysia, and other countries of the region and was vulnerable to attacks by the international financial capital. The cross-border flow of huge amounts of funds is one specific condition that made China vulnerable to such attacks. Early on, the Chinese Government realized the potential hazards from the large-scale cross-border flow of funds. Therefore, China took an extremely cautious approach for many years toward the issue of free convertibility of the RMB Yuan under capital accounts. Such caution alleviated the impact of foreign financial capital on China's financial system and national economy. It cannot be concluded, however, that it is feasible to reform a country's financial system without unleashing the flow of capital but it is necessary to acknowledge that hastily unleashing the flow of capital when the country's financial system remains rather vulnerable is likely to incur disastrous losses, which are far more than the loss of efficiency caused by the backwardness of a financial system. When Asia's financial crisis swept across the region, the Chinese Government had set up a powerful "firewall" system between financial institutions and entity economy. For example, China's "Law upon Commercial Banks" clearly provided that commercial banks were "not allowed to pour funds into the stock market or directly invest funds into the real estate market." Hence, the fluctuations in the stock market and variations of exchange rates would not be transferred to the entity economy sector through banks. In addition, when China's commercial banks accumulated many, large, bad loans, the Chinese government adopted practises to meticulously mitigate the pressure and did not request these

Financial expenditure and its contribution to GDP growth

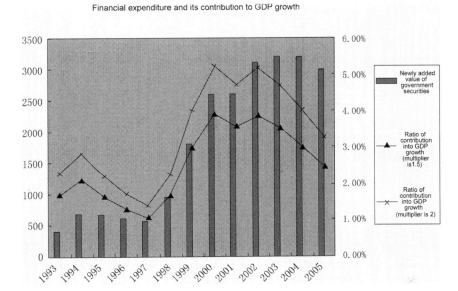

Figure 14.8. Central Government's financial expenditures and its contribution to growth of gross domestic product (with investment multipliers of 1.5 and 2).

commercial banks to immediately show rates of capital sufficiency that measured up to international standards. Instead, it worked out a pertinent schedule, requested these commercial banks to reform themselves gradually, and helped them enhance their rates of capital sufficiency by means of making government investments under certain terms and conditions. Thanks to such governmental investments, commercial banks managed to improve themselves and proceeded to help the entity economy sector avoid the impact exerted by the financial sector. This was China's unique experience in coping with the financial crisis.

Financial risks in a globalization scenario and establishment of domestic systems

Financial risks remain

Do financial risks still exist in the newly emerging market-oriented countries a decade after Asia's financial crisis? The answer is yes. Most of the newly emerging market-oriented countries around the globe undeniably posted rapid economic growth and quickly increased foreign exchange reserves. However, financial risks as a consequence of globalization have persisted. The only change is that such risks have changed in nature since the 1997 financial crisis.

There will be two types of financial risks in the world economic scene. The first may be termed "traditional financial risks," which are manifested in the forms of crisis in international revenues and expenditures, decreased exchange rates, and dramatically increased domestic interest rates. During Asia's financial crisis, there were such traditional financial risks, to which a number of countries are still vulnerable. One of these vulnerable countries is India. Although today's India is registering quick economic growth, it has suffered financial deficits for many years and does not yet have a balance of international revenue and expenditure. Moreover, India's capital market has relied on enormous overseas investments for a long time (a considerable portion of which are short-term speculative funds). In such circumstances, if there are relatively large fluctuations in major capital-exporting countries or if international investors change their view on the development perspective of India, funds could collectively flee India within a short period. The situation could result in a shortage of foreign exchange reserves, a drop in the exchange rate of India's currency, and a rise in interest rates.

The second type of financial risks can be termed "Japanese-style." These occur when the national economy is overheated and the domestic consumption is insufficient, thus causing the national currency to suffer a long-term upward pressure for re-evaluation. As a result, speculative capital would swarm into the concerned country, causing bubbles in prices of domestic assets. Bubbles in asset prices are hard to maintain. When such bubbles in asset prices burst, the domestic entity economy is seriously affected, giving rise to crisis (although the concerned country may have an adequate amount of foreign exchange reserves to cope with capital outflows, hence evading risks in terms of exchange rates). However, this constitutes a financial crisis in substance because it demonstrates the influence on the entire economy triggered by problems in the financial system.

Assuming China's economic scene sees a relatively large decrease in asset prices, including decreases in prices in the securities and real estate markets, the "wealth effect" to be incurred (excluding the investment effect) could affect China's gross domestic product by 4 percent, equal to about half of China's economic growth rate over the past few years (see Table 14.1).

Preventing and controlling "microscopic" financial risks

"Microscopic" financial risks refer to those arising from individual enterprises and generated in the process of financial and economic operations. These financial risks lay the foundation for "macroscopic" financial risks on the whole. In the final analysis, all types of integrative financial risks are largely inseparable from macroscopic financial risks.

In China's current economic environment, microscopic financial risks have loomed disproportionately large because an overwhelming majority of the investments made by Chinese enterprises have come from their profits or from profits made by other enterprises (see Figure 14.9). Such a mode of investment is not directly restricted by the financial market, and the responsibility for controlling risks has been transferred to the shoulders of non-financial enterprises.

Reducing microscopic and individual financial risks requires two types of efforts. The first includes intensifying the building of a modern enterprise system,

Table 14.1 The potential impact of a 50 percent decrease in China's securities and market, and a 30 percent decrease in real estate

Current market value of tradable A shares	RMB Yuan 6 trillion
Loss of wealth in the event of a 50 percent decrease in securities value	RMB Yuan 3 trillion
Total current value of urban residents' housing property	RMB Yuan 30 trillion
Loss of wealth in the event of a 30 percent decrease in the real estate market	RMB Yuan 9 trillion
Total loss of wealth	RMB Yuan 12 trillion
Marginal consumption tendency of wealth*	7%
Decrease of consumption as a result of decreases in the securities and real estate markets	RMB Yuan 840 billion
Decreases in Consumption/GDP	4%

* According to Zandi (1999), the extent of consumption growth as a result of the wealth growth brought forth by the increase of share prices in the stock market is far less than the extent of consumption shrinkage as a result of wealth shrinkage incurred by the decrease of share prices in the stock market; i.e. the marginal consumption coefficient of the negative wealth effect is 0.07.

enhancing the vigor and vitality of entrepreneurs, and increasing enterprises' capabilities in risk control. In fact, an enterprise's risk-control capability is not a technical concern. Instead, it is largely determined by internal governance, in line with the modern enterprise system. As far as an individual enterprise is concerned, heavy risks are more often than not incurred through non-scientific decisions, which are often the result of ill-conceived actions of staff members. The root cause is the failure to create a wholesome corporate governance structure. Another reason

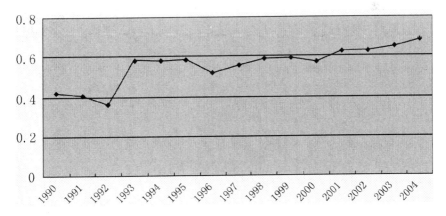

Figure 14.9 Sourcing of enterprises' investments: estimated self-raised funds as a percentage of their fixed asset investments.

Source: Li (2006).

is the unscientific or undemocratic way in which an enterprise's internal decisions are made. Meanwhile, pressures from outside the enterprise (including pressures and restrictions from the capital market) are not passed on to the enterprise. Therefore, reinforcement of corporate governance is able not only to enhance the level of the enterprise's skills in the internal control of risks, but also to reinforce the capital market's confidence in the enterprise's operation, thereby taking better control of operating risks of the enterprise and making a more rational judgment of the enterprise's value.

The second type of effort needed for the reduction of enterprises' microscopic financial risks is in the area of supervision. The microscopic supervision as such comes from within the concerned industry (e.g., supervision of operating practises, product quality, customer service and corporate reputation within the industry) and is conducted by the competent authority responsible for supervision of the capital market. As far as the capital market is concerned, the intensity of supervision and the enforcement force of supervision are two important factors directly determining whether the capital market is healthy.

After Asia's financial crisis, many corporate governance scandals took place in developed market economies, such as the United States. After reviewing the conditions that allowed these scandals to occur, some countries carried out various reforms to their market mechanisms. The reinforcement of supervision and legislation has largely alleviated the financial risks of enterprises.

Controlling macroscopic financial risks

Macroscopic financial risks refer to systematic financial risks stemming from poor mutual coordination among enterprises and among financial institutions. Such financial risks are controlled largely by the government.

The experience of many countries has shown that when it comes to taking control of financial risks, on the whole it is necessary to address three issues, starting with the overheating of the macro economy. When the macro economy is overheated, the conditions are ripe for blind demand for investments, thus giving rise to increases in asset prices or a huge influx of foreign funds. In such a scenario of overheated investments, the quality of fixed assets formed by such investments is sub-optimal, and it is difficult for poor-quality assets to maintain high-standing asset prices. When asset prices fall, poor-quality assets are inflated through positive feedback resulting from fluctuations in the macro economy, therefore resulting in a macroeconomic crisis.

The second issue to be addressed is the control and holding of financial risks on the whole. It is necessary to properly adjust and intervene in operations in the capital market, which has its own rational and irrational laws of motion. Fluctuations in asset prices are not only determined by various indicators of the macro economy (such as interest and exchange rates), but are also determined by market expectations. Market expectations cannot be 100 percent rational, particularly when observed in the short term. Under such an irrational market framework, asset bubbles are likely to occur (or asset prices will remain at a low level for a long period). By their nature, asset bubbles are hard to maintain in the long run. After asset bubbles are broken, the sharp decrease of asset prices is bound to influence the development of the entity economy in some way. The government, including competent supervisory organs, must keep an eye on the bubbles that arise from asset prices. There is a relatively wide variety of ways to stem bubbles from asset prices, such as appropriately enhancing the interest rate, increasing the costs of bank funds' entry into the capital market, strictly supervising operations of the capital market, preventing market speculation, and properly managing expectations. Expectation management is in and of itself an important responsibility of government.

The third type of effort deals with taking hold of economic and financial risks on the whole and is about managing the size of debt (particularly the size of exterior liabilities) in the entire economy. A basic lesson learned from Asia's financial crisis is that the size of exterior liabilities incurred by a country must not exceed a certain level. Because developing countries normally value their exterior liabilities in hard currency, their balance of international payments becomes barely able to support their repayments in cases where exterior liabilities reach a certain size. In such instances, countries inevitably cannot renew their borrowing of funds when debts come due, thus giving rise to financial risks. China has gained ample experience in this regard (see Table 14.2). Since China's economic reform and opening up, the Chinese Government has taken hold of the total amount of liabilities at all times. Through such a strict control regime, the Chinese government lost several types of control. For instance, the Guangdong International Trust Investment Corporation asked for loans from abroad in the country's name. Its ability to repay debt became suspect when it was discovered that the quality of its investment projects was rather poor. Meanwhile, the country's commitment was not honored in full. It is necessary to prevent such cases from occurring again in the course of China's future economic reform.

Table 14.2 Estimates of China's exterior liabilities: size, ratio to gross domestic product, and the ratio to foreign exchange reserves

Balance of exterior liabilities at the end of 2006	US$322.988 billion
GDP in 2006	US$2,670 billion
Balance of exterior liabilities/GDP	12.1%
Foreign exchange reserves at the end of 2006	US$1,066.3 billion
Balance of exterior liability/foreign exchange reserves	30.3%
Foreign direct investment balance at the end of 2006	US$660 billion
Profits available for remittance out of China (assumed to take up 30% of the balance)	US$198 billion
Profits available to be remitted out of China by foreign investors/ foreign exchange reserves	18.6%

Establishment of a firewall

A main measure for dissolving financial risks is to take strict control of the ratio of exposure of the national economy to external financial risks. There are many ways to measure the ratio of exposure of a country's macro economy to external economic interference, but among the more important ones is the ratio between the total sum of funds flowing into a country as a result of the short-term capital flows from abroad and the total sum of assets possessed by the same country. Under the precondition of incomplete convertibility in capital accounts, this ratio can accurately describe the degree of exposure to the international financial market. Undoubtedly, such a ratio of exposure to financial risks must be strictly controlled.

On the premise that the ratio of exposure stated above is strictly controlled, it is necessary to restrict the influence of fluctuations in the capital market on enterprises' operations and to control the influences on families' consumption from a national perspective. When fluctuations occur in the capital market, they can be transferred to operating practises of enterprises through various channels. One of the more frequently occurring channels is seen when the capital market turns downward. It then becomes hard for enterprises to issue (original) stock shares, thus making it difficult to raise funds. This mechanism is not the most important option around the world because most countries still adhere to a bank-centered financial system.

The second channel through which the fluctuations in the capital market influence enterprises is seen when bank capital enters the capital market directly or indirectly. When the capital market moves downward, bank capital falls; as a result, banks must reduce the size of related loans, which causes enterprises' investments to drop. China must set restrictions upon such a mechanism within a short amount of time. Specifically, enterprises should be encouraged to go through a strict supervision, examination and approval system to become listed on the stock market and to raise funds at relatively low costs. Even if stock prices go down, those companies that operate successfully and adopt proper business practises are still able to get listed on the stock market and raise a certain amount of funds. Besides, commercial banks should continue to resist re-determining their statutory capital in line with share prices in the short- and medium-terms, thus cutting off the influence of price fluctuations in the stock market towards the operations of banks. In this way, bank behaviors can become relatively independent of the capital market.

In fact, a basic lesson from the Great Depression in the United States in the 1930s is the necessity for cutting off capital market fluctuations' influence on the entity economy, thus reducing the influence of price fluctuations in the securities market toward banks. One often-used measure to reduce fluctuations in the capital market and consumption behaviors is the fostering of institutional investors, instead of mobilizing individuals and family consumers to straightforwardly enter the stock market. When institutional investors become comparatively mature, consumers can participate in the capital market by buying retirement funds and insurance funds. In case of price fluctuations in the capital market, because fund investments made by families are long-term, stable investments, families' consumption will remain constant in the face of fluctuations in the stock market, thus minimizing the influence on the entity economy.

In short, in this era of globalization, financial risks remain in newly emerging market-oriented economies such as that of China. Despite constant economic growth in China, there is a need to carefully study and prepare for possible financial crises in the future and minimize risks.

The new economic order and developing countries

The international economic order is more unfavorable to developing countries today than it has been since the 1990s, when globalization began to sweep across the planet. In this new economic order, developing countries will inevitably fall into "development traps." In large part, the so-called "medium-income trap" in developing countries is closely correlated with irrationality about such an order.

The system of trade

Prior to the 1990s, unfavorable terms of trade were an important factor holding many developing countries back. In those years, many developing countries' participation in the international economic division of labor was confined mainly to exporting raw materials. However, since the beginning of the 1990s, many developing countries, particularly ones that recorded rapid economic growth, have been involving themselves in the tide of economic globalization principally by providing processing services for developed countries by tapping their low-cost labor, thus earning foreign exchange. In the new global economic layout, terms of trade have been stacked against developing countries; the trading system has also been irrational to toward them, as these countries (including China) must face market pressures in regard to prices of raw materials. Meanwhile, market prices of products are sliding downward (see Figure 14.10).

Growing protectionism in developed countries' trade has posed a challenge to fast economic growth in developing countries. In the current course of globalization even developed countries are, per se, faced with a mission of economic restructuring. It is widely seen that industries whose added values are generated by cheap labor have gradually relocated from developed countries to developing ones and those with newly emerging market-oriented economies. Therefore, the production outputs of these industries in developed countries are decreasing all the time. This used to be the basic mode of development in the world economy. Unfortunately, because the governments of many developed countries failed to perform their duties in economic restructuring, local politics have become more influential in promoting protectionism.

Protectionism hampers developing countries' efforts to open up their economies and discourages improvement in their performance in the macroscopic circular flow of the world economy. A frequently seen reflection of increasing trade protectionism is the rise in anti-dumping cases. In recent years, developed countries lodged a growing number of anti-dumping suits against developing countries

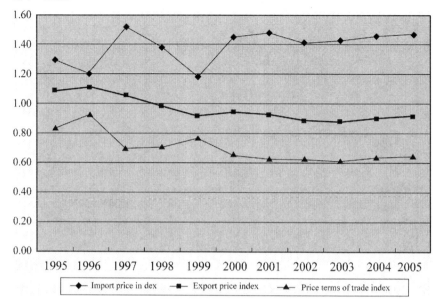

Figure 14.10 Evolution of China's foreign trade parity.
Source: Cui Jindu and Li Chengbang (2006).

(particularly against China) that employ export processing as a major means of export, thereby causing developing countries to suffer a series of setbacks in exports. Another important manifestation of trade protectionism is the manipulation of exchange rates in the so-called developing countries. Developed countries coerce developing countries into stemming growth of their export sales through increases in exchange rates. In reality, exchange rates are a relatively minor factor in regard to trade imbalances. The major cause of trade imbalances is not an exchange-rate discrepancy between countries. But exchange rate issues are nevertheless frequently used as a pretext by politicians in developed countries for restricting exports from developing countries.

Intellectual property rights

With the expansion of globalization and the increasingly detailed division of labor among countries, developed countries have become more fully aware that the intellectual property rights they have accumulated over the years are now the very core of their competitive forces. Therefore, developed countries often draw excessive attention to intellectual property rights, in an attempt to safeguard their economic competitiveness. There have been three types of problems in protecting intellectual property rights.

The first of these problems deals with irrational pricing. Today, developed countries persist in levying heavy fees for intellectual property rights in relation to rather mature technologies (such as the technology for manufacturing digital video disks and mobile telephones). Such fees have intangibly impeded economic progress in developing countries (see Table 14.3). Exorbitant pricing of intellectual property rights is a reflection of deep-rooted deterioration in terms of trade between developing and developed countries over many years. The truth is that developed countries paid no respect to intellectual property rights at all in the course of their own economic development. For example, the United States did not respect the United Kingdom's copyright agreement at all in the course of its own economic development in the nineteenth century and reprinted publications of the United Kingdom at will. Despite this disregard for intellectual property rights of other countries, the United States still levies royalties and patent fees on developing countries.

Another problem in relation to intellectual property rights is that developed countries insist on fees even with core technologies essential for social development. For example, giant corporations in developed countries have made no concessions on intellectual property rights related to technologies for environmental protection, energy conservation, and medicines to prevent or treat diseases such as HIV/AIDS. Overall, fees have generally impeded countries' economic development. In fact, developed countries' persistence in levying exorbitant fees for certain core intellectual property rights benefits neither developing nor developed countries. Exorbitant fees actually encourage the pirating of technologies, which are then

Table 14.3 Fees charged for intellectual property rights to produce digital video disk players in China in 2004

Payee in China	Patentee	Ratio of patent fee
3C	Philips, Sony, Pioneer	3.5% of the selling price; minimum fee: US$3.5 per unit
6C	Toshiba, Hitachi, Panasonic, Mitsubishi, Times Warner, JVC	4% of the selling price; minimum fee: US$4 per unit
1C	Thomson	2% of the selling price; minimum fee: US$2 per unit
Dolby	Dolby	About US$1 per unit
MPEG-LA	Administrator of the patent pool comprising 23 patentees	US$2.5 per unit
DTD	Digital Theater Systems, Inc.	US$2 to US$3 per unit
	Total patent fee on average	US$19.70 per unit
	Average selling price	About US$100 per unit
	Approximate percentage taken up by patent fee in the selling price	20 percent

Source: Wei Yanliang (2004).

used to churn out inferior-quality versions. But such pirating and mass production of inferior goods makes it impossible for developing countries to benefit from new technologies in the long run and makes it hard for developed countries to earn revenues from charging intellectual property rights because the volume of such rights transactions is too low. Therefore, when it comes to protecting intellectual property rights, developed countries should collaborate with developing countries toward a solution, which would guarantee lower costs and a greater transaction volume, thus resulting in a win-win situation. In this regard, some newly emerging non-profit welfare organizations, such as the Bill and Melinda Gates Foundation, have been wielding greater influence. Such organizations offer a promising perspective for the solution to problems related to intellectual property rights and toward the economic and social progress of developing countries.

Capital flow and risk-distribution system

Developing countries have occupied unfavorable positions in the world's economy. One of the main causes of the disadvantageous positions is that developing countries have taken on the entirety of exchange rate risks arising from financial relations with developed countries because most institutions in developing countries have been unable to receive loans via valuation in their home currencies. When a developing country such as India asks for a loan from abroad, the funds flowing into India are in US dollars. Once these funds flow out of India's stock market to other countries, it is necessary to convert the rupees into dollars, thus generating a pressure on India's international revenue and expenditure system. Once the rupee decreases in value, the losses will be borne by India as a whole. On the contrary, today's China has an international payments surplus, but China's foreign exchange reserves are valuated in dollars or Euros. Therefore, when the exchange rate of US dollars or Euros against the RMB Yuan drops, Chinese organizations holding RMB Yuan and US dollars will have to take the exchange rate losses.

Such a risk-distribution system is certainly unfavorable to developing countries. The ultimate measure for changing such a risk distribution system is to allow or assist certain developing countries to conduct financial transactions via valuation in their home currencies.

Currency policy and coinage income

Because currencies of developing countries have not yet become internationally accepted, the predominant currencies of the world's financial scene are US dollars and Euros. When the currency policies of the central bank of the United States or Europe undergo changes, these changes will naturally be passed on to developing countries in various ways. For example, if the US dollar interest rate rises, the interest rates in developing countries will also rise; otherwise, funds will flow back to the United States via diversified channels. Such an arrangement is unfavorable to developing countries, because the central banks in Europe or in the United States, when formulating their currency policies, naturally aim mainly to adjust their own national or regional economies without taking into account the influence their policies have on other countries. Therefore, fluctuations in currency policies will undoubtedly be passed on to developing countries, and thus generate an adverse influence upon developing countries.

In fact, one of triggers of the Asian financial crisis was the United States' tightening of its currency policies in mid-1997 with the goal of taking control of the bubbles in asset prices there were brought on by overheated investments in the Internet-based economy (they did not result from any judgment about the global economic climate). As shown in Figure 14.11, the ratio of "M2" to gross domestic product in the United States bottomed out, causing the exchange rate of the US dollar to rise and triggering Asia's financial crisis. M2 is the measure of the US money stock that consists of "M1," certain overnight repurchase agreements and certain overnight Eurodollars, savings deposits (including money market deposit accounts), time deposits in amounts of less than US$100,000 and balances in money market mutual funds (other than those restricted to institutional investors.)

Coinage income is another significant factor (see Figure 14.12). The US dollar has become the world's main currency in foreign exchange reserves and has served as a principal settlement currency for international trade. The Euro, as a freshly emerging currency of international reserves and for international trade, has been issued in an increasing volume. The coinage income out of such an increasing volume of issuance has been possessed by the Federal Reserve System in the United States and by the European Central Bank. Such coinage income flows back to the central banks in the United States and in Europe in various forms. For example, when Federal Reserve System augments its currency issuance volume, a large portion of the currency issued flows abroad, and the Federal Reserve System purchases US Government securities in the form of a currency issuance, thus

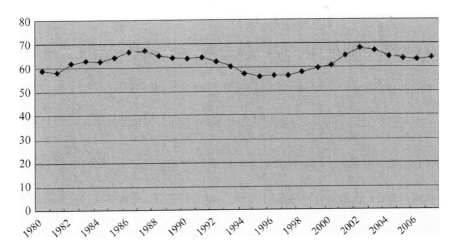

Figure 14.11 Ratio of M2 to gross domestic product in the United States.

Source: World Development Indicators 2006 and US Bureau of Economic Analysis.

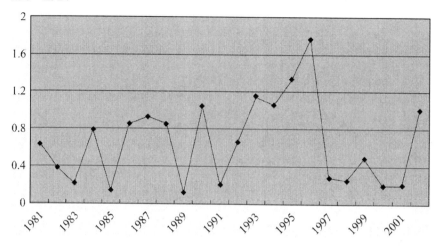

Figure 14.12 Estimated coinage income of the United States (International earnings of US
dollars, 1981–2002, as a percentage of gross domestic product).
Source: Chen Yulu, et al. (2005).

substantively protecting the US securities market. Such support to the US securities
market has been manifested in the fact that the earning rate on US Government
securities has remained at a rather low level for a long time. Such a low earning rate
has boosted the long-term boom of American economy. Figure 14.11 sets forth the
ratio between US dollar coinage income and gross domestic product of the United
States, which fluctuates around 1 percent. By the same token, the central bank
of Europe can buy European bonds by means of issuing Euros, thereby keeping
the interest rate of European bonds at a relatively low level while safeguarding
economic development in Europe.

Ex-post facto aid

The last front in which the international economic order is unfavorable to developing
countries becomes apparent after a financial crisis – when developed countries' aid
to developing countries was not based entirely on considerations of the interests of
developing countries. Instead, developed countries, when offering such aid, paid
more heed to how to guarantee that their creditors could recover loans. Historically,
developed countries' aid agencies, represented by the IMF, have overly emphasized
the necessity for developing countries to adopt tight fiscal policies in the short term
after having suffered a financial crisis. These policies included ones related to
fiscal restraint and currencies. Policies of restraint have indeed brought forth some
excessive, unnecessary economic pressure on developing countries (see Ito 2007)
and have aimed to reduce risks to creditors in developed countries and guarantee
the recovery of their investments within a short time.

Ostensibly, policies that overly emphasize short-term restraint have not been
accompanied by ordinary economic analysis. After the occurrence of a financial

crisis, the aiding party should make its best effort to reduce economic losses and stabilize the financial scene. Under certain circumstances, it is necessary to enlarge financial expenditures and to put into force various kinds of relatively loose currency policies to maintain the normal operation of the economy. However, because developed countries have the absolute right of control in the ex-post facto aid mechanism, economic aid provided after a financial crisis in today's world is often attached with overly uncharitable conditions. The root cause of these occurrences has not yet been definitively identified. Therefore, when the next financial crises occur in developed countries, their impacts will exceed those of a regular financial crisis.

Summary

Despite the sweeping tide of economic globalization, the international economic order of the day remains quite unfavorable to developing countries. Developing countries must repeatedly appeal to all countries and international policy makers to scrutinize irrational elements in today's economic order. Only when the international economic order becomes more rational can the world economy can step onto a path of long-term prosperity. Meanwhile, developing and developed countries could embrace common prosperity and development and create a shared harmonious environment. As a swiftly emerging developing economy, China has the capability and the reasons to adopt reasonable and well-structured measures to support its efforts to build a new, more rational, international economic order.

References

Chen, Yulu; Wang, Fang; and Yang, Ming (2005). "Internationalization of Currency as a Transnational Competition Strategy: Evidential Experience of the US Dollar on the Globalization of the Renminbi." *Economic Research*: 2.

Cui, Jindu and Li, Chengbang (2006). "Terms of Foreign Trade China Was Exposed To: An Analysis of the Scene from 1995 to 2005." *International Economic Cooperation*: 4.

Gill, Indermit and Kharas, Homi (2007). *An East Asian Renaissance: Ideas for Economic Growth*. Washington, DC: World Bank.

Ito, Takasoshi (2007). "Asian Financial Crisis and the International Monetary Fund, 10 Years After." *Asian Economic Policy Review* (2): 16–49.

Li, David Daokui (2006). "Large Domestic Non-Intermediated Investments (DNI) and Government Liabilities: Challenges Facing China's Financial Sector Reform." Working Paper, Centre for China in the World Economy, Tsinghua University.

Wei, Yanliang (2004). "Follow-up Report on Recent Disputes over Intellectual Property Rights of DVD players." *Electronic Intellectual Property Rights*: 11.

Zandi, Mark R. (1999). "Wealth Worries." *Regional Financial Review*, August: 1–8.

Index

Please note that a **bold** entry indicates a table or figure.